Graphic Novels and
Comics in the Classroom

Graphic Novels and Comics in the Classroom

Essays on the Educational Power of Sequential Art

Edited by CARRYE KAY SYMA *and* ROBERT G. WEINER

Foreword by ROBERT V. SMITH
Afterword by MEL GIBSON

McFarland & Company, Inc., Publishers
Jefferson, North Carolina, and London

LIBRARY OF CONGRESS CATALOGUING-IN-PUBLICATION DATA

Graphic novels and comics in the classroom : essays on the educational power of sequential art / edited by Carrye Kay Syma and Robert G. Weiner ; foreword by Robert V. Smith ; afterword by Mel Gibson.
p. cm.
Includes bibliographical references and index.

ISBN 978-0-7864-5913-1

softcover : acid free paper ∞

1. Comic books, strips, etc., in education.
2. Graphic novels in education.
I. Syma, Carrye Kay, editor of compilation.
II. Weiner, Robert G., 1966– editor of compilation.
LB1044.9.C59G73 2013   371.33—dc23   2013010027

BRITISH LIBRARY CATALOGUING DATA ARE AVAILABLE

© 2013 Carrye Kay Syma and Robert G. Weiner. All rights reserved

No part of this book may be reproduced or transmitted in any form or by any means, electronic or mechanical, including photocopying or recording, or by any information storage and retrieval system, without permission in writing from the publisher.

Cover illustrations—*clockwise from upper left:* "Thimble Theatre" comic strip panel, E.C. Segar, 1921; superhero © 2013 Digitalvision; female fire spirit © 2013 Antonis; zombie © 2013 Aaron Rutten; anime eye © 2013 Hemera; man in office © 2013 Dorling Kindersley

Manufactured in the United States of America

*McFarland & Company, Inc., Publishers
Box 611, Jefferson, North Carolina 28640
www.mcfarlandpub.com*

Acknowledgments

The editors would like to thank Dr. Robert V. Smith and Dr. Mel Gibson for their foreword and afterword. Thank you for taking time out of your busy schedule to take part in this project. It is an honor to work with you both. We would also like to thank all of the reviewers who also took time out of their hectic lives to take a look at these essays. We hope this is a volume of which you can be proud to have contributed.

* * *

I would like to dedicate this volume to my husband, Jake Syma, and our children, Leila and Jacob. Thank you for being so patient with me and for your continued love and support.

I would also like to thank my colleagues who have aided me throughout this process. A special thanks to all of the authors who contributed to this volume. I would like to thank Kevin Jones for his amazing art work for the graphic short we created. Rob, this project has been interesting, to say the least!

— Carrye Kay Syma

* * *

I would like to dedicate this volume to the memory of my father, Dr. Leonard Weiner, who was at the forefront of the computer revolution (having worked at IMB in the 1960s and helped with founding the Computer Science department at Texas Tech). Your contribution to the world of education and to the community is not forgotten. I remember all those late nights you stayed up grading. You were a true inspiration as an educator. I also dedicate this volume to the memory of my prairie dog Poncho (who warmed my heart). You were my constant companion for nearly eight years and the best pet I ever owned. Thanks to all my other critters still with me especially Sweet Girl, Mr. Eddie, and Blossom. Thanks to Dr. Jessica Thomas, Dr. Jimmy Gleason, Todd Klein, Nick Yanes, Matt Mceniry, and Denise Caspell.

Love and thanks to my mother Marilyn May Weiner (who is also an educator and inspiration), Larry and Vick Weiner, Tom Gonzales, Joe Ferrer, John Oyerbides, and Sara Dulin.

Thanks also to Joe Gulick, Shelley and Ian Barba, the deans of Texas Tech University Libraries, Dean Dyal Laura Heinz (for good advice), my colleagues in RIO (Ms. Cynthia Henry, Ryan Cassidy, Dr. John Hufford, Brian Quinn, [dedication to the memory of Sandy River], Sheila Hoover, Sam Dyal, Esmeralda Rodriguez, Jake Syma, Arlene Paschal, Innocent Awasom, Tom Rohrig, Kimberly Vardman, Minerva Alaniz, Jack Becker, Donell Callender), Mr. Ryan Litsey, Connie Kitten, Dulcinea A., Christiana P., Selena Kyle, Shannon Jones, Kevin Jones, Kaley Daniel, Ms. Amy Kim, Karin Slyker (thanks for your continued support), Eobard Thawne, Norrin Radd, Erik Lehnsherr, Max Eisenhardt, Jim Hammond, Bart Hill, Mark Todd, Doug Campbell, Cord Scott, Lance Eaton, Mr. B. Quinn, Ron Thomas,

Richard Graham, Kevin Flanagan, Patrick Grzanka, Liorah A. Golomb, Roberto Delgadilo, Jessica Olin, Alison Mandaville, Karen Gavigan, Gwen Evans, Francisca Goldsmith, Vivian Howard, Arianne Hartsell-Gundy, Phillip Troutman, Miss K. Vardeman, Barbara Mcarthur, and Dr. Rodney Donahue. Thanks to the Document Delivery Staff at TTU, LTMS department, Southwest Collection and all the faculty and staff of TTU Libraries, thanks to Joan Ormrod, David Huxley.

Thanks to John Cline, Susan Hidalgo, Carol Tilley, Lan Dong, Jacqueline Edmondson, Robert Moses Peaslee, Cindy Miller, Amy Nyberg, Elizabeth Figa, James Bucky Carter, and Chris Angel. It is a privilege to work with you.

Thanks to all the authors in this volume for their patience; it's been a long time coming.

Lastly, thanks to my co-editor, colleague and friend Carrye Syma for all her hard work. It's been great working with you. Thanks for believing in this project. I hope we do more together!

— Robert G. Weiner

Table of Contents

Acknowledgments — v

Foreword
    Robert V. Smith — xi

Introduction
    Robert G. Weiner *and* Carrye Kay Syma — 1

Part I: Significance of Graphic Novels and Comics: Then and Now

Using Comics to Teach the Language Arts in the 1940s and 1950s
    Carol L. Tilley — 12

Stigmatization, Multimodality and Metaphor: Comics in the Adult English as a Second Language Classroom
    Alice Leber-Cook *and* Roy T. Cook — 23

The Attitudes of Some Students on the Use of Comics in Higher Education
    Christina L. Blanch *and* Thalia M. Mulvihill — 35

Part II: Teaching Graphic Novels and Comics in the Classroom

"I can get college credit for reading *Batman*? That's a joke, right?" Confessions of a Fanboy Professor Teaching Comic Books
    David Whitt — 50

"What the —?" Pre-Service Teachers Meet and Grapple Over Graphic Novels in the Classroom
    James Bucky Carter — 58

Teaching Intertexuality and Parody Through the Graphic "Supertext": Martin Rowson's *The Waste Land* (1990)
    Kevin M. Flanagan — 73

Part III: Graphic Novels and Comics, Beyond the Text

"Remember, remember the fifth of November": Using Graphic Novels to Teach Dystopian Literature
    Daniel Ian Rubin — 84

Exploring the Art in Sequential Art: An Art Historical Approach to
Teaching Comics
 ABRAM FOX 91

On Teaching Comics and Graphic Novels in the Medieval and Renaissance
Classroom
 CHRISTINA C. ANGEL 101

Leagues, Evildoers and Tales of Survival: Graphic Novels and the World
History Classroom
 MARYANNE A. RHETT 111

"Indisciplinary" Teaching: Comics Studies and Research Writing Pedagogy
 PHILLIP TROUTMAN 120

Part IV: Specific Graphic Novels and Comics and Their Application in Educational Settings

Teaching "The Auto-Graphic Novel": Autobiographical Comics and
the Ethics of Readership
 REBECCA SCHERR 134

Teaching Theory Through *Y: The Last Man*
 TIMOTHY D. ARNER 145

Approaching Literacy Features Through the Graphic Novel *Logicomix*
 MARIANNA MISSIOU *and* YIANNIS KOUKOULAS 154

Manga, the Atomic Bomb and the Challenges of Teaching Historical Atrocity:
Keiji Nakazawa's *Barefoot Gen*
 JEREMY R. RICKETTS 174

Information Comics: Risks and Pitfalls
 FELIX KELLER *and* DOROTHEA OECHSLIN 184

Graphic N-extbooks: A Journey Beyond Traditional Textbooks
 JEREMY SHORT, DAVID KETCHEN *and* JEFF SHELSTAD 200

Part V: Cultural Implications of Graphic Novels and Comics

Beyond Borders: Teaching Global Awareness Through the Graphic Novel
 LAN DONG 220

The Benefits of Writing Comics
 DIANA MALISZEWSKI 233

Multicultural Education Through Graphic Novels
 REBECCA M. MARRALL 245

"So, Joss, why do you always write these strong women characters?" Using Joss
    Whedon's *Astonishing X-Men* to Teach Feminism
        ERIN HOLLIS   251
Sequential Art for Qualitative Research
        MARCUS B. WEAVER-HIGHTOWER   260

Afterword
        MEL GIBSON   274
About the Contributors   277
Index   281

Foreword

Robert V. Smith

If you are like me, when you pick up a newly published or newly acquired book, you fan through the pages, stopping here and there to look at the illustrations—be they diagrams, photographs, or comic images. They all draw us in! But, the comic illustrations often have the greatest impact because they are frequently used to vividly express ideas, emotions, and action in the context of the narrative. You are then presented with the mental invitation to start reading the text and if it is interesting, compelling, and coherent you're "hooked."

In this volume, Syma and Weiner provide us with a series of essays describing robust associations among authors and illustrators to produce graphic novels, novelettes, textbooks and other curricula materials. Through the collective works we are offered suggestions that graphic creations have enhanced power to engage and instruct learners of all ages, but perhaps most importantly the visually inspired members of the Millennial generation. Moreover, trends in the use of graphic aids and instruction throughout all walks of life and across many cultures, suggests an increasing, not diminishing, use of graphics in the future—all based on an abundance of scientific studies that support facilitated learning through combinations of image and text.

From a personal perspective, I attest to the power of graphics and specifically comic graphics to illustrate and reinforce meaning of the written and spoken word. Beginning in the early 1980s, and in a series of personal and professional books on topics from graduate research in the sciences to management of academic research groups to leadership development of professionals in private and public workspaces, comic illustrations have played key roles. One of the earliest works incorporated previously crafted comics that were adopted through licenses and fees. Another early work used cartoons commissioned by a publisher and crafted by a distant artist that I had little influence on, except for possible rejection of a cartoon or two.

In my most recent works, beginning in 2004, I have worked on three book projects with the Arkansas illustrator Dusty Higgins. Akin to the landmark association between L. Frank Baum and illustrator W.W. Denslow in the creation of *The Wonderful Wizard of Oz*, Dusty and I have collaborated in crafting characters and situations that have not only enlivened the resulting book-length works but also served to engage and entertain audiences during hundreds of presentations. Our most recent effort has led to *The Way of Oz—A Guide to Wisdom, Heart, and Courage* and a set of characterizations that enrich a work that incorporates history, biography, literary and artistic criticism in a synthesis containing advice on lifelong learning, caring and serving, all with a focus on the future and ethics in the lead. So, from my perspective the graphics elements of learning are worth exploring, adopting and assessing — for further refinements for learning — well into the future. Syma and Weiner offer us a primer that will be a helpful guide as we test the boundaries of graphics-assisted learning and understanding.

Robert V. Smith serves as provost and senior vice president at Texas Tech University. Examples of his use of graphics in learning and understanding can be viewed at thewayofoz.com.

Introduction

ROBERT G. WEINER *and*
CARRYE KAY SYMA

"I thought you could do things in comics that could be done in no other medium; that as an esthetic form, comics were irreplaceable..."
— Samuel R. Delany, "Introduction," *Miracleman: The Golden Age* (4)

"Basically comic books are a manifestation of popular culture, and as such deserve study in their own terms. But comics can also be studied as a reflection of our society, and their study can be a part of our attempts to understand ourselves and our society."
— Michael Uslan, *The Comic Book in America* 1973 (191).

"Graphic novels do give the brain a good workout. That's because readers are processing words in captions and in speech bubbles, while also taking in art through the series of panels. The brain is working through all this at the same time the reader is following a storyline, getting to know characters, interpreting facial expressions and predicting what comes next. That's a lot for the brain to do!"
— Linda Johns "Getting Serious About Comics," 2012.

First let's get one thing straight: sequential art, cartoons, comics, and graphic novels are not a genre, they are a format and a technique for telling a story or conveying information. Second, comics are a form of social history that can be used to impart knowledge about a particular era. *Captain America, Superman, Wonder Woman, Iron Man, Crime Does Not Pay,* etc., are time capsules in the same way that, say, John Steinbeck's *Grapes of Wrath* or Dante's *Inferno* are.

In the past 10 to 15 years, the use of sequential art in education has exploded. Teachers in secondary and elementary schools, professors in universities, and instructors of all kinds are using comics and graphic novels to illustrate points about gender, history, sociology, philosophy, mathematics, and even medicine. It is no longer a question of whether sequential art should be used in educational settings, but rather how to use it and for what purpose. (In addition, theses and dissertations related to comics have exploded as well. There is even an online comic for graduate students; see www.phdcomics.com.) As we know, for decades since comics started being big business in the 1940s, a large segment of educators, academics, librarians, and parents decried the use of comics for anything but turning one's brain into mush. To be sure there were those early works that used the sequential art format for purposes of instruction and enlightenment. Some of these early educational works include *Texas History Movies* (Figure 1), *True Comics, Real Heroes,*[1] the *Classics Illustrated* series, and *Picture Stories from the Bible.*

Figure 1

The U.S. government saw the potential to use comics and cartoons to teach Americans and government workers various concepts. This is most recently documented in Richard L. Graham's (2011) excellent *Government Issue: Comics for the People, 1940s–1960*. In addition, the Army published *PS Magazine, the Preventive Maintenance Monthly*, which taught correct preventative maintenance concepts in sequential art format (Eisner 2011, Fitzgerald 2009). Other early examples of educational comics include *Martin Luther King and the Montgomery Story*. Originally published in 1957, its 14 pages have been "credited with being one of the most influential teaching tools ever produced for the Civil Rights Movement" (*Seattle PI* 2010). In a similar vein, the *Golden Legacy* imprint published illustrated biographies (beginning in 1966) of important historical African American men and women. Its tactic was touted as not a traditional comic publication but as "a new approach to the study of history. The intention of our publication is to implant pride and self-esteem in black youth while dispelling myths in others" (Fitzgerald 2011). The series features biographies of notables like Harriet Tubman, Crispus Attucks, Robert Smalls, etc. In the 1970s the publisher Davco released a series of short biographies of prominent figures from American history in the sequential art format (these included presidents such as Andrew Johnson and Woodrow Wilson, as well as historical figures like Patrick Henry and Alexander Hamilton). Even Marvel Comics got into the act of producing comics in the 1970s that were designed to help with vocabulary and reading—*Spidey Super Stories* (a tie-in with the television program *Electric Company*, featuring the character of Spider-Man).

Full length books like the *Introducing* and *For Beginners* series were popular in the 1980s and 1990s. Larry Gonick published *Cartoon* guides about such diverse topics as American and world history as well as genetics and statistics, which have been in use for more than 30 years. In the last 15 years, educational stories and material published in graphic novel format have become commonplace. Some excellent examples include Jay Hosler's *Clan Apis*, Mark Schultz's *The Stuff of Life: A Graphic Guide to Genetics and DNA*, *Fallout*, on the history of the atomic bomb, by Jim Ottaviani, and, as discussed in this volume by Marianna Missiou and Yiannis Koukoulas, Apostolos Doxiadis' study of philosopher/mathematician Bertrand Russell, *Logicomix*.

An interesting trend in graphic literature includes the adapting of classic texts (in the *Classics Illustrated* vein) but in much more detail. We are not talking just about sequential art adaptations of Shakespeare or Shelley's *Frankenstein*, but heavy historical, scientific, and literary works like Charles Darwin's *Origin of Species* (Keller 2009), *The United States Constitution: A Graphic Adaptation* (Hennessey 2008), Allen Ginsburg's *Howl* (Drooker 2010) and Sun Zzu's *Art of War* (Clester 2012).

It seems as though today anything can be adapted and translated to the sequential art form. This applies to the traditional comic book format as well (those floppy magazine publications). The University of Nebraska-Lincoln teamed with the National Center for Research Resources (through a Science Education Partnership Award) to publish *The World of Viruses* series, the goal being "to increase public understanding about viruses and infectious disease" (Powell 2009, np). (Graphic adaptations of medical issues have become increasingly popular. There is even a conference devoted to it; see http://graphicmedicine.org/.) In addition, the Federal Reserve Bank published a series of comics explaining issues related to money and economics (this includes *The Story of Foreign Trade and Exchange*, *The Story of the Federal Reserve System*, and *The Story of Inflation*, 2007). "Fair use" law also gets the graphic novel treatment in *Bound by Law*, featuring an EC Comics *Tales from the Crypt*-style narrator (Aoki 2006). Even a study of *Health Care Reform* has recently received the sequential art treatment (Gruber 2011). We could write and publish a full annotated bibliographic monograph of educational graphic novels and comics and still not cover it all. The above, however, illustrates that sequential art as a format has been used as an educational tool for more than 70 years and is getting more and more popular all the time as an instructive tool.

Academics have had their hand in studying the educational impact on comics for almost as long. Academic journals like the *Journal of Educational Sociology* have been studying comics since the 1940s. Articles and books continue to appear, and a brief look at some of the recent literature provides an enlightening window into the various types of work being done (Cooper 1981, Sabeti 2011, Gavigan 2011, Rouke 2011, Carter 2007, Monnin 2009, Tabachnick 2009, Dong 2012, Bakis 2012). Librarian Kat Kan, in her 2010 edited volume *The Graphic Novel and Comic Books,* has a whole section on "Comics in the Classroom: Using Graphic Novels to Improve Literacy" (pp. 69–105). While it is not our purpose to go into a detailed literature review of books and articles related to graphic novels teaching and education, the above does illustrate just how important this topic has become in the last several years.

Other recent developments related to comics and education include the open-access peer reviewed journal *SANE* (founded by contributor James Bucky Carter). Its motto is "SANE journal publishes research- and practitioner-based articles covering all intersections of comics and education, from pre-kindergarten to post-secondary studies, from a variety of disciplines" (*SANE JOURNAL* 2012). Contributor Christina Angel is one of the founders of the Comic Book Classroom, an after-school program designed to promote literacy among young people using comics (see www.comicbookclassroom.org). In the summer of 2012, Dr. Angel spearheaded the Rocky Mountain Conference on Comics and Graphic Novels and the Denver Comic Con and literary conference, with proceeds going to the Comic Book Classroom. The Rocky Mountain Conference on Comics and Graphic Novels had an educational and literacy focus and featured such notables as RC Harvey, Charles Hatfield, Maureen Bakis, James Bucky Carter, and William Kuskin, as well as educators from all over the country from secondary to higher education discussing their work with comics in educational settings. Similar conferences with an educational focus are starting to pop up all over the world. Again, our focus is not to document all such programs, but these examples give readers a sense of just how important comics are for educators (and librarians).

Courses specifically on comics in colleges and universities are a fairly new phenomenon. Stan Lee, however, pointed out that as early as 1967, "more than a dozen college professors thruout (sic) America now use Marvel mags in their English Lit. courses as supplemental material…" (Lee 1967, np). Moreover, in the early 1970s, Michael Uslan (producer of the *Batman* films) taught the first accredited university course on comics at Indiana University and also wrote one of the very first textbooks on comics, *The Comic Book in America* (1971). Uslan's goal was to teach a course that looked at "history, folklore, art, sociology, psychology, and (comics') literary/educational value…. I wanted my students to receive an unprecedented three hours of college credit for it, which would make it [as] important as history, physics, or chemistry" (Uslan 1974, 26). In his article, "Confessions of a Comic Book Professor," Uslan outlines his experiences with administrators and the long, strange road to teaching the first accredited course on comics (Uslan 1974, 26–29). Every academic who has taught a course on comics owes a great debt to scholars like Uslan and so many others (Thomas Inge, John Lent, and Randy Scott, to name just a few) who paved the way to make comic studies a respected part of the academy. In fact, in *The Comic Book in America,* Ulsan argued in 1973 that there were four major reasons for using comics in education:

The case for comics is based on four related assumptions:

1. that comics can help people who are having reading problems learn to read more effectively
2. that comics can help improve grammar and increase vocabulary

3. that comics can be an introduction to the reading of more sophisticated materials and the to the study of literature in general
4. and finally, that comics could be used to teach various attitudes and facts (189)

As educators and librarians, we have all heard and seen the above arguments (which Professor Uslan put it so eloquently all those years ago) many times over at conferences, in the literature, and in discussions with colleagues.

In today's transmedia culture, the concept of just what it means to be educated and literate continues to change and mutate. As librarians, the editors are keenly aware of the need for information literacy, "the ability to recognize the extent and nature of an information need, then to locate, evaluate, and effectively use the needed information" (Plattsburgh 1996–2012). The Association for College and Research Libraries has put together its own guidelines and principles for information literacy, which are supposed to be the standard for teaching and learning (ACRL 2012). Along with information literacy is the concept of visual literacy, the "complex act of meaning-making using still or moving images" (Frey and Fisher 2008, 1). The combination of images with text in order for students to understand and interpret the world is probably the most important aspect of teaching literacy in the 21st century. In fact, one could argue:

> the primary literacy of the twenty-first century is visual. It's no longer enough to read and write text. Our students must learn to process both words and pictures. To be visually literate, they must learn to "read" (consume/interpret) images and "write" (produce/use) visually rich communications. They must be able to move gracefully and fluently between text and images, between literal and figurative worlds [Burmark 2008, 5].

Sequential art, of course, usually combines both the visual and the narrative in a way that readers have to interpret the images with the writing. With comics and graphic novels permeating all aspects of popular culture and the world it is almost impossible for even those who disdain the format to not be touched by it (for example, in 2012, *The Avengers* was one of the biggest movies in the history of popular culture, and its source material is comics). Even those who may never pick up a comic for pleasure reading or analysis are still touched by the world of comics. Comics are probably one of the purest forms an educator could use to teach visual literacy.

One of the things that make comics such a good fit for education is that students are using a format that provides an opportunity for active engagement. Their minds are lively when reading comics. The readers involve their minds with both the visual and narrative content, hopefully resulting in greater comprehension and interest. Even the *Chronicle of Higher Education* has come out in support of using comics (and creating them) in the university classroom, arguing:

> working in the comic form can accomplish as an exercise for students as well as for us: it demands the conscious structure of visual and textual data with intention. It can be a great form for experimenting with multimedia and in particular remembering that a picture can be more than illustration — it can illuminate something that complements, contradicts or otherwise engages with the text (Salter 2012).

One of the most exciting developments with regards to graphic novels and education is the use of the graphic novel textbook, such as *Atlas Black* (Short 2011), *University Life* (Payne 2011) (as discussed in this volume) and *Super-Powered Word Study* (Carter 2011). They provide a unique way for students to understand business management, college life, and build vocabulary through the form of sequential art. This does not mean the content is dumbed down in any way, but rather the content is presented in an eye-catching format. The editors have also experimented with the idea of using a mini-graphic novel textbook for our freshman information literacy course, Library 1100 (Figure 2). We discovered that students find its use in class to be more engaging as a supplement to our content (Weiner and Syma, forthcoming).

Above and opposite: Figure 2 (script: Carrye Syma, art: Kevin Jones, concept: Rob Weiner).

Conclusion

Although there are plenty of books, articles, and websites related to comics, education, and teaching, the editors hope this volume makes a noteworthy contribution to the literature and can stand proudly alongside the already great body of work. We are confident educators will find this volume readable, practical, and applicable to their practice. This volume is for all educators and librarians from all parts of scholastic spectrum (elementary, secondary, to the Ph.D.s and instructors in higher education). The essays in this volume come from a wide variety of the academic continuum including theory, pedagogy, anecdotal evidence, history, case studies, and applied application. The editors hope that they will invoke discussion and that this volume can be used for years to come. In addition, the editors hope that readers will dip into and savor these essays for their honesty and breadth.

Ultimately, comics are about telling stories, whether the content is about superheroes, zombies, managing a business, history, or genetics, and it is through these stories that students can have a greater grasp of the reality around them. As James Bucky Carter has expressed it so perfectly: "Teachers (*Professors, Librarians, and all types of educators*) need to find a place in their classrooms for comic books and graphic novels because it is a sound practice to do so" (Carter 2008, 47). Amen!

Notes

1. To see some digitized examples of *True Comics* and *Real Heroes* see the following websites: http://www.lib.msu.edu/branches/dmc/digital.jsp?coll=2 & http://digitalcomicmuseum.com/

References

Aoki, Keith, James Boyle, and Jennifer Jenkins. 2006. *Bound by Law: Tales from the Public Domain*. Durham, NC: Duke University Center for the Study of the Public Domain.
Association for College and Research Libraries. 1997–2012. "Information Literacy Resources." *ALA.org* Accessed June 26 2012. http://www.ala.org/acrl/issues/infolit.
Bakis, Maureen, and James Bucky Carter. 2012. *The Graphic Novel Classroom: Powerful Teaching and Learning with Images*. Thousand Oaks, CA: Corwin Press.
Burmark, Lynell. 2008. "Visual Literacy: What You See Is What You Get." In Nancy Frey, Douglas Fisher eds., *Teaching Visual Literacy*. Thousand Oaks, CA: Sage Press: 5–25.
Carter, James Bucky. 2007. *Building Literacy Connections with Graphic Novels: Page by Page, Panel by Panel*. Urbana, IL: National Council of Teachers of English.
_____. 2008. "Comics, the Canon, and the Classroom." In Nancy Frey, Douglas Fisher eds., *Teaching Visual Literacy*. Thousand Oaks, CA: Sage Press, 47–60.
_____, and Erik Evensen. 2011. *Super-Powered Word Study: Teaching Words and Word Parts Through Comics*. Gainesville, FL: Maupin House.
Clester, Shane, Sun Tzu, Cullen Bunn, et al. 2012. *The Art of War: From Smarter Comics*. Mundelein, IL: Writers of the Round Table Press.
Cooper, Vicki, and Carolyn Bradfield. 1981. *Comics as an Educational Tool: Laugh & Learn with Some Favorite Cartoon Characters*. Mobile, AL: Berkley/Small.
Cooper, Vicki, Carolyn Bradfield, and Mark Griswold. 1981. *Comics as an Educational Tool*. Lawrenceville, GA: Pawprints.
Delany, Samuel R. 1992. "Introduction." In Neil Gaiman and Mark Buckingham, *Miracleman: The Golden Age*. New York: Eclipse: 4.
Doxiadis, Apostolos, Christos H. Papadimitriou, Alekos Papadatos, et al. 2009. *Logicomix*. New York: Bloomsbury.
Davco. 1977. *Alexander Hamilton: The Gripping True-Life Story of the Man Who Strongly Influenced America's Government*. Skokie, IL: Davco.
Davco. 1977. *Andrew Johnson: The Intriguing True-Life Story of the President Who Fought Off Impeachment*. Skokie, IL: Davco.
Davco. 1977. *Patrick Henry: The Inspiring True-Life Story of the Leader Whose Oratory Set Young America Aflame*. Skokie, IL: Davco.
Davco. 1976. *Woodrow Wilson: The Warm True-Life Story of the President Who Went to War to Save Democracy*. Skokie, IL: Davco.
Dong, Lan, ed. 2012. *Teaching Comics and Graphic Narratives: Essays on Theory, Strategy and Practice*. Jefferson, NC: McFarland.
Drooker, Eric, and Allen Ginsburg. 2010. *Howl: A Graphic Novel*. New York: Harper Perennial.

Eisner, Will, and Eddie Campbell. 2011. *PS Magazine: The Best of the Preventive Maintenance Monthly.* New York: Abrams ComicArts.

Federal Reserve Bank of New York, Cedric Fan, Steve Malin, et al. 2007. *The Story of Foreign Trade and Exchange.* New York: Federal Reserve Bank of New York Public Information Department.

Federal Reserve Bank of New York, Ed Steinberg, Steven Malin, et al. 2007. *The Story of Inflation.* New York: Federal Reserve Bank of New York Public Information Department.

Federal Reserve Bank of New York, Ed Steinberg, Steven Malin, et al. 2007. *The Story of the Federal Reserve System.* New York: Federal Reserve Bank of New York Public Information Department.

Fitzgerald, Bertram A. 2011. "About Golden Legacy." *Golden-Legacy.com.* Accessed June 7, 2012. http://www.golden-legacy.com/about.html. The *Golden Legacy* series of 16 books is still available and even bound together in a hardback.

Fitzgerald, Paul. 2009. *Will Eisner and PS Magazine: An Ongoing Legacy of Nitty-Gritty Laughs and Deadly Serious How-To Comics for Generations of America's Warriors: An Illustrated History and Commentary.* Fincastle, VA: FitzWorld.US.

Frey, Nancy, and Douglas Fisher. 2008. "Introduction." In Nancy Frey, Douglas Fisher eds., *Teaching Visual Literacy.* Thousand Oaks, CA: Sage Publications: 1–4.

Gavigan, Karen, Mindy Tomasevich, and Robert G. Weiner. 2011. *Connecting Comics to Curriculum: Strategies for Grades 6–12.* Santa Barbara. CA: Libraries Unlimited.

Gonick, Larry. 1987–1988. *Cartoon Guide to U.S. History.* New York: Barnes and Noble Books.

Gonick, Larry. 1990. *The Cartoon History of the Universe.* New York: Doubleday.

_____, and Mark Wheelis. 1991. *Cartoon Guide to Genetics.* New York: Harper Perennial.

_____, and Woollcott Smith. 2005. *Cartoon Guide to Statistics.* New York: Collins.

Graham, Richard. 2011. *Government Issue: Comics for the People, 1940s–2000s.* New York: Abrams Comicarts.

Gruber, Jonathan, and H.P. Newquist. 2011. *Health Care Reform: What It Is, Why It's Necessary, How It Works.* New York: Hill and Wang.

Hennessey, Jonathan, and Aaron McConnell. 2008. *The United States Constitution: A Graphic Adaptation.* New York: Hill and Wang.

Hosler, Jay. 2007. *Clan Apis.* Columbus, OH: Active Synapse.

Jenkins, Richard, and Debra Detamore. 2008. *Comics in Your Curriculum.* Marion, IL: Pieces of Learning.

Johns, Linda. 2012. "Getting Serious About Comics." *momshomeroom.msn.com.* Accessed August 13, 2012. http://momshomeroom.msn.com/parenting-articles/reading/getting-serious-about-comics/251535497?wt.mc_id=msn.

Kan, Kat, ed. 2010. *Graphic Novels and Comic Books: The Reference Shelf, Vol. 82, No. 5.* New York: H.W. Wilson Company.

Kalogridis, Laeta, and Christopher Shy. 2006. *Pathfinder: An American Saga.* Milwaukee: Dark Horse Comics.

Keller, Michael, Nicolle Rager Fuller, and Charles Darwin. 2009. *Charles Darwin's* On the Origin of Species: *A Graphic Adaptation.* New York: Rodale.

Lee, Stan. May 1967. "Stan's Soapbox!" In *Marvel Tales 14.* New York: Marvel.

Monnin, Katie. 2010. *Teaching Graphic Novels: practical strategies for the secondary ELA classroom.* Gainesville, FL: Maupin House.

Ottaviani, Jim. 2001. *Fallout: J. Robert Oppenheimer, Leo Szilard, and the Political Science of the Atomic Bomb.* Ann Arbor, MI: G.T. Labs.

Payne, Tyge, Jeremy Short, Rob Austin, et al. 2011. *University Life: A College Survival Story.* Irvington, NY: Flat World Knowledge, Inc.

Plattsburgh State University. 2012. "Definitions of Information Literacy." *Plattsburgh.edu.* Accessed June 9, 2012. http://www.plattsburgh.edu/library/instruction/informationliteracydefinition.php.

Powell, Martin, et al. 2009. *World of Viruses: Never Ending Battle & Curse of the Tree-Man.* Lincoln: University of Nebraska.

Rourke, James. 2010. *The Comic Book Curriculum: Using Comics to Enhance Learning and Life.* Santa Barbra, CA: Libraries Unlimited.

Sabeti, Shari. December 2011. "The Irony of 'Cool Club': The Place of Comic Book Reading in Schools." *Journal of Graphic Novels & Comics* 2.2:137–149.

Salter, Amanda. June 25, 2012. "Comics in the Classroom and Beyond: Professor Hacker Tips About Teaching, Technology, Productivity." *Chronicle of Higher Education.* Accessed June 28, 2012. http://chronicle.com/blogs/profhacker/comics-in-the-classroom-and-beyond/40931.

SANE Journal: Sequential Art Narrative in Education. 2012. Accessed June 26, 2012. http://www.sanejournal.net/.

Schultz, Mark, Zander Cannon, and Kevin Cannon. 2009. *The Stuff of Life: A Graphic Guide to Genetics and DNA.* New York: Hill and Wang.

Seattle PI. January 18, 2010. "Libraries Keep MLK's Crucial Comic Book." *Book Patrol* (Posted by Nancy Matton. Accessed June 6, 2012. http://blog.seattlepi.com/bookpatrol/2010/01/18/libraries-keep-mlks-crucial-comic-book/. The actual comic can be viewed at http://issuu.com/hamsa/docs/mlkcomic-eng.

Short, Jeremy, Talya Bauer, David J. Ketchen, et al. 2011. *Atlas Black: The Complete Adventure.* Irvington, NY: Flat World Knowledge, Inc.

Tabachnick, Stephen Ely, ed. 2009. *Teaching the Graphic Novel.* New York: The Modern Language Association of America.

Uslan, Michael. 1971. *The Comic Book in America.* Bloomington: Indiana University Press.

_____. 1973. *A Study Guide for P.C. 1 The Comic Book in America.* Bloomington: Indiana University Press.

_____. November–December 1974. "Confessions of a Comic-Book Professor." *Amazing World of DC Comics* 1.3: 26–29.

Versaci, Rocco. 2008. "Literary Literacy and the Role of the Comic Book: Or You Teach a Class on What?" In Nancy Frey, Douglas Fisher eds., *Teaching Visual Literacy.* Thousand Oaks, CA: Sage Publications.

Weiner, Robert G., and Carrye Kay Syma. Forthcoming. "Graphic Novels and Introduction to Library Research." *LOEX Proceedings* 2012 *(Library Orientation Series No. 45).*

PART I
Significance of Graphic Novels and Comics: Then and Now

Using Comics to Teach the Language Arts in the 1940s and 1950s

CAROL L. TILLEY

Historical scholarship on the role that comics played in classroom-based teaching and learning in the United States has been largely superficial. Nyberg's (1998, 2002, 2010) examinations of librarians' and teachers' perceptions of comic books—especially during the years leading to the establishment of the Comics Magazine Association of America's 1955 editorial code—are perhaps the best known and among the most expansive of these research contributions. Nyberg asserts, in part, that the objections to comics overshadowed any acceptance of this medium by teachers and librarians. Yet, the basis for her arguments are never more than a few dozen sources, even though she acknowledges that "hundreds of articles about comics were published in trade, academic, professional, and popular periodicals" (Nyberg 2010, 28) during this time period. Dorrell et al.'s (1995) historical study of the integration of comics in primary and secondary classrooms relied on only a small portion of the literature available on the topic. Tilley's (2007) investigation drew on a large body of primary sources to offer a more nuanced understanding of librarians' perceptions of and relationship to comics than Nyberg has, but because of its focus on librarians rather than teachers, Tilley's work largely is excluded consideration of how comics were used in classroom settings.

This essay seeks to expand the work of Dorrell et al. (1995), Nyberg (1998, 2002, 2010) and Tilley (2007) on the use of comics in American elementary and secondary schools during the 1940s through the mid–1950s, the apex of the free voluntary reading of comics by young people in the United States. Rather than focusing on educational researchers, classroom teachers, and school librarians who disparaged comics without seeking first to test the medium's value, it concentrates instead on the positive integration of comics in language arts instruction in the 1940s and 1950s. First, it examines two important curriculum documents from the National Council of Teachers of English—*An Experience Curriculum in English* (Hatfield 1935) and *The English Language Arts* (Smith 1952)—that legitimized comics as a topic of inquiry and an instructional tool in language arts classrooms. Second, it describes three exemplar cases for the use of comics in language arts classroom settings during the 1940s and 1950s. Third, it highlights recommendations regarding comics from textbooks on reading pedagogy published in the 1940s and 1950s. In highlighting these examples, this essay argues for a reconsideration of the historical role played by comics in educational settings and demonstrates that there is indeed historical precedent for the contemporary uses of comics in classrooms.

Legitimizing Comics in the Classroom

Founded in 1911 by teachers, researchers, and others frustrated by the increasing effects college entrance examinations were having on the structure and contents of the pre-collegiate English curriculum, the National Council of Teachers of English (NCTE) quickly established itself as the representative voice for reading, literature, and language arts educators in the United States. As Alvermann (2010) argues, Charles Swain Thomas' (1917) "Articulation of Elementary-School English with Secondary-School English," which called for a comprehensive and unifying curriculum that spanned primary and secondary grades, served to provide "common ground in a goal to which he believed all English teachers, regardless of grade level, aspired: namely, teaching students to interpret and express themselves in relation to what they read" (Alvermann 2010, 63). Two documents—*An Experience Curriculum in English* (Hatfield 1935) and *The English Language Arts* (Smith 1952)—helped to establish the vision for that comprehensive and unifying curriculum. Additionally, and more important to this discussion, these documents encouraged and legitimized the inclusion of comics in classroom instruction.

The result of a commission established in 1929 by then–NCTE president Ruth Mary Weeks, *An Experience Curriculum in English* (Hatfield 1935) was the first comprehensive document to outline a course of study for primary and secondary school students in the English language arts. *An Experience Curriculum* drew on child-centered pedagogical theory such as that espoused by John Dewey to promote learning organized around "well-selected experiences" (3), which were to be based in everyday living and drawn from the disciplines of literature, reading, creative expression, and communication (i.e. speech, writing). In this curriculum, tools such as spelling, grammar, and vocabulary were considered instrumental—a means to a specific end—and therefore not worthy of study except as they were essential to the fulfillment of a particular experience. Example experiences included fanciful ones such as "to become friendly and intimate with fairies, elves, and goblins" (38) and "to be a satisfactory guest" (139), alongside more traditional ones such as "to trace the derivation or history of a word" (105) and "to make a speech in support of some school project" (157). Hatfield's report emphasized learning rather than teaching, activity rather than subject.

Less than two decades later, *The English Language Arts* (Smith 1952) supplanted *An Experience Curriculum* as the NCTE's articulation of core curriculum concerns resulting from a charge in 1945 to reevaluate the nature of English teaching. One superficial, but important difference between the two documents was the change in terminology: "English" became "language arts," an attempt to highlight the curriculum's emphasis on a fuller spectrum of communication modalities. In a more critical alteration, *The English Language Arts* downplays the more playful tone and child-centered ideals of its predecessor. In this new document, having the experiences of making a long-distance telephone call or writing a formal letter of regret, along with many others Hatfield outlined, disappear in favor of recommendations for communication experiences that contribute to a students' development as moral, responsible, and thoughtful citizens in an American democracy. Even still, an activity, rather than subject-focused, view of learning dominates the report.

What *An Experience Curriculum* and *The English Language Arts* share is an appreciation for the increasingly prominent role that the mass media were playing in young people's lives. Consider, for instance, that *An Experience Curriculum* included activities related to listening to radio broadcasts[1] (cf. 64) and discussing motion pictures (cf. 67) in its suggestions for primary and secondary literature learning. Similarly *The English Language Arts* includes a statement asserting the relevance of radio, film, and television in the literature curriculum (cf. 392). None of the learning experiences associated with non-print media proposed in these two documents included production elements often found in modern media literacy activities. Rather, the activities emphasized the value of enhancing young people's understanding of the different presentation strategies afforded by non-print media and improving their abilities to be critical consumers of the media that were occupying increasing hours of their leisure time. Importantly, these curriculum proposals also asserted the value of addressing another mass medium exerting great influence in the lives of young Americans: comics.

In the United States, the free voluntary reading of comics by young people, as determined through both market and educational research, reached its apex in the 1940s and 1950s. During these years, more than ninety percent of elementary-aged students and perhaps more than eighty-percent of high school-aged students read comic books regularly (cf. Armstrong 1944; Kessler 1948; Sones 1947). Comics reading was not a casual pursuit: for instance, for the two and a half thousand students in grades four, five, and six whom reading researcher Paul Witty studied in the early 1940s, the average number of comic titles they listed as reading was thirteen, with half of those read "often" or "regularly" (Witty 1941). Young people read comics not only in pamphlet form, but also in the newspaper. In the same study, Witty found that on average young people identified more than twenty comic strips they read, with two-third of these read "often" or "regularly." What makes Witty's figures especially striking is that at the time of his study, comic books were only beginning their ascent into popularity. Consider that in 1940 readers purchased more than seven million new comic books, but this figure continued to climb to a peak of ninety million issues sold monthly in 1954 (Bechtel 1941; "Comic Comics" 1954).

In Hatfield's *Experience Curriculum* (1935), comics are treated in the recommended activities for literature instruction in the primary grades. Specifically, in the section on "Enjoying Humor of Various Kinds," an objective states: "To enjoy newspaper comics, and other similar material. To develop some discrimination between the good and the poor" (27). Although newspaper comics were still at the publication of this guide the predominant format for comics publication, promotional comic books such as *Famous Funnies*, early experimental comics magazines including *More Fun Comics*, and hardbound collections of newspaper strips were available to readers, thus suggesting that the direction to "other similar material" acknowledged the availability of these other formats. The second half of the objective, encouraging the development of taste discrimination, is common to this time period with many teachers and librarians viewing their work, especially with children, as one of inculcating an appreciation for higher literary and aesthetic experiences. Interestingly, though the focus in this section is on humor, the enabling objectives related to comics include equipping students with the ability to recognize and interpret the structural and literary conventions of comic strips. Certainly the inclusion of one objective pertaining to comics does not place this medium in an integral position in the language arts curriculum, but it does serve to acknowledge the role comics played in the lives of young readers as well as to legitimize the use of comics in classroom settings.

The place of comics in Smith's *The English Language Arts* (1952) is somewhat more prominent. The text acknowledges that, "Comic magazines sell hundreds of thousands of copies to one children's book" (392), while earlier hopefully proposing that... Explicit discussion of comics is proposed in the section on the mass media. First, in "Questions for the Study of the Newspaper" (360), attention is given to personal, aesthetic, and instrumental aspects of comics: "What do the comics add to you enjoyment of the paper? Who reads them? By what standards do you select comics to read in the paper? Where do newspapers get comics? What purposes do they serve?" (362). Second, in the similarly titled "Questions for the Study of Magazines," comics explicitly appear in four of twenty questions. These include one question on the claims of advertisements in pulp magazines and another that proposes a comparison of the types of humor employed in comics generally as well as in more literary magazines such as *The New Yorker*. The other two questions, which both hint at the importance of aesthetic judgment, are:

11. How funny are the comics? For what purposes do people read them? What other books or magazines can supply the same needs?

12. What standards do you use in the selection of comics for reading? What proportion of a person's reading time should go to comics if he is to get all there is for him other magazines? In books? (364)

How Instructors Used Comics in Elementary and Secondary School Settings

Throughout the 1940s and until the mid 1950s, when national opprobrium for comics reached its zenith, the professional literature for and about language arts teachers carried occasional articles discussing the positive application of comics in classrooms. For instance, a teacher described newspaper comics as one source of reading material for enhancing the English-language facility among native-born Mexican children enrolled as first-graders in Texas (Netzer 1941). Similarly a junior high school teacher from New Jersey suggested the value of comic books to promote vocabulary development as well as tolerance (Friedman 1941). In the late 1940s, Katharine Hutchinson, a Pittsburgh teacher, led a national study of the use of *Puck Magazine*, a comic and humor magazine, in primary and secondary schools. Her findings suggested the positive use of the comics for vocabulary growth, the development of inferential skills, sources for interpretative writing and storytelling, as well as supplemental materials for remedial readers (Hutchinson 1949). Similarly, a New York junior high school teacher reported using the comics in *Weekly Reader* in addition to *Classic Comics* to connect with the personal interests of remedial readers (Frank 1950).

These examples serve to highlight some of the ways that language arts teachers employed comics in a variety of formats — editorial, newspaper, and pamphlets — to meet instructional objectives. Yet, in many ways, these uses are incidental: comics are instrumental to instruction, rather than the focus of instruction. The remainder of this section highlights three cases in which comics are at the center of longer, more fully developed language arts instructional units. In each instance, the teachers use comics to connect with students' interests in a deliberate and programmatic manner encouraged by both *An Experience Curriculum* and *The English Language Arts*. *English Journal*, a flagship journal of the NCTE, published each of these cases.

DISCOVERING THE APPEAL OF THE COMICS

Writing in *English Journal* in 1943, Fleda Cooper Kinneman, an experienced freshman English teacher at North Phoenix High School in Arizona, described an instructional unit she undertook with her freshman students. Initially, Kinneman surveyed her students about their comic books habits, learning that only nine of her one hundred and seventy five students, or about five percent, did not read comic books. Building from the principle that "the modern point of view in teaching is to begin with the child's interests" (331), she gave several days to a unit on the comics medium. To open the unit and seed discussion, Kinneman surveyed her students reading preferences for both newspaper strips and comic books, as well as to understand the relationship between comics and her students' lives and values. For instance, through the survey and the subsequent two days of discussing comic strips, she learned from her students that the *Superman* strip—which was second in popularity among her male students to *Mutt and Jeff*—provided them with "a delightful avenue by means of which they can escape the routine and monotony of everyday living" (332).

Like many of her contemporaries and consistent with then-existing NCTE curriculum and instruction documents, Kinneman viewed part of her role as an English teacher to move students to higher levels of aesthetic appreciation. The comics unit, then, while child-centered, had as one aim the *improvement* of students' reading choices, although Kinneman was clear in stating her belief that reading comics would lead neither to illiteracy or a long-term preference for this medium to the exclusion of others. Consequently, when Kinneman requested students to bring in their favorite comic books, she used their selections to spur an analysis of what students found especially appealing in the books as well as what weaknesses they identified in their examples. As her students identified what appealed to them in the comics they preferred, Kinneman worked with them to brainstorm suggestions for more traditional works of literature that had similar appeal factors. The strategy of identifying substitutes for comics was not uncommon—see, for instance, Dias (1946) and Carr (1951)—but having young people serve as the recommending sources for these substitutes was. Through their discussions, students provided titles and rationales for dozens of diverse books including Melville's *Typee*, Maugham's *Of Human Bondage*, DuMarier's *Rebecca*, Tarkington's *Penrod*, Remarque's *All Quiet on the Western Front*, and Wren's *Beau Geste*.

In the final portion of the unit, Kinneman shared her students' insights in a series of radio programs broadcast in the Phoenix-area, two on KOV and two on KTAR. These episodes were intended to enlighten parents and other adults in the community about the role of comics in young people's lives. Unfortunately Kinneman is vague about the extent of her students' participation in the development and execution of the broadcasts. She does refer assign responsibility beyond herself in developing the episodes, stating that, "we did" (335) the broadcasts; additionally, she regards the conclusion of the unit as falling after the broadcasts had aired. Given those subtle clues, one might reasonably assert that the students had at least some limited involvement in the scripting and production of the radio episodes, which included one on comic strips, a second on comic books, a third on the *True Comics* and related publications from *Parents' Magazine*, and a final one relaying students' reading recommendations.

Reading Pictures

Hailing from North Phoenix High School, the same school where Fleda Kinneman taught, journalism instructor John Raymond wrote in *English Journal* in 1948 about a two-week unit on visual literacy he conducted with two classes of students. Comics were not the sole focus of this unit, but they were integral to it. As Raymond argued for the increasing importance of visual images in then-contemporary society and the need to provide instruction in how they work, he asserted that the previous decade's developments in cartoons and comics coupled with the introduction of comic books — "a truly new kind of mass literature for children and unlettered adults" (394) — demanded the medium be given full consideration. Although Raymond praised the work of gag cartoonists like Peter Arno, his depiction of comic books betrays his hierarchical understanding of the comics medium. In another paper for *English Journal*, Raymond (1949) describes an instructional unit on radio serials through which he hoped students would become more discriminating listeners. In the opening paragraph, he lumps together sensational paperback reprints, radio soap operas, and comic books as formats through which teachers "can reconcile their desire to improve standards" (563) with their need to connect with students' everyday lives.

The central and shared object for study in the unit on reading pictures, however, was a book of cartoons, Bill Mauldin's *Up Front* (1945), which collected his Pulitzer Prize-winning war-time cartoons for *Stars and Stripes*. With this text, Raymond and his students were able to grapple with questions such as the relationship between image and text as well as the role of cartoonists in commenting on social and political issues. Students' evaluations of the unit — an example of his responsiveness to students' needs — indicated the discussion of Mauldin's book, which they all read, to be the most "significant" (396) group activity in the two-week unit. Students also engaged in small group and individual activities. Although many of these focused on more conventional forms of journalistic imagery including photographs and advertising, comics were not excluded. Thus, one student investigation addressed the question, "Who reads comic books and why?" (396). That student was tasked with surveying young people of different ages "for (1) scope of comic-book reading, (2) sources of such books, (3) ratings of comic books and/or other reading, (4) age and grade level and other factors that seem to have significance" and then preparing "charts of questionnaire results for class study" (396). Still another student attempted to answer, "What do readers learn through reading comic strips or comic books?" by "analyz[ing] contents of strips or books for types of characters and stories" (396). Students were also encouraged to engage with gag cartoons, such as those by James Thurber, William Steig, and Charles Addams, to learn, "What makes a successful cartoon?" For this activity, students would "collect and analyze cartoons or published collections by a notable artist" and share "[t]he results of this analysis ... with the class through an oral report illustrated by the cartoons, perhaps with the opaque projector" (396). Additionally in his extensive bibliography, Raymond included a trade volume of George Herriman's *Krazy Kat* (1946) strips and Coulton Waugh's influential book *The Comics* (1947) alongside several collections of editorial and gag cartoons.

Creating *Beowulf*

In a 1953 *English Journal*, Gertrude Overton remarked that she had almost given up on teaching *Beowulf* to her senior general English students in Iron Mountain, Michigan.[2] With a few minutes to spare near the end of a class period, she decided to read to them, however, from a simplified version of the story and their enthusiasm led her to continue her reading the following day. Upon completing the reading, Overton wrote that she was "mildly horrified to hear someone suggest, 'You know, that story would make a good comic book'" (392). Rather than quash their plans as other teachers might have done, Overton turned her student's suggestion into a teachable moment, replying, "How should we go about the task?" Through the next two weeks, students created the guidelines for a sixteen-page comic book version of *Beowulf*, which they wrote, illustrated, and printed.

Although Overton's article is brief, she provides extensive details about the process and her students' activities. For instance, students believed it imperative that their representation of the story be authentic to Anglo-Saxon culture. To that end, they conducted research in the school and public libraries to better understand the people and their times. In another matter, the artists for the project had to negotiate how Grendel would be visually depicted; a search of the Comic Book Database website[3] indicates that there was no *Classics Illustrated* version of *Beowulf* on which the students could draw inspiration. Overton's students even seemed to think critically about the comics' medium; for example, they understood the importance of creating a storyboard or dummy to develop the layout for the final product. Similarly, students discussed whether to signify text as narrative or as speech: "A boy who was not in any sense a scholar said, 'Well, you'll have to decide first whether it's a conversation. If it's conversation, you'll have to extend circles from the speakers' mouths; if it is not conversation, you use an unbroken line'" (393).

Comics and the Teaching of Reading

Beyond curriculum recommendations from NCTE and actual classroom practices as described by language arts teachers, textbooks on the teaching of reading offer insights into teachers employed comics in primary and secondary classrooms. Systematic textbooks devoted to reading pedagogy were largely a twentieth century invention, with Huey's *The Psychology and Pedagogy of Reading* (1908) one of the first. Yet, by the mid–1940s, the texts on this topic had proliferated, making a comprehensive survey of them for this chapter impossible. What follows then is only a sampling of comments from some representative reading pedagogy texts, consistently highlighting the role comics could play in recreational and remedial reading.

HARRIS' *HOW TO INCREASE READING ABILITY*

First published in 1940 and most recently revised in 1990—the year of his death— Albert Harris' *How to Increase Reading Ability* (1947) was one of the early textbooks on understanding and treating reading disabilities. In this textbook, Harris, who was a founding member and early leader in the International Reading Association, which had specific interests in both reading research and reading disabilities (cf. Jerrolds 1977), wrote about the role of comics in the reading classroom. To wit, he described classroom "Practices range from that of the teacher who tears up each comic book he finds in his classroom, to that of the teacher who helps his pupils to set up a cooperative library of comic books" (432). Harris concluded optimistically and enthusiastically, though, that, "Anything to which children respond as enthusiastically as they do to comic books must have educational values that can be developed. The comic books of today may be pointing the way to the textbooks of tomorrow" (p. 433).

WITTY'S *READING IN MODERN EDUCATION*

Paul Witty, a prominent education and reading researcher at Northwestern University, was no stranger to comics. During the 1940s, Witty conducted several studies that both directly and indirectly examined children's readership of comics (e.g. Witty and Kopel 1939;

Witty 1941; Witty et al. 1942). In *Reading in Modern Education* (1949), Witty summarizes his investigations of children's comics reading before suggesting that teachers view this reading as an opportunity to understand children's personal interests and needs. Once teachers have a more firm understanding of the motivations for comics reading, they can begin to "offer discriminating guidance ... [that] will be the first important forward move on the road to better reading and improved tastes" (40). Although Witty's suggestions for focusing on taste improvement might seem opposed to comics as reading material, he is quick to note that reading comics is not always problematic. For instance, he highlights a fifth grade boy [who] read more comics than any of his classmates. But his pattern of reading was quite varied and his choices of books were generally high in quality; his conduct and behavior at home and at school were superior; and he was a favorite with his peers. In his case, reading the comics was not viewed as a problem (39).

He also related an anecdote of a classroom teacher who, by embracing her students' interests in comics, was able to identify conventional children's books such as *Make Way for Ducklings* and *The 500 Hats of Bartholomew Cubbins* they found enjoyable. As Witty concluded,

> She was also ready to admit the justice of a child's remark: "Sure, *Little Toot* and *The 500 Hats* are swell books, but they cost a lot of money, and you can get a secondhand *Superman* at Herman's for two cents" [49].

Adams, Gray, and Reese's
Teaching Children to Read

Late in 1949, Fay Adams, Lillian Gray, and Dora Reese, who were all professors of education, published *Teaching Children to Read*, a comprehensive textbook that surveyed a variety of topics including the role of reading in American society, reading readiness, and materials for readers at different levels. In addition, the authors provided the requisite overview of instructional methods for teaching reading. Near the end of *Teaching Children to Read*, Adams, Gray, and Reese devoted six pages to a discussion of comic books, writing, "No discussion of reading and literature is complete without considering those arch enemies of good literary taste — the comic books" (483). Despite this seeming opposition to comics and the inclusion of a generous quotation from Sterling North's infamous 1940 anti-comics editorial, Adams, Gray, and Reese ultimately presented a moderate position on comics. For instance, they cited both psychiatrist Lauretta Bender's (1944) assertion that reading comics helps young people work through their angst and fears as well as Paul Witty's (1941) argument that the vocabulary of comics is sophisticated and reading them may build a bridge to other books. In conclusion, they recommended using comics to reach remedial readers as well as to serve as a springboard for introducing humor in other reading, providing more than two-dozen recommendations for further reading on the subject of comics.

McCullough, Strang, and Traxler's
Problems in the Improvement of Reading

In this 1955 revision of a textbook originally published in 1940 with Ruth Strang as the sole author, Constance McCullough, Ruth Strang, and Arthur Traxler's *Problems in the Improvement of Reading* sought to offer practical insights and strategies on the teaching of remedial reading. In this edition, the authors take care to assess both the comics landscape — for instance, remarking favorably on M.C. Gaines' experiments with publishing nonfiction comics in the mid 1940s[4] — and children's interest in this medium. The textbook even commented on the extensive barter and exchange system many young people created for trading comics, something Strang knew firsthand from a study she published the early 1940s. In this earlier work, Strang (1943) proposed, "that adults should advocate moderation rather than total abstinence. They should recognize that the values of the comics differ for individual children" (342). Strang's temperate view carried forward only in part, as McCullough, et al. concluded, "It is better for retarded readers to read the better type of comics than not to read at all. The policy of starting with the comics, if that is where the youngsters are, is generally recommended" (325–326).

Re-Examination and Foreshadowing

Previous historical analysis of the integration and acceptance of comics in educational settings has largely overlooked various efforts policy makers, classroom teachers, and reading experts made during the 1940s and 1950s to acknowledge comics as both a legitimate topic for inquiry and a valuable instructional tool in the English language arts. Rather than picking the low-hanging fruit, this chapter attempts to uncover neglected stories and evidence that clearly foreshadows modern interest in using the newly revitalized medium of comics to meet both the recreational reading needs of students (e.g. Gorman 2008) and to invigorate language arts instruction (e.g. Carter and Evensen 2010; Monnin 2010; Tilley 2008). The purpose in doing so is not only to offer a correction to our contemporary understanding of the legacy of comics in the lives of young people during the mid-twentieth century in the United States, but also to demonstrate this medium's long-standing potential in enhancing instruction. Clearly it would be overreaching to assert that comics were widely embraced by teachers and similar professionals during the 1940s and 1950s, but it would be equally irresponsible to dismiss or minimize the evidence. What is most unfortunate is that in the past when young people were avid readers of comics in all formats, educators were the ones who needed convincing of the medium's value; today, it is the reverse.

Notes

1. The section on radio broadcasts in *An Experience Curriculum* was quite prescient. For instance, it predicts that "soon one may expect to see people walking our streets with minute radio sets hung from their hats and going full blast as they step along" (Hatfield 1935, 64).

2. Somewhat strangely, less than a year after her article was published, Overton wrote a complimentary letter to Fredric Wertham, praising his work in speaking out against the comics industry. See Gertrude Overton, Letter to Frederic Wertham, July 31, 1954. In Box 124, Folder 3, Fredric Wertham Papers, Manuscript Division, Library of Congress, Washington, DC.

3. Comic Book Database, http://www.comicbookdb.com.

4. They also still praised *True Comics*, seemingly not realizing that this series had not been published since 1950.

References

Adams, Fay, Lillian Gray, and Dora Reese. 1949. *Teaching Children to Read*. New York: The Ronald Press Company.
Alvermann, Donna E. 2010. "The Teaching of Reading." In Erika Lindemann ed., *Reading the Past, Writing the Future: A Century of American Literacy Education and the National Council of Teachers of English*. Urbana, IL: National Council of Teachers of English.

Armstrong, David T. 1944. "How Good Are the Comic Books?" *Elementary English Review* 21: 283–285, 300.
Bechtel, Louise Seaman. 1941. "The Comics and Children's Books." *Horn Book* 17: 296–303.
Bender, Lauretta. 1944. "The Psychology of Children's Reading and the Comics." *Journal of Educational Sociology* 18: 223–231.
Carr, Constance. 1951. "Substitutes for the Comics I." *Elementary English* 28: 194–200, 214.
Carter, James Bucky, and Erik Evensen. 2010. *Super-Powered Word Study: Teaching Words and Word Parts Through Comics.* Gainesville, FL: Maupin House.
"Comic Comics." (1954. *Publisher's Weekly* 165: 2042.
Dias, Earl J. 1946. "Comic Books — A Challenge to the English Teacher." *English Journal* 35: 142–145.
Dorrell, Larry, Dan B. Curtis, and Kuldip R. Rampal. 1995. "Book-Worms Without Books? Students Reading Comic Books in the School House." *The Journal of Popular Culture* 29.2: 223–234.
Frank, Minna. 1950. "Remedial English Victories." *High Points* 32: 56–60.
Friedman, Irving R. 1941. "Comic Mags: I Let My Pupils Bring Funny Books to Class." *The Clearing House* 16: 166–168.
Gorman, Michele. 2008. "Graphic Novels Rule! The Latest and Greatest for Young Kids." *School Library Journal* 54: 42–49.
Gray, William S. 1943. "Educational News and Editorial Content." *Elementary School Journal* 43.9: 499–512.
Harris, Albert J. 1947. *How to Increase Reading Ability: A Guide to Individual and Remedial Methods* 2d ed. New York: Longmans.
Hatfield, W. Wilbur. 1935. *An Experience Curriculum in English: A Report of the Curriculum Commission of the National Council of Teachers of English.* New York: D. Appleton.
Hutchinson, Katharine H. December 1949. "An Experiment in the Use of Comics as Instructional Material." *Journal of Educational Sociology* 23: 236–245.
Jerrolds, Bob W. 1977. *Reading Reflections: The History of the International Reading Association.* Newark: International Reading Association.
Kessler, Clara Louise. 1948. "Leisure Time Interest Questionnaire." *Illinois Libraries* 30: 168–174.
Kinneman, Fleda Cooper. 1943. "The Comics and Their Appeal to the Youth of Today." *English Journal* 32: 331–335.
McCullough, Constance, Ruth Strang, and Arthur Traxler. 1955. *Problems in the Improvement of Reading* 2d ed. New York: McGraw Hill.
Monnin, Katie. 2010. *Teaching Graphic Novels: Practical Strategies for the Secondary ELA Classroom.* Gainesville, FL: Maupin House.
Netzer, Helen E. 1941. "Teaching Mexican Children in the First Grade." *The Modern Language Journal* 25: 322–325.
Nyberg, Amy Kiste. 1998. *Seal of Approval: The History of the Comics Code.* Jackson: University Press of Mississippi.
_____. 2002. "Poisoning Children's Culture: Comics and Their Critics." In Lydia Cushman Schurman and Deidre Johson, eds., *Scorned Literature: Essays on the History and Criticism of Popular Mass-Produced Fiction in America.* Westport, CT: Greenwood.
_____. 2010. "How Librarians Learned to Love the Graphic Novel." In Robert G. Weiner, ed., *Graphic Novels and Comics in Libraries and Archives: Essays on Readers, Research, History and Cataloging.* Jefferson, NC: McFarland.
Overton, Gertrude H. 1953. "Beowulf Can Be Fun: An Account of an Unorthodox Approach." *English Journal* 42.7: 392–393.
Raymond, John C., and Alexander Frazier. 1948. "Daytime Serials as Laboratory Material." *English Journal* 37.8: 394–399.
_____, and Alexander Frazier. 1949. "Reading Pictures: Report of a Unit." *English Journal* 38.10: 563–567.
Smith, Dora V. 1952. *The English Language Arts.* New York: Appleton-Century-Crofts.
Sones, W.W.D. 1943. "Comics in the Classroom." *School Executive* 63: 31–32, 82.
_____. 1947. "Comic Books Are Going to School." *Progressive Education* 24: 208–209, 212.
Strang, Ruth. 1943. "Why Children Read the Comics." *Elementary School Journal* 43: 336–342.
Tilley, Carol L. 2007. "Of Nightingales and Supermen: How Youth Services Librarians Responded to Comics Between the Years 1938 and 1955." Ph.D. Dissertation, Indiana University. Digital Dissertations (UMI Number: 3277995).
_____. 2008. "Reading Comics." *School Library Media Activities Monthly* 24: 23–26.

Witty, Paul. 1941. "Children's Interest in Reading the Comics." *Journal of Experimental Education* 10.2: 100–104.

_____. 1941. "Reading the Comics–A Comparative Study." *The Journal of Experimental Education* 10: 105–109.

_____. 1949. *Reading in Modern Education*. Boston: Heath.

_____, and David Kopel. 1939. *Reading and the Educative Process*. Boston: Ginn.

_____, Ethel Smith, and Ann Coomer. 1942. "Reading the Comics in Grades VII and VIII." *The Journal of Educational Psychology* 33: 173–182.

Stigmatization, Multimodality and Metaphor
Comics in the Adult English as a Second Language Classroom

Alice Leber-Cook *and* Roy T. Cook

Introduction

There is a growing literature on the use of comics in education generally, and on the use of comics in adult education in particular. Here we shall focus on the use of comics in adult English as a Second Language (ESL) classrooms. We shall concentrate on a specific theme regarding educational use of comics that has remained under-examined, and which has to our knowledge not been examined at all in the context of adult basic literacy education: the use of comics as a component of a larger curricular thrust towards providing learners with multimodal literacy competency.

Our examination of this issue shall proceed in three stages. In the first part, we will briefly look at how the reputation of comics, within both educational circles and society more broadly, has changed over the past half century, paying special attention to the difference between legitimating comics as a significant art form and legitimating them as a genuine form of reading.

In the second section we shall look at a parallel development in our understanding of literacy, one that shifted from a linear, writing-based model of reading to a more pluralistic understanding of literacy as involving multiple (often interwoven) modes of expression. This recent work on multimodal literacy promises to shed much light on the nature of comics and on their use in educational contexts.

Third, we shall look at some issues that are highlighted by thinking of comics as multimodal texts. In particular, a comparison of comics and digital technologies, and the difficulties that adult ESL learners may initially have with both, demonstrates that metaphor plays a crucial role in our understanding of both comics and computer technology. As a result, we will argue that an adult ESL curriculum that emphasizes the metaphors at work in comics can play a central role in introducing learners to abilities and concepts involved in a wide range of literacies, and this in turn will better prepare them for success in a world increasingly dominated by multimodality.

Past and Present Stigmatization

The various stigmas that have clung to comics find their roots in the anti-comics campaign that was spearheaded by the 1954 publication of psychologist Fredric Wertham's *Seduction of the Innocent*. The uproar created by Wertham's book and public appearances led to a U.S. Senate Subcommittee on Juvenile Delinquency hearing on the possible negative effects of comics. The resulting threat of government censorship led to the creation, by the comics industry, of the Comics Code Authority, whose actions led to a decades-long aesthetic crippling of the comics art form.

While the history of the anti-comics campaign is complex (Hadju 2009), and the controversy was not limited to American comics (Lent 1999), it will suffice for our purposes to note that one of the main themes underlying the attack on comics was that reading comics somehow "diluted" or "corrupted" true reading. The accepted view in the 1950s and beyond identified literacy with a single skill involving the linear scanning and comprehension of picture-free writing. While works containing illustrations to facilitate comprehension — that is, picture books — might be appropriate for very young readers, by adolescence such crutches were to be abandoned.

There are at least two ways that comics were thought to impede the development of "genuine" literacy skills. First, and most obviously, time spent reading comics was construed as time spent away from "real" literature. In addition, however, Wertham argued that comics foster the development of comprehension skills that conflict with, or prevent the development of, those skills required for genuine literacy, and as a result comics prevent their audience from appreciating supposedly higher forms of literature:

> [Reading comics] consists in gazing at the successive pictures of the comic book with a minimal reading of printed letters. Children may read the title, or occasionally an exclamation when the picture is particularly violent or sexually intriguing. This kind of picture reading is not actually a form of reading, nor is it a pre-stage of real reading. It is an evasion of reading and almost its opposite [Wertham 1954, 139–140].

This view of comics as a somehow debased form of reading only began to disappear with the critical acclaim and scholarly attention that comics began to receive in the mid-1990s. Nevertheless, this recently improved reputation should not fool us into thinking that comics have reached an equal footing with novels and other more traditional literature.

It is easy to think that that this battle has already been won: There is a growing academic literature on comics, and Art Spiegelman's *Maus*, Alan Moore's *Watchmen*, and Charles Schulz' *Peanuts* can be assigned in university courses with nary a raised eyebrow. In addition, comics play a central role in popular culture, as is evidenced by the substantial shelf space dedicated to their sale in bookstores and by the multitude of serious film adaptations. This evidence would seem to demonstrate that comics have shrugged off their bad reputation. Or so one would think. In actuality the picture is not quite so clear, and the complications arise due to two distinct, but often not clearly distinguished, ways in which comics scholars have tried to legitimate the medium.

A recent study of the use of comics in public school ESL classrooms by Bonny Norton and Karen Vanderheyden determined that, although children were open to the educational use of comics, they nevertheless retained older and supposedly outdated views about comics being inferior to "real" reading. Norton and Vanderheyden trace the roots of this problem to parents and teachers clinging to outmoded views of the nature of literacy. Their conclusion is striking:

we believe it is highly significant that these young language learners had accepted the dominant view that comics, in general, and *Archie* comics in particular, do not constitute "real reading" and hence have little educational value. It is clear that children are learning from a young age that "good reading" is associated with chapter books that are challenging, include lots of print, and have no pictures. When "good reading" is equated with "difficult reading," the second language learner is particularly disadvantaged... Further, it is possible to argue that while the use of chapter books, novels, and extended prose can have important pedagogical consequences for language learners, many teachers and parents may have shifted the focus of literacy instruction from meaning making to ritual [2003, 218].

In short, the general view is that comics might be serious and significant works of art, but they are not serious *texts*; thus comics can, and perhaps should, be the subject of serious study, but they are not, and cannot be, instances of *serious reading* (for additional evidence see Berninger 2010, Ziokowska and Howard 2010).

The issue is not merely a case of entrenchment, snobbery, or inertia. As Anne Frances Wysocki points out, the reluctance of educators and learners alike to see comics as on a par with other more traditional forms of literature stems at least in part from a natural, if ultimately misguided, comparison of comics with "serious" academic texts:

How might the visual appearance of most academic texts of the previous century — texts most often without photographs or illustrations or varied topography — have encouraged us to value (or devalue or repress) the visual in the circulation of academic and other "serious" writing? Is it perhaps because we have banished photographs and illustrations and typography from such texts that they have seemed appropriate for — and been able to play such a large part and continually return in — texts for children and advertising and other commercial work? [2004, 14].

If this view is right, then part of the blame for the continuing stigma attached to comics can be placed squarely at the feet of scholars and academics, even if the damage is unintentional. Even as scholars enthusiastically embrace broadened views of literacy (a phenomenon we shall discuss in detail below), they continue to produce scholarly work that for the most part fits squarely within older modes of categorization. If educators and learners continue to equate serious writing, and hence serious reading, with the sorts of un-illustrated texts produced by scholars (who study comics but who typically do not make them — Scott McCloud's *Understanding Comics* being the obvious exception here), then the idea that comics can be serious reading will likely continue to be viewed with suspicion by educators — even by educators who study comics or who use comics within their classroom for other purposes. After all, academic publications on comics often fall squarely within the picture-free model of serious writing (due, in part, to the difficulty of obtaining reproduction rights for comic art).

Of course, there are subtle issues at work here concerning the distinction between texts *generated* by scholars and texts *appreciated* by scholars. Nevertheless, it is clear that there are two different messages that comics scholars have been attempting to send to educators and the general public: That comics are worthy of study and inclusion in curricula, and that comics are a genuine form of reading. At present, it would seem that only the first message has truly taken hold.

These observations are quite general, but they have a particular relevance to teaching adult ESL learners. The reason is simple: although the majority of learners and educators in cultures with a robust comics tradition (including, but not limited to, English, French, and Japanese-speaking cultures) will have absorbed the first lesson about comics (that they are a legitimate art form and thus a worthy subject of study) even if they have not absorbed the second (that they are a legitimate form of reading), many adult ESL learners — at least, the majority that are not from French or Japanese speaking cultures — will not yet have absorbed even the first lesson.

The issue is a purely demographic one. Adult learners in ESL programs often leave their native countries because of a combination of poverty, oppression, violence, and other negative factors. This makes it especially unlikely that the learners in question will have had either the exposure to quality adult-oriented comics or the leisure time to appreciate them, and as a result it is unlikely that they will enter an ESL program with anything other than a Wertham-like view that comics are only appropriate for children and adolescents, if they are appropriate for anything at all.

Of course, the solution is simple, at least in principle: We need merely to convince these learners of the cultural and artistic importance, and of the educational and literary value, of comics. This is, of course, easier said than done. There is the obvious problem of communicating subtle cultural, aesthetic, and literary-theoretic points to learners who are newly learning English. There is an additional, even more difficult obstacle that needs to be overcome, however.

One of the most challenging aspects of teaching English to adult learners from other locales and other cultures is to balance the fact that the learners in question are autonomous adults with the fact that the material constituting the adult ESL curriculum is more commonly taught to much younger learners. As a result, there are issues of respect and sensitivity involved that are not found in other classroom environments. Special care must be taken to insure that adult ESL learner's do not feel that the curriculum or their treatment in the classroom is condescending — an outcome that could easily arise, for example, if the instructor used textbooks and other materials that were clearly designed with children in mind.

We shall not attempt to give a full solution to this problem here, since we have other fish to fry. Nevertheless, there is a general two-part strategy that recommends itself. In successfully incorporating comics into the adult ESL curriculum, care needs to be taken, first, in selecting which comics to present and, second, in deciding how these comics are to be presented.

With regard to the first issue, feelings of condescension can be minimized if the instructor chooses comics that are clearly aimed at an adult audience and deal with serious themes. As a result, superhero comics are best avoided in this context, if only because of the common perception that they are intended solely for children and adolescents. Other factors come into play in selecting appropriate comics for the adult ESL classroom, however. Issues of cultural sensitivity and conflict minimization make some comics ill-suited for learners in this environment. For example, it would be inappropriate to assign Marjane Satrapi's *Persepolis* to devout Muslim immigrants who might already feel conspicuous due to their religious beliefs. Other graphic novels with strong religious or political themes, such as Garth Ennis' *Preacher*, Howard Cruse's *Stuck Rubber Baby*, Joe Sacco's *Palestine*, Spain Rodriguez' *Che: A Graphic Biography*, and Keiji Nakazawa's *Barefoot Gen* are also ill-suited for use in a context where the risk of cultural conflict is already high.

With regard to the second issue, comics used in the classroom should be carefully integrated with other activities, such as vocabulary lessons, that will emphasize the fact that reading comics is a genuine form of reading, intimately connected with other forms of literacy. This can be achieved in a variety of ways. For example, the dialogue-laden nature of comics makes them a valuable ingredient in lessons on idiom and colloquialism. Along similar lines, lessons that involve learners creating their own comics allow learners with limited English-language vocabulary to create complex narratives. In these ways and many more, the instructor can clearly demonstrate to the learner that they are not simply learning to "read" comics, but that they are using comics to learn how to read and to learn how to write, where this understanding of reading and writing includes both traditional, predominantly written works and more multi-faceted works such as comics. We have provided a sample lesson plan along these lines — one which focuses on punctuation — in the appendix.

Although the discussion above only touches the surface of important practical issues regarding the effective incorporation of comics into an adult ESL curriculum, it pulls together two ideas that are central to the themes that will occupy us for the remainder of this essay. First, it emphasizes the distinction between approving of comics as a legitimate art form and object of study and approving of comics as a legitimate form of reading, and it highlights the complex changes that these attitudes have undergone over the last half-century — changes that are more complex than merely a shift from disapproval to approval. Second, it emphasizes the distinction between an understanding of reading centered on linear, image-free written works and a broader understanding of reading, literacy, and text that incorporates a wide range of works and an even wider range of skills. It turns out that attitudes towards this latter issue have also undergone striking shifts — shifts that are relevant both to the study of comics and to the role of comics in the adult ESL classroom.

Comics and Multimodal Literacy

There is no doubt that comics currently enjoy a better overall reputation than they had at the time of Wertham's anti-comics crusade, and that they are viewed as a significant art form worthy of serious attention. As discussed above, however, it is less clear that comics are viewed, by learners, educators, and the general public, as a genuine form of reading. Although we assumed above that comics *are* a genuine and valuable form of reading, it is worth looking at this claim in a bit more detail.

In the late 20th century, the rise of the Internet and other so-called New Media engendered a gradual shift in education research from a paradigm that devalues any media that does not fit the univocal "un-illustrated linear text" model to a paradigm that emphasizes multiple understandings of literacy corresponding to, amongst other things, the recent explosion in the number and complexity of available media. Particular attention has been paid to the notion of *multimodal* texts, and multimodal notions of literacy associated with these texts. Bill Cope and May Kalantzis, in the introduction to their influential anthology on multimodal literacy, characterize the new paradigm as motivated by:

> the increasing multiplicity and integration of significant modes of meaning-making, where the textual is also related to the visual, the audio, the spatial, the behavioural, and so on. This is particularly important in the mass media, multimedia, and in an electronic hypermedia. Meaning is made in ways that are increasingly multimodal — in which written-linguistic modes of meaning are part and parcel of visual, audio, and spatial patterns of meaning... To find our way around this emerging world of meaning requires a new, multimodal literacy [2000, 5].

Loosely put, a multimodal text is a single text whose decoding requires mastery of a number of different literacies. Multimodal texts can involve (but are certainly not limited to) two or more of: written language, spoken language, images (both fixed and moving), music, non-musical non-spoken sound, gestures, textures, and smells.

Web pages provide the paradigm example of a multimodal text: A website typically involves multiple types of information whose decoding requires distinct skills, such as blocks of linear (or non-linear!) writing, pictures or other images, and music or sound. In addition, however, these individual subtexts may be organized in highly complex, non-linear hyperlink-based structures, and as a result, comprehension of the website as a unified work requires new abilities — that is, multimodal literacy skills — that are not reducible to the skills required to comprehend the individual component subtexts. In short, competently understanding a website involves more than the mere skills required to decode each of the images, sounds, and writing that make up its individual parts (Jewitt 2003).

Multimodality is not limited to websites, however. Randy Bomer emphasizes the growing importance of a wealth of new types of multimodal texts:

> where print and image do the work of meaning together, where sound and music contribute to the perspectives readers are asked to take, where bodily performance works in tandem with the written word, where print itself is animated and choreographed... [2008, 354].

Needless to say, comics, with their unique and powerful combination of picture and word, are multimodal text *par excellence.* As a result, comics are, on this new understanding of literacy and text, not only genuine texts — experience of which constitutes genuine reading — but are also particularly interesting and important examples of this wider understanding of text.

While the extant literature on comics in education already addresses their status as multimodal texts, it tends to do so in the context of learners who are already familiar with, and minimally competent with, this newly recognized pluralism in literacy. As a result, researchers in this area have focused on the ways in which inclusion of comics in classroom curricula can increase the relevance and effectiveness of lessons on learners who are already immersed in, and saturated by, multiple literacies and modern multimodal literacy technologies (e.g. Schwarz 2002, 2006, 2007 and Schwartz and Rubinstein-Avila 2006). As a result, these studies tend to focus on comics as a means to make instruction more relevant to learners already familiar with and comfortable with multimodal communication. As Margaret Hagood emphasizes, however, in developing effective literacy curricula, we need to focus not only on new modes of literacy but also on how these new modes intersect with the learners we wish to serve:

> It is important ... to examine both the production and consumption of media and online communication of all users — not just of youth. In an age when adults and youngsters are concurrently learning how to use new media and online technologies, research on the topic needs to address multiple perspectives [Hagood 2003, 390].

As we shall see, when teaching adult learners at very basic levels of literacy, considerations of how the multimodal aspects of comics connect to these learners' consumption (or not) of other modern literacy technologies becomes crucial. As a result, comics turn out to be an immensely promising (and unfortunately, in our experience underutilized) ingredient of literacy instruction at this level.

Comics, Multimodality and Metaphor

In order to focus the remainder of this paper, we shall now shift from a general discussion to focus on a particular group of adult learners with which we are familiar: Adult ESL learners enrolled in the Minneapolis Public Schools Adult Education ESL programs. As a result, the particularities of the case will differ from other adult education scenarios.

We are confident that the general lessons to be learned, however, will hold in a broad range of adult basic literacy environments, including both ESL and Adult Basic Literacy (ABE) curricula for native English speakers.

A large segment of the ESL learners in the Minneapolis Public School program are adult learners whose skills are at or below the second grade (L2) level of literacy. In addition, many of these learners are Muslim East African women. As a result, there are two particular characteristics that strikingly differentiate these learners from the learners usually addressed in research on comics in education. The first is that these learners are at very basic levels of literacy competence. The second, and more important, is the fact that these learners typically cannot read or write in their native language and as a result are lacking many of the skills that we expect in adolescent or adult learners such as competence or even bare familiarity with computers and other technology.

The first distinguishing factor highlights how the multimodality of comics can be a direct advantage in the adult classroom. The phenomenon of learning new vocabulary through decoding the likely meaning of those expressions based on the larger environment in which they occur—learning words from context—is familiar. Research in this area has often focused on learners who already have some linguistic competence, and thus has examined the acquisition of new words based on their role in written texts comprised of otherwise familiar vocabulary (e.g. Nagy, Hermann, and Anderson 1985). Adult ESL learners at the very basic level, however, typically will not have the critical mass of basic vocabulary necessary in order to decipher meanings in this manner. What they do have is the ability to understand pictures. New information can be acquired at least as easily through a combination of words and pictures as through words alone (Mayer and Andersen 1992). As a result, comics have the potential to be an extremely useful tool for teaching new vocabulary to adult ESL learners (or anyone at very basic literacy levels) by facilitating vocabulary (and, at later stages, grammar) acquisition by encouraging learners to understand linguistic meaning in part through decoding visual information in the comics panel.

Before moving on, it should be noted that, in characterizing and attempting to understand the interaction between pictorial and verbal content in multimodal texts, it is important to avoid a number of misconceptions. First, we should not assume that decoding pictorial content is less difficult or cognitively less complex than decoding written content based on the fact that some learners are competent in the former but not the latter. Second, we should not assume that learners from other cultures will automatically interpret pictures in the same way Westerners do, since pictorial understanding is not uniform amongst cultures (see chapter 8 of Berry, Poortinga, Segall, and Dasen 2002 for a useful discussion).

The second distinguishing factor—the lack of familiarity with multimodal texts in general and digital technologies in particular—presents the instructor with both challenges and opportunities. One recurring theme in the literature on comics as a multimodal literacy tool is the idea that comics can be used to make instruction relevant to and interconnected with learners' digitally saturated, multimodal lives. As Bonny Norton and Karen Vanderheyden put it:

> if educators do not take seriously the social and cultural texts that are authorized by [learners]—which may simultaneously empower and disempower them—they run the risk of negating and silencing their students [2003, 204–205].

The use of comics as a tool to make lessons relevant and connected to broader concerns will be ineffective if the target learners lack the cultural background or technical skills to support these connections, however.

One of the most significant challenges for literacy instructors at the basic ESL level is the fact that learners often lack exposure to, and competence with, many of the kinds of texts and technologies that both instructors and more "traditional" learners take for granted. There are a number of reasons for this lack of exposure and expertise, including obvious ones such as poverty, general literacy issues, and lack of familiarity with keyboard skills and typed text. As a result, comics will not be effective in *reinforcing* pre-existing familiarities with multimodal texts, but they can be useful in *introducing* learners to multimodal texts incorporating multiple distinct literacy skills. This introduction, in turn, can play a central role in a larger curriculum involving the development of competencies with other multimodal literacies such as those associated with the computer and the internet.

There is a deeper (and theoretically much more interesting) reason for this widespread lack of competence with multimodal literacy amongst ESL learners. In addition to unfamiliarity with the relevant texts and technologies, learners are often unfamiliar with the metaphors associated with the multimodal texts themselves. Along with the development of multimodal texts has come a parallel framework of metaphors essential to understanding and working with these texts. For example, computer competence involves not just mastery of the keyboard, screen, modem, and disk, but also requires competency with a complex system of metaphor associated with the "office" design of computer applications such as Microsoft Word. Jonathan Keats traces the origin of this complex network of meanings to the introduction of the Macintosh computer and the office metaphors governing its operating system and applications. He locates the origins of these metaphors and themes in the now-famous 1984 Super Bowl advertisement introducing the Macintosh via an Orwellian motif. The advertisement features a Big-Brother-like view screen on which actor David Graham (representing IBM) proclaims "uniformity of thought" to a drone-like population. Actress Anya Major, wearing a shirt emblazoned with the Apple Macintosh logo and chased by riot-geared police, hurls a sledgehammer through the viewscreen, silencing the broadcast and freeing the masses from conformity (and hence from IBM). Keats notes:

> That the ad operated in such overtly metaphoric terms was apt, for it was with metaphor, rather than technology, that Apple made the computer accessible to anybody who cared to use one. How? By making it similar to the old-fashioned desktop. Gone was the need to memorize command lines, let alone programming languages as foreign to everyday life as Sanskrit. Managing data became as intuitive as manipulating physical files and folders. With the mouse as a prosthetic limb, anyone could get ahold of the computer power once hoarded by technological elite [Keats 2007, 57].

These metaphors only work when the computer user is familiar with common Western office environments. In addition, the web of metaphor involved in the design and understanding of computers and digital technology has long since outgrown its office-inspired origins, and involves metaphors from a number of distinct sources. Thus, concepts such as: desktop, folder, file, web, information superhighway, clipboard, cut, and paste—while familiar and relatively straightforward to most Westerners—will be alien to many learners from other cultures.

Interestingly, comics are comparably saturated with similar metaphorical devices and non-literal (or at least non-obvious) conventional symbolism. This, perhaps, should not be surprising: There is a growing body of interesting research on the role of metaphor in multimodal discourse, focusing on the particular skills required to decode metaphors that depend on two or more distinct literacies, the reasons why such metaphors are so prevalent in multimodal texts, and the ways in which our understanding of and analysis of such metaphors might differ from more traditional, linear-writing-based understandings (e.g., Forceville and Urios-Aparisi 2009).

The classic catalogue of such metaphorical devices in comics is Mort Walker's *The Lexicon of Comicana* (1980), which introduces humorous terminology for a number of such devices. Although Walker, the creator of the newspaper strips *Beetle Bailey* and *Hi and Lois*, first introduced these terms in a humorous piece written for the National Cartoonists Society, the fact that other comics creators began using his terms as serious taxonomical tools motivated him to create the *Lexicon* (which retains the humor of the original publication even as it is more ambitious in scope). For our purposes, however, it is not the humorous nomenclature that is of interest, but rather the broad cataloguing of common metaphorical and symbolic devices used in (Western) comics. A number of the devices that Walker catalogues in the *Lexicon* clearly function in much the same manner as office-based metaphors function within computer design and architecture. A few typical examples:

Briffits:	Motion-oriented dust clouds, even when indoors.
Hites:	Horizontal motion lines.
Lucaflext:	A window reflected on a shiny surface, even when no window is present.
Plewds:	Flying sweat droplets used to indicate embarrassment.
Squeans:	Stars indicating disorientation
Waftarons:	Curved lines representing an odor [from Walker 1980: 28 – 32].

The prevalence of such metaphors within comics provides the instructor with the opportunity to utilize comics as a powerful tool for introducing complex aspects of multimodal literacy into a basic ESL classroom. In addition to introducing learners to multimodal texts involving multiple modes of information presentation, comics can also be used to introduce learners to the rich roles that metaphorical devices can play in multimodal texts. Thus, comics are a promising means for providing ESL learners, who might have anxieties regarding the acquisition of unfamiliar technological skills, with the conceptual abilities requisite for mastering these other forms of multimodal literacy.

Equally importantly, the existence and accessibility of comics from other cultures — in particular, Japanese manga — not only allows instructors to introduce learners to the central role that metaphor plays in multimodal texts, but it also provides an easy way to demonstrate a central aspect of such metaphors — their conventionality. In comparing comics from different cultures, learners can experience firsthand how the metaphors used by one culture differ from those used by another culture. A typical example is the use of an image of sawing a log above a sleeping character's head to designate sleep in Western cartoons versus the use of "snot bubbles" to denote sleep within Japanese comics. These sorts of comparisons can serve a dual purpose, by usefully demonstrating the role that such metaphors play within comics (and, by extension, within other multimodal texts) and by emphasizing the cultural contingency of such metaphors. This latter role is important in demonstrating to the learner that these metaphors are (at least partially) culturally bound, and thus are not something that ought to be immediately recognized and understood. Instead, like other aspects of literacy, they must be learned.

Of course, as already emphasized above, the advantages of using comics in adult ESL classrooms (on in any classroom, for that matter) are not limited to their role in providing skills required for mastery of computer technology and other multimodal texts. First and foremost, we should not forget that comics are a significant, and woefully understudied and underappreciated, art form, and as a result any instruction involving quality comics is worthwhile for its own sake. In addition, the role that comics can play in providing learners with competencies specific to multimodal literacy should not be misconstrued as merely a novel route towards introducing computer and internet skills to learners. Just as comics are a serious art form, they are also an important type of multimodal text in and of themselves. Finally, comics and digital texts are themselves merely two examples from a much larger continuum of multimodal texts, including films, newspapers, and a multitude of multimedia technologies and environments. Lessons learned through the study of comics, and metaphor within comics, will thereby transfer to these other formats.

Conclusions

In this essay we have tracked two gradual and interconnected changes in our attitudes towards comics: our view of comics as legitimate both as an art form and as a form of reading, and our view of literacy as encompassing more than merely linear written texts. In doing so we have drawn a number of lessons about how comics can be fruitfully incorporated into adult ESL classrooms and about the specific benefits that can be expected upon doing so. In particular, viewing comics as a node in a complex network of interconnected types of multimodal texts — texts whose understanding depends fundamentally on new and often unfamiliar metaphors — has allowed us to gain a deeper understanding of comics themselves, but it has also provided insight into the ways in which comics can be used to strengthen connections between comics and other (multimodal) media. This essay has only scratched the surface of these issues, however, and it is clear that there remain deep theoretical and practical strata to be explored.

Appendix A: Word Balloon Punctuation Lesson

Learning Level: Pre-lit to Level 1 Adult Learner. This lesson is intended to supplement introductory lessons on sentence punctuation while introducing learners to complex meaning-creating mechanisms at work in comics.

Learning Objectives: To strengthen learners' understanding of punctuation marks by associating them with non-verbal content; to develop learners' abilities to decipher narrative content in comics based on non-verbal cues.

Materials: A few pages of a content-appropriate comic with the thought and speech balloon text deleted (either digitally or with correction fluid), one copy for each learner. One copy of the original unaltered comic.

Lead In: Review the differences between ".," "!," and "?."

Procedure

Step 1: Learners are given a few minutes to read their copy of the text-free comic. Learners then write one of ".," "!," or "?" in each empty speech or thought balloon based on whether they think that character is making a statement, making an exclamation, or asking a question. It should be emphasized to learners that there is no "right" answer here. Instead, the activity should be viewed as a puzzle where the clues might not determine a unique answer.

Step 2: Learners post their filled-in comics on the classroom wall, and discuss how they decided which punctuation mark to use in each balloon. The instructor should focus discussion on instances where learners disagreed about a particular balloon, and encourage students to discuss the type of data they used in choosing a punctuation mark (e.g., body position, facial expression, background information, metaphor, conventional symbol, etc.).

Step 3: The original comic, with text intact, is posted on the wall. The instructor leads the learners in examining how the actual dialogue in the original comic differs (or not) from their interpretation of it, and what reasons might underlie any differences.

References

Berninger, Mark. 2010. "Workshop II: Comics in School." In Mark Berninger, Jochen Ecke, and Gideon Haberkorn, eds., *Comics as a Nexus of Cultures: Essays on the Interplay of Media, Disciplines, and International Perspectives.* Jefferson NC: McFarland: 245–252.
Berry, John, Ype Poortinga, Marshall Segall, and Pierre Dasen. 2002. *Cross-Cultural Psychology: Research and Applications.* 2d ed. Cambridge: Cambridge University Press.
Bomer, Randy. 2008. "Literacy Classrooms: Making Minds Out of Multimodal Material." In James Flood, Shirley Brice Heath, and Diane Lapp, eds., *Handbook on Teaching Literacy Through the Communicative and Visual Arts.* New York: Lawrence Erlbaum Associates: 353–361.
Cope, Bill, and Mary Kalantzis, eds. 2000. *Multiliteracies: Literacy Learning and the Design of Social Futures.* New York: Routledge.
Forceville, Charles J., and Eduardo Urios-Aparisi, eds. 2009. *Multimodal Metaphor.* Berlin: Walter de Gruyter.
Hadju, David. 2009. *The Ten Cent Plague: The Great Comic Book Scare and How It Changed America.* New York: Picador.
Hagood, Margaret. 2003. "New Media and Online Literacies: No Age Left Behind." *Reading Research Quarterly* 38.3: 387–391.
Jewitt, Cary. 2003. *Technology, Literacy, and Learning: A Multimodal Approach.* London: Routledge.
Keats, Jonathan. 2007. *Control+Alt+Delete: A Dictionary of Cyberslang.* Guilford, CT: Lyons Press.
Lent, John. 1999. *Pulp Demons: International Dimensions of the Postwar Anti-Comics Campaign.* Lanham, MD: Farleigh Dickinson University Press.
Mayer, Richard, and Richard Anderson. 1992. "The Instructive Animation: Helping Students Build Connections Between Words and Pictures in Multimedia Classrooms." *The Journal of Educational Psychology* 84.4: 444–452.
McCloud, Scott. 1994. *Understanding Comics: The Invisible Art.* New York: Harper.
Nagy, William, Patricia Herman, and Richard Anderson. 1985. "Learning Words from Context." *Reading Research Quarterly* 20.2: 233–253.
Norton, Bonny, and Karen Vanderheyden. 2003. "Comic Book Culture and Second Language Learners." In Bonny Norton and Kelleen Toohey, eds., *Critical Pedagogies and Language Learning.* Cambridge: Cambridge University Press: 201–221.
Schwartz, Adam, and Eliane Rubinstein-Avila. 2006. "Understanding the Manga Hype: Uncovering the Multimodality of Comic-Book Literacies." *Journal of Adolescent and Adult Literacy* 50.1: 40–49.
Schwarz, Gretchen. 2007. "Media Literacy, Graphic Novels, and Social Issues." *Studies in Media and Information Literacy Education* 7.4: 1–11.
_____. 2006. "Expanding Literacies Through Graphic Novels." *The English Journal* 95.6: 58–64.
_____. 2002. "Graphic Novels for Multiple Literacies." *Journal of Adolescent and Adult Literacy* 46: 262–265.
Walker, Mort. 1980. *The Lexicon of Comicana*, Lincoln, NE: iUniverse Books.
Wertham, Fredric. 1954. *Seduction of the Innocent: The Influence of Comic Books on Today's Youth.* New York: Rinehart & Company.
Wysocki, Anne Frances. 2004. "Opening New Media to Writing: Openings & Justifications." In Anne Frances Wysocki, Johndan Johnson-Eilola, Cynthia L. Selfe, and Geoffrey Sirc, eds., *Writing New Media: Theory and Applications for Expanding the Teaching of Composition.* Logan: Utah State University Press, 1–23.

Ziolkowska, Sarah, and Vivian Howard. 2010. "Forty-One-Year-Old Academics Aren't Supposed to Like Comics: The Value of Comic Books to Adult Readers." In Robert G. Weiner, ed., *Graphic Novels and Comics in Libraries and Archives: Essays on Readers, Research, History, and Cataloguing.* Jefferson, NC: McFarland, 154–166.

The Attitudes of Some Students on the Use of Comics in Higher Education

CHRISTINA L. BLANCH *and*
THALIA M. MULVIHILL

> It never felt like an assignment. It was more like an adventure. Like you're discovering things as they play out.
> — Mickey Smith

Comic books have generated a unique, innovative and highly analytical subculture in the United States that is too often belittled as the last refuge for "geeks" and "weirdos" or simply thought of as fodder for young children. There is much more to the field of comics than that. They are not just for kids anymore. They have not really been just for kids for decades. And from personal experience, the diversity amongst comic book readers is startling.

There have been several studies on deconstructing comics and their reflection upon what is occurring in culture (Heer and Worcester 2009; Wolk 2007; Wright 2001). Comic creators not only invent their own cultures, but borrow themes from traditional and contemporary cultures to which readers can relate. In fact, to understand most comic cultures, the reader must be familiar with current events. For example, recent issues of Captain America have seen the title hero take on fiendish plots related to the financial crisis, the tea party movement, and even saw him pardoned by President Barack Obama himself (Issues *Captain America* #34, *Captain America* #601, *Siege* #4).

There is a sparse but growing amount of research on using comics as teaching tools that focus mainly on lower grades. This area of research, however, is lacking in higher education. We believe that this form of learning is beneficial to students of all ages. They have been used as reading tools for younger children, but comics have use in the higher education classroom as well. We argue that comics, also referred to as graphic novels or graphica, are legitimate forms of literature and can be used as teaching tools in higher education. They are manifestations of popular literature and they are becoming legitimate forms of literary and pictoral art. We believe comics are simply modern forms of narrative and that the educational potential of comics has not yet fully been realized.

There are several research questions for this study relating to the use of comics as textbooks in the higher education classroom. The first research question is, can comics promote lifelong learning by engaging students? The other aspect of this research project focuses on the learning methods and the retention of information. This aspect deals with the idea of comics as whole brain activities. The final question is, how is the idea of using a comic book as a text book in a college class received by the students? Hopefully this study will shed some light on these questions by looking at a group of students who have used comics as a textbook and analyzing their perceptions.

Literature Review

When someone mentions the word comics, several meanings may be derived by the listener. They usually associate it with superheroes such as Batman, Iron Man, Wonder Woman, Green Lantern, or Spider-man to name a few. They could think of comics as in "comic strips" including *Peanuts* or *The Far Side*. They could even think of comics as people who make them laugh, such as Steve Martin or "The Last Comic Standing" television show. All of the aforementioned definitions could be applied to the word comics. Comics are most often equated with superheroes. Yet, to read comics you do not have to read about superheroes. *American Splendor* by Harvey Pekar, *Maus* by Art Spiegelman, *Sandman* by Neil Gaiman, and *A Contract with God* by Will Eisner are extremely popular, non-superhero comics and they hold a great influence over the medium.

For this essay, we are using Scott McCloud's definition. He defines comics as "juxtaposed pictorial and other images in deliberate sequence, intended to convey information and/or to produce an aesthetic response in the viewer" (McCloud 1993, 9). A simpler definition would be using a combination of art and prose to tell a story or narrative.

HISTORY OF COMICS IN EDUCATION

Soon after the comic book industry began in 1933, educators began thinking of creative ways to use them to teach students. W.W.D. Sones (1944) was one of the first scholars to conduct studies on the use of comics in the classroom. Curriculums were designed to include comics (Hutchinson 1949) and the *Journal of Educational Sociology* devoted an entire volume to the topic of comics in the classroom (1944). Even the director of the Child Study Associates of America believed that due to the popularity of comics they could be used in the classroom as educational tools (Gruenberg 1944).

As with any new teaching method, some educators approved of the use of comics and some vehemently opposed it. Some educators, and many librarians, believed that comics were rubbish and impeded learning (Dorrell, Curtis, and Rampal 1995). Many of these educators agreed with the psychiatrist Frederic Wertham, the figurehead for the charge against comic books, who warned America of their dangerous nature. Wertham testified in 1954 against comics and by the time the investigation was over, it was decided that comics were bad for children and any thoughts regarding the educational value of comics stopped.

In the 1970's some scholars began reintegrating comics into their curriculum (Alongi 1974; Brocka 1979; Haugaard 1973; Koenke 1981). However, these uses were scarce and the words of Wertham still lingered. In 1992 when Art Spiegelman's *Maus* (1986; 1991) became the first comic book to win a Pulitzer Prize people began to take another look at comics as literate works that could be used in the classroom.

Today, educators have started to see comics as valuable teaching tools. They can be applied at any education level and incorporated into practically any subject. They are used in many different areas of study including Media studies or Language Arts (Ballenger 2006; Monin 2010; Norton 2003; Schoof 1978; Versaci 2001), Popular Culture (Brocka 1979), Art Education (Williams 2008), Communication (Duncan and Smith 2009), the Foreign Language Classroom (Ellman 1979; Marsh 1978), Physics (Kakalios 2002), History (Dobrowolski 1976), and Business Ethics (Gerde and Foster 2008) to name a few. There is even a new trend emerging in Comic Studies (Heer and Worcester 2009; Pustz 1999) as more universities recognize comics as a serious medium.

There is still a stigma attached to comics, however. In the past, and even today, comic books and graphic novels have been looked down upon by literary scholars. It did not help the validity of comics when in the 1940's and 1950's it was feared that comics would lead to mental stagnation and moral decay (Wertham 1954). Finally, after comics changed due to the new "comics code" that publishers were made to follow, comics began to be thought of as a stimulation for unmotivated learners by some educators (Ellman 1979). Yet, they still remained amusing toys to the majority of scholars. Advocates of using comics in education still see a stigma retained on the use of comics among educators and even some students (Viadero 2009). Matt Smith, comics scholar and co-author of *The Power of Comics*, says "There's no denying there's still a stigma to comic arts studies" (McGinn 2009). In fact, Smith would not even bring up the topic of using comics in the classroom until he was granted tenure. But as he became empowered by tenure, he now offers comic studies classes including Comics as Culture, Comic Studies Fieldwork courses, and a course on the books of comic creators such as Alan Moore (*Watchmen*).

Why Comic Books?

In a visually saturated world, students today have been weaned on a fully stimulated mind experience. The majority of the students that educators are teaching have grown up watching MTV and playing the Xbox. In this visual age of computers, internet, and television, education must change fundamentally in order to be effective (Murr and Williams 1988). The education system that emphasizes reading, lecturing, and ideas that have been around since antiquated times needs to be balanced by something more compatible with our visual culture. This does not mean giving up on the basics of reading and writing, but altering it to a system that is more compatible with today's visual culture.

Still, teaching culturally diverse students can be challenging and basic differences in the teacher's background and the student's background can cause stress and failure in the classroom (Svinick and McKeachie 2011). Comics can help to bridge those cultural differences as the graphics and the language that they communicate can be easier to convey. Comics can also bridge socioeconomic and generational gaps (Gerde and Foster 2008).

We are not arguing that one type of teaching method, specifically using comics, should replace all others types, but they should be included in the teaching arsenal. Even though people have been warned that television will vulgarize society and our children's intellect, many educators include television and movies in their curriculum. Educators do not only use one teaching method, they use many different types to engage the different basic learning styles of students—visual, auditory/verbal, tactile, and kinesthetic (Dunn and Dunn 1993).

Comic books can address these different learning styles at once, while engaging students at the same time. Some of comic books' strengths as teaching tools are that they are motivating, they are popular and reflect popular culture, they are visual and have a permanent component, and they are a whole-brain activity.

Motivation and Engagement

There are many reasons comics are good teaching tools. Comics are inherently interesting and the pictures are eye-catching. Students are interested in them and they become motivated. Comics create opportunities for students and educators to engage in meaningful dialogue (Williams 2008). Kay Haugaard, a teacher and early proponent of comics in the classroom, wrote in her article *Comic Books: Conduits to Culture* that "if educators ever find out what constitutes the fantastic motivating power of the comic book, I hope they bottle it and sprinkle it around schoolrooms" (1973, 55). By using comic books in the classroom, educators can benefit from this motivation.

Motivating students is a topic that concerns most educators (Svinicki and McKeachie 2011). The complex media environment surrounding today's students sometimes make traditional classroom materials seem dull or boring to the students. Using comic books as classroom teaching tools catches the students off balance and leads them to become more engaged and motivated (Versaci 2001). Disengaged students and those who are nonparticipants in classroom discussions can be distracting to educators. Many students lose motivation to speak in class for many reasons such as fear of being embarrassed, lack of knowledge, cultural norms, and boredom (Svinicki and McKeachie 2011). By using comics as a teaching tool, many of these fears are allayed because of the ideology attached to comic books. This breakdown of the norms of culture can motivate students to take part in classroom dialogue.

With comics, the words give substance to the meaning and sequences of actions. Veteran comic book writer Mark Waid commented that "the medium is novel in that it in some ways provides more information to the reader than prose and in other ways, less. Good graphic novels such as *Maus* and *Watchmen* engage the imagination in ways that no other medium can" (Personal communication). When students' imaginations are engaged, they take part in conversations and realized that their lives and stories are sources of knowledge, something that education seldom treats as so (Palmer 1998).

Popular Culture and Real life

Students are drenched in popular culture in their everyday lives. By incorporating popular culture into the classroom, educators can bridge the divide between the student's lives in and out of school (Morrison, Braun, and Chilcoat 2002). There should be a continuum between what is going on in the student's life and their experiences in school. Hutchinson states that "new learning always is a continuation or expansion of learning already possessed by the learner (1949, 236). Using comics is a way for educators to incorporate popular culture into the classroom and lead students in discussions about lifestyles, myths, and values that they already possess (Brocka 1979).

Students often have a difficult time transferring what they have learned into the real world or even to other classes (Svinicki and McKeachie 2011). This is due to the context in which the information was learned. Making a connection between what the students are learning and their own lives should be a goal of educators (Palmer 1998). By incorporating comic books as popular culture into the classroom, the students relate their learning to the real world and then can see the concepts of what they are learning in everyday activities, therefore, applying what they have learned. Although most comic book worlds are not reality, the students can relate to the characters.

Comic books can also instill a love of reading which can translate into life-long learning. As young children learn to read using the comic book, they also learn to love reading and this will then be transferred to reading more and more. World leaders such as Desmond Tutu and President Barack Obama have both been quoted as saying that they read comic books when they were young and for them, it instilled a love of reading (http://www.usa today.com/life/books/news/2009–01–07-obama-spiderman-comic_N.html).

Learning Methods

The combination of text and graphics can be powerful. They can "literally 'put a human face' on a given subject" (Versaci 2001, 62). Comic books can increase learning for the visual learner while also addressing the needs of the verbal learner (Mayer and Massa 2003).

Besides helping visual and verbal learners simultaneously, comics also have visual permanence. Instead of time happening sequentially for a predetermined period, the reader takes in the information at the student's own pace, thus giving the student control (McCloud 1993). This is very similar to reading a literary novel, but the graphic elements add a visual layer. It comes down to the point that visual learners benefit from visual media. In a world that has so much information available visually at one time and with an increase in the diagnoses of ADD and ADHD, comic books provide focused "snapshots" that help to keep the mind from wandering.

Reading comics is a whole brain activity. Our human brain has two sides and is asymmetrical. This is one of the characteristics of our genus, *Homo*. Our previous ancestors, the Australopithecines had symmetrical brains, both sides being like a mirror image of the other. However, 2.4 million years ago, the first of the human line evolved with an asymmetrical brain. It is at that point in time that human culture began to flourish.

The two hemispheres of the brain work in different ways and are used for different tasks such as problem solving logically or by hunches and splitting or lumping. The left hemisphere is logical and works in processing mathematical information, using language, writing, and performing logical deductions. The right hemisphere is responsible for imagining, artistic, and intuitive abilities. Most people favor one hemisphere or the other. Traditionally, the educational system has favored left hemisphere activities such as reading, writing, and listening (Williams 1983).

Linda Verlee Williams, author of *Teaching for the Two Sided Mind: A Guide to Right Brain/Left Brain Education*, describes the left side of the brain as a computer working lineally and sequentially, while the right side is a kaleidoscope, "combining parts to create a rich variety of patterns" (1983, 6). Certain tasks, like complex thinking however, take cooperation from both sides of the brain.

To make full use of whole brain cooperation does not mean that an educator needs to stop using books or giving lectures, but to balance those things with activities that stimulate the right hemisphere. When educators present information to students both visually and verbally, student's brains make those connections and "develop a full and varied repertoire of thinking strategies" (Williams 1983, 10). When using comics, the whole brain is engaged. The right brain is engaged with the graphics and left brain is engaged with the storyline, making use of both hemispheres. To read a story and see the story at the same time forces sensory connections to both the left and right hemispheres processors (Murr and Williams

1988). This makes learning more effective, and might even make it fun. If educators can make learning "something we do as a matter of living a useful, happy, productive life," it becomes beneficial to society as a whole (Murr and Williams 1988, 418).

Methodology

This qualitative study was conducted through semi-structured, face-to-face interviews (Patton 1990) which were recorded and transcribed. The participants were volunteers from a group of students who had participated in and successfully completed an Introductory Cultural Anthropology class in which the comic book *Y: The Last Man* was used as a textbook. In this series, Yorick Brown and his monkey are the only males left alive on the planet after a devastating plague hits. Gender roles are thrown for a loop, women are the only ones left to share experiences with, the full effect of discrimination is seen in what jobs must be filled, and there is the realization that the planet is doomed without a reproducing species is not lost on its inhabitants. Some accept their fate, some fight to find a way to reverse the annihilation, and some even denounce any fight to survive as opposition to God's will.

In total, six participants were recruited through sending an introductory e-mail and the students who responded were selected to be interviewed.

The interview instrument was formulated through incorporated themes found while conducting a literature review on the use of comics in the classroom. In all cases, the of the participants was assured, and the names of the participants' real names and the names of any other persons/places mentioned in the interview did not appear on the transcripts. Inductive analysis was used with the data for this study as it allows critical themes to emerge (Patton 1990). All of the interviews were analyzed and coded using an inductive data analysis process: a system of open, axial, and thematic coding (Strauss and Corbin 1990). The codes were engagement and life-long learning, love of reading, real literature, learning methods, social, mini-communities, involving others, and connections between classes.

Theory is an "ever-developing entity" (Glaser and Strauss 1967, 32). In qualitative research the goal is not to test a theory, but to generate a theory. For this study we are using the approach of grounded theory developed by sociologists (Glaser and Strauss 1976; Strauss and Corbin 1990). The approach of grounded theory is to produce transcripts of interviews, identify analytic categories or themes, pull the data from those categories together and compare them, use the categories to build theoretical models, and present the analysis using quotes from interviews for illumination (Bernard 2006).

DESCRIPTION OF PARTICIPANTS

All six of the participants were over 18 and enrolled at Ball State University. They all had attended and successfully completed "Introduction of Cultural Anthropology" in the Spring of 2009. Of the six participants, two were male and four were female. The below table is a short summary of the participants, including pseudonyms, majors and minor, interest in comic books, and if they had used comics for a class previously.

Name	*Major(s)*	*Minor(s)*	*Interest in comic books*	*Comics used in classes previous*
Donna Noble	English Studies	Spanish	None	No
Jack Harkness	Secondary Education	None	Avid	No

Name	Major(s)	Minor(s)	Interest in comic books	Comics used in classes previous
Amy Pond	Anthropology Biology	None	None	No
Martha Jones	Wildlife Biology and Ecology	Anthropology French	Somewhat interested	No
Mickey Smith	Computer Science	None	None	No
Rose Tyler	Telecommunications	Anthropology Entrepreneurship	None	No

Participants in the study.

Findings

> I felt like I was having fun while completing classwork and actually furthering my knowledge of anthropology.
> — Jack Harkness

All of the six participants were asked questions and their answers were analyzed according to the criteria provided in the previous section. While each participant had a unique perspective, there were some clear patterns of similarities detected. First all of the participants read the comic and believed that it contributed to their education in a way that provided life-long learning. Second, all the participants thought that they retained the information better due to the presentation in the form of a comic book. Finally, a surprising result of a social nature was found to have occurred in the classroom due to the commonality of everyone reading the comic book.

Engagement and Life-Long Learning

> Learning is not designated to like, only prescribed areas and if you can find ways to teach those in unique ways, kids are going to learn it a lot better.
> — Donna Noble

Before taking this class very few students had read a comic before. In fact, while some students viewed them like Mickey, as the things that "a pasty, white guy stuck ... in the basement of their parent's house" read, others were afraid that they were not going to understand them. Both of these responses were expected as the former is the typical stereotype of comic books and their readers (Lopes 2006) while the latter is due to lack of the skills required to obtain a proficiency in visual literacy (Eisner 1985). One student said that comics were just simply not real literature. Donna commented that "I was an English major and I read a lot of books and comics just weren't part of my canon."

While some were anxious either positively or negatively about reading the comic book, some were excited. "Awesome" and "Hooray" along with "Really?" were a few responses when asked what they first thought upon discovering a comic book was being used as a textbook. Most of the students were like Martha who was "excited 'cause it wasn't a boring textbook." Mickey thought it "was new and strange so it made it more interesting."

For those who were unsure about using the comic, after they read it they had different opinions. Rose said she now likes comics and doesn't think they are geeky anymore. It was more academic than she thought it would be, it "made me think outside the normal textbook," and being a Freshman it taught her "how you have to think differently in college." Mickey was surprised that you could pull out so much important information from a comic book—skills like analytical skills and creative skills. For Jack, who was already an avid comic book reader, he was surprised everyone liked it, not just nerds, but even several "Greek" kids he knew loved it.

During the study it was found that of the six participants and their friends, only one student reads all of their textbooks, three read some of them, and six read none of them. Getting students to read can be a challenge. This is one of the benefits of the different approach of using a comic as a textbook in the classroom. The students are engaged and want to read. In fact, several students read the whole comic in one day. Mickey read the book in one day. So did Amy. She actually read it more than once. Donna, the English studies major, also did and remarked that the "only way that would happen is if I enjoyed what I was reading." Martha spread out reading it over several days but instead of selling the book back, as she does with all of her textbooks, she kept the comic. Jack said that he thinks everyone in the class read it and said that "everyone I talked to in the class actually read all of the assigned reading for that comic book."

Can comic books motivate students to read the texts? Rose felt that "people might see comics in classes as a new thing and they would be willing to try it and they'll realize that it's not bad having to read for class." She added that reading the comic would make her want to read the other books. Martha thought maybe the comic was too fun and students would then be let down by a textbook.

Love of Reading and "Real" Literature

> Well, I started reading different types of books and it got me back into more teeny stuff which I know sounds weird. But it just got me reading again which is kind of a big deal 'cause that semester I hadn't taken a lot of English classes. So, it got me back into reading. It reminded me why I loved English language so.
> — Donna Noble

The comic book combines "the subtlety and intimacy we get from good literary books while providing the speed of apprehension and the excitingly scramble, hybrid reading experience we get from watching, say, computer screens that are full of visuals as well as text" (Tabachnick 2007, p. 25). While at first Donna did not see comic books as real literature, she views them differently now. "It was probably the best book I've read that has been assigned to me in my entire, like, educational experience."

Jack believed that it helped him to understand that many different forms of media can have academic purposes. As a secondary education major he said that he believes that they are such a good learning tool that he is considering trying to work them in his curricula when he teaches upon seeing "how much of a positive reaction it can get from the students." It helped this future teacher to realize that learning is all around us, not just in textbooks.

Martha believes that reading the comic made reading fun. "It's actually made me want to read more of them. But learn, not just for fun, but you're learning and you're having fun. Which we don't get enough of here in school." She went on to say that enjoying the reading made her want to understand the material we were learning in class more and opened her up to other reading materials. As Donna said "Learning is not designated to like, only prescribed areas and if you can find ways to teach those in unique ways, kids are going to learn it a lot better." You can have fun and learn at the same time.

Learning Methods

> As soon as you said it, like, I would think about it in the graphic novel and it made it all easier. I could just reference that in picture form like in my head.
> — Amy Pond

Just as a teacher writes information on the board or shows a powerpoint presentation and then explains the information, a comic book uses both visual and written (akin to spoken) language at once. Donna mentions that if there is a tangible way to see what is being taught it is easier as you are not just reading but seeing. "It was multiple ways of learning, different ways of leaning, all combined in one thing. And it was really interesting." She said reading the comic expanded her mindset on different ways of learning materials. Martha thought the marriage of pictures and text made her want to understand the material more and helped her to understand the material. Jack agreed. He thought it was a different way to learn where you were not just absorbing information thrown as you, but that it was "secretly talking about anthropology" which allowed you to understand the information and relate it to the topic being studied.

Retention

> I've read books for classes before and I don't even remember reading them. And I remember everything about the comic and I remember why I thought it was interesting because we talked about it and we just looked at it so carefully about what it meant, what the culture was in it. And so feel like it's one of those few books that I've actually retained throughout my entire education.
> — Rose Tyler

Rose went on to say that other students in her Anthropology classes do not seem to have retained as much as she did. She said that the concepts learned from the comic have helped her in her other classes. Rose is not the only one who thinks that they retained the information from the comic more than they would from a textbook. Mickey said that the comic helps you to remember because it is applied and not just a definition.

Students know how they learn. Martha explained that she is a kinesthetic learner. She explained that she still has the information in her head from the comic "when a lot of information from my other classes and other textbooks are gone." She wondered "would I be better in my classes, or would I retain the information better if ... there wasn't just a teacher there who is just giving us this big old book to just read through or would it be more interesting if it had a more interesting context for us. For students. Hopefully more teachers will be doing this."

While the students agree that the comic helped them to retain information, most agreed that textbooks were still important to "set up the background information you need in order to draw those conclusions from a comic book" because you need to "know what you're looking for in order to find it."

Social Aspects

> Not always can I just walk outside and just do something and reference it to my class. It's very difficult to do that.
> — Amy Pond

Richard Light (2001) assumed that memorable learning took place inside the college classroom. He interviewed college students for a research project and found that learning outside of the classroom was vital. Events outside the classroom are so important to a student's college experience. Getting students to take what they are learning in the classroom into their lives outside the classroom.

An aspect of the use of comics in the classroom that was unexpected was a social one. We assumed that reading is a solitary activity or at least an activity that would not be openly talked about due to the attached stigma. However, the students seemed to talk quite a lot about the comic both in and out of class. One social aspect was telling others about the comic book. All of the participants told others about reading the comic for class. Donna told her boyfriend about it and he even read the comic, too. Rose told her father and he was skeptical about it until he read her final paper, and then he also read the comic. Other participants said they had fun telling people about the comic and how it related to class. Many thought it was unique and others were jealous. Donna told her English class about it a year later when they were talking about different way of writing and how to present ideas in various ways.

People in class seemed to form mini-communities when talking about how the comic would end. For example, Martha talked about how the biology majors thought certain suggestions about the ending were impossible, and theology majors would then veto other ideas. She said there was a lot of talk regarding the book and everyone had their own ideas about what would happen. Students would use references from class to deny or confirm what could happen and "it became kind of like a huge debate."

Rose heard the same type of debates. "I really think that people enjoyed it. Or at least they, I would hear discussions about how they thought it would end because it was only the first book. And I would hear debates about it before and after class about how the rest of the series would go. And I think that really shows how interested people were in, um, in the comic and what was going to happen. And so it made them really think about the characters and the culture and the comic."

Jack mentioned that he would talk to people in his dorm that were in the course with him and how they would all talk about the comic outside of class. Donna mentioned how she and her friend in the class would talk after class and one day spent "a good 45 minutes talking about the book. And how much fun we had had in class that day and talking about the charts that you make, like the kinship charts, talking about the kinship charts and how messed up the *Y: The Last Man* guys kinship chart would look."

In addition to social life outside of the classroom, there was another social aspect inside the classroom, or really between classrooms. Making connections between classes is hard to get students to do. Many of the students said that the comic book made them realize that there are connections between classes, like Donna.

Jack also thought it helped with other classes. "I guess it just made me think about culture more, like when other events came up in other classes I related it on more to how different cultures would handle them. I guess I just used the cultural aspect a lot more and how I related it to my other classes more." He used the concepts from *Y: The Last Man* in his other classes "and I don't think I would have ever done that if I just taken the standard anthropology course instead of using the comic." These connections not only happened in the classroom, but in their outside lives. Amy mentioned that things outside of class that are "normal and fun could actually be referenced to something I learned in class. Not always can I make that connection to my life."

Another connection the students made was even more important. It was used to inspire them to do better in their field. Martha said that "as I was writing the paper (the *Y: The Last Man paper*) and as I reread it, like, the way I was talking about the comic book and what we learning about globalization and how you know 90 percent of the really, like, very important jobs that we take for granted today are mainly men ... I'm really trying my best to be the best in my field so that I can be a better example for other women who want to do the same thing."

Summary

Print based texts are extremely important in education, but it is also true that "new concepts of language must be developed with the emergence of the visual culture" (Ornstein 1977). Just as the invention of the alphabet and the printing press altered educational methods in the past, with the invention of a plethora of visual tools, it must be altered again. Socrates did not write books and "believed that they were inferior to the spoken word as a means of education" and that they would "vulgarize learning" (Boorstin 1983, p. 529). He was wrong. Methods change as diffusion and invention occur and we must change the way that we educate students in this process. Students from this study seem to agree. Simply reading plain textbooks and lecturing to classes is not the way for this new generation to learn. Most students feel like Martha does about textbooks. She falls asleep while reading them. But, when Martha was reading the comic book she "wasn't like about to fall asleep. It was a lot more interesting and I learned the exact same material." Students today have different needs and educators need to meet those needs.

Several research questions were posed in this study. We believe the results from this study answer those questions. The results show that using comics as teaching tools in the college classroom is a positive idea for both instructors and students. The comics engage students. Comics help with the retention of information. And the idea is something different and is well received by the students.

So, to answer the question can using comics as textbooks in the higher education classroom promote lifelong learning by engaging students? We believe the answer is simply yes. Using comics as a textbook has inspired many students to not only read more comics, but to expand what they read. It converted Donna, the English Studies major, who started off thinking comics were not real literature. After reading the comic for class, she was not only motivated to read more comics but remembered why she loved the written word in the first place. I think that anything that can do that deserves a second look. In addition, after reading the comic, students are more accepting of other forms of literature than simply what they have been told is literature. Some educators worry that reading graphic novels will discourage reading other genres (Schwartz 2002) but this study shows otherwise.

As with all teaching materials, comic books are not for every educator or every subject. But, as a literary form that is changing and maturing all the time, comic books communicate universal ideas while capturing the student's attention in an engaging way. Teaching with comics will give an opportunity to relate to students in a meaningful way and open the door to a new way of communication with the new "media" generation. Whole brain learning makes us effective learners. Outside of the classroom today's students have grown up on a combination of visual and auditory stimulation. So, can using comics as educational tools help to remedy this "problem" and simultaneously help with the retention of information?

It helped Amy to stay focused while she was reading instead of falling asleep. She would see the pictures in her head. Martha said she remembered things immediately after reading them in the comic book. Jack thought that more students would be drawn to the material because it is something they can relate to instead of being disengaged. As much as educators think that the "old ways" should work, they have to realize that this is a new generation. These media driven kids are smart and need to be challenged but in different ways. Many may say that reading a comic book could not possibly be challenging. We beg to differ and challenge them to read one themselves before they judge. We have seen many educators converted to using comics in the classroom once they finally gave them a chance.

The social aspect of using the comic was something that very surprising. We had always thought of reading as a solitary event. Additionally, because of the stigma attached to comic book readers, as mentioned by Mickey in his earlier perception of comic book readers, we believed that the students might tell people but keep it to themselves if they liked it. We were proven wrong. As Jack said, even people he thought would hate it liked it and talked about it.

The most amazing thing was that not only did students talk about the comic with each other and their friends, but they took what they learned from the comic and applied it to other classes. As educators, we attempt every day to get our students to understand that what they are learning in college is more than just to take tests and get a grade. We want them to apply what they are learning to their lives and apply what they are learning in other classes. That is what happened with the comic book. And it happened unintentionally. It made Martha want to be a better example to women in her field of study. That alone makes it a success.

References

Alongi, Constance V. 1974. "Response to Kay Haugaard: Comic books Revisited." *The Reading Teacher* 27.8: 801–803.
Bendis, Brian, Olivier Coipel, Mark Morales, et al. May 2010. *Siege 4*. New York: Marvel.
Bernard, H. Russell. 2006. *Research Methods in Anthropology: Qualitative and Quantitative Approaches.* Lanham, MD: AltaMira Press.
Boorstin, Daniel J. 1983. *The Discoverers.* New York: Random House.
Brocka, Bruce. 1979. "Comic Books: In Case You Haven't Noticed They've Changed." *Media and Methods* 15.9: 30–32.
Brubaker, Ed, Steve Epting, Butch Guice, et al. January 2008. *Captain America 34*. New York: Marvel.
_____, Gene Colan, Dean White, et al. July 2009. *Captain America 601*. New York: Marvel.
Cary, Stephen. 2004. *Going Graphic: Comics at Work in the Multilingual Classroom.* Portsmouth, NH: Heinemann.
Colton, David. July 7, 2009. "Obama, Spider-Man on the Same Comic-Book Page." *USA Today.* Accessed February 10, 2011. http://www.usatoday.com/life/books/news/2009-01-07-obama-spiderman-comic_N.htm.
Dobrowolski, Alex. 1976. "The Comic Book Is Alive and Well and Living in the History Class." *The Social Studies* 67.6: 118–20.
Dorrell, Larry D., Dan B. Curtis, and Kuldip R. Rampal. 1995. "Book Worms Without Books: Students Reading Comic Books in the School House." *Journal of Popular Culture* 29.2: 223–234.
Duncan, Randy, Matthew J. Smith. 2009. *The Power of Comics: History, Form, and Culture.* New York: The Continuum International Publishing Group Inc.
Dunn, Rita, and Kenneth Dunn. 1993. *Teaching Secondary Students Through Their Individual Learning Styles: Practical Approaches for Grades 7–12.* Boston: Allyn and Bacon.
Eisner, Will. 1985. *Comics & Sequential Art.* Tamarac, FL: Poorhouse Press.
Ellman, Neil. 1979. "Comics in the Classroom." *Audio Visual Instruction* 24.5: 24–25.
Gerde, Virgina W., and R. Spencer Foster. 2007. "X-Men Ethics: Using Comic Books to Teach Business Ethics." *Journal of Business Ethics* 77.3: 245–258.
Glaser, Barney G., and Anselm L. Strauss. 1967. *The Discovery of Grounded Theory.* Chicago: Aldine Publishing Company.

Gruenberg, Sidonie Matsner. 1944. "The Comics as a Social Force." *Journal of Educational Sociology* 18.4: 204–213.

Haugaard, Kay. 1973. "Comic Books: Conduits to Culture?" *The Reading Teacher* 27.1: 54–55.

Heer, Jeet, and Kent Worcester, eds. 2009. *A Comics Studies Reader*. Jackson: University Press of Mississippi.

Hutchinson, Kay. 1949. "An Experiment in the Use of Comics as Instructional Material." *Journal of Educational Sociology* 23.4: 236–245.

Kakalios, James. 2002. "Adding Pow! to Your Physics Class with Comic-Book Lessons." *Curriculum Review* 42.2: 14–15.

Koenke, Karl. 1981. "The Careful Use of Comic Books." *Reading Teacher* 34.5: 592–595.

Light, Richard J. 2001. *Making the Most of College: Students Speak their Minds*. Cambridge, MA: Harvard University Press.

Lopes, Paul. 2006. "Culture and Stigma: Popular Culture and the Case of Comic Books." *Sociological Forum* 21.3: 387–414.

Marsh, Rufus K. 1978. "Teaching French with the Comics." *French Review* 51: 6: 777–85.

Mayer, Richard E., and L.J. Massa. 2003. "Three Faces of Visual and Verbal Learners: Cognitive Ability, Cognitive Style, and Learning Preference." *Journal of Educational Psychology* 95.4: 833–846.

McCloud, Scott. 1993. *Understanding Comics: The Invisible Art*. New York: Harper Collins.

McGinn, Andrew. August 7, 2009. "Wittenberg Professor Gets Serious About Funny Books." *Springfield News-Sun*.

Monnin, Katie. 2010. *Teaching Graphic Novels: Practical Strategies for the Secondary ELA Classroom*. Gainesville, FL: Maupin House.

Morrison, Timothy G., Gregory Bryan, and George W. Chilcoat. 2002. "Using Student-Generated Comic Book in the Classroom." *Journal of Adolescent and Student Literacy* 45.8: 758–767.

Murr, Lawrence, and James Williams. 1988. "Half-Brained Ideas About Education: Thinking and Learning with Both the Left and Right Brain in a Visual Culture." *Leonardo* 21.4: 413–419.

Ornstein, Allan C. 1977. *An Introduction to the Foundations of Education*. Chicago: Randy McNally College Pub. Co.

Palmer, Parker. 1988. *The Courage to Teach: Exploring the Inner Landscape of a Teacher's Life*. San Francisco: Jossey-Bass: A Wiley Company.

Patton, Michael Q. 1990. *Qualitative Evaluation and Research Method*. Newbury Park, CA: Sage.

Pustz, Matthew. 1999. *Comic Book Culture: Fan Boys and True Believers*. Jackson: University Press of Mississippi.

Schwartz, Gretchen E. 2002. "Graphic Novels for Multiple Literacies." *Journal of Adolescent and Adult Literacy* 46: 262–265.

Sones, W.W.D. 1944. "The Comics and Instructional Method." *Journal of Educational Sociology* 18.4: 232–240.

Spiegelman, Art. 1986. *Maus*. New York: Pantheon Books.

_____. 1991. *Maus II*. New York: Pantheon Books.

Strauss, Anselm C., and Juliet Corbin. 1990. *Basics of Qualitative Research: Grounded Theory Procedures and Techniques*. Newbury Park, CA: Sage Publications.

Svinicki, Marilla, and Wilbert J. McKeachie. 2011. *McKeachie's Teaching Tips: Strategies, Research, and Theory for College and University Teachers*. 13th ed. Belmont, CA: Wadsworth Cengage Learning.

Tabachnick, Stephen. 2007. "A Comic-Book World." *World Literature Today* 81.2: 24–28.

Versaci, Rocco. 2001. "How Comic Books Can Change the Way Our Students See Literature: One Teacher's Perspective." *The English Journal* 91.2: 61–67.

Viadero, Deborah. 2009. "Scholars See Comics as No Laughing Matter." *Education Week* 28.21: 1–2.

Waid, Mark. June 17, 2010. Personal communication.

Wertham, Fredric. 1954. *Seduction of the Innocent*. New York: Rinehart.

Williams, Linda Verlee. 1983. *Teaching for the Two-Sided Mind: A Guide to Right Brain/Left Brain Education*. New York: Simon & Schuster.

Williams, Rachel Marie-Crane. November 1, 2008. "Image, Text, and Story: Comics and Graphic Novels in the Classroom." *Art Education*.

Wolk, Douglas. 2007. *Reading Comics: How Graphic Novels Work and What They Mean*. Cambridge, MA: Da Capo Press.

Wright, Bradford. 2001. *Comic Book Nation: The Transformation of Youth Culture in America*. Baltimore, MD: Johns Hopkins University Press.

PART II

Teaching Graphic Novels and Comics in the Classroom

"I can get college credit for reading *Batman*? That's a joke, right?"
Confessions of a Fanboy Professor Teaching Comic Books

DAVID WHITT

The second epigraph on my course syllabus for "Not Just Kids Stuff: Comic Books and Popular Culture" is a quote by computer expert extraordinaire The Drummer from the comic book series *Planetary* by Warren Ellis and John Cassady. In issue #4 (July 1999) titled "Strange Harbours," Planetary researchers are attempting to unearth a mysterious ancient ruin discovered after a building explosion. Meanwhile, several blocks away Private Investigator Jim Wilder is witness to a mugging, decides to intercede, and begins chasing the attacker. Wilder follows the assailant into the Planetary excavation site and, oblivious to the investigation team, steps on the ruin and disappears, to which The Drummer comments, "Well, I wasn't expecting that." This rather understated reaction perhaps best reflects my attitude toward teaching a class on comic books. My goal is that each student, like The Drummer, will be surprised at what he or she discovers reading the various graphic novels selected. While this is arguably a bit idealistic, it has provided me with the motivation and enthusiasm for teaching this rather unique subject.

A course on comic books is obviously not part of the traditional Nebraska Wesleyan undergraduate curriculum, but instead offered as a Liberal Arts Seminar (LAS) designed to introduce first-year students to the college experience through a unique topic selected by the individual instructor. Additionally, students learn about the variety of campus resources and opportunities available to them with sessions on library research, studying abroad, the speaking/writing workshop, service learning, the career center, registering for classes online, and surviving finals. LAS classes have studied such diverse subjects as: utopia and dystopia, the Olympics 1968, poverty in the U.S., Don Quixote, Japanese Anime, standup comedy, the television series *Buffy the Vampire Slayer*, the Beatles, and America before Columbus. My LAS, "Not Just Kids Stuff: Comic Books and Popular Culture" (taught each Fall from 2004 to 2008) explored the rich history and cultural significance of comic books through the analysis of several popular and influential texts including *Watchmen, Marvels, Sandman,* and *Maus*. The mainstream popularity and critical response toward these works, and many others, supports Thompson's (2007, 29) contention that "comic books and graphic novels are beginning to take their rightful seat at the table of quality literature of our time." As "quality literature" we read, interpret, and analyze comic books as "serious fun" instead of simplistic stories of adolescent fantasy, where students learn to appreciate the complex narratives, visual styles, and social commentaries within this unique artistic and literary genre.

The purpose of this essay is to discuss the challenges designing and teaching an entire course on comic books for an undergraduate audience. I will first examine the student-centered challenges of developing a course on comic books, and then describe student reaction to the various graphic novels selected for analysis. Hopefully, my experience will encourage others to consider incorporating comic books into their instruction, and also provide me with feedback as to how I can improve my course in the future.

As a reader of comic books since I was 9, and a self-proclaimed fanboy geek, I never thought my love of *The Fantastic Four*, *Teen Titans*, and *ROM* would translate into designing a course offered for college credit. The first LAS I taught was entitled *Star Trek: Communicating Across Generations* (1999 and 2000). Then, needing to finish my doctoral dissertation, I took several years off teaching LAS until finally deciding the time was right to teach the comic book course I had been organizing in my mind for years. However, to base an entire class around comic books had unique pedagogical challenges. The more traditional classes I teach like Mass Media, Persuasion, and Communication Theory have instructor's manuals with sample syllabi and assignments, computerized test banks, and CD-ROMs. Unfortunately there are no such materials for anyone interested in designing a class on comic books, meaning I would have to design the entire course from scratch.

While each LAS focuses on a different topic, all sections are relatively standardized; each must have some type of public-speaking element and various writing assignments, including a 7- to 9-page research paper. The individual instructor has discretion in the amount of reading, writing, and testing required. One unique and beneficial component of the LAS is that all sections typically have a student assistant, an individual selected by the instructor to help teach the course. This person can either be a former LAS student, or someone with a sincere interest in the subject matter. In my class the responsibilities of the student assistant include guiding discussion of specific graphic novels, reading and providing feedback on papers (but not grading), answering questions and offering advice to first-year students as the "voice of experience," and serving as a liaison between professor and students. I value the insights of the student instructor and have, on several occasions, adopted their suggestions for how to improve the course.

I ultimately decided to conduct the class like a book club, with some slight variations. First, although the entire class reads the same graphic novels, two to three students are assigned to one specific book, each responsible for covering specific chapters or sections. Depending on the book's length each graphic novel could be covered in two to three class periods, with class discussion generating additional analysis and interpretation. Next, students write a short paper (3–4 pages) on this graphic novel based on specific questions I assigned. These questions require students to move beyond description of plot and character and reflect upon on a graphic novel's themes, symbolism, and art. In addition to these short papers students are also required to write a paper on their history with and attitudes toward comic books due the second week in the semester, and also develop a major research paper (a LAS requirement) based on a graphic novel(s) outside of the regular course readings due before the end of November.

Along with these writing assignments there is also a group presentation (another LAS requirement). Based on their interest level each student is placed in one of five subject areas: the Comics Code of the 1950s, Marvel Comics, DC Comics, Japanese Manga, or Underground Comix. The 4 to 5 person groups then meet outside of class to conduct and compile research exploring the history, influential writers/artists, characters, and cultural influences of these comic companies and genres. To engage the audience, groups are encouraged to make their presentations highly visual and interactive using PowerPoint, VHS/DVD (if possible) and design group activities to facilitate learning (draw your own manga character, for example).

With the various writing and public speaking assignments determined, my next challenge is to evaluate the attitude and comic book experience of the 16 to 18 first-year students in the course. LAS has a unique system of registration whereby students rank in order their top five course topics and then a computer selects which students are placed in which classes. However, the system is not perfect. Some students who preference a LAS topic high (1 or 2) may not be selected, while others who preference it lower (4 or 5) are disappointed, and sometimes upset, at having been placed in a course s/he never wanted to take in the first place. In the case of my course, I typically have about a third of the students who ranked it high, a third in the middle, and a third toward the bottom. Consequently, those students who want to be there have some history with comic books (rather few), while the reluctant others have little to no experience (surprisingly many).

The negative attitude of some students becomes even more pronounced when they visit the campus bookstore with their parents. Mothers and fathers see the stack of the graphic novels their child is required to purchase and express concern they are wasting their hard-earned money on comic books instead of more serious literature. After all, their child is at Nebraska Wesleyan University for a liberal-arts education, not to waste time reading *Batman* or Japanese manga. Such reports are quite common from students, especially during our discussion on the first day of class regarding their attitudes and experience with comic books. Thus, my first hurdle each semester is attempting to justify the value of a college course on comic books and convince the students their time and money are being well spent. To accomplish this goal on the first day of class I spend time discussing the domestic and international appeal of comic books. I begin with examples from higher education to demonstrate how college professors at other institutions such as the University of Minnesota and DePauw (Indiana) have used comic books to teach physics and biology, while Washington State and Palomar College (California) English professors use graphic novels to teach literature, science fiction writing, and film adaptations (O'English, Mathews, and Lindsay 2006). Additionally, because Nebraska Wesleyan is a Methodist-founded university, all students are required to take a religion or philosophy course. Consequently, I briefly mention the dramatic growth of Christian comics, and how two pastors, one in Kentucky and the other in Tennessee, use comic book superheroes in their sermons. Finally, I discuss how art teachers in various junior high and high schools in Maryland and Virginia use comic books to teach students how to draw and brainstorm ideas.

The appeal of comic books on an international level is also addressed as I explain how DC Comics joined forces with UNICEF to promote mine awareness in Bosnia (1996) and Latin America (1998), while in 2004 Marvel Comics developed an ethnic adaptation of a comic book series *Spider-Man India*. I also mention my travels abroad seeing American comic books in Costa Rica, and stumbling upon comic book stores in Nice, France, and Waterford, Ireland.

While these facts may not be particularly impressive or interesting to some students, or sway their skepticism about the value of a comic book course, what does get their attention is the financial bottom line. Student's eyes widen, and some jaws even drop, when stating the monetary value of *Action Comics #1* (first appearance of Superman), *Detective Comics*

#27 (first appearance of Batman), or *Amazing Fantasy #15* (first appearance of Spider-Man). I also share a list of personal collector "hits and misses," comics that were a wise investment (*Wolverine* Limited Series 1982) and those, for one reason or another, I now regrettably did not purchase (*Ultimate Spider-Man #1*). I discuss collecting comics in terms of playing the stock market, that there is never a "sure thing," and how value of a comic book can rise and fall.

After providing an initial foundation for the scope of comic books the next several class periods explore the medium's history by watching the video *Comic Book Confidential* (1988) that, as an instructional tool, is something of a mixed bag. Its discussion of early comic book history, the 1950s Senate hearings, and the 1960s underground comics scene are interesting and, at times, humorous. However, compared with more contemporary educational programming, like The History Channel's *Comic Book Superheroes Unmasked* (2003) (I do not show this program because students in the Marvel and DC groups use it for their group presentations), the overall production value makes the video both look and sound dated. Still, despite its flaws *Comic Book Confidential* has value as a basic introduction to comic book history through the late 1980s.

After using the first week to justify the academic value of the course, the second week we delve into writing and, more importantly, reading. As mentioned earlier, the first writing assignment is a short paper that asks the student to discuss their history and attitudes toward comic books. The first book we read is Scott McCloud's *Understanding Comics* (1993). McCloud does an excellent job of not only examining comic history, but also discussing the various narrative and artistic elements within comic books. The fact that the book is humorous, engaging, and designed as a comic book certainly adds to its appeal. Many students have never read a comic book, but appreciate McCloud's simple yet informative approach. An added benefit of *Understanding Comics* is that through its paneled format students become "trained" to read comic books, thus easing their transition into reading other graphic novels. McCloud's book becomes a foundational text for the entire course, and I make reference to concepts such as closure and iconic abstraction when creating various critique questions.

After briefly examining comic history, reading *Understanding Comics* and also the book chapter "Introducing Comics and Ideology" by McAllister, Sewell, and Gordon from *Comics and Ideology* (2001), our first official graphic novel is Judd Winick's *Pedro & Me*. Released in 2000, *Pedro & Me* is the story of Pedro Zamora of MTV's *The Real World: San Francisco* (1994), who, at age 17, was diagnosed with HIV, and died of AIDS at 22. Zamora's *Real World* roommate, comic artist Judd Winick, decided to honor his friend with a graphic novel that tells Pedro's life story. Winick tells how Pedro arrived in the United States from Cuba as a young boy, contracted HIV as a teenager, became an informational speaker about HIV/AIDS, was selected as a cast member of *The Real World*, and finally succumbed to AIDS in November 1994. At its heart *Pedro & Me* is a story about friendship, but also has educational value showing Pedro teaching others about HIV/AIDS, misconceptions about the contracting the virus, and how to protect oneself. It is also an award-winning graphic novel recognized by the GLAAD, Publisher's Weekly, the American Library Association, and the National Consortium of Latin American Studies.

Upon first reading in *Pedro & Me* in 2003 I immediately decided this was the first graphic novel I wanted students to read. My rationale was simple. By beginning with this short, yet emotionally powerful story I hoped to alter significantly, if not shatter, student perceptions of what a graphic novel could be. I wanted students to be introduced to graphic storytelling not through costumed superheroes and their fantasy adventures, but through real people, facing real challenges. While Winick's narrative is both lighthearted and somber, it is most importantly honest, not shying away from frank discussions of sexuality, relationships, and HIV/AIDS. Additionally, his art vividly captures Pedro's pain and brave struggle to combat AIDS, with images of his arm and face covered in shingles, his body soaked with perspiration after experiencing night sweats, and his gaunt face from weight loss. During our class discussion over *Pedro & Me* I have had many students comment that the story made them cry or was personally meaningful. For some, the book becomes their favorite of the entire semester, which is surprising because it is competing against the more popular superhero stories.

Next, we read an article by Gordon (2001) entitled "Nostalgia, Myth, and Ideology: Visions of Superman at the End of the 'American Century'" from *Comics and Ideology* (2001), and Reynolds' chapter on "Masked Heroes" in his book *Super Heroes: A Modern Mythology* (1992). These readings assist in transitioning from the real world to the imaginary world of costumed heroes who are both super and serious, fascinating and flawed. What better way to exemplify these characteristics than by then reading *Watchmen* (1986)? Written by Alan Moore and drawn by Dave Gibbons, this groundbreaking and influential graphic novel certainly needs no introduction, having been analyzed and critiqued extensively for the past two decades. During *Watchmen* week we examine Moore's deconstruction of the superhero genre, how the book's themes resonate in a post–9/11 world, study Gibbons' art and use of repetitive imagery (the smiley face), and debate whether its inclusion on *Time* magazine's Top 100 Novels is deserved. Overall reaction to *Watchmen* is typically split as some students enjoy Moore's complex narrative, while others are confused from Chapter One. Not surprisingly, *Watchmen*'s ending (spoiler alert!) generates the most discussion with some students feeling "let down" by the revelation of a psychic monster designed by scientists and artists that kills millions to bring peace to the world. *Watchmen* challenges students to think about superheroes not as infallible and indestructible, but as people with real problems and issues. Because I taught this LAS from 2004 to 2008, the 2009 *Watchmen* film had not yet been released. However, when I teach this course again it would be interesting to show the *Watchmen* film and have students discuss how the adaptation tapped into or diverged from the themes and visual style of the original graphic novel.

For our next book we stay in the DC Universe, but analyze the psychological complexities of a more familiar comic book character for the students, Batman. For the first two years of the course we read Frank Miller's influential *The Dark Knight Returns* (1986) (*DKR*) and then switched to Grant Morrison's *Arkham Asylum: A Serious House on Serious Earth* (1989) (*AA*). Student reaction to *DKR* was surprisingly negative, while the opposite was true of *AA*. Miller's older and edgier Batman generally failed to resonate with students who did not care for his interpretation of the Dark Knight. *AA*, on the other hand, has been an overwhelming success. Morrison's complex psychoanalytical and mythic narrative challenges the student to look deeper into the text for meaning. Students also appreciate the art of Dave McKean with his nightmarish images of the Joker, the inmates, and the asylum itself. Class discussion of *AA* moves from analyzing Morrison's labeling the story as a modern passion play, to McKean's religious symbolism, to the line between sanity and insanity reflected in both the Joker and Batman. Additionally, we also read "Guilt and the Unconscious in *Arkham Asylum*" by Rollin (1994, 4), who argues that the graphic novel's power lies in an "intense exploration of the unconscious" analyzing McKean's art and the book's psychoanalytic themes of the mother and the infant. For their written critique students must defend whether Batman is sane, or as Joker says, belongs in Arkham with the rest of the inmates.

After examining *Watchmen* and *Arkham Asylum* from DC comics we move to Marvel comics focusing on *Marvels* (2001) by Kurt Busiek and Alex Ross. Busiek's narrative moves from the 1940s to the 1970s examining the history of the Marvel Universe not through the adventures of its superheroes, but through the perspective of an "everyday man," photographer Phil Sheldon. Busiek's writing, combined with Ross's distinct artistic style, makes for a graphic novel that is not only socially relevant, but also visually impressive. Despite students' being, at times, confused by the story, as their knowledge of the Marvel Universe is limited, they appreciate Ross's realistic and detailed artwork. In their critiques I ask students to compare the art of Ross to that of Winick and Gibbons and whether his lack of "iconic abstraction" (McCloud 1993, 46) is a strength or weakness. The vast majority of students argue it is a strength, drawing them into the story more closely and appreciating even more the time and patience necessary to create each panel and page of a comic book.

After four weeks of reading and writing about American comic books, our attention next shifts across the Pacific Ocean to "The Land of the Rising Sun" and Japanese manga.[1] First, the Japanese manga group will have informed the class about its history, style, artists, and popularity among children and adults. Additionally, I refer back to McCloud's discussion of aspect-to-aspect storytelling that creates a mood or sense of place that reflects the Japanese tradition of "being there" rather than "getting there," as well as the Eastern tradition of cyclical and labyrinthine art. Next, we read Katsuhiro Otomo's cyberpunk classic *Akira: Volume One* (2000). Students not familiar with manga are surprised by its adult themes, graphic violence, and page after page of action sequences. There is also surprise at how quickly this thick 364-page book can be read. The following week we watch the *Akira* (2001) DVD to see how the book was translated into film, and, if there is time, view a supplemental feature on the film's art. Students are not required to write a critique of *Akira* because at this point in the semester they are researching and writing their major paper due in a little more than one week.

The second-to-last graphic novel we read is Neil Gaiman's *Sandman: Preludes and Nocturnes*. I begin by providing a brief history of Gaiman, his critically acclaimed work on *Sandman* as well as the popular *Death* series, and finally listing his work as a novelist and screenwriter. Like *Watchmen*, *Sandman* divides the class. Some students praise Gaiman for his creativity, weaving together of history, mythology, and religion. Others are disturbed by the content, particularly the story "24 Hours" and its horrific images of blood lust, self-mutilation, and mass murder. Gaiman takes the reader on a dark journey in *Preludes and Nocturnes* following Morpheus, the immortal protector of dreams, on a mythic quest to reclaim his tools of power (a pouch of sand, helmet, and ruby) stolen from him in Chapter One. Not surprisingly, Dream's sister Death "steals the show" at the end of the graphic novel making an immediate impression upon many students who are motivated to read more about this whimsical character and her dour brother even more.

We finish the semester the same way we began, reading a graphic novel based not in the world of fiction, but historical fact, Art Spiegelman's Pulitzer Prize–winning *Maus*. According to Versaci (2001, 63), "More so than any other graphic novel, Spiegelman's work has entered academia and is taught in various types of courses at colleges and universities throughout the country." Interestingly, there are usually several students who have either heard of *Maus*, or have read it in a high school English or history class. Spiegelman's personal and emotional story and his unique artistic portrayal of mice as Jews and cats as Nazi's generates fascinating class discussion. I try to bridge 60 years of history from World War II to today discussing the nine-hour documentary *Shoah* (1985), Steven Spielberg's Academy Award-winning *Schindler's List* (1993), my own visit to Dachau concentration camp outside Munich in 1994, and most recently, the 2007 conference hosted by Iran examining the "truth" of the Holocaust. Many students share their experiences touring the Holocaust Museum in Washington, D.C., which makes Spiegelman's graphic novel that much more powerful.

Aside from reading and writing about graphic novels we also engage in other comic related activities including visiting a comic book store in downtown Lincoln, Nebraska, and watching scenes from films with comic book references including, *Mallrats* (1995), *Chasing Amy* (1997), *Kill Bill: Volume 2* (2004), and *Unbreakable* (2000). The final assignment of the semester requires students to draw, either individually or in pairs, their own comic book. The content and style is entirely of their choosing, the only requirement being each book has to be a minimum of three pages, or if students pair up, six pages. On the last day of class we pass around the comic books for everyone to read. Of all the assignments this one might be the most popular, and for some, the most time-consuming. Students spend hours not only thinking about what story they want to tell, but also drawing their comic, obsessing over every detail from panel size and story length to characters and dialogue. I do not grade these comic books in a traditional sense since these students are not professional writers or artists. Instead, I give each student credit for completing the project and kudos to those who were particularly creative.

Since first teaching "Not Just Kids Stuff" in 2004 I have learned a great many things about comic books, first-year students, and myself. I have never claimed to be a "comic book expert." If I were to grade my own comic expertise I would probably be above average, with a "B," or, on a good day, a "B+." However, my strengths as an instructor are enthusiasm for the subject matter and an ability to connect with students. Hopefully, when added together, these characteristics create a learning environment that challenges students to think of comic books as more than just a juvenile pastime and to consider their larger, and more meaningful historical and cultural influence. If at then end of the semester a student reflects back upon their experience and views comic books in a more positive way, I have done my job.

Occasionally I run into a former LAS student who proudly proclaims he or she still reads comics, shares titles with me, and asks for my recommendations. In fact, in spring 2007, my student assistant walked into my office and enthusiastically handed me three bagged and boarded comic books (a *Spider-Man*, *Superman Annual*, and *Sandman*). She explained they were a gift from one of the LAS students the previous semester who purchased them at a comic book store while visiting Chicago. Considering this student's, at times, negative attitude in class and the general quality of his written work, we both thought he disliked the course, and were genuinely surprised by his generosity. At that moment the words of The Drummer resonated, and like a proud parent I thought to myself, "Well, I wasn't expecting that."

Notes

1. The first year teaching my LAS, before switching to Japanese manga, students read Harvey Pekar's *American Splendor* and then watched the 2003 film upon which it was based. Reaction to the graphic novel was overwhelmingly negative, although students did like the film. Pekar's narratives failed to connect with

students who were bored, and somewhat annoyed, with his personality, attitude, and slice-of-life observations. Based on their reaction I decided not to keep *American Splendor* on my required reading list. However, occasionally a student will select one of Pekar's graphic novels for their major paper.

References

Ellis, Warren, and John Cassady. July 1999. *Planetary 4*. New York: Wildstorm Productions and DC Comics.
Gordon, Ian. 2001. "Nostalgia, Myth, and Ideology: Visions of Superman at the End of the 'American Century.'" In Matthew McAllister, Edward Sewell, and Ian Gordon, eds., *Comics & Ideology*. New York: Peter Lang.
Mann, Ron. Director. 1988. *Comic Book Confidential* [VHS]. Los Angeles: Pacific Arts Video.
McAllister, Matthew, Edward Sewell, and Ian Gordon. 2001. *Comics & Ideology*. New York: Peter Lang.
McCloud, Scott. 1993. *Understanding Comics*. New York: Paradox Press.
O'English, Lorena, Gregory Matthews, and Elizabeth Linsday. March 2006. "Graphic Novels in Academic Libraries: From *Maus* to Manga and Beyond." *The Journal of Academic Librarianship* 32.2: 173–182.
Reynolds, Richard. 1992. *Super Heroes: A Modern Mythology*. Jackson: University of Mississippi Press.
Rollin, Lucy. February 1994. "Guilt and the Unconscious in Arkham Asylum." *Inks: Cartoon and Comic Art Studies* 1.1: 2–13.
Thompson, Terry. January 2007. "Embracing Reluctance When Classroom Teachers Shy Away From Graphic Books." *Library Media Connection* 25.4: 29.
Versaci, Rocco. November 2001."How Comic Books Can Change the Way Our Students See Literature: One Teacher's Perspective." *English Journal* 91.2: 61–67.

"What the —?"

Pre-Service Teachers Meet and Grapple Over Graphic Novels in the Classroom

JAMES BUCKY CARTER

Pre-, During- and Post-Contact Zones at Work in the English Education Classroom

One of the major hurdles of the English educator is assisting pre-service teachers in revising some, if not all, of their notions on what constitutes good teaching. Many of my students reveal that their English classrooms were places where content was not integrated seamlessly from one element to the other, where student choice was extremely limited, or where teaching to the end-of-the-year test was the most important thing on the teacher's mind. Indeed, a common response after I have just explained the rationale behind a best practice technique versus how a given element has been taught traditionally is "That's [the traditional way] how we did it." Vocabulary lists completely divorced from in-class readings; every student reading the same text regardless of interest or ability; grammar for twenty minutes a day, followed by writing, followed by reading: this is the perception of "excellent" teaching for many future English teachers before they take their methods classes.

Often "That's how we did it" is muttered with a bit of exasperation, as if to say "*I never knew there was a better way!*" but sometimes the tone is a bit more confrontational, as if the student is really telling me, "Those techniques were good enough to help me get into college, where now I have to listen to you tell me they don't work? If it worked for me, it'll work for my students too!" This, of course, leads to other notions we often need to have our students reconsider: that what works for one student will work for all students and that all students will share the interests and passions of the pre-service teacher currently engrossed in college-level content considerations.

There is also the fact that, once they leave the university, many of my students are likely to note a schism between what I taught them and what they can do in their classrooms. Either through prescribed curricula, the mentorship or policies of traditionalist leaders, or seemingly useless trial-and-error, many will note that "Too often the reality simply does not match the expectation [if I have successfully moved them towards more progressive teaching ideas]. Such disappointments are demoralizing; they can cause teachers to be wary of new approaches and even create cynicism toward teacher education conferences, classes, and pedagogical books" (Alsup and Bush 2003, ix). Poor students! I've promised them a better way, asked them to change their thinking, and now it seems I've tricked them. Woe to these students, and it is easy to say that woe to the teacher educator who must continually meet, clash, and grapple (Pratt 2002) with stale, ineffective, but pervasive methods of teaching.

Luckily, many of us are stubbornly persistent in our pursuit of pedagogical reform (or are we gluttons for punishment?). Surely Thomas Philion was correct to assert that "English Studies is itself a contact zone" (2002, 79), a "site of intense power struggles and vigorous discussions about the proper allocation of time, resources, energy and ideological commitments" and that "secondary English teacher education" constitutes one of those "frontiers" (80). Philion points out that methods courses and student teaching illustrate "that sociocultural conflict and negotiation are recurring features of secondary English teacher education" (81). This fact is not likely to change any time soon.

In the summer of 2007, a group of mostly pre-service teachers gathered in an expansive, high-tech, theatre-style classroom in Hattiesburg, Mississippi, to take what they thought was a typical young adult literature class. When it was revealed that the texts for the course were all graphic novels, "book-length sequential art narrative featuring an anthology-style collection of comic art, a collection of reprinted comic book issues comprising a single storyline (or arc), or an original, stand-alone graphic narrative (Carter 2007, 1), students soon had to meet their preconceived notions of textuality, literacy, and pedagogical worthiness and resolve how they clashed with their ideas of sequential art narratives. A contact zone was established as these students learned about various types of literacy, encountered the terms *New Literacy*, *Visual Literacy*, and *Multimodal Literacy* for the first time, tried to see those terms' connections to critical literacy, and attempted to see how graphic novels could help bridge the gap between real-world literacies and values and school-centric literacies and values. For some students, the reaction to a class reading list with over twenty graphic novels took the form of a classic line from super-hero comics in which the hero, shocked to his or her core by a recent happening but still needing to make sure the book in which he or she appeared was kid-friendly, would reply, "*What the—?!?*" This chapter will share the sources, lessons, and activities these students engaged in during our two-week, four-hour-a-day sessions, the progress students made in this particular contact zone as described above, and how they worked to resolve some of the outstanding issues associated with graphic novels and literacy instruction.

Pre-Teaching Consternation and Meeting the Class

Before introducing the students, I should mention that contact zones were already entrenched in the course before it even made enrollment. I was thrilled that my chair had allowed me the opportunity to teach what may have been the first-ever "Graphic Novels as Young Adult Literature" course in the United States. However, not all shared my enthusiasm. Students in my "Contemporary Trends and Issues in the Graphic Novel" class (a critical theory and popular culture- heavy "Comics as Literature" section I was able to offer through one of the department's variable-content courses) had already informed me that another member of the department had remarked to his class that it "made his blood boil" that the university was even offering courses in graphica. When I tried to advertise the course via flyers in and around the English department, they disappeared quickly, even as other flyers

> **SUMMER '07! MINI-SESSION!!**
> **ENG 418 SPECIAL TOPICS: TEACHING GRAPHIC NOVELS IN MIDDLE AND HIGH SCHOOL!**
>
> **LEARN WHAT EDUCATION RESEARCH HAS TO SAY ABOUT USING GRAPHIC NOVELS IN THE CLASSROOM, AND LEARN HOW YOU CAN USE THEM TO BUILD LITERACY CONNECTIONS WITH STUDENTS RANGING FROM RELUCTANT READERS TO GIFTED!**
>
> **E-MAIL JAMES BUCKY CARTER AT JAMES.B.CARTER@   .EDU FOR MORE INFO! OPEN TO ANY EDUCATION STUDENT. DIFFERENTIATION AVAILABLE!**

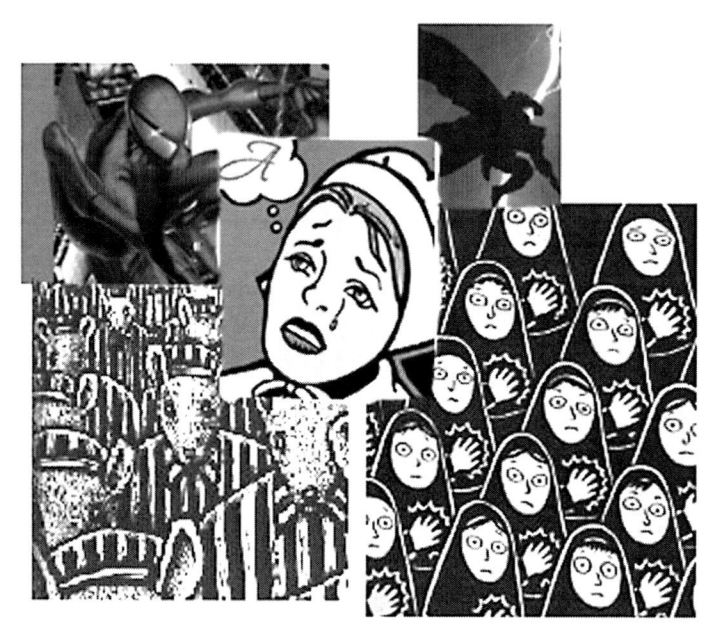

Figure 1. A Flyer for the Possibly Historic Course.

placed elsewhere around campus remained. I was assured by my chair that it was probably the doing of some irate student, but I went to the office over spring break and put up more flyers in and around the department, when no students would have access to the building, and they too disappeared before student access was granted again. It appeared I had at least one person on campus with whom I shared a difference of "ideological commitment" (Philion 2002, 80) to the course. Frustrated and a little furious, I sought alternate methods of advertising the course, placing two advertisements in the campus newspapers for just under $200. The class made enrollment, and though several students dropped after the first day, due to my grappling with ways to get over the clash, it was never in danger of being closed before it even started.

Meet the Class

Sixteen students became the core of the historic course that asked them to consider the pedagogical potential of an often maligned art form, one that never shook its early American colloquialisms of "the funnies" or "the funny papers." Fifteen students were female. Two identified as African American females; the rest identified as Caucasian. Fourteen were pre-service teachers in either elementary education, History or English. The sole male was an English major but expressed interest in possibly teaching in Texas one day. One Caucasian female was a career school librarian. Most of the students were traditional, but several were older, including the female school librarian and the male, Chris, who was a military veteran. Three students — Chris, a History education major named Melissa, and an English Education major — had taken my "Contemporary Trends and Issues in the Graphic Novel" course previously.

Information for this essay comes from fifteen of the sixteen students' journals and assignments, which I combed over using methods associated with analytic induction (Robinson 1951; Ragin 1994). I coded recurring themes and comments and organized points of data accordingly. One student did not allow permission to cite her work, while the others signed consent forms on the last day of class. These consent forms were sealed and not reviewed until final grades for the course had been posted.

First Contact for Most

Students were instructed to write journals on each graphic novel we read, on each secondary article we read, and on each day's activities. On the first day, I asked students to journal on what their exposure to comics was before we began reading any graphic novels. The data reveal that only two students considered themselves "serious comic book fans." *Archie* comics and strips from the Sunday newspaper were the most often cited examples of previously read sequential art (excluding comments from the three students who had taken my other graphic novel course). The class had a substantial female majority, and notions of gendered identity and its connection to comics were quickly revealed in their earliest journals:

- "I have never had any interest in comic books. They are in my house because my husband reads them. I have never thought about using comic books in my classroom as reading material."
- "I really do not know much about graphic novels except that they are colorfully illustrated and usually tell the story through bubbles coming out of the characters' mouths."
- "I have never conceptualized them as novels because they look so short, and pictures are never really in novels, with a few exceptions."
- Paraphrase of multiple responses: "I was more interested in Barbie."
- Paraphrase of multiple responses: "I always thought comics were for boys."

Herein it is apparent that there were value judgments at play regarding not just gendered reading, but literacy, textuality and textual worth. Though there is some indication that

Manga is very popular among young girls (Accomando 2008), many students felt that comics were a male's domain. One student's remark seems to imply that if her husband didn't read them, comics wouldn't even be allowed in her home. It is true that much of super-hero comics' readership is male, but this dynamic shifts when we consider the wide range of comics genres available, graphic novels, and the aforementioned Manga. Jeffrey D. Wilhelm and Michael W. Smith (2002) have noted that comics and other highly visual texts do seem to draw and keep the interest of boys, but nowhere in their research do young men seem to assert an ownership over the form like these students seem to have assigned to comics. These students may be under the assumption that all comics are either cartoons or super-heroes, as I have found is often the case when speaking with in-service teachers, but their entries do not offer evidence for this. Comics do not seem to be appropriate reading material for the student whose husband brings them into her house or for other female classmates, who were more interested in Barbie, apparently a more acceptable signifier of gendered habits with this group.

Comics do not seem to enjoy the status of literature among these students, either. They are "not thought of as novels," have never been considered for classroom use, and tell their stories in different ways (via bubbles) than do traditional print-based texts. "Pictures are never really in novels," says one student. The concept that the pictorial is separate from the alphabetic, the wordly, so to speak, reveals schemata about text and textuality. Rather than seeing the pictorial elements of graphic novels as texts to be read, they are something that precludes them from consideration as a novel in the minds of many of my students in this course. So is their length. I have found both these issues to be a tension that in-service teachers have about sequential art as well, so much so that I have offered solutions to the way of thinking via an online draft of a presentation I give around the country that can be accessed here: *http://www.archive.org/details/NhcteTalk08GraphicNovels*. At the beginning of our course, my students were being prepped to meet their preconceived notions on comics and literacy and grapple with two weeks' worth of content that would ask them to clash with those ideas on gender, literacy, literature, and pedagogical potential.

Authentic Comics Crafting Experiences

Though many articles examining the graphic novel in education deal with the format as a way to engage reluctant readers, it is reductive to think that is their only value in the classroom. Graphic novels also offer authentic reading and writing opportunities, with "authenticity" herein defined as Brian Cambourne defines it:

> Authenticity refers to the degree to which learning activities used to promote reading resemble the kinds of reading activities and learning that occur outside the traditional, institutionalized school setting. The more an activity is like an everyday activity, the higher degree of authenticity it possesses. With respect to reading, writing and the other accoutrements of literacy, the more that an activity requires the students to engage in the kind of reading-writing-literacy behaviors that highly literate, proficient adults use to address their needs, the more authentic the activity is judged to be [2002, 38].

Though it may be hard for some to believe, many comics and certainly graphic novels are written and drawn by highly intelligent, talented adults who manage to make a good living at their craft and are even offered exclusive contracts and form-specific awards for their work. Some even win Pulitzers, like Art Spiegelman's *Maus*, or are National Book

Award finalists, like Gene Yang's *American Born Chinese*, make *Time*'s "best of" lists like Alan Moore and Dave Gibbons' *Watchmen* and Alison Bechdel's *Fun Home*, or get attention from Oprah Winfrey, like Sara Varon's *Robot Dreams* (*http://pwbeat.publishersweekly.com/ blog/2008/08/13/almost-there-robot-dreams-makes-oprahs-listkid-division/*). As such, asking students to engage in production of sequential art is to ask them to work through an authentic writing and composing process. Using the ReadWriteThink.org activity "The Comic Book Show and Tell" as their framework, after their journal entry and a brief introduction to the history of sequential art and education (again, see *http://www.archive.org/details/ NhcteTalk08GraphicNovels*), students were asked to write a short comic responding to the prompt "Peter Parker awakes to his alarm clock going off, and it's bad news!" I have detailed this process elsewhere (Carter 2007), but the activity essentially defines the roles of those associated with comics production, asks students to become amateur script writers, then to hand their work over to a partner who will then draw it based on the writer's written prompts (writers must show and tell, give direction, dialogue, and details to get their vision across). The artist then gives the drawn pages to the writer, who can evaluate his or her level of detail based on how well the drawing matched their initial visions. Students were asked to journal on their reactions to the activity. I felt the journals would express anxiety based on some of the students' murmurings. I certainly had to answer the "What if I can't draw?" question, as I always do when endeavoring through this activity. Teachers may meet with this clash of ideas of artistic talent and its perceived value by modeling their own drawings and assuring students that they should do their best, even if that means stick figures. There is also some pressure that can be released by reminding the artist that it's the writer who is ultimately responsible for the work, not the artist, who must only use what the artist has provided. This activity was the second of two authentic sequential art pieces I asked the student to produce. The Comic Book Show and Tell acted as a sort of "pre-test" of their skills and an initial experience with the form. They were also asked to produce three-page mini-comics on the topic "How I became a Reader." These were to be scripted, drawn, and inked (and colored if desired) by the story-teller only, as are many good graphic novels. Each student was given an authentic piece of 11 x 17 Blue Line Pro comic book board etched with non-photo blue guidelines for panels and page layout and two additional pieces of 11 x 17 copy paper pages to complete their comic story in the actual size that most professionals work. The final products were due and shared during our exam activities the last two days of class, acting as a kind of post-test. As always, students were to journal on the experience.

Revealing Samples

The common or recurring themes of the three-page "How I Became a Reader' mini-comics reveal compelling evidence of many aspects considered standard fare in contemporary reading and adolescent literacy research. Being read to as a child was of great importance, and family members were often depicted as playing a major role in the students' literacy development, either through active modeling or reading bedtime stories, or via practicing basic literacy skills like the alphabet. The value of the pictorial was again revealed to be less than that of the traditional print-based textual, and value judgments on authors like R.L. Stine revealed young readers clashing with their teachers' concepts of literacy. In-school reading was revealed to be enticing for some students but restrictive for others.

Accelerated Reader (AR), a program designed to increase kids' reading output, was mentioned in multiple instances, sometimes as a motivator and confidence builder, other times as an oppressive means of stifling interest. The stories reveal that literacy itself is a contact zone, where various values are in play and assorted definitions of worth, reading, and identity are intertwined. As for connections with graphic novels, many of the form's exemplars are memoirs or autobiographies, works with strong elements of realism, even if the characters are drawn in economical or metaphorical manners (see *Safe Area Gorazde*, *Persepolis*, and *Maus*, respectively). Michael Bitz's work (2004a, 2004b, 2009) has shown that when given the opportunity and the proper training, middle and high school students prefer to write autobiographic comics or comics with true-to-life messages rather than super-hero stories. Several students used the phrase, "Once upon a time..." as a device to time-travel the reader back to their respective youths, but only one student in my

Above and next page: Pages from Jessica and Melissa's Mini-Comics Reveal Students' Influences Concerning Notions of Literary Merit and the Benefits of Programs like Accelerate Reader.

class told their story in an alternate form other than autobiography, crafting a fictional fairy tale.

Perhaps offering evidence to the class's early assertion that comics was "boy's reading," and offering more evidence to Wilhelm and Smith's research, only one student considered comics as an important part of his evolution as a reader: the singular male. In Chris's narrative, a young fellow of modest means accompanies his mother to the Salvation Army. He is attracted to the "gag a maggot" smell of the cheap, yellowing paper of old comic books. He buys a stack and makes friends for a lifetime.

Chris's compelling story is reminiscent of several narratives from world leaders in Stephen Krashen's *The Power of Reading*, 2nd edition (2004) and reminded me of an interview with Joan Kaywell in which she mentioned the saving power of books (Carter 2008), a concept of currency with many young adult literature and English Education scholars. She mentioned being saved by a particular text, and, in transcription, I found that I had replied to her by telling her how Chris Claremont's run on *Uncanny X-Men* had offered me solace and comfort as a youth. Indeed, several of the words that surround young Chris as he reads his comics in the last panel of his narrative are the names of X-Men characters, testament to that series' influence and quality.

Above and opposite: Chris's Comics

SENSES REELING... MIND SPINNING... CHRIS COULD ONLY EXCLAIM
WHAT IS THAT SMELL?!
STAR WARS
REPEATLY ...:)
DEAR GOD!! DON'T MAKE ME COME OVER THERE! GET OVER HERE NOW AND BE QUIET.
BOOKS MAGAZINES MUSIC
THANKS TO THAT GAG-A-MAGGOT SMELL I WOULD SOON DISCOVER SOME-THING LIFE CHANGING
COMICS / FUNNIES MAD MAGAZINE CRACKED $1.00
HELLO!!! WHAT DO WE HAVE HERE? MOM!
STAR WARS

Students' Reactions to Their Sequential Art Work

Journal entries on the two comic-making activities reveal a shifting perspective on the value of sequential art in the classroom. After completing the Comic Book Show and Tell, students responded accordingly:

- "I really liked seeing the pictures to go along with my script in comparison to what I had pictured in my mind."
- "It was more challenging than I expected it to be because of the importance of giving very explicit details about what is happening."
- "It makes the writing process fun for students."
- "I feel this is a great way to show real world applications of literacy. There are so many steps to creation and this could help the students focus on attention to detail."
- "It is interesting to see the process of what all goes into creating a great comic book. I never knew that comics could be used for more than a good read."
- "I so wish teachers were doing these things when I was in school. I've already had some teaching experience, and the biggest problem I have encountered with student writing is descriptive language and detail."

For many of these students, comics are now more than reading material; they've become process material. Having experienced for themselves a lesson actually geared for grades 6 and up, they have first-hand knowledge of how the activity can help students compose, revise, and metacognitively consider aspects of creating. One student catches on to the authenticity behind the activity, perhaps bringing together previously separate schema for "school" and "comics." Perhaps also telling is that there are no comments associated with gender as there were in beginning journal entries, just a focus on what "students" could get out of the activity.

The theme of respect for the form also emerges in the above comments, and this is reiterated when students respond to being the author, artist, and inker for their three-page mini-comics on becoming a reader:

- "I now know all of the time and effort that goes into making a comic book.... I think it would take me an entire year to make an entire comic.... This was a really fun activity and a great learning experience."
- "I now have an even stronger admiration for those artists who also write the script. Making graphic novels is something to be handled with care because every small detail counts."
- "The most important thing I realized about my classmates' comics was that most of them weren't artists either. That made me feel a lot better about mine."
- "It would make a great project for students so they could not only learn something new, but create something that they can be proud of and share with others.... This exercise really gave me a new insight on the different ways, not only that students can learn, but the different ways that I can teach."
- "It allowed each student to express their creative abilities.... I feel 100 percent positive I would use this activity in my classroom."
- "I worked so hard putting my comic together. Panel by panel, I painstakingly drew and lettered my story. When I finished, I was so proud of it! I had created a comic book. I really think students would experience this same pride."

Pride in their work is another theme, and they seem sure that their own students might feel similarly if asked to compose a piece of sequential art. Again, there are no gendered assumptions at play. The time and effort spent in producing their comics appears to have offered a respect for the form that might not have been present before, and the potential for exploring the form as a means of engaging students in meaningful work is now a strong consideration. Having clashed and grappled with the form, they seem more willing to let their future students meet it. Recently, at my current institution, I taught a graduate-level course entitled "Teaching the Graphic Novel" in which the students reiterated the idea that one can never truly understand the work that goes into comics and their value in examining elements of composition until they have tried it themselves.

Ramifications for Practicing Teachers

My students' shifting perspectives reveal to me that when people educate themselves on the potential classroom utility of comics art and composition, they tend to be more willing to accept the form. Actually engaging in the comics creation process reveals the challenges and skill associated with production and helps illustrate what students might gain from trying and studying the medium. Classroom teachers might consider this and try the form themselves, perhaps using the Comic Book Show and Tell as a primer before sharing the lesson or similar ones with their students. Certainly there is no shortage of texts available now to help those not familiar with the comics medium learn about its composition. Katie Monnin's *Teaching Graphic Novels* (2010) deconstructs the form marvelously such that anyone can learn how comics creators use space, panels, narration and sound elements to various affect. Other books that blend how-to elements with formal instruction and consideration of the medium include *Comics and Sequential Art* (Eisner 1985), *The Art of Making Comics* (Pellowksi and Bender 1996), *Graphic Storytelling and Visual Narrative* (Eisner 1996), *How to Create Comics From Script to Print* (Fingeroth and Manley 2006), *Making Comics* (McCloud 2006), *Drawing Words and Writing Pictures* (Abel and Madden 2008), *Adventures in Cartooning* (Sturm, Arnold, and Frederick-Frost 2009), *The Complete Idiots Guide to Creating a Graphic Novel* (Gertler and Leiber 2009) and *The Insider's Guide to Creating Comics and Graphic Novels* (Schmidt 2009). Other resources are listed in the "References" section of this chapter.

Curriculum specialists and others responsible for teachers' professional development might consider asking teachers to craft a story in comics form too in order to help them see the value of comics' creative processes. English Educators might do well to test their and their pre-service students' conceptions about the form by endeavoring to craft mini-comics. With the medium gaining so much attention from educators (something, by the way, it has been garnering with various degrees of fervor since the 1930s) and many more education-related texts integrating comics elements on the horizon, it appears to be a reality that not learning a little about sequential art narratives and sharing it with pre-service teachers may be an action moving away from the acceptable toward the irresponsible.

Students' Final Comments

Toward the end of the course, I asked students to write a final journal reflection on their thoughts and feeling associated with using comics in the classroom. Two elementary education majors admitted that they were still struggling with finding ways they could integrate comics into their future classrooms, but most seemed to find at least one idea or activity suitable for practice. For example, one student who remarked that she was still having trouble thinking of graphic novels for early elementary classrooms (alas, TOON Books wasn't going strong as a publisher of comics for emergent readers yet), stated, "I love the idea of testing comprehension by having students rewrite (in comic book form) something just read." This student and another elementary education major used the phrase "do whatever it takes" in describing what they will do to get students to learn, and while it might be disconcerting for some to see them possibly considering teaching comics only as a desperation strategy, no one expounded enough to suggest that is exactly what they were suggesting. Many students admitted an initial lack of knowledge or familiarity with the form but said exposure to it and interaction with it influenced them to change their opinions:

- "After being exposed to these books I will be more willing to incorporate this genre into my curriculum."
- "I definitely have a greater appreciation for graphic novels than I had in the past and I am definitely planning on incorporating them into my future classroom."
- "My views on graphic novels have changed a lot over the past two weeks. I just did not know a lot about graphic novels and all they could offer a classroom. I am now a lot more accepting of them."

Not being a future English teacher did not deter the history major. She too found herself considering integrating sequential art narratives into her future classroom: "Although I am not an English major, many of the texts and articles we read were helpful in preparing to incorporate graphic novels into a history class."

Furthermore, as I hypothesized regarding students' earlier comments, some admitted to having associated the comics form with very narrow notions of genre:

- "The first day of class, I associated all comic books w/ superheroes and had never dreamed about using them in my class. Now I wouldn't dream of going without them. Their [sic] is so much variety to choose from…"
- "I have been so surprised to find such difficult topics being explored in the books we read…."
- I have come so far from when this class began. I did not know anything about graphic novels. I was one of those close minded people who thought you couldn't learn anything from graphic novels. Now I see that I was wrong!"

Notice that gendered notions of reading are absent from these comments as well. No longer does it seem to be a general impression that comics are only for boys, or that they're not proper reading for girls. Further thoughts about utility and variety have superseded thoughts about quality. Literacy value seems to have trumped literary value, and there is no mention of comics still being viewed as a low form.

Two other quotes are particularly telling. The last student quoted above wrote further in her journal,

> Most of the people I have told that I'm taking this class have had negative attitudes toward it. Their initial reaction is "Comic books! I can't believe they teach that in college!" But they just don't understand the depths and concepts that can be taught from these books we read.

Distinctions of quality regarding sequential art versus traditional forms are now placed in the other, a genderless, resistant other, not the self. Further, the writer is not aggravated with this opinion, which might have been popular among the class in its early sessions. Rather, the student feels that the skeptics' sense of conflict regarding the medium is rooted in ignorance. The write seems to suggest, "If only they'd seen what I have seen." Another student wrote, "I never realized just how valuable graphic novels could be in the classroom. They engage students in so many different ways that now I think that teachers who don't include them in their classrooms are doing their students a grave disservice." While it is important to note these students had an instructor for the course who is very pro-comics-in-the-classroom and who has written some of the secondary texts they read, and that that could have influenced what information they chose to share in their final reflective pieces, it seems clear to me from examining their comments that the best way to learn about the potential of this form in the classroom is to study it overtly and thoroughly, allowing one to directly challenge preconceived notions of quality, form, and appropriate classroom materials.

As simple as it seems, the "walk a mile in my shoes" adage might be the best advice a teacher educator can glean from this chapter. English educators and those who teach young adult literature may want to consider giving more time to sequential art narratives in their teacher education courses, letting students read the books and articles written on their literacy benefits along with *multiple, varied* examples of graphic novels themselves, as did my students. Those who teach young adult literature may seek to teach all-graphic novel "special topics" sections from time to time, and those with the ability to allow such courses to appear in course catalogues may need to loosen their grip on what constitutes the traditional young adult course, which typically is a survey, to allow for a thorough examination of the comics form. Or, perhaps the field of young adult literature has grown and has accepted so many forms that one young adult literature course is no longer sufficient to prepare future English teachers.

Furthermore, to fully understand the complexity of the medium, students and their teachers may need to create comics and metacognitively study the composition processes they used to make them via reflection and discussion. While none of my students nor I advocate for a full-scale revolution in which all canonical or traditionally print-based texts are replaced with comic books and graphic novels, it seems increasingly silly, ignorant, and stubborn to meet comics and graphic novels with resistance. As John Milton so often reminds us, active virtue is best. Virtue that is untested in no virtue at all. Certainly my data suggests that my students learned the virtue and value of meeting, clashing, and grappling regarding considerations of the form. They further illustrate that the "contact zones" surrounding cogitation of sequential art narrative in education can be rough-and-tumble, sure, and it probably ought to be, but the important part of the challenge is that it begins with a bit of willingness to embrace.

Special note

To see the syllabus for the course referred to herein, complete with graphic novels read, visit this address: *http://ensaneworld.blogspot.com/search?q=All-GN's+Ya+Lit+Class*

References

Abel, Jessica, Matt Madden. 2008. *Drawing Words and Writing Pictures.* New York: First Second.
Accomando, Beth. July 28, 2008. "Librarians Harvest New Manga Titles At Comic-Con." *National Public Radio*. Accessed July 28, 2008, at *http://www.npr.org/templates/story/story.php?storyId=92998234*.

Alsup, Janet, and Jonathan Bush. 2003. *"But Will it Work With REAL Students?" Scenarios for Teaching Secondary English language Arts.* Urbana, IL: NCTE.

Bitz, Michael. 2004a. "The Comic Book Project: Forging Alternative Pathways to Literacy." *Journal of Adolescent and Adult Literacy* 47.7: 574–586.

_____. 2004b. "The Comic Book Project: The Lives of Urban Youth." *Art Education* 57.2: 33–39.

_____. 2009. *Manga High: Literacy, Identity and Coming of Age in an Urban High School.* Cambridge, MA: Harvard Education Press.

Cambourne, Brian. 2002. "Holistic, Integrated Approaches to Reading and Language Arts Instruction: The Constructivist Framework of an Instructional Theory." In A.E. Farstrup and S.J. Samuels, eds., *What Research Has to Say About Reading Instruction, Third Edition.* Newark, DE: International Reading Association: 25–47.

Carter, James Bucky. 2007. "Introduction–Carving the Niche: Graphic Novels in the English Language Arts Classroom." In James Bucky Carter, ed., *Building Literacy Connections with Graphic Novels: Page by Page, Panel by Panel.* Urbana, IL: NCTE: 1–25.

_____. 2007. "Ultimate Spider-Man and Student-Generated Classics: Using Graphic Novels and Comics to Produce Authentic Voice and Detailed, Authentic Texts." In James Bucky Carter, ed., *Building Literacy Connections with Graphic Novels: Page by Page, Panel by Panel.* Urbana, IL: NCTE: 145–156.

_____. 2008. *Analyzing the Role and Processes of General Editors of Book Projects Related to the English Language Arts.* Accessed February 13, 2006, via Proquest dissertations and theses: AAT 3312162.

Eisner, Will. 1985. *Comics and Sequential Art.* Tamarac, FL: Poorhouse Press.

_____. 1996. *Graphic Storytelling and Visual Narrative.* Tamarac, FL: Poorhouse Press.

Fingeroth, Danny, and Mike Manley. 2006. *How to Create Comics from Script to Print.* Raleigh, NC: Twomorrows.

Gertler, Nat, and Steve Lieber. 2009. *The Complete Idiot's Guide to Creating a Graphic Novel.* 2d ed. New York: Alpha Books.

Krashen, Stephen D. 2004. *The Power of Reading.* 2d ed.. Portsmouth, NH: Heinemann.

McCloud, Scott. 1993. *Understanding Comics.* New York: DC.

_____. 2006. *Making Comics.* New York: Harper.

Monnin, Katie. 2010. *Teaching Graphic Novels.* Gainesville, FL: Maupin House.

Moore, Alan, and Jacen Burrows. 2003. *Writing for Comics.* Rantoul, IL: Avatar Press.

Pellowski, Michael M., and Howard Bender. 1995 *The Art of Making Comics.* Minneapolis, MN: Lerner.

Philion, Thomas. 2002. "Frontiers of the Contact Zone." In Janice M. Wolff, ed., *Professing in the Contact Zone: Bringing Theory and Practice Together.* Urbana, IL: NCTE: 79–101.

Pratt, Mary Louise. 2002. "Arts of the Contact Zone." In Janice M. Wolff, ed., *Professing in the Contact Zone: Bringing Theory and Practice Together.* Urbana, IL: NCTE: 1–20.

Ragin, Charles C. 1994. *Constructing Social Research.* Thousand Oaks, CA: Pine Forge Press.

Robinson, W.S. 1951. "The Logical Structure of Analytical Induction." *American Sociological Review* 16: 812–818.

Schmidt, Andy. 2009. *The Insider's Guide to Creating Comics and Graphic Novels.* Cincinnati, OH: Impact.

Sturm, James, Andrew Arnold, and Alexis Frederick-Frost. 2009. *Adventures in Cartooning.* New York: First Second.

Wilhelm, Jeffrey D., and Michael W. Smith. 2002. *Reading Don't Fix No Chevys: Literacy in the Lives of Young Men.* Portsmouth, NH: Heinemann.

Teaching Intertextuality and Parody Through the Graphic "Supertext"
Martin Rowson's The Waste Land *(1990)*

KEVIN M. FLANAGAN

The following essay is a thought-experiment relating to the place of graphic novels in upper-division undergraduate education. While graphic novels and comics are increasingly taught in relation to the discrete properties unique to their medium, they continue to have much to offer other areas of the humanities. As such, this essay proposes a theoretical framework from which we might think about a graphic novel as a structuring determinate in the process of course creation. I have focused my discussion on one specific graphic text, Martin Rowson's *The Waste Land* (1990: a wholesale re-imagining of T.S. Eliot's epoch-defining poem of 1922), and have related it to the one specific course (a semester-long survey of European modernism). However, I hope that this specific idea — that a graphic novel might, in some senses, *become* the syllabus — is portable to a variety of different contexts.

From Rowson to Eliot

Near the middle of Martin Rowson's gonzo novel *Snatches* (2006), in a chapter appropriately called "Film Studies," the imposing academic Sykes-Wolsey delivers a rambling lecture that investigates the cultural value of the blockbuster James Bond and *Carry On* franchises. In this multi-page performance, which is an evident riposte to the self-involved, insular discourses that characterize a less-than-charitable view of the contemporary humanities, Sykes-Wolsey manages to align the accessible populism of these two British film institutions with the deeply modernistic, indeed highly serious, linguistic sensibility of no less a figure than T.S. Eliot (Rowson 2006, 131–135). Sykes-Wolsey's tirade ends with a comedic meditation on the potential incoherence of intertextual analysis (a sensibility ultimately undone over the course of reading this playful, robustly intertextual novel): "it is still valid to imbue partially what Bond says with what Eliot and his muddle-headed followers still maintain that what they call text might now have or ever have had any possibility of meaning, as such" (135).

Despite this parodically negative sentiment, Rowson is aware of his own reliance on the legacy of other texts. In addition to his mastery of caricature — he is a regular political cartoonist for *The Guardian*, in addition to his frequent credits as an illustrator, graphic novelist, and formidable prose stylist in his own right — Rowson's work produces re-representation of known historical and literary precedents. Michael Moorcock, in a review of *Snatches*, has noted that Rowson's work is "reminiscent of Smollett's glorious vulgarity, with echoes of Gillray, Swift, Sterne, and Peacock," all while bearing the countenance of "a modern original" (Moorcock 2006). Graphic novel scholar Stephen E. Tabachnick — who regards the tradition of English caricature and cartooning to be absolutely central to the evolutionary trajectory of subsequent narrative intersections of word and image (he lists William Hogarth, Thomas Rowlandson, and the aforementioned James Gillray as central to this generic movement) — considers Rowson's graphic novel adaptations of classic literary texts as far more than simple exercises in the visual transposition of the verbal (Tabachnick 2009, 2; 8). Most importantly, Tabachnick refers to Rowson's *The Waste Land* as "brilliant," and credits it with lending some degree of classroom appropriateness to the very form of the graphic novel (13).

At first glance, Rowson's engagement with Eliot's poem seems an aberration, a stalwart exception to the lamentable tradition of straightforwardly "faithful" graphic novel adaptations of canonical literary texts. In *Reading Comics: How Graphic Novels Work and What they Mean* (2007), Douglas Wolk has (understandably) railed against this practice. He writes: "comics adaptations of prose books are almost uniformly terrible, from the old *Classic Illustrated* pamphlets to the contemporary versions of *Black Beauty* and *The Hunchback of Notre Dame*; they don't run the same current, basically, and they end up gutting the original of a lot of its significant content" (Wolk 2006, 13). This observation speaks to the operative assumptions of medium specificity. The classic "realist" novel of the 19th and 20th centuries is good at what it does — imploding personal space, giving a platform to unspoken psychologizing, demonstrating a willingness for long gestating emotional evolution — while the graphic novel thrives in other arenas. Specifically, sequential graphic texts are ideal conduits for kinetic narratives, externalized spatial relationships, and the visual contextualization of the spoken word (the ubiquitous "speech bubble"). With this in mind, how can Eliot's *The Waste Land*, a poem that eschews conventional narrative, revels in arcane cultural allusions, and resists obvious spatial and temporal explanation be rendered intelligible for a medium that has, historically, been more aligned with action and heroism than with contemplation and self-serving introspection?

Martin Rowson seems to short-circuit this potential feedback loop by thoroughly altering the apparently central focus of *The Waste Land*. In his text, private eye Christopher Marlowe leaves his grubby Los Angeles offices in search of revenge for the murder of his partner Fisher. Arriving in London, he becomes embroiled in an escalating series of killings and double-crosses, before eventually finding himself in the midst of an obtuse quest for the Holy Grail which takes him deep into the criminal underworld. For readers already familiar with Eliot's *The Waste Land*, some of the references to the original poem are immediately evident: the dislocated and somewhat aimless life of an American in London; the retreat into arcane introspection in the face of the technological imperatives of modernity; and the application of a massive textual inheritance onto the contours of daily life (Maddrey 2010).[1] However, for readers who have not previously been exposed to Eliot's works, and who may not have the historical, contextual, and critical vocabulary to parse it, Rowson's *The Waste Land* is a godsend: in place of largely abstract verbiage, he offers a multimodal detective story. But while the adaptation obviously elucidates aspects of the poem to which it corresponds, it also offers a convenient method, a sort of structuring principle, for the investigation of aesthetic modernism on the whole. In Rowson's representation of modernism, wild intertextuality and grotesque parody become crucial sites of struggle for this sometimes obtuse body of literary texts.

Tracking the Detective Story

Casting an interpretation of *The Waste Land* in terms of a detective story is not wholly inappropriate to Eliot's life and legacy. Eliot reviewed numerous detective stories for *The Criterion* in 1927, and even compared Thomas Kyd's *The Spanish Tragedy* to contemporary stories of detection (Preston 1959, 397–398). In writing about T.S. Eliot's formative influences, Robert Crawford notes that "Sherlock Holmes was to be a favourite with Eliot all his life," whose powers of detection, mastery, and intellectual curiosity meant that "Holmes, for Eliot, was not only the scientist but *the* urban man" (Crawford 1987, 10).[2] But an interest in Holmes (and his creator, Sir Arthur Conan Doyle) signaled more than just an appreciation for the procedural aspects of the detective story. Like Conan Doyle — who published a wide-ranging history of spiritualism in 1926 — Eliot, in both personality and prose, seemed at times suspended between a poetic, sometimes occult set of influences (Eastern religions, mysticism, the folkloric and mythopoetic world of James George Frazer's famous *The Golden Bough* [originally published 1890]) and the rationalist, material concerns of his capitalist reality (most famously, his day job as a banker).

Thus, Rowson's choice to build a methodological means of decryption into the narrative and characterizations of his version of *The Waste Land* draws attention to a recommended program of reader-response: in order to "get" his text, and by extension that floating signifier called modernism, his audience must work backwards to understand the implied connections between texts. On a wholly naïve level, his graphic novel of *The Waste Land* can be read as a rather spare, disjointed potboiler. But — as with an understanding of literary modernism itself — the text only becomes fully polysemic with an understanding of how it interacts with others.

The Place of the Supertext

The governing logic of what has been called the "supertext" is useful for explaining Rowson's *The Waste Land*. In an oft-cited formulation by John G. Cawelti, the supertext (in this case referred to as a genre or macro-text) "claims to be an abstract of the most significant characteristics or family resemblances among many particular texts, which can accordingly be analyzed, evaluated, and otherwise related to each other by virtue of their connection with the supertext" (Cawelti 1997, 68). Here, Cawelti does not necessarily refer to historically originating texts so much as those that interrelate the salient aspects of form and content of an otherwise recognizable genre. While his use of the term can denote the larger, governing set of principles and ideas that constitute an idealization in the aggregate (i.e., a set of characteristics not present in any one example), the concept *can* be applied to *individual* works that show a remarkable reflexivity in this regard. These supertexts demonstrate internally comprehensive understandings of larger, more diffuse formations. In a sense, they are the sorts of texts that often yield the "best example" so often desired by classroom instruction. Given the regrettably limited time available for demonstration and example in a semester-long course, a supertext can be offered as a convenient anchor for a number of concerns. Cawelti offers that "the supertext can be treated like an individual text: Its history can be constructed; its impact and influence can be explored; it can be compared with other texts; it can be used as a source for constructing histories and theories of art and culture" (68).

The sheer scope, range of reference, sense of self-awareness, and deep engagement with canonized literary texts on display in Rowson's graphic novel situate it as a teachable supertext *par excellence*. In fact, *The Waste Land's* text and images present themselves in-and-amongst so many other key works by modernist artists — Wyndham Lewis and his vorticist *Blast* periodical, Marcel Duchamp's scandalous painting *L.H.O.O.Q*, and Eliot's own *Old Possum's Book of Practical Cats*, to name but three — that it stands, on its own, as a road map for a course in modernism. Rowson's supertext can introduce and exemplify aspects of modernist cultural production; it can draw attention to a wider sphere of works that differently attend to the stylistic and conceptual bases of modernism; it directly relates to the ways in which modernist artists utilize intertexts in constructing "original" meanings, or how and why such artists adapt already existing texts toward new ends; and it dramatizes one definitional distinction that arguably separates the "modern" from the "postmodern," namely the conceptual difference between parody and pastiche.

While one could argue that a textbook or historical survey could just as easily put forth some of these discussions, Rowson's *The Waste Land* has two notable advantages. For one, the fact that it is an engaging graphic novel certainly helps: it addresses students in visual and verbal terms simultaneously, intrinsically positions modernism as a transmedia phenomenon that is spatially aware, and does all of this efficiently, in familiar-but-challenging narrative terms. Moreover, this supertext formally (and obviously) embodies many of the contradictions and contestations that are present in any study of modernism. It displays the uneasy co-presence of "high" cultural forms with "low" modes of mass and popular culture, and, to defer to Peter Childs, the excitingly visceral tensions that arise from the contradictory alliance of "revolutionary and reactionary positions, fear of the new and delight at the disappearance of the old, nihilism and fanatical enthusiasm, creativity and despair" (Childs 2000, 17).

Meeting with Modernism

On one level, Rowson's *The Waste Land* is an exemplary modernist (or, depending how you and your students eventually classify it, postmodern) text. Following Childs, we might broadly introduce students to modernism (as opposed to allied-but-different concepts like modernity and "the modern") as a "cultural reaction" to the new productive, industrial, and historical conditions in place, especially in Europe, at the beginning of the 20th century (Childs 2000, 17).[3] Some basic definitional parameters should be introduced before leaping too deeply into a wider set of primary texts. Before any readings occur, brainstorming with students as to their preliminary ideas about modernism, their previous engagements with the concept, and their personal encounters with relevant texts can help frame the eventual terms of discussion. Further, Michael H. Whitworth's concise formulations about modernist stylistic tendencies — which he puts forth with the disclaimer that they might appear to be overly indebted to formalist critical methodology — are useful for giving students some sense of what modernism looks and reads like. He lists an engagement with (and ambivalence about) contemporary urban life; willfully difficult style dependent on allusion and fragmentation; the presentation of an intelligible past in the face of an unintelligible present; the possibility of artistic transcendence of the constrictingly quotidian aspects of everyday life; organizing structure based on classical myth or legend; the differentiation between individual consciousness and the mass; and, the assumption of an exclusive access to cultural literacy (the assumption, in short, of a "writerly" reader) (Whitworth 2007, 11–16; Barthes 1974, 4). Students will quickly recognize some of these features upon their first read-through of Rowson's text: it follows an alienated, privileged protagonist through a nightmarish urban environment, is explicitly modeled on the quest for the Holy Grail, constantly alludes to other texts, uses episodic ellipsis without fully motivating all action or plot elements, etc. It does what other modernist texts do, and this resemblance can be revisited throughout the semester, especially once more "primary" texts have been consulted.

Note, too, that Rowson's text need not initially be presented to students as an adaptation of an antecedent work. While instructors familiar with adaptation studies might be tempted to introduce Eliot's *The Waste Land* and Rowson's *The Waste Land* in a one-to-one correspondence, and might want to position the course around an initial reading of Eliot followed by a reading of Rowson, an almost opposite approach will likely yield better results. My gambit is that the course might cover more conceptually compelling terrain — both for teacher and student — if the intellectual investigation begins solely within Rowson's framework. Therefore, I suggest introducing Rowson's texts along with a preliminary discussion of modernism. Since one likely goal of the course is to have students display their own understanding of how the term modernism gets used in literary and academic contexts, a program of working backwards can help feed this larger issue. Given a preliminary amount of information — a "set of clues" if one keeps up the spirit of detective work — students can work through the supertext/syllabus, at each turn "reverse-engineering" Rowson's work. Put another way, students will unpack the tenets of modernism via Rowson's framework, through a careful reading of Rowson's text in consultation with the more traditionally taught superstars (Woolf, Yeats, Joyce, and so on) of Eurocentric modernism.

This unpacking of reference, allusion, and influence has more to do with Robert Stam's reformulation of the process of adaptation than it does with older models based on textual fidelity (Stam 2005, 24–28).[4] What students are asked to undertake is a sustained program of transtextual interpretation, one that has an eye to both the meanings of the course's explicit supertext (Rowson's *The Waste Land*) and at the same time a more abstract supertext (the "ideal" or "most typical" instantiations of modernism). Again, this impulse can be traced back to the ways in which scholars have attempted to understand Eliot and his version of *The Waste Land*.[5] Noting that he "adapted" elements from many sources, and set his work within the recognizable milieu of the Grail quest, one path to interpretation has been to trace the meanings of these constitutive texts, and to read the resulting work as a negotiation of past artistic production combined with the talents of the modernist author.

"Talent" or "genius" are words that are often idly thrown around, but they have a specific significance to the study of the canonized form of modernism. In fact, the course should begin with two other preliminary texts that can be used to more fully realize Rowson's framework, and which can be revisited at nearly every juncture. The first is Eliot's own "Tradition and the Individual Talent," which offers his theory of how originality works for writers that have no choice but to recognize the massive textual inheritance to which they are privy. The insights found therein, which deal with the tempering of intrinsic talent *vis a vis* a long history of exceptional, original artists, can just as easily be ported for a discussion of Rowson as it can for Eliot and other canonical modernist authors. Alongside of this, one might offer students the preface ("A Meditation upon Priority, and a Synopsis") to Harold Bloom's widely discussed *The Anxiety of Influence: A Theory of Poetry* (1973), in which he outlines another, in some senses more antagonistic, thesis about how great writers deal with the achievements of past artists. Again, the questions typically asked of Eliot and his contemporaries work equally well for Rowson: which elements of work by antecedent artists (visual and literary) does Rowson replicate (or parody)? Are there specific ideas, styles, or methodologies that he adopts? Are these replications foregrounded and acknowledged? Does Rowson appear to disown any of his fore-bearers? Does he subconsciously reproduce notable work by others?

Rowson's Magic Moments

With this skeletal outline — an initial reading of Rowson, introductory discussions of salient characteristics of modernism, and a reading of Eliot and Bloom's critical texts — the class can begin with the investigative work prompted by the text. Since Rowson's graphic novel touches on so many subjects, the possibilities are vast, yet conducive even to texts and contexts not explicitly featured in the book. An example of this might take the form of a unit on the historical context out of which modernism emerged. For example, the bar scene in "Chapter Two: A Game of Chess" — the first such scene upon Marlowe's arrival in London — showcases a room full of famous authors (among them Gertrude Stein, Robert Graves, and Herman Melville), but is most interesting for the presented wall decorations, which are exclusively comprised of reproductions of famous Pre-Raphaelite paintings (Rowson 1990).[6] This seemingly throw-away detail in the text can actually be positioned as a key means of working out Whitworth's point about how modernist texts approach the past. The Pre-Raphaelites, a group of painters and poets who began to work as a loose unit in the 1840s, reacted to industrialization and the coming of the Victorian metropolis with an explicit retreat into a neo-medievalism that shunned machines and the urban in favor of an invented, idealized alternative. Here, students might think about how reactions to (or arguments against) modernity get contained in modernist texts; how and why a graphic novelist might decide upon underdetermined visual detail instead of straightforward verbal statements; and how submerged detail (more generally) often comments upon the larger historical and theoretical issues at work in a text.

Two potentially strong "teachable moments" in Rowson's *The Waste Land* are its explicit gesture to Vorticism in Chapter One, and its general visual representation of the city in the second half of the book. Although Rowson's graphic style is typically uniform in terms of the organic sinuousness of his lines and shading, there is a compelling moment where he abandons his initial visual modality in favor of a wholesale adoption of Vorticist abstraction. The panel in question is diagonally split: in the lower right-hand corner is a hand holding several tarot cards, while the bulk of the left part of the frame contains portraits of several members of the Vorticist group (mixed with other persons associated with other contemporary artistic and literary movements), rendered in the style of some of Wyndham Lewis and Henri Gaudier-Brzeska's drawings and paintings (both of whom are represented). This is a wonderful opportunity to discuss the interplay between visual and literary form/content. In addition to showing works by artists like Lewis, his publication *Blast* (1914–1915) can be examined. Here, issues pertinent to the graphic novel can be discussed in parallel terms of the avant-garde art journal: suddenly, Rowson's lapse into a quoted stylistic flourish corresponds to the formal experimentation at work in the canonized modernist texts. The uneasy distinctions between text and image in Lewis's journal can be thought about in relation to Rowson's parallel juggling of the two.

Chapter Three, "The First Sermon," is notable for Marlowe's vast amble around London. As such, it can frame a discussion of other modernist texts that are predicated on the encounter between the sensitive individual and the city. In particular, two famous texts might be examined (in whole or in part): James Joyce's inexhaustible *Ulysses* (1922) and Virginia Woolf's lauded *Mrs. Dalloway* (1925). In a compact manner, the class can examine corresponding excerpts from both texts, namely parts of the monstrous "Circe" chapter in *Ulysses* (in which physical space implodes, and the city is experienced in psychical terms as hallucination and internalized journey) and the famous opening section of *Mrs. Dalloway*, in which Clarissa Dalloway walks across a section of London (Joyce 1986, 650–497; Woolf 2005, 3–28). With *Ulysses*, students might question conceptual assumptions about urban space, while *Mrs. Dalloway*'s locatability in London might draw a more direct discussion between Rowson's rendering of the place and Woolf's verbal evocation.

After teaching a number of units that relate issues in Rowson's *The Waste Land* to other modernist texts, I suggest wrapping up the course with a reading of Eliot's poem and a total re-reading of Rowson's graphic novel. By this point, students have a more comprehensive vocabulary with which to talk about modernist aesthetics, have been introduced to historical and contextual issues that aide in the reading of a work like Eliot's, have made connections between Rowson and his intertexts (which might lead them to a similar approach to Eliot and his allusions, influences, and quotations), and have seen examples of visual, prose-based, and poetic iterations of modernist work. The withholding of Eliot until the end means that students will ask a different set of questions about this famously ambiguous poem.

Modernism or Postmodernism? Debating Parody and Pastiche

Throughout this course, Rowson's text has been used to propel students into bigger, on-going debates in the study of, and definitional parameters for, modernism. But the status of Rowson's graphic novel — which effortlessly moves between hard-boiled crime and references to obscure literature — could almost as readily be offered as postmodernist as modernist. How can we have students debate the minute differences between the modern and the postmodern, given that they've just spent weeks constructing a set of definitions for modernism and have been given no explicit instruction on the salient characteristics on postmodernism? It might be most manageable to isolate one (multimodal) aspect of the debate — in the case of Rowson's graphic novel, the difference between parody and pastiche works best — and have students offer their own readings of the text through the introduction of a common theoretical framework. The most useful source here despite (or because of) its difficulty is the "Culture" chapter of Fredric Jameson's *Postmodernism, or the Cultural Logic of Late Capitalism* (1991). He outlines a distinction between a teleological mode of parody — a barbed, textually stable form of comedic exposure and exaggeration that held sway during the modernist moment (and before) — and puts these against the postmodern frame of pastiche, a practice that posits a seemingly endless and ungrounded quotation to ulterior referents, devoid of deeper meaning (Jameson 1991, 17). He writes "for with the collapse of the high modernist ideology of style ... the producers of culture have nowhere to turn but to the past: the imitation of dead styles, speech through all the masks and voices stored up in the imaginary museum of a now global culture" (17–18).

Rowson's *The Waste Land* is, certainly, one such "imaginary museum." But are its allusions just the equivalent of window-dressing, "red herrings" or Hitchcockian "MacGuffins" that make the expected postmodernist gestures? On the contrary, do its explicit references to a cultural inheritance — the very same tradition to which Eliot responds, and from which he writes his poem *The Waste Land*, a work that is almost always upheld as its own kind of poetic modernist supertext — position it as yet another late example of the still-ongoing project of modernism? In this regard, is Rowson our contemporary Eliot, albeit in the form of an artist more reliant on caricature and his sense of humor? There is no easy or entrenched place to go from here. In short, leave your students with an indeterminate cliffhanger, a properly modernist *dénouement*: anxious, complex, darkly comic, and unresolvable.

Notes

1. As Joseph Maddrey demonstrates throughout his *The Making of T.S. Eliot* (2010), part of the opacity of Eliot's work — and, consequently, one of the reasons why it is so difficult to teach to a heterogeneous group of undergraduate students — is that it constitutes itself through a lifetime's worth of reading. Eliot's own "Tradition and the Individual Talent" affirms the conceit that all genuinely creative writing is the result of a negotiation of textual precedents and influences with one's immutable creative energies (1094–1095).
2. Italics mine.
3. It is important to note — and emphasize to students — that the critical consensus as to what does and does not constitute itself as engaged with modernist sensibilities is always subject to modulation and expansion. For a recent discussion, see Douglas Mao and Rebecca L. Walkowitz's article "The New Modernist Studies" (2008), an important "state of the field" piece published in *PMLA*.
4. Note that Stam is explicitly discussing adaptation in the context of film and cinema's engagement with other media and textual forms. He challenges us to consider poststructuralist, Bakhtinian, and paratextual frameworks (especially modeled after work by Gerard Genette, in books such as his *Paratexts: Threshold of Interpretation*).
5. See Maddrey's *The Making of T.S. Eliot* for an example of this approach, especially the chapter "Beyond Good and Evil," which traces Eliot's most recent textual involvements in and around writing *The Waste Land* (99–124).
6. Rowson's *The Waste Land* is unpaginated. Note that it contains an indispensable appendix in which Rowson names his "Cast" of characters, pointing to the likenesses of famous authors and describing how they function in the narrative. This, too, is unpaginated.

References

Barthes, Roland. 1974. *S/Z: An Essay*. Trans. Richard Miller. New York: Hill & Wang.
Bloom, Harold. 1997. *The Anxiety of Influence: A Theory of Poetry*. New York: Oxford UP. [1973].
Cawelti, John G. 1997. "The Question of Popular Genres Revisited." In Gary R. Edgerton, Michael T. Marsden, and Jack Nachbar, eds., *In the Eye of the Beholder: Critical Perspectives in Popular Film and Television*. Bowling Green, OH: The Popular Press: 67–84.
Childs, Peter. 2000. *Modernism. The New Critical Idiom*. New York: Routledge.
Crawford, Robert. 1987. *The Savage and the City in the Work of T.S. Eliot*. Oxford: Oxford University Press.
Eliot, T.S. 1991. "*The Waste Land*" In *T.S. Eliot: Collected Poems, 1909–1962*. New York: Harcourt Brace Jovanovich, 51–69.
_____. 2001. "Tradition and the Individual Talent." In Vincent B. Leitch, ed., *The Norton Anthology of Theory and Criticism*. New York: Norton, 1092–1098.
Frazer, James George. 2003. *The Golden Bough: A Study in Magic and Religion*. London: Wordsworth Books. [1922, 1890].
Gennette, Gerarld. 1997. *Paratexts: Thresholds of Interpretation*. Trans. Jane E. Lewin. New York: Cambridge University Press.

Jameson, Fredric. 2003. *Postmodernism, or the Cultural Logic of Late Capitalism*. Durham, NC: Duke University Press. [1991].
Joyce, James. 1986. *Ulysses*. Ed. Hans Walter Gabler. New York: Random House.
Maddrey, Joseph. 2010. *The Making of T.S. Eliot*. Jefferson, NC: McFarland.
Lewis, Wyndham, ed. 2009. *Blast 1*. Berkeley, CA: Gingko Press. [1914].
Mao, Douglas, and Rebecca L. Walkowitz. 2008. "The New Modernist Studies." *PMLA* 123.3: 737–748.
Moorcock, Michael. April 22, 2006. "Weird History: Michael Moorcock Enjoys Martin Rowson's Satirical Rampage, *Snatches*." *The Guardian*. Accessed January 31, 2011.
Preston, Priscilla. July 1959. "A Note on T.S. Eliot and Sherlock Holmes." *The Modern Language Review* 54.3: 397–399. Accessed through JSTOR, January 31, 2011.
Rowson, Martin. 1990. *The Waste Land*. New York: Harper & Row.
_____. 2006. *Snatches*. London: Jonathan Cape.
Stam, Robert. 2005. "Introduction: The Theory and Practice of Adaptation." In Robert Stam and Alessandra Raengo, eds., *Literature and Film: A Guide to the Theory and Practice of Film Adaptation*. Malden, MA: Blackwell: 1–53.
Tabachnick, Stephen E. 2009. "Introduction." In Stephen E. Tabachnick, ed., *Teaching the Graphic Novel*. New York: MLA Press: 1–15.
Whitworth, Michael H. 2007. "Introduction." In Michael H. Whitwork, ed., *Modernism*. Blackwell Guides to Criticism. Malden, MA. Blackwell Publishing.
Wolk, Douglas. 2007. *Reading Comics: How Graphic Novels Work and What They Mean*. New York: Da Capo.
Woolf, Virginia. 2005. *Mrs. Dalloway*. New York: Harcourt. [1925]

Part III

Graphic Novels and Comics, Beyond the Text

"Remember, remember the fifth of November"
Using Graphic Novels to Teach Dystopian Literature

Daniel Ian Rubin

Like many of my colleagues teaching English/language arts at the secondary level, I was never taught in my teacher preparation program to use graphic novels to teach literature. Actually, the use of graphic novels in the classroom was never even approached. Many years ago as a rookie teacher, it was my belief that there was absolutely no reason to even discuss graphic novels. The literary canon was there for a reason, and graphic novels had no place within it; graphic novels had absolutely no literary or educational value. Growing up, I was a huge fan of comic books, but I have to admit that as an inexperienced educator, I never gave any thought to introducing comics/graphic novels in the classroom alongside traditional novels. Graphic novels were looked down upon by my colleagues, and since I never saw my peers using them, I let this color my vision as to their usefulness in the secondary classroom.

All of that changed a few years ago when a student in my sophomore English class suggested that I read a graphic novel that he had just finished, *V for Vendetta* (Moore 2008). I had previously heard of the title since the film version had recently premiered in theaters, and I thought that the text would be a nice diversion from what I normally read, so I decided to give it a try. I was immediately engrossed with the storyline, and in my own mind, I began to draw major thematic parallels between *V for Vendetta* and a text I was currently teaching in my senior-level English/language arts class, *Nineteen Eighty-Four* by George Orwell (2003). I mocked my own narrow-minded arrogance and realized that "comic art can carry as much truth, beauty, mystery, emotion, and smart entertainment as any other, more traditional, media of expression" (Arnold 2007, 12). Without a second thought, I quickly ordered a class set of *V for Vendetta* for use in my senior-level British literature classes.

Since I continually search for new texts that I hope will be engaging to my students, I knew immediately that reading *V for Vendetta* could help my students further analyze the topics of discrimination, government control, mind control by the media, and religious/political corruption, some of which I was already approaching in my *Nineteen Eighty-Four* unit. My only hope was that, by using the format of a graphic novel, my students would be as engaged, if not more so, than reading the traditional texts that they (and I) were accustomed to. As I anticipated, one of my students stated that, "I was more enthused to be reading a graphic novel just because it was different and it was something I had never done before." Bucher and Manning (2004) affirm this notion when they posited that, "educators can use [graphic novels] to offer alternatives to traditional texts and mass media and to introduce young adults to literature that they might otherwise never encounter" (68). Although graphic novels had never been taught at my high school before, I thought it was time for me to give it a chance. I was ready to teach *V for Vendetta* for the first time in my senior-level British literature classes during the 2009–2010 school year, and as I will discuss in this essay, the response that I received was simply overwhelming. Note: All student names are pseudonyms

Benefits of Graphic Novels

It is becoming widely understood that the appropriate use of graphic novels can be highly beneficial for middle and high school aged students (Boatright 2010; Bucher and Manning 2004; Carter 2007; Schwarz 2007), especially those with hearing impairments and those that are English Language Learners (ELLs) (Dresang 2006; Smetana, et al. 2009). Graphic novels are engaging to our youth (Dresang 2006) since, "for many young adults, graphic novels represent a welcome move away from what they consider traditional 'school' reading" (Bucher & Manning 2004, 67), and therefore, they are appealing because they are perceived as being somewhat subversive (Smetana, et al. 2009). It is believed that reading graphic novels promotes literacy (Schwarz 2002) and a love for reading (Dresang 2006), and they also help improve students' writing skills (Carter 2007). Using graphic novels in the classroom can also "provide a context-rich, high-interest story environment for acquiring new vocabulary" (Smetana, et al. 2009, 230), and they can help introduce new literary terms as well as literary techniques such as the use of dialogue (Bucher and Manning 2004). According to Seyfried (2008), graphic novels are also turning "out to be a heavyweight in the teaching of advanced themes in literature and visual literacy" (45). It is quite evident that using graphic novels in the elementary and secondary classroom provides a wide variety of positive learning experiences for students.

Graphic novels can also be used in various subject areas across the curriculum, such as English/Language Arts, social studies, science, art, and even math (Bucher and Manning 2004; Carter 2007; Christensen 2006; Schwarz 2002, 2007). Christensen (2006) sums up the use of graphic novels when she stated that, "Most important, they are books about important social and political issues that can be understood and discussed by all reading levels and are in a format that teens love to read. It is a winning combination for both students and teachers" (230). I couldn't agree more.

Introducing V for Vendetta

Written by Alan Moore and David Lloyd (2008), the graphic novel *V for Vendetta* takes place in an alternate future near the turn of the twenty-first century (for a deeper look at the work of Alan Moore, I suggest you refer to the text by Di Liddo). In England, a nuclear war has just ended, and a fascist, dictatorial government, led by the "Head," has taken control. "V," a man who has recently escaped from an internment camp, dons a Guy Fawkes' mask and begins to attack symbols important to the government (e.g., by blowing up the houses of Parliament). Under constant video surveillance by the ruling class, V hides in his home, called the "Shadow Gallery," while trying to plan and orchestrate a revolution against England's totalitarian regime.

Before my students in my British literature class even opened up *V for Vendetta*, I asked them to get a copy off of the bookcase and place it on their desks. Then, at the same time, I had them open the books up, and I asked them about their initial responses. The predominant reaction was that of shock and surprise. Sandra expressed how, "When I first saw we were reading a graphic novel, I was a little confused. I was not sure how to read it or if I was even going to like it." Yesenia went on to explain that:

> I have never read a graphic novel, so it took me a little bit of time to get used to reading it picture by picture.... It looked like a regular book from the outside and a comic book in the inside, and I wasn't sure what order the pictures went in.

Furthermore, Katy had the preconceived notion that "this [was] going to be more of a boy book that I [would] have to force myself to read.... I thought reading a graphic novel was going to be childish, since it was basically a comic book or picture book." Due to these concerned responses, I thought that I had my work cut out for me. So, in order to assist my students become more comfortable with the idea of reading a graphic novel, I explained how to read the graphic novel, from left to right and top to bottom. Since many of the students had never read a comic book before, I also had to explain how to read the text in each frame (from top to bottom and so on). Once they got the hang of decoding a graphic novel, we were able to begin reading it as a whole class and discuss it as a work of literature; the novelty of being a graphic novel quickly became secondary to the storyline. Eventually, Lorena commented that, "I had some first doubts about *V for Vendetta* because of the graphics, but now that I understand how to read it, I have really enjoyed it." Another student added quite succinctly that she had also prematurely "judged the book by its cover" and found great enjoyment in reading *V*.

Major Sociopolitical Themes

According to Schwarz (2007), "The graphic novel is especially useful for secondary students because many titles touch on important social-political issues" (1). I feel that *V for Vendetta* is an incredibly strong text for discussing social and political issues that are important to our society today. As a class, we were able to identify several pertinent themes. For example, we were able to discuss and analyze corruption of our religious leaders. In the graphic novel, a prominent Bishop sexually assaults young girls who are provided to him by the government; that is, until V eliminates him. The novel provided the students with the opportunity to more deeply discuss the sexual abuse cases which have been ravaging the image of religious leaders in various churches across the country.

Another major theme introduced in *V* that we discussed and researched was the notion of ever-present video surveillance and a lack of privacy. In the story, London's citizens are constantly monitored by video cameras and hidden microphones. I presented the students with several pictures of video cameras that I had taken personally during a recent trip to London, and we discussed the ominous presence of the cameras and the possible implications to individual privacy. Under the same theme of privacy, I had my students do some internet research on National Security Agency (NSA) wiretapping and how that is a factor in American life today. Let's just say that my students were shocked to find out that our government has the power to watch us and listen to our conversations quite easily and efficiently if it suits their purpose. We also discussed the concept of vigilantism and if it is an appropriate way to solve one's problems. In the graphic novel, V destroys various landmarks and murders corrupt politicians and other government officials in order to create a new system of democratic government in England. Therefore, by reading *V*, my students were able to critically assess their own personal beliefs about freedom, race, ethnicity, and sexual orientation and question to what extent they would go to ensure those beliefs. As Luna commented, "Although I personally don't think I would ever go to the same lengths to get revenge, it does make me think of how far I really would go to get vengeance for myself and others that were hurt."

Besides being able to teach *V for Vendetta* from a purely literary standpoint, teaching *V* allows for a great amount of cross-curricular research and discussion. In that same vein, Carter (2007) affirmed that, "English and history or social studies teachers should work together to exploit the potential of titles that make clear political statements or get at issues of national and international import" (51). Although I worked alone in creating this unit, I connected the reading of *V* to history/government, sociology, and even technology. One of the first points that I addressed was the fact that V wears a mask which resembles Guy Fawkes, a conspirator who, in 1605, attempted to blow up Parliament in London. Only one or two of my students knew who Guy Fawkes was, so I assigned all of the students to do some background internet research to learn more about Fawkes along with the meaning of this important quote in the story: "Remember, remember the fifth of November, the gun-powder treason and plot. I know of no reason why the gun-powder treason should ever be forgot" (Moore 2005, 14). Then, as a whole group, we discussed why V would decide to wear this mask, what it might symbolize in the story, what it might signify to the leaders and the citizens in London, and what it means to V personally.

We also talked about the use of nuclear weapons and their deleterious affects on the populace, both locally and globally. Since London and much of its people were destroyed during a nuclear war, it allowed us to focus on why we still have these weapons of mass destruction, who deserves to own them, and what happens to the human body once the bomb drops (as well as its after-effects). In the story, homosexuals and people of color were interned, became victims of harmful medical experimentation, and were eventually killed to make way for the new White society. Therefore, we also discussed racism, homophobia, and the use of involuntary human research subjects (or "guinea pigs"), which ultimately led us to a discussion about how the internment camps in the novel were similar to the concentration camps in the Holocaust. This facilitated a rigorous discussion about the value of human life, justice, and morality. Schwarz (2007) stated, "the graphic novel offers an exciting new means for teaching ... topics like social justice, in the secondary classroom in particular. [They often] address questions citizens need to be asking and researching about war, genocide, stereotyping, poverty, and justice" (3). By reading and analyzing *V for Vendetta*, my students were able to address these issues as well as question their own personal beliefs on larger societal issues.

Use with Nineteen Eighty-Four

According to Bucher and Manning (2004), teaching graphic novels can help "serve as a bridge to other classics" (68). I decided to teach *V for Vendetta* right after reading *Nineteen*

Eighty-Four in my British literature classes because of their similar themes of totalitarianism, subversive rebellion against the government, torture, and lack of privacy. In brief, the novel *Nineteen Eighty-Four* is a story about government control and the leadership's unflinching grasp over its citizens. Originally published in 1949, this text is still taught in secondary schools, both in this country and around the world, because of its powerful depiction of truth, love, power, self-determination, and the struggle of the individual against the government (Ingle 2007). According to the Modern Library 100 Best Novels list, *Nineteen Eighty-Four* is ranked as the thirteenth greatest novel of all time (randomhouse.com/modernlibrary/100bestnovels.html). I firmly believe that *Nineteen Eighty-Four* is the most chilling and gripping dystopian novel ever written and that *V for Vendetta* deserves to be discussed alongside such a classic.

At the completion of my *V for Vendetta* unit, I created a large-group assignment which asked the students to analyze *V* and *Nineteen Eighty-Four* side by side. I asked that the students break up into small groups of 3 to 4 members and brainstorm the similarities between the two works. They created large, colorful compare/contrast posters and presented them to the class. The students came up with ideas ranging from the use of slogans—"*War is peace,* Freedom is slavery, and Ignorance is strength" in *Nineteen Eighty-Four* and "Strength through Purity, Purity through Faith" in *V* to Big Brother's use of constant surveillance via telescreens and microphones in *Nineteen Eighty-Four* to the Head's constant monitoring of people via cameras and audio devices in *V for Vendetta*.

Student Reflections

Upon completion of the dystopian unit comprising of *Nineteen Eighty-Four* and *V for Vendetta*, I asked my seniors to reflect upon what they learned, if anything, from reading a graphic novel. As Sandra commented, "I like the graphic novel *V for Vendetta* because it has some mystery to it. I didn't know what was going to happen next and that made me want to keep reading it." Addressing the important issue of social justice, Steven explained that:

> After reading this, it kind of gave me an idea of the possibility of how bad [life] could get. It made the injustice stand out in our world—by that I mean how anybody with enough money could easily escape years from jail or possibly a life sentence, while a lower class person would commit a smaller crime and still get worse punishment. You could say that *V for Vendetta* opened my eyes a lot more about the real world.

Lorena approached the notion of a single person being able to have a positive influence on the larger society. She stated that:

> V himself is really an idea for the people. You weren't supposed to look at him as a person but as the ideal that he was trying to represent and did set [for the people]. It doesn't really matter who the person is, but it's their ideas that they set out for the rest of the world that matters, and that makes a difference.

Lorena saw that V was more than a vigilante trying to eliminate corrupt public officials in order to settle a personal vendetta. V was able to stir up the masses to fight against a corrupt government because he represented individuality and civil liberties. He transcended the power of the individual in order to move the masses.

One of the most exciting responses to the reading of the graphic novel was a student purchasing a V costume for me to wear in class (and future classes). Since we culminated

Figure 1. Dressed as V for one of my British literature classes.

our *V* unit around Halloween time, and Irene worked at a Halloween store, she decided to get me a costume. When Irene presented it to me in front of the class, I was so flattered and excited to don the outfit worn by V, that I put it on immediately. It is now in my personal collection to be worn each time I read *V for Vendetta* with my students.

Conclusion

On a person/professional level, I am fascinated with critical pedagogy and its critique of capitalist society as we know it. I want to study further how critical pedagogy and social justice can be woven into our schools, English literature classes in particular, and how they can lead to the production of more critically engaged citizens. Schwarz (2007) supports this belief when she theorized, "Beyond passing standardized tests, students today need to engage with social issues and media literacy, critical thinking about information/communications and about society if our democracy is to have a future" (10–11). Students need to be able to think critically and evaluate issues in society which are concerning to them. Teaching *V for Vendetta* allows me the opportunity to engage students in conversations which are conducive for personal reflection and analysis.

Even though I am the only English/language arts teacher in my high school using graphic novels as academic texts, I find immense value in the their use to teach dystopian literature. From my personal experience and discussions with colleagues, it appears that many educators are hesitant to use graphic novels in their classrooms (Bucher and Manning

2004) and that they are often seen as "controversial in the curriculum" (Schwarz 2007, 1). Despite this hesitancy and concern, I am glad to see that some of:

> Our teaching colleagues have begun using graphic novels to increase students' confidence as readers and to develop their enjoyment of reading. Instead of heralding a regression from the art of the written word, we are finding that graphic novels are providing a bridge to it. (Seyfried 2008, 48)

I am very fortunate that I gave graphic novels a chance in my classroom, and I got past my arrogant notion of what appropriate or acceptable literature was. I assert that the appropriately chosen graphic novel can be more engaging and influential than a "classic" text due to the exciting storylines, detailed artwork, and heavily complex storylines. Hopefully, *V for Vendetta* is just the first of many graphic novels that I will introduce to my students in the coming years and that they will be exposed to a more wide variety of literature in other classes that they encounter in the future.

References

Arnold, Andrew D. 2007. "Comix Poetics." *World Literature Today* 81.2: 12–15.
Boatright, Michael D. 2010. "Graphic Journeys: Graphic Novels' Representations of Immigrant Experiences." *Journal of Adolescent & Adult Literacy* 53.6: 468–476.
Bucher, Katherine T., and M. Lee Manning. 2004. "Bringing Graphic Novels into a School's Curriculum." *The Clearing House* 78.2: 67–72.
Carter, James Bucky. 2007. "Transforming English with Graphic Novels: Moving Toward our 'Optimus Prime.'" *English Journal* 97.2: 49–53.
Christensen, Lila L. 2006. "Graphic Global Conflict: Graphic Novels in the High School Social Studies Classroom." *The Social Studies* 97.6: 227–230.
Di Liddo, Annalisa. 2009. *Alan Moore: Comics as Performance, Fiction as Scalpel*. Jackson: University Press of Mississippi.
Dresang, Eliza T. 2006. "Graphic Novels for Children: Should They Be Considered Literature?" *Children & Libraries* 4.3: 49–51.
Ingle, Stephen. 2007. "Lies, Damned Lies and Literature: George Orwell and 'The Truth.'" *British Journal of Politics and International Relations* 9: 730–746.
Moore, Alan, and David Lloyd. 2008. *V for Vendetta*. New York: Vertigo.
"100 Best Novels: The Board's List." 2007. *Modern Library*. Accessed October 1, 2010, from http://www.randomhouse.com/modernlibrary/100bestnovels.html
Orwell, George. 2003. *Nineteen Eighty-Four: Centennial Edition*. New York: Plume.
Schwarz, Gretchen E. 2002. "Graphic Novels for Multiple Literacies." *Journal of Adolescent & Adult Literacy* 46.3: 262–265.
_____. 2007. "Media Literacy, Graphic Novels, and Social Issues." *Simile* 7.4: 1–11.
Seyfried, Jonathan. 2008. "Reinventing the Book Club: Graphic Novels as Educational Heavyweights." *Knowledge Quest× Visual Literacy* 36.3: 44–48.
Smetana, Linda, Darah Odelson, Heidi Burns, and Dana L. Grisham. 2009. "Using Graphic Novels in the High School Classroom: Engaging Deaf Students with a New Genre." *Journal of Adolescent & Adult Literacy* 53.3: 228–240.

Exploring the Art in Sequential Art

An Art Historical Approach to Teaching Comics

ABRAM FOX

To engage in the study of comics is to perform the role of an art historian. Practitioners of comics scholarship may not realize it, but art historians they are nonetheless. What, exactly, *is* art history? To paraphrase textbook author Fred Kleiner's simplistic answer to that same question, art history is the study of works of art (including "architecture, sculpture, the pictorial arts ... and the craft arts") and their historical, cultural, and social contexts (Kleiner 2011, xxxvi). Art history is concerned with visual manifestations of human creativity in all forms, and comics unquestionably fall under this broad categorization. But even within that categorization, comics only appear in survey textbooks as a contextual accompaniment to Roy Lichtenstein and the other artists of the Pop Art movement (Kleiner 2011; Davies, Denny, Hofrichter, et al. 2011), which is a disappointing treatment for such a wide-ranging artistic medium.

Despite the inherently visual nature of comics, a great deal of academic research and teaching on comics and other visual forms of popular culture happens outside the discipline of art history,[1] and "[as] a result, the rich visual aspect of comic art has been neglected in favor of an approach that stresses narrative content" (Roeder 2008, 5). Comics are fodder for tantalizing discussions on social, gender, and political issues, historical events, and many other subjects of academic inquiry. Though the introduction of comics to other fields is undoubtedly a boon, divorcing them from art history overlooks a vital point: comics introduce an unmistakable element to disciplines primarily concerned with texts (Freedman 2003).

It's not a bad thing that art historical inquiries are being made into comics by other disciplines, because the position of comics within the academic discipline is undefined. The language of comics is in the canon — itself a problematic concept — thanks to Lichtenstein, Andy Warhol, and other pop artists (Goldstein 2009), but the medium itself has little presence other than to accentuate pop art's challenge to the normative rift between painting as "high art" and comics as "low art."

With that in mind, what form should the incorporation of comics into the discipline of art history take? A purely historical or stylistic chronology, in the vein of traditional art history pedagogy, seems unsatisfying. To discuss comics purely on visual terms could be promoted by removing images from their narrative context, but to ask students to think critically about a page or panel from Alison Bechdel's *Fun Home: A Family Tragicomic*, for example, without knowledge of the page's relationship to the story is similarly unproductive. The sequential aspect of any comic cannot be denied, regardless of the form it takes. More broadly, art history's signature pedagogy of projecting images on a screen categorically fails when dealing with comics, particularly multi-page ones. Reading a comic is a private and individual experience (Pratt 2009; Hatfield 2009a) whether in print or on a computer screen, which is fundamentally different from how students encounter works projected on a large screen or reproduced on a different scale in a textbook.

A challenge in studying comics in art history is managing their wide-ranging relevance for a more suitable inquiry. "Comic art provides ample ground for interrogating a range of issues including high and low art, the mass reproduction and circulation of images in a global marketplace, democracy and visual culture, the political and ethical implications of humor, the architecture of the comic-strip page, child development, and visual literacy" (Roeder 2008, 6–7). The debate between high and low art comes quickest to the forefront when dealing with art from the past hundred years or so, particularly since the appearance of the modern superhero comic book. Is it possible to think about Cy Twombly's sequential *Three Studies from the Temeraire* (1988–89), the juxtaposition of image and text in Barbara Kruger's *Untitled (You Invest in the Divinity of the Masterpiece)* (1982), or Damien Hirst's workshop-produced spot paintings without considering whether the way we understand those works is grounded in how we understand comics? Beyond their kinships to works and artists already in the art historical canon, comics deserve their own place in the canon if only because stylistic innovations of the past few decades of comic art play much larger roles in the *oeuvre* of contemporary artists (Goldstein 2009). But even if comics were included in the art history canon, what good is the effort if the result is a brief mention in a lecture or an additional image in a textbook? Is there a more productive way of incorporating comics into the discipline?

A major obstacle is that the development of comics cannot be understood in the same way as other forms of art. David Carrier has emphatically made the point that, although the content of comics changes, their format and the techniques used to create them have largely remained the same since the 1890s, and had been available for centuries prior. "One of the reasons that comics are difficult to analyze is that the working tools of art historians are designed to deal with historical development," something absent in comics (Carrier 2000, 114). While it would be interesting to delineate a taxonomy of comic book styles — imagine teaching students about Jack Kirby's Renaissance and Baroque periods — the idiosyncrasy of individual artists is arguably of more interest than attempts to group artists by similarities (Wolk 2007).

In teaching comics in an art history classroom, my approach foregrounds the conceptual and practical aspects of comic creation and explores relationships between comics and the canon of "high art," as delineated by the types of works of art found in museums and survey textbooks. Students grapple with the basic structure of comics, introduced in light of attempts at definitions (McCloud 1994; Carrier 2000; Kunzle 1973) and anti-definitions (Hatfield 2009b; Meskin 2007). Hatfield writes against the utility of defining comics, which can bog down class discussion and deflect attention from broader aims of academic inquiry. The definitions suggested by McCloud, Carrier, Kunzle, and others provide launching points for understanding how comics relate to other art forms, but by acknowledging the limitations of these definitions, students can examine "how different definitions serve different ends and reveal historical and critical situations" (Hatfield 2009b, 24). Such an approach is powerful for understanding how any artistic medium is viewed at various places and time in history. Once students have been encouraged to challenge definitions and definition-makers in a medium with which they are familiar, they are further empowered to challenge other assumptions presented in class and feel more comfortable about the validity of their own perceptions and opinions on academic subjects (Freire 1970).

The translation of my intended approach for teaching comics as art history into a practical course has been an ongoing process. Initially, because of a condensed summer semester schedule, my original syllabus included only two graphic novels, Scott McCloud's *Understanding Comics: The Invisible Art* (1994) and David Mazzucchelli's *Asterios Polyp* (2009), along with a few short stories and articles on comics history, appreciation, and theory.[2] Since then, the number has increased greatly. *Understanding Comics* has an awkward relationship to the academic study and teaching of comics, detailed best by Hatfield in "Defining Comics in the Classroom; or, The Pros and Cons of Unfixability" (2009a). I nonetheless find it a valuable book for the course, as an inquiry into the nature of comics presented as a comic, rather than purely text. My approach in teaching *Understanding Comics* is similar to the one recommended by Hatfield and Marc Singer (2010), and students do not encounter McCloud's text until after they have had the opportunity to consider other definitions of comics and become comfortable with the notion of challenging a didactic graphic novel that can otherwise be overbearing.

Assigning a comic to students is not like assigning a journal article or a book. Students feel like they *have* to read journal articles, while they *get* to read comics, and this in turn fulfills the constructivist principle of making course material relevant to the student (Uno 1999). I also assign comics from anthologies like Ivan Brunetti's *An Anthology of Graphic Fiction, Cartoons, and True Stories, Volume I* (2006) and *Volume II* (2008) for extended in-class discussions and short writing exercises. When students come to class having already read the material at hand, class time can be spent more productively with student discussion and analysis rather than instructor review (Richlin 2006). Crucial readings include Richard McGuire's "Here" (Brunetti 2006, 88–93) and Ware's "Thrilling Adventure Stories/I Guess" (Brunetti 2006, 364–369), two influential short comics that challenge fundamental theories of how time, space, and the normative relationship between text and image work in comics, as delineated by McCloud (1994), Hatfield (2009a), and other theorists that students encounter earlier in the semester.

"Here" is a six-page comic that depicts the past, present, and future of a single point in space. The first panel is a textless view of a corner in a room, followed by several panels captioned "1957" showing moments surrounding the birth of a child. Though McGuire retains the simple basic format of six panels arranged in three rows of two, each panel contains multiple subpanels stacked and juxtaposed to show moments that occur in the same spot. Caption panels locate each image in specific years, at first bouncing throughout the twentieth century and eventually ranging to absurd extremes, as far back as 500,957,406 B.C. and as far forward as 2033. Several characters reappear throughout the story, but the real focus of the narrative is time itself (Wolk 2007).

"Here" addresses the nature of time in comics, and "Thrilling Adventure Stories/I Guess" destabilizes the relationship between image and text on the comic book page. In the short story, also only six pages long, Ware attempts "to portray simultaneity—to portray an instance in which perceived experience is colored by intellectual action" (Kannenberg, Jr., 2009: 313). The images in "Thrilling Adventure Stories/I Guess" show a straightforward superhero story of a spandex-clad champion saving a helpless woman from the clutches of a mad scientist. The text, on the other hand, relates a first-person retelling of various incidents in a young boy's childhood. Though the boy's narrative is told naively, the reader recognizes disturbing themes of racism, domestic violence, and possible child molestation underlying his recollections. Every word on the page, from text in speech bubbles to sounds effects that accompany gunshots and explosions, work toward this narrative end. There is no direct connection between word and image, except that "while the images show a super-heroic way to re-order a person's unacceptable behavior, the text presents the viewpoint that such problems have few easy solutions but many long-term and difficult consequences" (Kannenberg, Jr., 2009, 313).

"Thrilling Adventure Stories/I Guess" highlights the major role that the relationship between image and text has played in the creation of art. When a painting or sculpture is explicitly connected to a work of literature, like a scroll depicting *The Tale of Genji* or an altarpiece showing the Annunciation, a fair assumption is that the image will correlate to the words written by Murasaki Shirabu or recorded in the Gospels of Luke or Matthew. "Thrilling Adventure Stories/I Guess" subverts that assumption, and by successfully challenging norms of how images are read, both "Here" and "Thrilling Adventure Stories/I Guess" can provide an engaging entry into discussion of works from the fine art canon. Discussion of the treatment of time and space in "Here" can foster understanding of a work like Masaccio's *The Tribute Money* (ca. 1425) as an image that combines multiple narrative moments in one pictorial composition, or the reverse of Duccio's *Maestà Altar* (1308–11), in which the narrative panels are read in an unexpected sequence that can be confusing to any viewer. In my own field of eighteenth-century British art, "Thrilling Adventure Stories/I Guess" provides a compelling analog to James Barry's *The Progress of Human Culture* (1777–1784) murals at the Royal Society of Arts, a series of six narrative paintings showing the historical progress of society and culture from antiquity through the modern day and into the spiritual realm. Barry wrote a 50-page description of the painting series for the members of the Society of Arts, but twentieth-century scholarship has revealed that the artistic program in the room actually depicts a religious sub-narrative completely obfuscated by Barry's text (Pressly 1981). When discussed in conjunction with "Thrilling Adventure Stories/I Guess," the concept of an artist representing simultaneity through the presentation of a seemingly-related series of images and texts becomes a more palatable theme for discussion.

One of the positive aspects of discussing comics in the classroom — their familiar presence from popular culture — can also be a hurdle for students unfamiliar with the material. When I prepare to teach a class in British painting, I feel confident that most of my students will possess a common unfamiliarity with the course material. The same cannot be said for a course that touches on aspects of contemporary popular culture. It is important to ensure that no students feel lienated due to a lack of prior experience reading comics, or privileged because of experience (Witek 2009).[3] On a pedagogical level, a comics class can operate effectively along the lines of Paolo Freire's liberation pedagogy, in which the instructor functions as a facilitator rather than a professor and in which students are recognized as important arbiters of cultural value whose experiences are equally valid to each other and to the instructor (Freire 1970).

In aligning myself with Freirian pedagogy, I take care to avoid presenting myself as an objective expert on comics. Freire's approach celebrates each individual's background equally, and I do explain to students how my academic background colors my personal reading of comics. Early in the semester I introduce William Hogarth's 1743 print *Characters and Car-*

icatures, which features dozens of individualized faces stacked upon each other filling the space of the composition. The image asserts Hogarth's mastery of "characterization," which is grounded in naturalistic likeness, as a rebuttal to his rivals' accusations that he created "caricature," which is grounded in exaggeration. Hogarth also reproduces several faces, from paintings and prints executed by Renaissance artists, that he argues fall under each category, including "caricatures" by Annibale Carracci and Leonardo da Vinci. The juxtaposition of such major "high" artists with "low" genres and techniques can be shocking to those who associate Leonardo solely with the *Mona Lisa* (ca. 1503–06). Students are put on notice that the course thus goes both ways, incorporating comics into the art historical canon while also leading from comic books back to related issues from throughout the history of art.

An early assignment in the semester is a formal analysis paper, another of art history's signature pedagogies, which challenges comics' relationship to the canon. Students are asked to select an image from Marvel's 2009 Wolverine Art Appreciation Month variant cover program, a series of cover images in which the character of Wolverine was illustrated in the style of historical artists. Marvel promoted the program as if it were a transgression of comic books into the realm of high art, and artist Ed McGuinness is quoted in a Marvel publication as saying his contribution was "probably the closest I'll ever come to 'real' art" (O'Dell, et al. 2009). Despite such statements, the Wolverine images provide insight into how contemporary comic artists understand and construct their own artistic canon (O'Dell, et al. 2009) based on their interests and experiences. Laura Martin's homage to Vincent Van Gogh is a portrait combining the blue and yellow palettes of Van Gogh's late 1880s self-portraits with the famous biographical note of the artist's severed ear, except in this case Wolverine's ear is impaled on one of his adamantium claws even as his accelerated healing process has regenerated a new one on the side of his head. The homage to Salvador Dali, painted by Paolo Rivera, replicates the surrealistic landscape of *The Persistence of Memory* (1931) with Wolverine's mask, gloves, a maple leaf, and the X-Men's Blackbird jet among the objects taking the place of melting clocks.

Students are generally able to elucidate their chosen cover illustration's iconographical relationship to the character and its stylistic relationship to the historical artist, either because of familiarity with Wolverine or by making the educated guess that none of Van Gogh's original portraits included metal claws. Through formal analysis assignments, students are able to develop a familiarity with art history's formal vocabulary, which in turn serves as a launching point for further stylistic analysis. They struggle to reconcile the totality of the image with their preconceptions of painting and comics as two disparate realms of art, and that struggle can be particularly difficult for those students whose primary exposure to comics is via superhero comics. According to Douglas Wolk, "what matters most in superhero comics is *what happens to whom* and *what it looks like*—the actual plot and dialogue, and the content of the images," not their style (Wolk 2007, 110). Within the genre of superhero comics there is great stylistic diversity, and artists such as Frank Miller, Todd McFarlane, and Jim Lee have cultivated large fanbases that snap up any of the artist's work regardless of subject matter. But when compared with the world of comics creation at large, however, superhero comics demonstrate a limited range of styles designed to support the narrative subject matter (Wolk 2007).

Later in the semester, once students have become familiar with *Understanding Comics* and worked through a shorter text like Daniel Clowes's *Wilson* or James Sturm's *Market Day* as well as the much longer and denser *Jimmy Corrigan: The Smartest Kid on Earth* by Chris Ware, the class focuses on David Mazzucchelli's *Asterios Polyp*. Mazzucchelli started his career illustrating superhero comics, and he best known to mainstream audiences for his collaborations with Frank Miller on *Daredevil* and *Batman* in the mid–1980s, and to literary audiences for his 1994 co-adaptation of Paul Auster's novella *City of Glass* (Kuhlman 2009). He has since transitioned into academia, teaching illustration at the School of Visual Arts in Manhattan, and his book has been suggested, for better or for worse, as a textbook for the creative possibilities within the comics medium (Martin 2010).

Asterios Polyp's titular protagonist is thrust into a journey of self-discovery that includes a cast of mostly-superficial character stereotypes, flashbacks to his tenuous relationship with his ex-wife, and dream narration from his dead twin brother. His journey is less about physical movement than a change in his worldview, from strict dualism to a more organic, decentralized understanding of the world. Asterios's binary vision symbolizes the perceived severe divide between the literary and artistic worlds, and *Asterios Polyp* is a "self-consciously heavy-handed refutation of [Mazzucchelli's] protagonist's dualist worldview" (Wivel 2010). Mazzucchelli challenges and breaks down the frameworks of panel and page layout, font design, color usage, and even the dust jacket, all to draw attention to process of creation.

Asterios Polyp serves as a fulcrum for in-depth discussion on the multifaceted ways comics operate across visual and narrative levels in ways neither literature or fine art can. Students initially have trouble coming to grips with this argument because Mazzucchelli never states it outright. Rather, he assigns the counterpoint view to Asterios and uses the novel itself to argue against this view. At one point Ignazio, the dead twin, conjures the content of a lecture Asterios, an architecture professor, delivers on the difference between "factual" and "fictional" art:

> Factual art makes an honest, transparent statement about itself, e.g. a building whose structure is evident from its exterior and materials, or an abstract painting whose content is its form: paint on canvas. Fictional art creates an illusion, as in a building whose structure is hidden or covered by a skin; or in a figurative painting that asks you to see arrangements of pigment as an apple or a mountain or a saint... Anything that is not functional is merely decorative [Mazzucchelli 2009].

Students are asked to assess this argument in relation to the text, both within the context of the narrative and of the physical book. The fervor with which Asterios argues for the supremacy of factual art reflects Mazzucchelli's interest in deconstructing the printing process, even though the narrative is nothing if not a multi-layered aggregation of symbols, allusions, and cross-references. Rarely is a page illustrated without a detail that recalls an earlier image or predicts later events. The conceit is extended to the structural framework of the text itself. Each character has a unique font and word balloon shape: Asterios's lower-class mother's words are in a looping cursive font, for example, and his upper-class father's dialogue is in a quasi–Phoenician script. Asterios himself speaks in bold and all caps, his speech "bubbles" taking the form of rectangles that frequently adjoin the edges of panels in a manner reminiscent of caption boxes containing disembodied narration, with singing indicated by rising and falling text in front of a musical staff.

Students enjoyed the process of identifying and exploring passages in which the visual elements gave them difficulty or challenged their personal notions of the form of comics. One of my first students called these passages "only-in-comics" moments. In particular, students were drawn to one "only-in-comics" sequence in which Mazzucchelli explores the depiction of memory. The short chapter begins with an image of Asterios in a seated pose floating in a void and saying "I have a blister on my foot," before looking up to see that he is in the empty room he is renting in the small town of Apogee. Once the page is turned the second image is repeated, except Asterios is in his Manhattan loft and speaking to his ex-wife Hana, fifteen years prior. The narrative continues over the next few pages as Hana panics when the end of a cotton swab falls off in her ear. She pleads with Asterios to remove it, which he does with the tweezers from a Swiss Army knife that she had found earlier in the day, and several chapters prior, while the two were at the beach. It is an absolutely mundane scene loaded in meaning. The narrative sequence is presented a small strip of panels that runs through the middle of six consecutive pages. Jumbled across the same pages are multiplicities of magenta-washed panels, all of which contain images of Hana. The reader eventually realizes these images are Asterios's memories of his ex-wife, stirred up from his fleeting memory of a similar time when he had a blister. The student who called it an "only-in-comics" moment referred back to it a later project, writing:

> I find myself repeatedly returning to the pages of *Asterios Polyp* during the "I have a blister on my foot" sequence. On these pages it becomes clear how juxtaposed static images can create an artistic experience that is unique to the medium. Asterios' positioning on each of the pages remains the same though the context of the moment is changed. The introduction of a series of seemingly unrelated frames surrounding a single more linear narrative stream serves as one of the most accurate and fascinating representations of memory I have ever seen. Each image is associated with every other image, but mostly in a non linear [sic] fashion. Mazzucchelli utilizes spacing, size, and color to create an experience in which we find ourselves browsing back and forth across Asterios and Hana's entire relationship. I would be hard pressed to imagine how one could possibly produce the same effect in another medium.

Asterios Polyp is a recent example of how the comic books can be used to challenge the formal underpinnings of art. Continuing that line of inquiry is one of the possible approaches for the final project students complete by the end of the semester. The project is designed to allow each to pursue his or her individual interests in the intersection of comics and "high art." The project guidelines are designed to allow a maximum of creativity and allow the student to pursue his or her specific comics-related interests. In the guidelines I suggest a number of possible approaches, including:

- Curating a museum exhibit juxtaposing a comic book artist with a historical artist, multiple comic book artists with an historical style or school, or comparing themes in comic book art and "high art";
- Examining a comic book or body of work along art historical critical lines of inquiry (feminist, formalist, queer theory, etc.);
- Proposing a comic book, with or without images, that consciously deals with any of the issues or theories discussed in class, along with explanations;
- Creating works of art, in any medium, that also address the aforementioned issues;
- Any other topic of the student's choice dealing with style, narrative, themes, imagery, etc. that engages in dialogue between comic books and "high art."

Some students choose to create visual works of art, including those who profess no previous artistic experience or inclinations. They return to the formal arguments of *Understanding Comics* or *Asterios Polyp* to work out for themselves some of the ideas presented by McCloud or Mazzucchelli. Others look outside the bounds of the course to personal interests such as hobbies or membership in niche comic readership groups.

It is difficult to describe an ideal project because of the open-ended nature of the assignment. Instead, I will discuss one outstanding project from the first year of the course. Michael, a senior theater major, was fascinated by several points of contention that came up throughout the semester and produced a series of one-page comics addressing each incidence. He often characterized himself as an occasional comic reader and his project was his first foray into the medium as a creator. He wrote in his project description that: "My primary concerns in creating this comic were first, to simply have the experience and be open to discovering and learning anything new about comics, and second, to establish further for myself what it is that I think make comic book aesthetically unique."

Michael titled his project *A Collection of Failed Experiments in Comic Book Aesthetics*, but it was an inspired success. His single-page comics included revisiting McCloud's definitions of comics with a short essay framed on the page within comic panels, and a short story in which he "sampled" images (borrowing the concept from hip-hop music) from comics and fine art to create a "post-modern" comic that "acknowledges that it is only able to exist through the previous creation of other works." The pages Michael felt were his strongest were those in which he applied the practice of his academic major, theater. He created *A Series of Improvised Comics!*— a response to Dali's paranoiac-critical method and R. Crumb's *Abstract Expressionist Ultra Super Modernistic Comics* (Molotiu 2009), both of which were discussed briefly in class — and adapted the climactic scene from Henrik Ibsen's *A Doll's House* with the protagonists Torvald and Nora rendered as cartoonish blobs juxtaposed with their dramatic dialogue. He wrote that the process of creating the comics further expanded his artistic vocabulary by thinking of how the "beats" and pregnant moments in theater translate into the pacing mechanisms of the page. For Michael and other students who were previously only readers (or non-readers) of comics, the act of creation provided new insight to the medium.

Comics have a role in the teaching of contemporary art, just as they have one in other disciplines interested in visual culture or any of the other nitty-gritty aspects of the comic book. Art history as a discipline has been slow to embrace comics, perhaps because of the strengths of literary examinations of the medium as well as comics' incongruence with the traditional art historical canon. Comics *can* work in art history, as long as we accept that they do not fit cleanly into the canon because of their hybrid literary-pictorial nature. Comics themselves are a methodology, providing new ways of thinking about, and new vocabulary for talking about, how art functions. Students are enthused by the experience of looking at familiar material in a completely new light. The excitement and creativity demonstrated by students free of the burdens of traditional disciplinary paradigms is reason alone to find a better place for comics at art history's table.

Notes

1. Even within academia, the study of art history can vary depending on departmental or college organization. At some schools, art history is taught under the aegis of the art department. At others, such as the school at which I teach, art and art history are independent academic departments.

2. This syllabus is reflective of the American comics tradition and ignores the Japanese *manga* and Franco-Belgian *bande dessinée* traditions for the most part. I am up front to my students about this sin of omission, as well as the homogenous set of white, middle-class, male authors. I provide opportunities for students interested in those schools to bring their interests into class throughout the semester, and do my best to keep my syllabus fluid and present more diversity in future iterations.

3. The first year I taught a course on comics, one of the students asked at the end of the first day if I could create a cheat sheet of various superheroes, their powers, affiliations, and publishing companies. This student was fearful of being left behind during discussions of superhero comics, a subject matter which largely dominated the class's discussion on the first day, and our conversation served an indicator that I needed to be clearer about my expectations for the course and of following Witek's precept of not privileging insider knowledge (in this case, of superhero comics).

References

Bechdel, Alison. 2006. *Fun Home: A Family Tragicomic*. Boston: Houghton Mifflin.
Brunetti, Ivan, ed. 2006. *An Anthology of Graphic Fiction, Cartoons, and True Stories, Volume I*. New Haven, CT: Yale University Press.
_____, ed. 2008. *An Anthology of Graphic Fiction, Cartoons, and True Stories, Volume II*. New Haven, CT: Yale University Press.
Carrier, David. 2000. *The Aesthetics of Comics*. University Park: Pennsylvania State University Press.
Clowes, Daniel. 2010. *Wilson*. Montreal: Drawn and Quarterly.
Davies, Penelope J.E., Walter B. Denny, Frima Fox Hofrichter, et al. 2011. *Janson's History of Art: The Western Tradition*. 8th ed., Volume II. Upper Saddle River, NJ: Prentice Hall.
Freedman, Kerry. 2003. *Teaching Visual Culture: Curriculum, Aesthetics and the Social Life of Art*. New York: Teachers College Press.
Freire, Paolo. 1970. *Pedagogy of the Oppressed*. Trans. Myra Bergman Ramos. New York: Herder and Herder.
Goldstein, Claudia. 2009. "Comics and the Canon: Graphic Novels, Visual Narrative, and Art History." In Stephen E. Tabachnick, ed., *Teaching the Graphic Novel*. New York: The Modern Language Association of America, 254–261.
Hatfield, Charles. 2009. "An Art of Tensions." In Jeet Heer and Kent Worcester, eds., *A Comics Studies Reader*. Jackson: University of Mississippi Press, 132–148.
_____. 2009. "Defining Comics in the Classroom, or, The Pros and Cons of Unfixability." In Stephen E. Tabachnick, ed. *Teaching the Graphic Novel*. New York: The Modern Language Association of America, 19–27.
Kannenberg, Gene, Jr. 2009. "The Comics of Chris Ware." In Jeet Heer and Kent Worcester, eds., *A Comics Studies Reader*. Jackson: University of Mississippi Press, 306–324.
Karasik, Paul, and David Mazzucchelli. 2004. adapts. *City of Glass: The Graphic Novel*. By Paul Auster. New York: Picador.
Kleiner, Fred S. 2011. *Gardner's Art Through the Ages: A Global History*, Enhanced 13th ed., Volume II. Boston: Wadsworth.
Kuhlman, Martha. 2009. "Teaching Paul Karasik and David Mazzucchelli's Graphic Novel Adaptation of Paul Auster's *City of Glass*." In Stephen E. Tabachnick, ed., *Teaching the Graphic Novel*. New York: The Modern Language Association of America, 120–128.
Kunzle, David. 1973. *The Early Comic Strip: Narrative Strips and Picture Stories in the European Broadsheet from c. 1450 to 1825, History of the Comic Strip, Volume 1*. Berkeley: University of California Press.
_____. 1990. *The Nineteenth Century, History of the Comic Strip, Volume 2*. Berkeley: University of California Press.
Martin, Robert Stanley. June 6, 2010. "Inchoate Thoughts on Asterios Polyp." *The Hooded Utilitarian*. Accessed June 20, 2010. http://hoodedutilitarian.com/2010/06/inchoate-thoughts-on-asterios-polyp/.
Mazzucchelli, David. 2009. *Asterios Polyp*. New York: Pantheon Books.
_____, and Frank Miller. 2007. *Batman: Year One*. New York: DC Comics.
_____, and Frank Miller. 2010. *Daredevil: Born Again*. New York: Marvel Comics.
McCloud, Scott. 1994. *Understanding Comics: The Invisible Art*. New York: Harper Paperbacks.
McGuire, Richard. 2006. "Here." In Ivan Brunetti, ed., *An Anthology of Graphic Fiction, Cartoons and True Stories*. New Haven, CT: Yale University Press: 88–93.
Meskin, Aaron. 2007. "Defining Comics?" *The Journal of Aesthetics and Art Criticism* 65.4: 369–379.
Molotiu, Andrei, ed. 2009. *Abstract Comics: The Anthology, 1967–2009*. Seattle: Fantagraphics Books.
O'Dell, Brian, Eric O'Dell, John Rhett Thomas, et al. October 2009. *Wolverine Art Appreciation*. New York: Marvel.
Pratt, Henry John. 2009. "Narrative in Comics." *The Journal of Aesthetics and Art Criticism* 67.1: 107–117.
Pressly, William L. 1981. *The Life and Art of James Barry*. New Haven: Published for the Paul Mellon Centre for Studies in British Art by Yale University Press.
Richlin, Laurie. 2006. *Blueprint for Learning: Constructing College Courses to Facilitate, Assess, and Document Learning*. Sterling, VA: Stylus Publishing.
Roeder, Katherine. 2008. "Looking High and Low at Comic Art." *American Art* 22.1: 2–9.
Singer, Marc. January 21, 2010. "Weeks 1–2: Scott McCloud, Understanding Comics." *I Am NOT the Beastmaster*. Accessed September 27, 2011. http://notthebeastmaster.typepad.com/weblog/2010/01/weeks-12-scott-mccloud understanding-comics.html.
Sturm, James. 2010. *Market Day*. Montreal: Drawn and Quarterly.

Uno, Gordon E. 1999. *Handbook on Teaching Undergraduate Science Classes: A Survival Training Manual.* San Diego: Harcourt, Brace and Company.

Ware, Chris. 2000. *Jimmy Corrigan: The Smartest Kid on Earth.* New York: Pantheon.

———. 2006. "Thrilling Adventure Stories/I Guess." In Ivan Brunetti, ed., *An Anthology of Graphic Fiction, Cartoons, and True Stories.* New Haven, CT: Yale University Press: 364–369.

Witek, Joseph. 2009. "Seven Ways I Don't Teach Comics." In Stephen E. Tabachnick, ed., *Teaching the Graphic Novel.* New York: The Modern Language Association of America: 217–222.

Wivel, Matthias. June 8, 2010. "Hooded Polyp: Beyond the Binary." *The Hooded Utilitarian.* Accessed June 20, 2010. http://hoodedutilitarian.com/2010/06/hooded-polyp-beyond-the-binary/

Wolk, Douglas. 2007. *Reading Comics: How Graphic Novels Work and What They Mean.* Cambridge, MA: Da Capo Press.

On Teaching Comics and Graphic Novels in the Medieval and Renaissance Classroom

Christina C. Angel

I admit now to being a disinterested student as an undergraduate. I would love to tell you that I was thrilled to have to stumble through Shakespeare the first time I read him or beyond excited to challenge myself to read *Beowulf* in its then-odd poetic structure (or better yet, translate the entirely foreign Old English), but that simply would not be true. Despite having always been an avid reader, as a young adult I could not see the point in trying to comprehend the socio-political milieu of early modern London or trying to read a language no longer spoken or even written. I would also love to tell you that I learned to adore both of these and many more texts of these periods because I had great teachers of them, but that too would not necessarily be accurate (at least until well into graduate school). I had to discover their magic mostly on my own, and this happened for me as soon as I realized not only their importance relative to their time periods, but also the great influence they held over the more modern texts I read with such zeal. As an undergraduate, I always felt inferior to my classmates because they seemed to innately comprehend that which proved difficult for me; furthermore, many of them also seemed to be instinctively engaged with texts in a way I was not.

In short, I had to *learn* how to be a student of literature, and this alone informs so much of my current teaching practice. When students in my lower-division, non–English major literature courses struggle or complain of a text's difficulty, I do not roll my eyes (literally or figuratively) and complain about how they just don't get it; instead, I find myself empathetic and sympathetic to their plight and opt instead to try to teach them how to appreciate that which challenges them by sharing how I came to such a place. My own experience as a once-reticent and fearful reader of "old" texts is what makes me uniquely suited to the claims below.

My philosophy of teaching, like any good philosophy, is grounded mostly in accumulated wisdom and informed largely from experience. As a university English professor of nearly ten years, of course I have read scholarship on pedagogy and discussed various theories in and out of the classroom; furthermore, I have engaged the processes of "best practices" and "assessment" regarding the learning of literature and these are fine things. Useful things. Things that keep us employed. But any teacher or professor with hundreds (or even thousands) of hours in the classroom can tell you, all the pedagogy and definitions of usefulness in the world do not create an effective teacher any more than the reading of law books makes one a good lawyer. There is always the indefinable, the un-quantifiable element that creates magic in a classroom. At this point in my career, this is what most concerns me: the moment in the literature course when something just *clicks*, where proverbial light bulbs illumine over heads and not just learning but *understanding* occurs.

In my experience, these moments come not from what I learned in graduate school about theory and practice, mind you; they arrived, as I suspect they do for many others beside myself, out of a kind of "winging it"— of following some basic instinct to get students to not just read and apply literary terminology, but to find and understand something more. When it came to my own early experiences in front of undergraduates with Medieval and Renaissance texts, I stepped into the room armed confidently (I thought) with the strength of my hard-earned degrees and engagement in discussion groups of "best practices" and "learning outcomes." I found that despite this preparation, I had no idea how to actually teach any of those students anything. Such a discovery and how I fumbled my way out of it is the essence of this essay; therefore, the bulk of what will follow is anecdotal in nature and I do this not out of scholarly laziness but a sense of sharing experience—to offer an adjunct perspective to the typical theorizing that occurs in this field. In short, I want to explain how I came to be a successful teacher through experience and my willingness to trust my instincts over learning when necessary, in the hopes of inspiring others to do the same. One way I got there involves the use of comics.

Medieval and Renaissance Texts and Comics

English Medieval and Renaissance studies has perhaps always been plagued with a certain disinterest by many students, likely due in part to a perceived inaccessibility, both in terms of their cultural relevance and also in language barriers. I remember the first time someone told me that Shakespeare wrote in what is deemed "modern" English in the large scope; I wondered: "then why is it so hard to understand?" and I know that many of my students often experience the same. Furthermore, and after many years of actually teaching this material to others, it would seem that student disinterest is growing in general toward these older literatures. After all, in an age of increasingly more prevalent technology that garners our attention to Facebook, text messaging, and YouTube, spending the kind of time it takes to read *Beowulf* in Old English may seem tedious or even pointless. While Shakespeare in particular used to be the cornerstone of Western learning, students can now graduate from high school, and sometimes even college, without encountering so much as a single couplet of The Bard's immortal words. Further, I regularly meet students well into their adult years who have not only never heard of *Beowulf*, but have no concept of the history of the English language and what Old English represents. A rather funny illustration of this comes most recently from a university student in a general literature course complaining rather too loudly to another student that she could not finish reading *Bartleby, the Scrivener* (written in 1853) because the "Old English is too hard" to read.

In the past decade, I have experienced teaching literature to a wide range of undergraduate students, from the inner-city community college to the expensive private school trust-fund set. In that time, I discovered one thing about which I am absolutely certain: few students out there — regardless of their life experience and educational locale — will engage with a text that doesn't seem relevant. Yes, there are those who will simply do what you ask because their grades matter, and others who will genuinely love what is offered on the syllabus because they are already appreciative readers. But what of the rest of the students? The ones who claim they are not readers or the ones who major in education but seem to have no real taste for understanding literature, or worse yet — the group of English majors who love to read but have never been taught *how* to read. I cannot relate how many conversations I have had over the years with colleagues who feel that whether or not a student likes the book(s) a teacher offers them for analysis is utterly irrelevant. In an age where we (educators) are perpetually competing with variable-quality public education, television, and the internet for our students' attention, their ability to "like" and connect with what we offer them to read is far from irrelevant: it is *crucial*.

In the field of Medieval and Renaissance studies, it is often difficult to engage students in new and meaningful ways, particularly since the traditional method of teaching these subjects — that is, rote memorization and slogging through texts, often line-by-line with no relevance offered — provides little opportunity for engagement to the average student. The great challenge of teaching in general and certainly in this field is that it is distant, both in language and in relevance, and the general availability of SparkNotes and popular film in the evasion-of-doing-the-reading tactics department makes "cheating" easy. The question is, as it once was for me, how can we get students to read the greats — for now I will stick to the canonical figures of *Beowulf* and Shakespeare — and find meaning and relevance in them?

The answer is both simple and complex. Too often professors of literature labor under the assumption that students should read Shakespeare, for example, because it is "good for them," without a second thought or care about whether or not students like, appreciate, or even comprehend the artistic relevance of the subject. If we want a student of literature (particularly an initially disinterested, reticent, or fearful one) to be engaged, we must first attempt to engage them, and while there are many best practices out there for how to do this, I had to discover how to do it on my own.

Enter the comic or graphic novel. I currently teach at an open-enrollment university that is largely nontraditional in its demographic. I teach a wide range of courses in Humanities, Classics, Medieval, and Renaissance literature, as well as Children's Literature and for all of the aforementioned, I use comics to teach a number of the texts in each, and I do this often in underhanded ways. I have recently added a course dedicated to the study of comics and graphic novels alone, but that is a different matter altogether. Unlike many other professors who teach comics, I only had a minor interest in the field until an experience in graduate school changed this. I admit to falling victim to larger perceptions of comics as a lesser literature, prone to unreasonable superhero fandom and simplistic story lines to appease children. I knew also that there was a keen difference between the superhero fare and more "mature" storylines like *Maus*, or *The Sandman*, and I had read them, but I never thought that I would find myself learning to read these types of texts with the same sense of frustration and wonder that I learned to read Old English ones. Furthermore, ten years ago I never thought I would find myself teaching an entire course on comics and graphic novels and confessing to a classroom full of students that I am no expert on either one but rather a Medieval and Renaissance professor. Like many other folks who teach comics, I find myself defending the practice frequently and the most common defense is that they are not just "fun" reading. Comics *are* "fun" reading, but because they offer both visual and textual reading opportunities, they seem to reach a larger audience initially than other forms of literature. Secondarily, however, and like all good literature, a study of comics and graphic novels affords students opportunities for so much more than entertainment. Stephen Tabachnick (2009) notes in *Teaching the Graphic Novel*: "The graphic novel ... treats nonfictional as well as fictional plots and themes with the depth and subtlety that we have come to expect of traditional novels and extended nonfictional texts" (2). Similarly, Joseph Witek (2009) highlights what comics readers have known for a long time, which is that "the study of sequential art manifestly is an interdisciplinary field, sharing conceptual and methodological boundaries with drama, film, art and art history, journalism, and cultural studies, among others" (218). This kind of interdisciplinary approach that combines various modes of study makes the graphic novel an ever-changing site of discourse in a number of fields, and allows it to function in a wide range of academic contexts.

The Story

I would like to back up here to discuss how such an anomaly occurred — about how a Medieval and Renaissance professor learned to use comics in the classroom. While working on my doctorate, an opportunity arose to teach an open-ended course that could be on any topic but had to include elements of public speaking, writing, and reading. My first response was to teach Revenge Tragedies (and particularly those of the early modern period such as *Titus Andronicus, The Duchess of Malfi,* and *Macbeth*). I chose these not just because they were my current topics of study personally, but because I thought the premise of revenge tragedy in general would resonate with students who in large part seemed to gravitate toward the likes of *South Park* and Quentin Tarantino movies. I assumed that they would see this connection immediately and I counted on spirited discussions of such. In so many ways, I was completely wrong. In fact, when I came into class excited about how the students would find *The Duchess of Malfi* disgusting and funny and even disturbing, what I got was a sea of blank faces in response to every open-ended question I asked. Then it hit me: not only did they have no context for the topic of the play, but they lacked one for the socio-cultural context of Shakespeare's time too. In the same vein that explaining a joke removes its humor, trying to give them these contexts only further diminished any hope of enjoyment from the play. About midway through that first class period on *The Duchess of Malfi*, I found myself resorting to the worst sort of teaching: going through each of the passages I had tabbed in my book and methodically explaining them while the students took notes. Even I nearly fell asleep from boredom.

At the time, I had recently read Alan Moore's *V for Vendetta*, and what struck me as interesting about the book in the first place was its dialogue with early modern England, not just thematically but intertextually as well. In an act of sheer desperation, it occurred to me to pause in the syllabus to read this book and/or watch the film version, which many students admitted to liking. I figured that since the notion of contextualizing the play in order to see it in contemporary literature was not working, I thought perhaps it might work in the other direction: show them something contemporary that intentionally has its roots in early modern English culture. So we did. Only one student in the room had ever seriously read a comic book and after a brief primer on how to accomplish this task, we engaged the text, reading words and images together. A few of them were hesitant at first, but most were at least giving it a try. The first task was to discuss the situation and setting of the book (oppression, darkness, a sense of impending doom) as it compares to an early modern sensibility (even more so than the Orwellian milieu clearly employed in the opening pages).

Because our only reference point so far had been *The Duchess of Malfi*, I asked them to first journal about how the play opens in relation to how *V for Vendetta* opens, in fear and oppression and that ever-present impending doom. The light bulbs started to flicker and I managed to wrestle some discussion out of them, by asking questions like, "What do these opening images make you think of?" and "How does this compare to the opening of Webster's play?" and "Why do you suppose they both open in this way? What does it mean?"

By the time we met the central character of V in the book, we had to discuss his mask. I offered them first a brief explanation of Guy Fawkes, and while I assumed they would find this less interesting, I was wrong there as well. Soon they had laptops out and were suddenly intrigued by this real-life "terrorist" (or patriot, depending on your position on the matter). I decided to make a game of it and asked them to look up specific things, like the year, the Gunpowder Plot, and Catesby, and report back to the class. Before I knew it, they were enthusiastically relating these and other points of interest, such as King James I and his unpopular ascension; this led them naturally to learn something about Queen Elizabeth I and why her passing had been considered such a great tragedy to England. Immediately the result was notable; in bringing together this information, they could then contextualize the time period and the text (*V for Vendetta*) was illuminated for them; in other words, they could speak intelligently about how *V for Vendetta* was in conversation with early modern plays. Soon it seemed I had opened a proverbial Pandora's box for getting these 18-year-olds excited about early modern political intrigue and culture (not to mention the literature it produced). And this was after only a few pages of reading the graphic novel.

One of the main reasons I chose the book was because V's opening lines are: "The multiplying villainies of nature do swarm upon him… And fortune, on his damned quarrel, smiling, showed like a rebel's whore… Disdaining fortune with his brandished steel, which smoked with bloody execution" (Moore 1988, 11–12). These lines, of course, are excerpted from *Macbeth*, and when I asked them why they thought that might be, or what the passage had to do with the comic, they naturally shrugged and agreed that none of them had ever read *Macbeth*. Thus we paused in our reading of *V for Vendetta* and I sent them home to read the play, to find that passage, and figure out (a) what it had to do with the play itself, and (b) why it might be the first bit of dialogue out of V's mouth in the comic. 'Twas here the monster was born: most of them read the play in its entirety before the next class, and the majority of them were excited to explain and share their findings. In the general sense, they found that this instance from the play was part of a speech by a lesser character designed to both set the stage for Macbeth and also to create that sense of impending doom and of rapid change. Further, they discerned that V and Macbeth had rather a lot in common in terms of their "morality" position in that they both claimed to do immoral things for a supposedly moral purpose; that the play was written for King James and his audience links it in time and place to the real story of the Gunpowder Plot and Guy Fawkes (which is all quite complicated and multi-layered, they decided); and finally, that V utters these words to establish his character intertextually to Shakespeare's play and to express the feeling of general anxiety of the time period (first decade of the 1600s) that is present also in V's story. It's a purposeful and complicated allusion. Did I mention that this was a class full of freshmen?

The class went on to finish *V for Vendetta* and evaluate the film, but they also read the other plays I assigned, and with the similar zeal given to *Macbeth*. It was the first time a student ever said to me, "You made reading Shakespeare *fun*." And it was fun—for them and for me—and I got them to understand not just the play but the entire social/

political/cultural milieu of its composition; they learned not just poetry and literature, but history, religion, and philosophy in the mix. This kind of interdisciplinary and intertextual approach to the early literature encouraged my previously mentioned freshman class to find other references and resonances in their lives. Some presented me with clips from *Family Guy, Robot Chicken, South Park,* and *The Simpsons*; one student even brought me a hip-hop song that he was absolutely *certain* was about Hamlet. These students left my class not just having read revenge tragedy and understanding its various nuances; they left with a kind of global comprehension I could otherwise have only dreamed about.

What the class inadvertently accomplished and what the process taught me has informed much of my teaching ever since. I didn't explain this part to the students, of course, but what we engaged in is a *hermeneutical* inquiry model that links things together thematically and symbolically and then asks how they go together and why. Hermeneutics is, in the simplest of terms, the study of interpretation and about how we gather meaning between two objects of knowledge. I now explain the concept to students in the following way: I draw a map on the board with each bubble as a single item (in the aforementioned class experiment, it would be "*Duchess of Malfi*" and "Fawkes mask" and "oppression" and "socio-political shift" and "revenge," for a start). Then as a large group, they assist me in drawing the lines that connect these ideas, at which time they also have to explain the connection. I define this for them as the hermeneutical map and that the lines which connect these bubbles and how we explain them is hermeneutics in general. This is a basic explanation to be sure, but it introduces not just the concept of seeing how texts can be in conversation but also that how we interpret them (which is ever-changing) speaks to a certain posture of understanding. I show them that where we begin to discuss the map we have made influences what we have to say about the connections, and that each time we travel through this map, it will be different. This may not have worked as well with my freshmen as it does with upperclassmen, but the concept itself is what now governs how I teach. The map is still there, but I tend to leave out the lesson on hermeneutics, even if it is what they are doing in the classroom.

Following the smash success of my aforementioned freshman class, I immediately sought to prove that the phenomenon was replicable and expanded the syllabus for the course for the following term. I added Neil Gaiman's *Marvel 1602* and James O'Barr's *The Crow*; the former helps add to the early modern context and the contemporary superhero world, and the latter is itself a revenge tragedy. It may seem at first as though more reading would in fact hinder the ability to cover ground, but this proved not to be the case here. In reading *Marvel 1602* we were able to explore not only more of the period of transition between Elizabeth I's reign and James I's ascension, but it also added another pair of contextual elements to the discourse: the morality play tradition and the burning of witches, both of which students were avidly interested in. We discussed the history of morality plays as the secular rising of the church plays in the late middle ages and that the allegorical figures transformed into naturalized ones in the Renaissance but without losing some of their "morality" roots. Such an exploration leads naturally (and chronologically) to the revenge tragedy, which is heavily steeped in morality tradition, with characters who represent particular vices and virtues clearly at odds in a host of settings.

Such a connection seems evident as the character V in *V for Vendetta* "is, after all, the progeny of the villain hero of Shakespearean drama, the Vice" (Keller 2008, 9), and this is not just one more thing that the "V" stands for here. What Keller notes about V's Shakespearean roots actually goes much deeper, as the figure of Vice is the essence of the morality play. As regards *Marvel 1602*, this is also important; the story is set up to be about "morality" itself—that is, what is right and wrong, and it is no mistake that the story essentially vilifies the Holy Church and the monarchy of the period (both of which were fairly corrupt) and elevates the superheroes, who have arrived several centuries early. In this case, I had students looking up the morality play, James I's particular interest in and distaste for the supernatural and witchcraft, as well as what they did not know about superheroes themselves. Perhaps the great revelation of this term for the students was that the superhero narrative of the 20th century is absolutely influenced by the morality play and revenge tragedy specifically. *The Crow* helped solidify this, particularly when paired with Webster's *The White Devil*, which is a play about trying to define what is good and evil when these distinctions must lie against the backdrop of a corrupted world.

The experiences of these two courses in particular led me then to believe that the positive and rich learning experiences had could not be limited solely to the open-ended freshman classroom, and soon I made the graphic novel part of my Shakespeare teaching in general, to similarly enthusiastic results, and I have since added comics for teaching *Beowulf* and even *The Canterbury Tales*.

Two Developing Approaches

I have two working theories of my own on using comics in the traditional classroom setting: Version Approach and Allusion Approach. The Version Approach, which simply explores a comic version of a text alongside the original, has to do with teaching Medieval and Renaissance texts themselves and *as comics*. This provides a landscape for various readers to find their place, and perhaps allow students who might not otherwise like a text to like or at least appreciate a literary work. The Version Approach here gives students an opportunity to read the text in a different way that is shorter and at times more accessible. Such an interaction between text and image does more here than a film version can do in several key ways: (1) students are forced to engage the text and image simultaneously and both require interpretation before moving on, whereas a film moves on whether or not the viewer is comprehending all s/he sees; (2) the reader of the comic is forced to consider whether the comic artist's rendering of the story meets with the reader's formulation of ideas and this creates a critical context, requiring examination of particular frames and panels in some detail; and (3) the length of the comic is often much shorter because of its ability to allow images to speak for lengthy descriptive passages, thus allowing a student to engage the work in less actual time. One complaint I will head off at the pass here is the one that sounds like this: "But what if students never read the original text and engage only with the comic book?" The answer in many ways is a simple one: on the levels that truly count, such as being able to critically read texts in conversation with one another, it does not matter. That is, whether or not a student reads the textbook version of Shakespeare's *Macbeth* or a well-chosen comic version that maintains the plot and dialogue of the play, s/he is still getting the play. What is important is that the student learns the story, its motifs and symbols, and is able to speak intelligently about the play in the end, and while the purist in me would rather the student read *Macbeth* and simply love it because I tell him/her to, sometimes we have to use alternative means to get the student there.

Another example of how the Version Approach can illuminate the course work is in the teaching of *Beowulf*. I used to believe that this story sold itself—a tale of a likeable, great warrior who battles monsters and dragons seems immediately appealing. I believed that at least until I started teaching it and quickly realized that many students do not get excited about *Beowulf* the same way that I do (alas). Like many medieval texts, and depending on the translation, *Beowulf* is often challenging for the same reasons that revenge tragedies are: it seems too distant to be relevant, and in this case in particular, there are no film versions of the story that do it any kind of justice. Recently, I added Gareth Hinds's *Beowulf* graphic novel to the assigned reading of Seamus Heaney's translation, and as I expected at this point, wonderful things began to happen. I had them read the text first and then the graphic novel; the emphasis I wanted to make was twofold: (1) compare the text's description of Grendel and compare it to Hinds's interpretation; and (2) compare the text of the battle with Grendel to the wordless 22 pages of the comic that depicts those events. This opened the discussion, ironically, on the text itself rather than the comic, as students carefully tried to unpack Heaney's translation of the poem. For example, I asked them to find descriptions of Grendel as they read. There are, of course, remarkably few; he is referred to in the Old English as *Caines cynne* ("Kin of Cain") and as *feond on helle* ("fiend from Hell") or *mearcstapa* ("boundary-walker"), but few concrete descriptors are provided. Such an activity is important when trying to determine the "accuracy" of Hinds's depiction of Grendel and necessarily sends students back to the text. Such a discussion also illuminates the more modern issues of Grendel himself— is he a literal monster or a figurative one? Is he humanoid or entirely human and just an outcast? Better yet, is he altogether a metaphor for what plagues a community? Hinds's work goes a long way to contextualize *Beowulf* through imagery, and J.D. Schraffenberger (2007) agrees that "This leaning on visual storytelling is, in itself, one way that Hinds combats the major obstacle of the original text for student readers of *Beowulf*— its language" (69). Thus we can use the graphic novel as a means to engage the sometimes difficult language of the text.

Clearly the applications of a Version Approach are endless, particularly as the field of comics grows in both popularity and literary value. Perhaps a bit more elusive, however, is what I call the Allusion Approach to incorporating comics into the classroom, and this directly relates to that first freshman class I referenced before. Many students do not immediately grasp allusions in literature, not because it is difficult, but because they lack the foundational education to recognize what is being alluded to — that is, one cannot identify a reference to Egyptian mythology if one has never encountered it. If a student is an English major, there is more often than not a required course that instructs them in this way, but for the average tourist student in English literature, no such thing exists. What the allusion approach offers us is a way to look at allusions from the reverse angle: point out what is allusive, and then send the students to find out what's important about the allusion (e.g., students looking up Guy Fawkes after encountering *V for Vendetta* versus recognizing Guy Fawkes first). In many ways, I would argue that this kind of learning is perhaps more critically important than the other way round because it requires the apparatus of not just accepting an allusion when one encounters it but rather actively seeking out what is not known and discovering how to know it.

The Allusion Approach can go far beyond the scope of the freshman or introductory course, which has been the subject matter to this point. Even in upper-division, English-major courses, the integration of comics can create even more sophisticated forms of discourse. In teaching, for example, *The Canterbury Tales*, it can be useful to compare what Chaucer is doing with both metafiction and frame narrative to any number of comics series, not the least of which is the recently popular *Scott Pilgrim* comics and subsequent film:

because Chaucer is immediately seen as inaccessible, even if read in a modern English translation, a link to the modern sensibility is necessary. After speeding students through the concept of a frame narrative and the lengthy General Prologue, I tend to focus at that point less on the stories themselves than on the structure of the *Tales* and how they fit together and within the frame. Similarly, Neil Gaiman's *The Sandman* works in just such a fashion (and has many additional uses than just this example, by the way), as the lengthy series offers several frame narratives, not the least of which is *World's End*. *The Sandman* series works also as a source of multiple allusions, not the least of which are ancient Greek and Egyptian mythology, the Bible, and of course, Shakespeare. For our purposes here, it is important to note the parallels and direct influence on Gaiman from the likes of Chaucer in terms of storytelling itself; one could even go so far as to note that Chaucer himself was a latecomer to this type of storytelling by opening the discussion to Boccaccio's *Decameron* as well. Therefore, the allusion does not have to be a singular moment, image, or line of text, but can be structural as well. Likewise, this kind of sophisticated reading extends to other areas of study. Ovid's *Metamorphoses*, while not a medieval text per se, wielded great influence over our popular Medieval and Renaissance writers and is a text I often include in my teaching as such. Not only does reading Ovid provide a basis of knowledge for much of Greco-Roman mythology, but also sets up Chaucer's frame narrative and the concept of interlacement in literature. Recently, I paired Alan Moore's *Watchmen* with Ovid and experienced the now-usual result of enthusiastic students. Not only could they interpret the stories as being similar thematically—about the fate of fallen gods and changing public opinion about their value—but they could also read the allusions as being structural, and I consider this a great leap in terms of their understanding and critical reading skills.

Ultimately, this brief and often anecdotal discussion only scratches the surface of what I intend to be a career-long study of the incorporation of comics into the classroom. My limited but successful ventures thus far inspire me to continue to find new ways to get students back to learning Medieval and Renaissance literature, perhaps even voluntarily. I can imagine a world, in secondary education specifically, that hearkens back to a more classical, or even philosophical approach, in which students are expected not to be passive, note-writing, Power Point–watching grade-seekers, but engaged critical thinkers who are able to synthesize their learning across disciplines for a purpose other than getting a job. Most of us who teach do so because we are convinced we can change the world—not in a sweeping, radical fashion, but simply by inspiring one student at a time to be intellectually curious. We teach because we understand what education has afforded us, not in terms of material success (obviously), but by being engaged, respected, and intellectually fulfilled in ways that no amount of Facebook, cable television, or video games can provide. No student should be deprived of Shakespeare, not because it is good for them to read the way Brussels sprouts are good for them to eat, but because the experience of this kind of reading alters one's sense of him- or herself, and inspires thought the way that nothing else can. Similarly, students should know and love *Beowulf* and Chaucer because it shows us that pre-modern cultures are not primitive but every bit as intellectually sophisticated as we are (if not more so in the absence of perpetual technological distraction). Most importantly, these texts remind us that no matter where we live or when, the *experience* of being human never really changes.

References

Heaney, Seamus. 2001. *Beowulf.* New York: WW Norton.
Hinds, Gareth. 2003. *The Collected Beowulf.* Cambridge, MA: THECOMIC.COM.

Keller, James R. 2008. *V for Vendetta as Cultural Pastiche: A Critical Study of the Graphic Novel and Film.* Jefferson, NC: McFarland.

Moore, Alan, and David Lloyd. 1998. *V for Vendetta.* Vertigo: DC Comics.

Schraffenberger, J.D. 2007. "Visualizing Beowulf: Old English Gets Graphic." In James Bucky Carter, ed., *Building Literacy Connections with Graphic Novels: Page by Page, Panel by Panel.* Urbana, IL: National Council of Teachers of English: 64–82.

Tabachnick, Stephen E., ed. 2009. *Teaching the Graphic Novel.* New York: The Modern Language Association of America.

Witek, Joseph. 2009. "Seven Ways I Don't Teach Comics." *Teaching the Graphic Novel.* Ed. Stephen E. Tabachnick. New York: The Modern Language Association of America: 217–222.

Leagues, Evildoers and Tales of Survival

Graphic Novels and the World History Classroom

Maryanne A. Rhett

World history and sequential art (graphic novels, comic books, etc.) face many of the same challenges in academia. Both categories are maligned for being too broad, too general, and too unsophisticated to be relevant in terms of truly *academic* pursuits, namely critical thinking, analytical reasoning, and thoughtful synthesis. However, the challenges that confront both are telling more of their *challengers* than they are of the *challenges*. The use of comics and graphic novels in the classroom is a relatively new phenomenon, although their inherent academic qualities have been scrutinized for much longer (as can be attested to by their inclusion in academic works seeking to garner understandings about cultural and popular temper and will). Similarly, world history, as a recognized subfield of history, is only about forty years old, although historians have undertaken writing world histories for millennia. After all Herodotus and Ibn Khaldun produced early "world histories," which used larger lenses for understanding historical trends than the regional or political scopes often in practice then and as today, but are the exception to the rule. Challengers of world history contend that it is impossible to "know" everything, much less write about everything. This contention ignores the basic point raised by world historians that they never claim such lofty goals. Instead, world history is a different way of looking at the same questions others have raised. Unbound by regional, state, or thematic constraints a world historian follows the thread of historical events across the time and space of the *world's* history. After all, war rarely stops at a nation's boundaries, a disease never recognizes state sovereignty, and popular culture is almost always the product of cultural transmission across. Likewise, critics are concerned about the "absolute realism," or lack thereof, in sequential art and contend that in a history class, where objectivity should be the standard, comic books and graphic novels too greatly distort reality. While fictional works like the *Iliad* are considered classics, the *X-Men* is derided as immature and lacking nuance. It is the aim, therefore, of this work to address the confluence of the graphic novels and their utility in the world history setting. Focusing on the natural cross-cultural and multi-thematic nature of graphic novels, we see a pedagogical tool that addresses the need to examine history and text, and thoughtfully synthesize knowledge gleaned from the class. While it is the aim of this piece to specifically address the undergraduate classroom, the work described herein is useful for some K-12 settings as well graduate classes.

The Critiques

World history is both a theoretical approach to history, much like nation-state or thematic history, and a style of teaching particularly common in general education curricula. While academics pursuing degrees and research agendas in world history do their own work in the theory and practice of the field, the theory cannot be separated from the pedagogical challenges it faces at the undergraduate level. Prominent world history collections, like Patrick Manning's *Navigating World History: Historians Create a Global Past* and Ross Dunn's *The New World History: A Teacher's Companion,* include examinations of these theoretical and pedagogical concerns underscoring the need to keep both theory and practice in mind when conducting world history.

Often the nature of world history is largely misunderstood as a generalist field. In 2006, Peter N. Stearns examined the critique of world history in his article "World History: Curriculum and Controversy." Stearns, writing a little over a decade after the firestorm of controversy related to the attempts, in 1994, to set standards for the ways in which both world history and U.S. history were taught, noted that the very essence of what is "standard" in world history (and U.S. history) was at the heart of critiques of the field. According to Stearns, "Conservative commentators argued that the world history approach detracted from the special emphasis that was essential to highlight Western achievements and landmarks. The World Standards were additionally seen — with some justification — as tending to describe non–Western civilization traditions positively while recurrently noting flaws in the Western approach, such as racism or slave trading" (Stearns 2006). At the time the Standards were being debated, the United States Senate weighed in on the matter. In a 99–1 vote the Senate turned down the standards. While the vote was aimed at questions related to the standards for U.S. history, as much as those about world history, the essence of the critique of the world field did not disappear. Notable world history communities, like the H-World listserv (*www.h-net.org*) frequently teem with discussions about the tension between "the West and the Rest," and yet the field only seems to grow in response (see: David D. Buck 1999 for further detail on this debate).

The perception that world history is generalist arises from two difficulties. The first is the critiques made during the debate over the Standards, and the second is the time constraints and pressures to pass students through general education curricula. World history survey courses rarely have the opportunity to develop fully the skills necessary for academic learning — critical thinking, analytical reasoning, and thoughtful synthesis; a possible shortcoming of all survey courses, despite their content driven qualities. At the undergraduate level, however, learning world history typically stops with the surveys, and bachelor's programs usher their students into "specialized tracks" like American, European, or gender history. World history, therefore, lingers as survey content until a student reaches the graduate level. In a growing number of graduate schools world history makes an analytical return; the field is one of the fastest growing history graduate programs in the United States, Canada, Europe, and Asia, although the programs are themselves relatively new. The number of trained world historians remains relatively low, thus continuing the deficit at the undergraduate level, with few world history professors to teach the surveys, let alone upper level offerings.

Graphic novels, comic books, and other forms of sequential art as academic texts face criticism from those unfamiliar with their utility and academic viability. Outside of the comics scholars' circle, popular perception, and non-comics related scholastic reception tend to downplay the significance of the comic book as a viable scholarly source. James Sturm's 2002 article, "Comics in the Classroom," argues that academia does not recognize the legitimacy of comics and graphic novels (Sturm 2002). Comic books retain much of the aura that they are pleasurable, fun reading that are enjoyed behind the spines of "real" works like *Moby Dick, War and Peace,* or *The Iliad.* While "gaudy escapism, whether superheroic, fantasy-based, science fictional," or fluff-driven comedy with "little depth or humanity" may indeed describe some comic books, graphic novels, and the like, they do not themselves define it (Gravett 2005, 8). Even pieces of "escapism" and "fluff" that lack "depth of humanity" are themselves important cultural artifacts that can be usefully wielded to elucidate details about popular perception, myth, and understanding.

The confluence of these two perceptions — the anti-intellectual quality of comics and the generalized vision world history is thought to produce — is well illustrated by the controversy over the recent additions to the *Batman, Inc.* series. *Detective Comics Annual #12, Batman Annual #28,* and *Batman and Robin #26,* introduced readers to a new member of the growing global Batman franchise, Paris' own caped crusader, Bilal Asselah, or "Nightrunner." Asselah, a young man of Algerian descent from the Parisian projects, sparked a whirlwind of controversy from conservative commentators who feared the Islamiziation of a "western" hero. The controversy surrounding David Hine and Detective Comic's choice of the French-Algerian Muslim is significant for several reasons. Within the classroom, the controversy and comic book itself provide content. Using this one simple story line, exploration of many themes is possible, including French imperial history, particularly *vis a vis* Algeria; increased immigration of non–Europeans to Europe due to labor shortages following World War Two; recent legal and cultural issues between France (and other European states) and its Muslim citizenry; the disparity between rich and poor in "developed countries," including the United States, and the realities this disparity produces. In terms of what the story offers as a focus of this essay, a quick return to the 1994 Standards question is in order.

In Lynne Cheney's 1994 *Wall Street Journal* op-ed "The End of History," through the voice of anonymous member of the National Council for History Standards, historians generally, world historians specifically, were vilified for pursing revisionist history at the expense of "traditional history" and "Western civilization" (Cheney 1994). This fear that history was being hijacked by the ivory tower and the forces of politically correctness echoes in the backlash to "Nightrunner." In December 2010, blogger Warner Todd Huston, in "Batman's Politically Correct European Vacation," maintained the argument that Bilal Asselah represents the forces of political correctness winning out at the expense of "white pride" and a "real understanding of Islam" (Huston 2010). In much the same vein as Cheney's concerns that the new world history standards would alter historical perceptions, Huston argued that D.C.'s choice in a Muslim Batman would mislead "people from any understanding of why riots are *really* going on in France" (Huston 2010). Huston's vision of French history rests the blame for the riots, which occurred in France on a large scale in 2005, squarely on a minority group's religious beliefs, rather than the fact that the group experiences severe poverty and political inequality. The legitimacy anti-"Nightrunner" contingents, like Huston, give to the power these characters could wield reinforces the necessity to examine popular culture in a historical context, and as it turns out, add it to the general historiography of a field.

Changing Perceptions

Although the perception that real academic learning is not possible when using comics continues to pervade textbook selection and they remain underutilized in institutions of higher learning, they are finding a place of prominence in K-12 settings (e.g. *comicsinthe classroom.net, teachingcomics.org*, or *comicbookclassroom.org*). However, at the college level, like world history, this is changing. According to a 2006 article, "an informal poll of the LES [Literatures in English Section] listserv members showed that a number of universities, including Duke, MIT, Michigan State, Chicago, UC Berkeley and Rutgers are collecting graphic novels fairly extensively" and academics have been continuing to "reassess the value and use of graphic novels" as visual media effective for developing scholastic messages (O'English, Matthews, and Blakesley 2006, 175).

In 2007, Virginia W. Gerde and R. Spencer Foster spoke to the utility offered by the *X-Men* series for understanding business ethics. According to Gerde and Foster the X-Men proved useful for elucidating complex socio-economic historical and contemporary issues (Gerde and Foster 2007). Likewise, in his 2008 article "Graphic Novels in the Classroom," Gene Yang noted that two qualities made graphic novels (and for that matter, sequential art more generally) useful for classroom learning: visual attributes, that combined the media read with the media watched, and visual permanence, allowing time to progress as quickly as one's eyes move across the page (Yang 2008, 187–8). The visual permanence component of this argument not only allows the rate of information transfer to be in the hands of the reader/viewer but it can alter the perception of time passage, an important feature of historical understanding.

As it happens, what world historians attempt in the classroom can be readily done by using the graphic novel. Such forms of sequential art offer unique and varied approaches to traditional themes, content, and timelines and their versatility is only added to by the wide distribution of topics and approaches they undertake. Moreover, the diversity of approaches graphic novels offer give professors who are initially reticent about using them a variety of means for testing the waters.

Historical Context and Fictional/Nonfictional Graphic Novel Sub-Genres

Not all graphic novels are "novels." The very fact that a large number of what are broadly termed graphic novels are actually nonfiction proves that, particularly in the history classroom, re-segmenting parts of the genre into sub-genres would be useful for reaching out to academics. While historians are not averse to using fiction in the classroom, fiction and nonfiction are taught in very different ways. Fiction is typically taught as the artifact of the history, and thus requires context in time and space. Nonfiction, conversely, presents the artifact *and* provides its own historical contextualization. In using graphic nonfiction, gaps in context remain, as in using non-documentary film. The groundwork laid by historians who brought fictional film into the classroom is analogous to the efforts of teachers who use sequential art in the classroom.

Rasmus Falbe-Hansen's article "The Filmmaker as Historian," notes that historians have treated historical films as they would traditional written history, but that they tend to focus their energies on the historical inaccuracies of the film (Falbe-Hansen 2003). This, while useful for providing basic context, does not really further the academic agenda of must professors. Instead, like historical film, graphic novels should be used as supplements to or extensions of other historical sources. In 1989 Joseph Witek noted that, "sequential art does what prose inherently cannot do; it supplies a visual and immediate image of cause ... followed by effect" (Witek 1989, 26). The other visual cues in addition to the verbal text indicate truth and falsity in causality, time and space are broken in new ways, and point of view within the narrative shifts with visual and verbal ease " (Witek 1989, 26).

It is, therefore, best if we begin to understand the field of graphic novels, and how they can be used in the world history classroom, as both fiction — an area that includes traditional comic books and graphic novels, that is "superheroes," fictionalized fiction, historical fiction, and/or re-conceptualized history — and nonfiction — including graphic history, graphic journalism, and graphic biography/autobiography/memoir. When it comes to fictional forms of sequential art, some sub-genres are straightforward, while others blur distinctions. The "superheroes" are works that likely spring to mind when the term "comic book" or "graphic novel" is mentioned. Material like *X-Men, Batman,* and *Superman,* are notable examples of this category. Despite their grear popular reception, moreover, these works do not inherently lack scholastic depth, as they are often written questioning social conventions. The *X-Men*, after all, address questions of Civil Rights, Jewish history, and/or the nature of genetic engineering and the debates which surround it. That said, the characters in such works still inhabit fictional worlds and their characters often exhibit impossible super-hero/god-like qualities. The fictional qualities that we freely associate with "superheroes" are not limited to those texts, however. A series of historical fiction has been written in the last twenty years in the graphic novel format. These works allow scholars and students to explore using both literary devices and visual rhetoric. Such works include: volumes one and two of Joann Sfar's *The Rabbi's Cat* or Jason Lutes' *Berlin* series, and Jean-Philippe Stassen's *Deogratias:A Tale of Rwanda.*

Fiction Examples

The story of a young child growing up before, during, and after the Rwandan genocide, *Deogratias,* provides a space to examine identity and humanity (or lack thereof) which defined that tradgic era. A fictional account, not unlike Joseph Conrad's *Heart of Darkness,* allows students to explore the work in and of itself, but also as a means of understanding Stassen, his motives for writing it, and the larger questions fiction and nonfiction raise about humanity. It has become common for publishers of graphic novels, particularly historical fiction, to offer lesson plans on their websites to be used in conjuction with their books. *Deogratias* is no exception. Using the format to the advantage of the teacher, the First Second publishing house's lesson plan asks the students to analyze the effectiveness of the author's non-linear narrative, "juxtaposing scenes of a pre genocide [sic] Deogratias engaging in typical teen behavior with a Deogratias who has obviously been driven mad" ("Deogratias — Lesson Plan..."). The visual quality of the graphic novel, no matter what sub-genre we are talking about, must be addressed. The visual rhetoric provides not simply a reiteration of the text, but is itself a vehicle of the narrative. What is more, using works like *Deogratias* in conjunction with pieces like *Heart of Darkness or* Adam Hochschild's *King Leopold's Ghost,* could, for example, complete the intelletual curcuit which leads from imperial absolutism (the Belgian Congo under Leopold) to the psychological distruction and insanity which allows humans to perpetuate inhumanity. A professor could ask students to reflect on Franz Fanon's contention in *The Wretched of the Earth* that "violent revolution [is] theraphy for the victims of Western power" (Pomper 1995, 4). While Fanon is not typically used in survey classes, his work is certainly appropriate for upper level undergraduate courses, particualrly as the nuance of imperialism, violence, and decolonization is explored.

Further historical fiction, or *allohistory* ("conjecture history," stories which speculate on alternative versions of history, like the Confederacy winning the Civil War), include Frank Miller's *300*, Brian Wood's *The Northlanders*, or the Japanese manga series *Hetalia* by Hidekazu Himaruya. While *300* is based, however loosely, on an actual historical event it is most assuredly fictionalized. It is no secret that the author, Frank Miller, was inspired to re-conceptualize history in part by the 1962 film *The 300 Spartans*, and had no intention of creating a historically accurate novel. Indeed, Miller's lack of intent for historical accuracy is precisely what fellow graphic novelist Alan Moore has criticized. The question of intentionality is useful for classroom analysis. On the one hand, knowing what Miller intended (as he has written extensively on the subject) can allow students to explore his reasons for choosing the historical setting he chose, the cultural reactions his choices instigated, and the viability of his work in the history classroom setting as a result. On the other hand, as the intentionality of the author is so frequently unknown in historical documents, examining the work as it is without knowing Miller's vision, allows the reader/viewer to develop an alternative understanding of the work. In fact, assignments which have the students first engage with *300* in the latter way, and then expose them to Miller's intentionality in a later stage can offer valuable lessons on the production of history as well as the producers of history. Can, for example, *300* represent a reinterpretation of history? If so, what does this insight offer in understanding the nature of historical "accuracy?" It is occasionally useful to assign such blatantly historically inaccurate works, whether they are graphic novels, traditional literature, or film. Their use opens a conversation between the students and professors about the nature of historical accuracy, the idea of subjectivity, and why and how history can be, and often is, manipulated.

The manipulation of history, moreover, is becoming an increasing common topic in popular literature and history. *Steam Punk*, a wholly separate sub-genre popular culture is useful to consider in terms of its impact on graphic novels, and how its themes alter historical perceptions. The kernel of Victorian era dress, technology, mannerisms, and cultural reference that is found in most Steam Punk literature and art acts at the historical launch pad for re-conceptualizing history. In graphic novel terms, *League of Extraordinary Gentlemen* fits well into this category, along with Hiromu Arakawa's *Full Metal Alchemist*, Bryan Talbot's *Grandville*, and Chris Bachalo and Joe Kelly's *Steampunk*.

In the case of *League of Extraordinary Gentlemen*, not only does the work represent Steam Punk, but it is also its own sub-genre of fictional graphic novels: "fictionalized fiction." While the characters possess super-hero or god-like qualities (fiction), they are in some ways real (historical) by virtue of their previous lives as literary characters. They have their own histories separate from the graphic novel they now inhabit, which adds a layer to their new incarnations and storylines. For example, one of the central characters in *League*, is Alan Quatermain, the hero of H. R. Rider's late nineteenth century imperial adventure novels. Quatermain is, in the original novels like *King Solomon's Mines* and *She*, the literary personification of the great white hunter, a symbol of the "civilized" European world, taming the "savage" and "uncivilized" African continent. In *League*, Quatermain continues in that vein, but carries new vices and flaws that situate him even more snuggly in the late nineteenth century imperial European world. Moreover, the rest of *League* is populated with characters from and references to *20,000 Leagues Under the Sea, The Strange Case of Dr. Jekyll and Mr. Hyde, Dracula, The Invisible Man, Gulliver's Travels,* the *Sherlock Holmes* series, and *Moby Dick,* not to mention Victorian erotica, leaders of the scientific community like Thomas Edison, and examples exploring the political climate of *fin de siècle* Europe (e.g., references to suffragettes).

Such fictionalized fiction offers a variety of ways to explore historical topics. It is difficult to imagine a student who has read all of the literary works discussed in *League*, but using the novel allows students to explore each piece of literature and historical reference as if he or she were conducting an intellectual scavenger hunt. The scavenger hunt, itself would need to be multifaceted. Asking students to do a general survey of the book, for example, would allow them to find, say twenty references, to literary or historical people, places, and events. There are a number of useful guides on the Internet that have mapped out the various references in *League*, but even if a professor would prefer the students not use those, every mentioned name or named graphic image can be traced back to its historical or literary root. The once the references are found further detail can be developed in conjunction with other course readings or lectures. The scavenger hunt's results give the students a reference sheet they can add to as the course/semester unfolds.

Nonfiction Examples

Like fictional graphic novels, nonfiction graphic novels fall into several sub-genres including graphic history, graphic journalism, graphic memoir, graphic biography, and graphic autobiography. Graphic history as one such sub-genre explores historical events and accounts, yet depicts the narrative graphically. Three examples of this genre include Jim Ottaviani's *Suspended in Language: Neils Bohr's Life, Discoveries, and the Century He Shaped*; Trevor Getz's *Abina and the Important Men*; and Will Eisner's *The Plot: The Secret History of the Protocols of the Elders of Zion*. Each work explores a historical theme — the life of Neils Bohr and the development of modern atomic theory and creation, the life of an African woman in the 1800s trying to secure her freedom, and history of one of the most notorious pieces of propaganda ever produced (respectively). From a historical perspective, in terms of the data conveyed there is no difference between these books and similar works which cover the same topics, expect that these works use the "graphic novel style" to add emphasis and nuance to the narrative, and perhaps more importantly, to offer new ways of interpreting the data covered. The visual components added to historical narrative act as persuasive tools to further the agenda/thesis of the work.

Suspended in Language allows us to consider not only the history of atomic discovery, but the rise and fall of European political powers and their impact on scientific discoveries and advances. Of particular importance to world history classes which find themselves part of general education curriculum surveys, moreover, *Suspended in Language* delves deep into the role of humanities (specifically language) in influencing and shaping science, scientific knowledge, and ethics and, conscience, and duty as they relate to the pursuit of academic knowledge.

A significant point to *Suspended in Language* is the indelicacy of both image and text. Bohr's atomic model, with the nucleus in the center and whirling electrons in knowable paths around it, is ultimately overturned when Werner Heisenberg presents his Uncertainty Principle. Still, Bohr's atom is the recognizable, if inaccurate, symbol of atomic theory.

Conversely, Heisenberg, and the intangible "language," have to step in and pick up where Bohr's image leaves off, offering more accurate, if less reconginzable, avenues for understanding subatomic study. In terms of teaching *Suspended in Language*, students can be asked to do a general survey of the work — an introductory essay or an intellectual scavanger hunt. Then, from this general survey students can be asked to choose one or two specific references to focus on further. This is particularly aided by the extensive foot and endnotes Ottaviani incorporates. Then, as a class, individual work can be shared and a class project — a website, reference guide, or other collaborative project using "group sourcing" techniques — will culminate in thoughtful synthesis. Moreover, as a test of historiographical analysis it would be interesting to ask students to compare the bibliographies and footnotes of graphic histories, like *Suspended in Language*, with those of history journal articles or monographs.

Conclusions

Despite the persistant assumption that world history only offers a "big picture" approach, lacking the nuance and depth of focused nation-state or thematic fields, world history encourages critical thinking, analytical reasoning, and thoughtful synthesis. What is more, the parallel criticisms which face world history and graphic novels stregthens the utility of both in academic settings. This combination of perspective and source provides a platform from which historical events and trends may be examined both in their historical contexts and in their representations, reinterpretations, and alternative visions and historical perspectives. What is more, the convergence of the field of world history and the genre of graphic novels no only remains theortical. In 2011, Trevor R. Getz released *Abina and the Important Men*. Billed by the publisher, Oxford University Press, as a graphic history, *Abina* explores colonialism, slavery, and questions of gender inequality through both text and visual rhetoric. Getz, a prominent member of the world history community, represents only a beginning in a relationship forged by parallel critiques and attempted outcomes. As world historians begin to take into account the unique trajectories of their own field and the textual development of graphic novels and comic books it is likely more graphic histories, from the world historical perspective will begin to emerge.

References

Arakawa, Hiromu. 2005. *Fullmetal Alchemist*. San Francisco: Viz Media LLC.
Bachalo, Chris, and Joe Kelly. 2001. *Steampunk*. New York: WildStorm.
"Batman's French Muslim Ally Angers Us Bloggers." 2011. In *Breitbart*. Accessed July 28, 2011. http://www.breitbart.com/article.php?id=CNG.f69208842037734646079b7605c64e54.11&show_article=1.
Buck, David D. 1999."Was It Pluck or Luck That Made the West Grow Rich?" *Journal of World History* 10.2: 413–30.
Cheney, Lynne V. October 20, 1994. "The End of History." *Wall Street Journal*.
"Deogratias — Lesson Plans: Graphic Literature as a Mirror of Current Events with Deogratias." 2011. First Second. Accessed September 20, 2011. http://www.firstsecondbooks.com/teachers/deogratiasLesson.html.
Dunn, Ross. 2000. *The New World History: A Teacher's Companion*. Boston: Bedford/St. Martin's.
Eisner, Will. 2005. *The Plot: The Secret Story of the Protocols of the Elders of Zion*. New York: W.W. Norton.
Falbe-Hansen, Rasmus. December 2003. "The Filmmaker as Historian." *p.o.v.* 16.
Fanon, Frantz. 1963. *The Wretched of the Earth*. New York: Grove Press.
Gerde, V.W., and R.S. Foster. 2008. "X-Men Ethics: Using Comic Books to Teach Business Ethics." *Journal of Business Ethics* 77: 245–58.

Getz, Trevor R. 2011. *Abina and the Important Men: A Graphic History*. Oxford: Oxford University Press.
Gravett, Paul. 2005. *Graphic Novels: Stories to Change Your Life*. New York: HarperCollins.
Himaruya, Hidekaz. 2010. *Hetalia: Axis Powers*, Vol. 2. Tokyo: TokyoPop.
_____. 2010. *Hetalia: Axis Powers*, Vol. 1. Tokyo: TokyoPop.
Hine, David. December 2010. *Batman Annual #28*. New York: DC Comics.
_____. December 2010. *Dectective Comics Annual #12*. New York: DC Comics.
_____. September 2011. *Batman and Robin #26*. New York: DC Comics.
Huston, Warner Todd. 2010."Batman's Politically Correct European Vacation." In *Publius Forum*: WordPress. Accessed March 14, 2011. http://www.publiusforum.com/2010/12/23/batmans-politically-correct-european-vacation/.
Khouri, Andy. 2010. "Racists Totally Freak Out Over Muslim 'Batman of Paris.'" In *ComicsAlliance*. Accessed July 28, 2011. http://www.comicsalliance.com/2010/12/28/racists-batman-muslim-paris/#ixzz1L34iM5Z5.
Lutes, Jason. 2000. *Berlin: City of Stones*, two vols., Vol. One. Montreal: Drawn and Quarterly.
_____. 2008. *Berlin: City of Smoke*, two vols., Vol. Two. Montreal: Drawn and Quarterly.
Manning, Patrick. 2003. *Navigating World History*. New York: Palgrave Macmillan.
Miller, Frank. 1999. *300*. New York: Dark Horse.
Moore, Alan, and Kevin O'Neill. 2000. *The League of Extraordinary Gentlemen*, two vols. La Jolla, CA: America's Best Comics.
O'English, Lorena, J., Gregory Matthews, and Elizabeth Blakesley Lindsay. 2006. "Graphic Novels in Academic Libraries: From *Maus* to Manga and Beyond." *Journal of Academic Librarianship* 32.2: 173–82.
Ottaviani, Jim. 2009. *Suspended in Language: Neils Bohr's Life, Discoveries, and the Century He Shaped*. Ann Arbor, MI: G.T. Labs.
Pomper, Philip. May 1995)."World History and Its Critics." *History and Theory* 34.2: 1–7.
Sacco, Joe. 2000. *Safe Area Gorazde*. Seattle, WA: Fantagraphics Books.
_____. 2001. *Palestine*. Seattle, WA: Fantagraphic Books.
_____. 2005. *War's End: Profiles from Bosnia, 1995–96*. Montreal: Drawn & Quarterly.
_____. 2009. *Footnotes in Gaza: A Graphic Novel*. New York: Metropolitan Books.
Satrapi, Marjane. 2003. *Persepolis*. New York: Pantheon Books.
_____. 2004. *Persepolis 2*. New York: Pantheon Books.
_____. 2005. *Embroideries*. London: Pantheon
Sfar, Joann. 2005. *The Rabbi's Cat*, two vols., Vol. One. London: Pantheon.
Spiegelman, Art. 1992. *Maus I: A Survivor's Tale My Father Bleeds History*. Rev. pbk. ed. New York: Pantheon Books.
_____. 1992. *Maus II : A Survivor's Tale and Here My Troubles Began*. London: Penguin.
Stassen, J.P. 2006. *Deogratias: A Tale of Rwanda*. First Second.
Stearns, Peter N. July 2006. "World History: Curriculum and Controversy." *World History Connected* 3.3.
Sturm, James. April 5, 2002. "Comics in the Classroom." *The Chronicle of Higher Education*.
Witek, Joseph. 1989. *Comic Books as History: The Narrative Art of Jack Jackson, Art Spiegelman, and Harvey Pekar*. Jackson: University Press of Mississippi.
Yang, Gene. January 2008. "Graphic Novels in the Classroom." *Language Arts* 85.3: 185–92.

"Indisciplinary" Teaching
Comics Studies and Research Writing Pedagogy

PHILLIP TROUTMAN

Graphic novels and comic books now appear with some frequency on college syllabi, positioned variously as literature, art, rhetoric, and historical evidence — in short, as objects of disciplinary analysis. The teaching of comics has benefitted enormously from these perspectives (e.g., Tabachnick, ed. 2009), but I would like to describe a complimentary approach, one that instead leverages the peculiarly interdisciplinary status of comics studies *as a scholarly field* in order to introduce students to academic writing and research. Comics studies, at least among Anglophone scholars, is always coming but never quite arriving; it is routinely described as emergent, nascent, embryonic. It maintains a long-standing but sometimes tendentious relationship with the popular realms of criticism (that of fans, journalists, and practitioners) from which it originally developed and from which it occasionally takes pains to distinguish itself. Moreover, it sits somewhat uneasily within the academy, both because of the medium's image/text composition, which sets it outside traditional disciplinary purviews, and because of its popular nature, which has engendered both an ivory-tower skepticism on the one hand and an "anti-academic" response by some popular culture scholars on the other. Comics studies, then, seems an unlikely "model discipline" for introducing students to academic writing and research — the stated goal of my first-year college composition course.

And yet, as I suggest here, it is precisely these qualities of liminality — characterized by Charles Hatfield (2010) as the "indiscipline" of the field — that make comics studies a rich point of departure for undergraduate students working to understand and enter realms of academic discourse. By having students read closely and write in response to the varied ways other writers approach comics, students can learn not only to exploit the benefits of particular frameworks, but also to see more clearly where the boundaries of academic work may lie, how those boundaries can shift, and how they can be negotiated to empower the students' own work. I will lay out some pedagogic "first principles" at the end of this essay, but I would like to emphasize here at the outset that my use of comics studies' indiscipline is predicated on a rhetorical approach to the disciplines, one that sees academic writing as a set of structured intellectual conversations in which students can learn to participate (Bartholomae 1995; Harris 2006). Like rhetoric scholar Van Hillard, my goal is to help students "awaken and orchestrate these conversations in their own writing, as they bring others' texts into connection with one another and their own work." Rather than researching in order to summarize authoritative pre-existing answers, students are "positioning themselves as active rhetorical agents whose responsibility as researchers is to access, define, and enter ongoing intellectual discussions and controversies" (Hillard 2009, 17).

This essay, then, will briefly describe the "indiscipline" of comics studies — the mixture of approaches, genres, and other means by which scholars and other critics converse about comics — and lay out an arc of assignments that help students enter those conversations. My course is designed as a first-year composition course (and is grounded in rhetoric/composition scholarship), but the outline and principles are readily adapted for upper division courses as well.

Indiscipline in Comics Studies

So, what exactly does the field look like, and how does that lay the groundwork for introducing students to academic writing and research? When Charles Hatfield (2010) describes comics studies as characterized by "indiscipline," he means its current state of "unexamined eclecticism" as opposed to a principled eclecticism, its "mere multidisciplinarity" as opposed to a principled interdisciplinarity (para. 27, 36). But rather than calling for fuller disciplinary development, Hatfield is optimistic about the field's potential for thoughtful, purposeful interdisciplinary work: a self-conscious, practiced *in*discipline. Borrowing Lisa R. Lattuca's categories of interdisciplinarity, Hatfield sees most of them already at work in comics scholarship, albeit in under-theorized and even unconscious ways. *Informed disciplinarity* is perhaps the most common, where discipline-bound scholars asking disciplinary questions reach outside their disciplines to borrow discrete "methods, theories, concepts, or other disciplinary components" (para. 28, quoting Lattuca). While this might seem to be the simplest and most conservative form, it can be quite useful in helping undergraduates understand and exploit disciplinary discourses to craft original arguments. For example, students analyzing comics adaptation can readily draw on concepts already developed in scholarship on film adaptations of literature, whether from film studies or literary studies.

Synthetic interdisciplinary is, for Hatfield, the "de facto" mode of comics studies development, since the comics medium has been claimed as an object of study by many disciplines yet has also "fallen through the cracks" between those disciplines. Hatfield sees this institutionally in the comics journals and conferences, where "comics studies has been simply the sum total of 'links' between the various disciplines interested in comics" (para. 33). But we need not dismiss the synthetic mode, especially if it works at least to accrete unto itself a vocabulary of shared terms and concepts, a lexicon deriving from the characteristic demands of the object of study itself. Even in the episodic debates over definition, for example, the terms of debate — panel, gutter, sequentiality, juxtaposition, mass production, narrative, word-image interaction — have been largely shared by comics critics both within the academy and without. These shared terms also lead to questions and methods that mark this as a space between the disciplines, not unlike film studies. And learning such jargon is step one in students' analytical writing process when taking on an unfamiliar field.

The most "provocative" and most promising mode for comics studies Hatfield sees is a *conceptual interdisciplinarity* that challenges disciplinary boundaries themselves in order to "carve out a new intellectual 'space.'" Here he argues for a "rigorous pluralism" and a studied "eclecticism" in scholarship that encourages the "questioning of the disciplinarity system, ongoing self-critical engagement with one's own discipline and its approach to knowledge production, and continual expeditioning across disciplinary borders," ultimately transforming the disciplines "from within" (para. 34–39). Few undergraduates, of course, possess the kind of insider disciplinary knowledge required for this kind of critical work, but students occasionally can see a broader version of this stance. Once student in my course, for example, analyzed the rhetoric of educators who guardedly defended comics in the 1940s, finding that their marginalized status in the public debate was as important to them as their study of the medium. Here we can see a kind of meta-disciplinary approach that comics studies' liminal status might encourage.

While Hatfield addresses indiscipline only within the academy, it seems useful — especially in the service of introducing students to comics studies — to extend that notion to the relationship the field bears to discourses outside the academy as well. Craig Fischer (2010) points out that comics criticism resonates in multiple registers, as academics, fans, and critics (by which he means both journalists/bloggers and practitioner-theorists) speak to each other in a braided discourse that joins and separates audiences depending on the forum and context. Thoughtful comics criticism and theory-building began among fans and practitioners (Lent 2010), and these traditions are showcased in blogs like *The Comics Reporter*; in print serials like *The Comics Journal*; and in anthologies like *The Best American Comics Criticism* (Schwartz, ed. 2010), which includes no academic criticism. But these kinds of forums also constitute a platform for academic crossover. *The Comics Reporter* regularly features essays by academic writers along with reviews and discussions of their books. Even *The Comics Journal*— whose editor frequently positions himself against the academy — includes essays and blogs by academic writers, as long as they meet his standards of intellectual but accessible prose (Fischer 2010, para. 17–23). The reverse is also true, evidenced by *A Comics Studies Reader* (Heer and Worcester, eds. 2009), where academic writers predominate but non-academic critics contribute significantly, too. The mix of styles and genres is even more promiscuous in the *International Journal of Comic Art*, which intersperses theoretical and analytical research articles with narrative biographies, archival discoveries, in-depth artist interviews, and national and regional bibliographic surveys. Significantly, this journal — as well as the *Journal of Popular Culture*, which publishes quite a bit of comics scholarship — follows the more open publishing practices of the American Popular Culture Movement, a movement often described as anti-academic from within the academy (Brown 1989). The more accessible prose often found in these venues opens the door to students, who may not be familiar with academic criticism but have read critical reviews of other popular media, such as films and video games. They may serve as models for students just learning the medium, as a kind of gateway into academic writing, where certain precepts — argument and evidence, for example — may be shared but others — citation practices, tone — may not.

One of the more problematic effects of mixed audience and open publishing practices, however, is the introduction of vagueness about the purpose of individual works of scholarship appearing in those journals. In a survey I conducted of the introductions to scholarly research articles in comics studies, only one third of them placed their research in the context of any existing scholarly lines of inquiry — one of the hallmarks of academic writing, indicating the exigency and significance of the work (Troutman 2010). This suggests that while comics scholars may have several audiences and purposes in mind, their articles don't always make clear what those audiences and purposes are. Indeed, two comics scholars have leveled sharp critiques at their colleagues' uncritical adoption of non-academic discourses. Benjamin

Woo (2008) calls for the abandonment of the fan- and industry-generated "Age" system of periodization ("Golden Age," "Silver Age," etc.), arguing that it offers little analytical use. More broadly, Joseph Witek (2008) responds to the caustic criticism practitioner-theorists like R. C. Harvey have leveled at academic writing, countering that American comics scholarship has been "under- rather than over-theorized" (218). He argues that by deferring to a (sometimes imagined) non-academic audience and its (sometimes assumed) aversion to specialized or technical language, comics scholars have "disabled ourselves from talking to each other" (223). Significantly, these two critiques, along with my study, were published in the *International Journal of Comic Art*, which itself caters to that mixed audience. But since the purpose of the academic writing seminar is to train students in "talking to each other"—and to us—in a language of analysis and argument situated in established traditions of academic inquiry (Bartholomae 1985), this poses a problem.

With its multi-disciplinary and inchoate shape, marginal place within the academy, and problematic relationship with non-academic discourse, comics studies seems an unlikely candidate for modeling academic writing to students just learning college-level research and writing. Yet it is precisely those characteristics that can help students recognize the differences between academic discourses (including disciplinary and inter-disciplinary varieties) and discourses outside the academy with which they are already more familiar (including fandom and journalistic criticism). Students can learn to recognize the differences between, say, literary, historical, and sociological approaches to comics analysis and to the ways some scholars may draw on methods and concepts from multiple fields. Students can also draw on familiar discourses by analogy in order to see, for example, the similarities between the ways popular critics offer evidence and the ways academic writers do (or the different ways academic writers do so in scholarly versus popular genres of writing). Students might even begin to think more critically about disciplinary approaches in the ways Hatfield wants comics scholars to, and in their prose, they might develop an attention to the multiple registers of discourse—even within one piece of writing—in the cross-fertilization that Fischer sees as carrying so much potential. So, how can we encourage this cross-fertilization? How can we have students begin to experience and make use not only of the boundaries between academic disciplines, but the boundaries between academic and other written discourses?

Arcs and Assignments

To make comics studies work for these purposes, my course follows two concentric arcs. First is an arc of writing development, with assignments staged to build upon one another and scaffolded with supporting materials that encourage increasing independence at each step of the way. Second is an arc of initiation into the study of comics, starting in non-academic discourse and moving into disciplinary academic discourses, with opportunities for crossing among these boundaries in the final project. Each project represents a phase in both arcs, moving students forward in developing their inquiry and analytical writing while asking them to locate that inquiry, analysis, and argument in the context of an existing discourse where it is valued. How each of these exploits the indiscipline of comics studies will, I hope, become clear as I describe the these in a bit more detail, but briefly first, those projects are:

- Formal analysis ("crit"): a five- to seven-page critical essay developed by analyzing selected formal qualities of a comic book or graphic novel in response to Scott

McCloud's claims in *Understanding Comics* (1994). Students choose the graphic novel from GW Libraries' collections or from my own small collection. Examples of two students' crits are posted to my blog, *CXStudies*, http://cxstudies.blogspot.com/.

- Academic abstracts: 300-word summaries of two published academic research articles on comics, each focusing not only on what the article is *about* but also what it *argues*. Students choose these from a list I compile from academic journals and academic anthologies. Two model student abstracts are posted to *CXStudies*, http://cxstudies.blogspot.com/.
- Research proposal and annotated bibliography: developed through guided library research and organized by the *use* students will make of those sources — e.g. those used for arguments, concepts, and methods versus those used as evidence or targets of analysis. (Proposal/bibliographies are ungraded and developmental; they do not reach "final" status.)
- Research essay: a fifteen- to 20-page argument that frames a question or issue in light of scholarly literature, substantively analyzes relevant evidence in order to make reasoned claims, considers objections and alternate points of view, reflects on the implications of the argument, and (usually) integrates images multi-modally as integral components of the argument. Two student examples have been published (Laser-Robinson 2005–2006; Kowalik 2010).

With this overall developmental arc in mind, I will discuss key details of the assignments.

Formal Analysis:
Scott McCloud vs. Comic Books

Understanding Comics (McCloud 1993) serves the first project in multiple ways: introducing students simultaneously to the subject matter (comics), an approach (comics as an art form or communication medium), a method (formal analysis of visual features), a vocabulary (*panel, gutter, closure*, etc.), and a form of discourse (practitioner-theorist, aimed at a broad audience). The assignment prompt and supporting materials introduce students to a key concept used throughout the course, the idea that *claims*— good, interesting claims, at least — must be contestable, substantive, and specific: they must be open to more than one point of view, must matter to someone, and must be viably sustainable with concrete evidence (Booth, Colomb, and Williams 2003). Students must closely analyze one or two formal features or techniques (e.g., panel transitions, image/text interaction, or the iconic/realistic spectrum) and use that descriptive analysis to develop a claim in response to specific idea in *Understanding Comics*. To train students up for this work — for even students familiar with comics are generally unfamiliar with formal analysis — we first read a graphic novel assigned in common. (*Watchmen* works well, but I have recently used *The Photographer.*) Students write a non-graded two-page visual analysis of the graphic novel, which we discuss. Students then read McCloud and re-examine the assigned graphic novel, now looking to substantiate or counter their first reading by citing specific visual techniques identified by McCloud. By looking closely at the graphic novel again, students almost immediately find evidence to contradict or at least complicate any number of McCloud's claims, or even to discover realms of formal analysis not even broached by McCloud (design across two-page spreads, for example).

In addition to focusing students on specific writing practices used in analysis — description, quotation, paraphrase, linking evidence to claims — this project has students position

McCloud's work as an argument and his ideas as claims, not as a set of facts to accept at face value. *Understanding Comics*, both in its ideas and its presentation, is so compelling that on first reading it seems unassailably authoritative, like all the other textbooks students have been asked to absorb over the course of their high school writing careers. Yet semester after semester, students who begin with very little sense of where McCloud could be wrong or incomplete wind up, over the course of four weeks and seven pages, revealing new categories of image/text interaction, new types of panel transition, and examples of character depiction that have no place on his iconic/realistic pyramid. Even more modest, hedged claims—that certain techniques, in certain cases, don't necessarily have the effect McCloud claims for them—are significant and show students how they might listen in and add to the critical conversation, respecting and using what knowledgeable writers have already said, but also finding a way to make a real contribution.

The amazing thing, really, with using *Understanding Comics* for these purposes is that all it takes for students to turn his sweeping truths into contestable claims is to read some comic books. I have students browse graphic novels in our library and in the collection in my office. (GW Libraries has dedicated a small annual budget to acquisition of literary, autobiographical, and historical graphic novels, and has also begun acquiring selected reprint compilations of superhero titles. My own collection fills in gaps that the library cannot fill, tending towards independent and artsy genres.) Student interests span the gamut—there are always a few dedicated superhero and manga fans—but I encourage them to choose a genre they are unfamiliar with, so they don't focus on plot and character to the detriment of the formal qualities that are the object of this assignment. (Since this is not a literary analysis, they can write about plot and character development only to the extent that those bear on the formal qualities or vice versa.) Inevitably, with very little direction in most cases, students find examples that don't quite fit McCloud's definitions, categories, and claims, and from there they start to build their own analysis.

While all these goals are accomplished with only two sources—McCloud and a comic book or graphic novel—occasionally I also assign a selection of scholars' responses to McCloud published in *The Comics Journal* (Beaty, et al., 1999). These can help jump-start students' re-assessment of *Understanding Comics*, highlighting both the contestability and substance of his ideas. They also introduce the idea of comics studies as an academic field, especially as one that has developed in this space—has, in fact, developed the space itself—between the academic realm, where these scholars teach and do their research, and the popular-critical realm, where both Scott McCloud and *The Comics Journal* aim their work. The peculiar "place" of comics studies is revealed not only in the fact that scholars felt comfortable writing for this publication, whose editor has no love lost on the academy, but also that the editor would invite such participation in a roundtable format common to academic publishing.[1]

Academic Abstracts

The second major project—two 300-word abstracts of academic research articles—always takes students by surprise. Writing "only" 300 words each seems like a very small task at first, and yet it is one we spend roughly three weeks on and, some students say, is the most difficult work of the term. For each article, the assignment requires students to:

- Restate the article's central question or topical problem
- Identify the articles' central claims or conclusions

- Describe the article's source base — e.g., genres, dates, authors
- Describe the research and/or analytical methods — e.g., theoretical concepts, quantitative techniques
- Set the article in the context of its larger aims, if any are apparent
- Optional, when appropriate: name any significant and obvious limitation to the article, e.g. failing to address a question it poses.

This format more closely matches that of the natural and social sciences, where journals generally require abstracts that perform these tasks, mirroring the format of articles themselves. Humanities and history journals rarely require abstracts, and scholars in these fields rarely write them with this level of specificity when required — a fact students readily pounce on once they get into the academic databases. Admittedly, then, this assignment might be read as an attempt at reforming humanities abstracts in the long term. But more immediately, it simply serves the purposes of walking students through a "hands-on" introduction to argument within a specific discourse community. That is because the writing part of the problem — reducing a 20-page article to only ("*only!*") 300 words manifests itself only as students use their writing to struggle with the larger intellectual problem: demonstrating comprehension of unfamiliar and often complex ideas articulated in unfamiliar specialized vocabulary. In a nutshell, this is the problem for every student entering into any discourse for the first time, whether within the academy or without — comic book fans, after all, use jargon, too (Fisher 2010, para. 28). Here students are also facing the problems of disciplinarity and inter-disciplinarity, for articles that approach comics from distinctive disciplinary perspectives may not only differ in format, but also in the ways they conceive of their objects of study, how they position their audience, and even the purpose of the research article genre itself (Bazerman 1981).

On a practical note, I should point out that students are selecting articles from a list I have developed over time. This is in part so I have already read any article the students will be abstracting and don't have ninety new articles to read every term just to grade the abstracts. It is also to ensure that each article articulates a discernable claim that students can recognize and, if possible, a particular research method or conceptual theory that students can learn to identify (as noted above, not all articles do). I also seed the list with a variety of disciplinary and inter-disciplinary perspectives, with special emphasis on formal analysis students could use in a variety of projects. The list of about 80 articles draws heavily from three major anthologies (Magnussen and Christiansen 2000; and Varnum and Gibbons 2001; McCallister, Sewell, and Gordon 2001), from the *International Journal of Comic Art*, from *ImageTexT*, and, more selectively, from the *Journal of Popular Culture*. It also includes single articles from a number of journals spanning a variety of disciplines and often featuring interdisciplinary work, e.g.: *Social Science Japan Journal, Rethinking History, Rhetoric Review, Journal of Gender Studies, Sociological Forum, Social and Cultural Geography, American Imago: Studies in Psychoanalysis and Culture,* and *Extrapolation: A Journal of Science Fiction and Fantasy*. The anthologies are placed on reserve; students access all the journals via J-STOR and other databases. (The *International Journal of Comic Art* is an exception; while it is indexed in some databases, some of the articles are not available electronically. GW has a print subscription, and students otherwise use inter-library loan.)

Grappling with these divergent approaches to comics by abstracting them is students' first entrée into developing their research project proposals. While students generally choose the listed articles based on topical interest, the abstract requirements and subsequent library work require students to focus on analytical methods, conceptual concepts, and interpretative claims. Abstracting encourages students to look closely not only for features that set academic writing apart from non-academic criticism in general, but also those features that mark certain disciplines in particular. Students will see many academic writers acknowledge and cite other scholars' work in order to define their own projects, but they will also see, for example, sociologists describe "content analysis" as a particular method of analysis, or literary scholars invoke Barthes to establish a specific framework of analysis. This helps re-orient students' research approach away from their default of reading and researching for "information" (i.e., authoritative fact) and towards researching for argument. While students do not always pursue research topics closely related to the articles they abstract, abstracting in this way does give them a sense of how such projects are defined and what they are designed to accomplish.

RESEARCH PROPOSAL, BIBLIOGRAPHY AND ESSAY

The two assignments discussed above take the first half the semester to complete, ungergoing multiple in-class workshops, focused "sketch" work on specific aspects of the writing, and extended peer-response workshops on full drafts. The rest of the term is dedicated to the research project, which begins with a research proposal and annotated bibliography. This is where students are encouraged to exploit both the multi-disciplinary and developmental "indiscipline" of the field of comics studies. Students researching academic journals with topical keywords — particular comics characters, titles, authors, genres, etc.— will see relatively few results (Art Spiegelman's *Maus* being one exception). In high school, students finding little already written on a topic were generally encouraged to abandon that topic. I want them to see instead that an absence of existing scholarship is *the reason to pursue* that topic. The point of research is to discovery, not repetition, and one key mode of academic writing is to work in response to a gap in the existing scholarly literature (Swales 1990). By identifying gaps in comics studies — and there are endless numbers of such gaps — students can begin to position themselves as creators and not just consumers of knowledge, potentially adding to the field. More importantly, perhaps, is the multi-disciplinary kind of indiscipline. Students finding little existing comics scholarship on a given genre or work or phenomenon will need to look to other fields for conceptual help. Film studies provides additional language of visual analysis. Literary scholars have studied adaptations. Cultural studies scholars have studied fan subcultures. Students looking to gain traction on comics might do well to make lateral moves into these fields, pulling relevant concepts and arguments in for focus and comparison.

To structure the proposal and encourage engagement with the peculiarities of the field of comics studies, I use a schema that asks students to categorize sources by the way the student plans to use them. A four-category version, *BEAM*, was developed by rhetoric scholar Joe Bizup; a colleague and I have modified it as *I-BEAM*:

- *Instancing* is the practice of using other sources in a constitutive manner, to signal and even to create the particular opportunity the student/writer wants to seize upon, the niche they want to carve out for their own work, making clear the exigency of that work.[2]
- *Background* sources are "materials whose claims a writer accepts as fact, whether these 'facts' are taken as general information or deployed as evidence to support the writer's own assertions. Writers regard their background sources as authoritative and expect their readers to do the same" (Bizup 2008: 75).

- *Exhibit*: "materials a writer offers for explication, analysis, or interpretation" (75).
- *Argument*: "materials whose claims a writer affirms, disputes, refines, or extends in some way" (75).
- *Method*: "materials from which a writer derives a governing concept or a manner of working. A method source can offer a set of key terms, lay out a particular procedure, or furnish a general model or perspective" (76).

I ask students to organize their bibliography with *I-BEAM* because attention to these categories highlights by contrast the student's own project and analytical voice in their research essays. For example, Alex Laser-Robinson's research essay, subsequently published (2005–2006), analyzes racial stereotyping in Hergé's Tintin comics. His only *exhibit* source in this case is the one Tintin work he focuses on, *The Blue Lotus*. His *background* sources include biographical works on Hergé and the artists' friend, Chang Jong-Jen, who served as a model and inspiration for the story. Laser-Robinson makes innovative use of Will Eisner's *Comics and Sequential Art* as a *method* source, one whose categories of analysis he uses to structure the components of his own analysis. As importantly, he starts out the paper with *argument* sources in the form of other scholars' work on Hergé's earlier career, in order to establish a key question to ask of any Tintin work: whether Hergé ever successfully overcome his early racist assumptions in his cartooning. Because this question had not yet been answered for *The Blue Lotus*, this scholarship nicely serves as Laser-Robinson's *instancing* source as well, documenting what is already known and implicitly indicating what has not yet been discovered.

While academic writers in most fields signal exigency by referencing prior academic work by others in the field, *instancing* sources might conceivably come from anywhere, including journalism, politics, or popular culture. For example, in another student essay subsequently published, Jessica Kowalik introduces her topic — the question of Frank Miller's politics as conveyed in his *Dark Knight* comics — by discussing a *Wall Street Journal* review of the recent *Dark Knight* films (Kowalik 2010, 338). Rather than analyzing the films (or conflating them with the comics), she simply uses their popularity and the political questions they raised in the wake of 9/11 to demonstrate the general importance of understanding the personal politics of creative artists working in mass media in that context. Similarly, students can frame their research with questions raised by popular reviewers (instanced by citing comics review websites like *The Comics Reporter* or essays in *The Comics Journal*), consensus held in the broader culture (instanced perhaps by citing Wikipedia or other compendiums of conventional wisdom), or issues relevant to non-academic discourse communities like fan groups (instanced by citing blogs and online forums).

Of course, students can also frame the exigency of their research by discussing scholarly literature, especially when the students have noticed a gap in that literature or a problem with existing academic arguments. And since the field of comics studies is still nascent, there are plenty of gaps and plenty of problem with existing academic arguments. Jessica Kowalik's essay, while initially (in the opening paragraph) framing the question through journalistic and popular sources, reframes it (in the second paragraph) not only in terms of the relative lack of scholarship on Frank Miller's political ideology, but also in terms of what she thinks the existing scholarship has gotten wrong about Miller's political ideology. Interestingly, she brings in yet another kind of source to do this — an interview with Miller himself. So here we see, in one place, how a student can "orchestrate" (to use Hillard's term again) academic, popular, journalistic, and practitioner realms of discourse in order to frame a particular research question. Likewise, her essay draws on works in a number of disciplines and fields — cultural studies, gender studies, sociology, political science, philosophy, and popular psychology — in order to carry out her own analysis. In its "indiscipline" — instancing her project by reference to discourses inside and outside the academy and drawing together sources across disciplines — Kowalik's essay demonstrates the potential comics studies has for helping students see both the value of academic and disciplinary writing, but also to make use of its connections to writing beyond the university.

Finally: First Principles

Much of this essay hinges upon a particular orientation towards the first-year writing course and towards undergraduate students' research potential in general. Having students enter any academic field forces them to confront and navigate the "social turn" emphasized in rhetoric and composition studies — the notion that researchers write in response to what others have written, within discourses whose traces are marked through acknowledgement and citation. In composition studies, Kenneth Burke's metaphor of the parlor has gained widespread currency: you arrive at a party late; an animated argument is underway; you listen to catch the drift; you jump in, participate, and influence the conversation; eventually you leave and the discussion continues on (Harris 2006, 34–36). In practical terms, this means we must teach students "to think of the page as crowded with others," as David Bartholomae puts it, but also to take the words of those others "as points of deflection, appropriation, improvisation, or penetration" (1995, 63, 66). This may require a reorientation on our part as instructors.

First: trust that your students have a greater capacity for doing original research and making original contributions than the system of undergraduate education has generally given them credit for. Of course, they will not have the dedicated time and expertise to conduct research with the depth and breadth we might expect of graduate students or peers in the profession. But they can learn to make the same intellectual moves, learning to read critically and to intervene in relevant scholarly literature with insights of their own.

Second: prior expertise in the topic is not prerequisite to making original observations. Granted, students with a depth of prior knowledge about a particular artist or series can draw on that to perform analysis at a satisfying level of detail. But some of the greatest insights come from students who have no knowledge or background in a certain work or even in comics in general, who will notice things "experts" may take for granted. And some of the most frustrating (and, I'm sure, frustrated) students are those who cannot see their way out of an uncritical, committed fan discourse; they may need directive encouragement to shift focus onto *unfamiliar* material or into ways of putting fan discourse in dialogue with academic discourse.

Third: students need practice working with and responding to sophisticated but flawed texts. Introduce the intellectual work of the course with texts that are simultaneously authoritative (foundational, even) and yet problematic in ways students can readily learn to see. Scott McCloud's *Understanding Comics* is almost the perfect text for this, as it proves so insightful, so right in so many ways, and yet is so replete with unsubstantiated claims, underdeveloped ideas, and bald assertions. His comics format proves enormously compelling, carrying us along with the flow, but also problematic, as we often need more explanation, more evidence, and more countervailing points of view than his pace allows. Some students also begin to see McCloud's work as rather conservative in form — dominated by his talking head — despite his emphasis on the boundless possibilities of the medium.

Fourth: stage and scaffold the research and writing assignments to train students to find and enter whatever realms of discourse you are interested in having them enter. They need guidance not just to find the sources — the blogs or review websites or academic journal articles — but also to find the gaps or problems or issues dealt with there that warrant further pursuit. I call this "researching for argument, not information." Comics studies, with its multiple points of entry, its multiple and overlapping discourses, and its vast incompleteness, seems tailor-made for this kind of work by undergraduates.

Finally, the status of comics as pop-culture artifacts or as visual material is not sufficient justification for using them in the writing classroom. Occasionally, I hear teachers say they use comics because they are more accessible (than prose texts) to students so immersed in visual culture. Students may be multi-media consumers, but that does not make them more media literate, and it does not necessarily make comics a more accessible medium. My students often report that comics are *more difficult* to analyze than prose fiction — or at least that visual analysis is less familiar to them — and the academic study of comics is entirely unfamiliar territory. It is the difficulty of interpreting and analyzing comics, not their purported accessibility, that energizes my use of them in teaching academic writing and research. This lack of familiarity allows us to focus on what all scholars must do in a field unfamiliar to them: pick up the established terminology, learn the prevailing frameworks of analysis, and discover the gaps in knowledge that will sustain further investigation.

Together these values and practices reflect an orientation that takes seriously the idea that undergraduates can contribute genuine knowledge to the field and accordingly challenges them to engage in ongoing scholarly conversations. Comics studies, lying as it does both at the intersection of academic and popular criticism and at the intersection of multiple disciplinary approaches, provides students with a rhetorical field full of choice, allowing them to follow approaches and interests, but also encouraging them to encounter other voices, other perspectives, with which they must come to terms before they can add to and enrich the conversation.

Acknowledgments

Collaborative faculty-librarian partnerships have proved enormously productive in developing this pedagogy. Dolsy Smith and I have worked together on an approach to database research called "imagining argument," which teaches students to parse article titles for implied claims, concepts, and approaches. Meanwhile, Cathy Eisenhower and John Danneker have been steadily adding graphic novels to GW Libraries' collections with student research purposes in mind. I am also deeply grateful to colleagues and friends in the writing programs at George Washington University and Duke University. Finally, I would like to thank this anthology's anonymous referee for the thorough reading and critique of the essay draft.

Notes

1. More recently, I have been shifting the formal analysis assignment away from the academy and towards popular criticism. After reading McCloud, students will browse a number of blogs that focus on formal analysis (for examples, see those linked from Tong 2011 Jan. 18 and 19; my thanks to critic Noah Berlatsky

for these and many other references). Students will write with blog criticism as the model and might seek publication on blogs that accept unsolicited submissions.

2. My colleague Mark Mullen and I borrow the term *instancing* from online video game design, where it designates the way programmers maximize limited server space by creating niches whereby smaller groups of players take part in a quest without having to compete with the many thousands of other players online at that time. We have drafted an article on this concept for publication.

References

Bazerman, Charles. 1981. "What Written Knowledge Does: Three Examples of Academic Discourse." *Philosophy of the Social Sciences* 11: 361–387.

Bartholomae, David. 1985. "Inventing the University." In Mike Rose, ed., *When a Writer Can't Write*. New York: Guilford: 134–165.

_____. February 1995. "Writing with Teachers: A Conversation with Peter Elbow." *College Composition and Communication* 46: 62–71.

Beaty, Bart, et al. April 1999. "Critical Focus: *Understanding Comics*." *The Comics Journal* 211: 57–99.

Bizup, Joseph. 2008. "BEAM: A Rhetorical Vocabulary for Teaching Research-Based Writing." *Rhetoric Review* 27.1: 72–86.

Booth, Wayne C., Gregory G. Colomb, and Joseph M. Williams. 2003. *The Craft of Research* 2d ed. Chicago: University of Chicago Press.

Brown, Ray B. 1989. *Against Academia: The History of the Popular Culture Association/American Culture Association and the Popular Culture Movement, 1967–1988*. Bowling Green, OH: Bowling Green State University Popular Press.

Fischer, Craig. 2010. "Worlds Within Worlds: Audiences, Jargon, and North American Comics Discourse." *Transatlantica* 1: n.p. Accessed February 23, 2011. *http://transatlantica.revues.org/4919*. [No pagination; cited by paragraph number.]

Harris, Joseph. 2006. *Rewriting: How to Do Things with Texts*. Logan: Utah State University Press.

Hatfield, Charles. 2010. "Indiscipline, or, The Condition of Comics Studies." *Transatlantica* 1: n.p. Accessed February 23, 2011. *http://transatlantica.revues.org/4933*. [No pagination; cited by paragraph number.]

Heer, Jeet, and Kent Worcester, eds. 2009. *A Comics Studies Reader*. Jackson: University Press of Mississippi.

Hillard, Van E. 2009. "Information Literacy as Situated Literacy." In Kathleen A. Johnson and Steven R. Harris, eds., *Teaching Literary Research: Challenges in a Changing Environment*. Chicago: Association of College and Research Libraries: 11–21.

Kowalik, Jessica. 2010. "Miller Misunderstood: Rethinking the Politics of *The Dark Knight*." *International Journal of Comic Art* 12.1: 338–400.

Laser-Robinson, Alexander S. 2005–2006. "An Analysis of Hergé's Portrayal of Various Racial Groups in *The Adventures of Tintin: The Blue Lotus*." *Euonymous: An E-Anthology of First-Year Writing*. http://www.gwu.edu/~uwp/fyw/euonymous05-06.html. Re-hosted at *Tintinologist.org*, http://www.tintinologist.org/articles/.

Lent, John A. April 2010. "The Winding, Pot-Holed Road of Comic Art Scholarship." *Studies in Comics* 1.1: 7–33.

Magnussen, Anne, and Hans-Christian Christiansen, eds. 2000. *Comics and Culture: Analytical and Theoretical Approaches to Comics*. Copenhagen: Museum Tusculanum Press.

McCallister, Matthew P., Edward H. Sewell, Jr., and Ian Gordon, eds. 2001. *Comics and Ideology*. New York: Peter Lang.

McCloud, Scott. 1994. *Understanding Comics: The Invisible Art*. New York: Harper.

Schwartz, Ben, ed. 2010. *The Best American Comics Criticism*. Seattle: Fantagraphics Books.

Swales, John M. 1990. *Genre Analysis: English in Academic and Research Settings*. New York: Cambridge University Press.

Tabachnick, Stephen E., ed. 2009. *Teaching the Graphic Novel*. New York: Modern Language Association of America.

Tong, Ng Suat. 2011. "Best Online Comics Criticism 2010: Introduction and Runners Up." http://hoodedutilitarian.com/2011/01/best-online-comics-criticism-2010-introduction-and-runners-up/.

_____. 2011. "Best Online Comics Criticism 2010: The Final List." *The Hooded Utilitarian*, http://hoodedutilitarian.com/2011/01/best-online-comics-criticism-2010-the-final-list/.

Troutman, Phillip. 2010. "The Discourse of Comics Scholarship: A Rhetorical Analysis of Research Article Introductions." *International Journal of Comic Art* 12.2–3: 432–444.

Witek, Joseph. 2008. "American Comics Criticism and the Problem of Dual Address." *International Journal of Comic Art* 10.1: 218–225.

Woo, Benjamin. 2008. "An Age-Old Problem: Problematics of Comic Book Historiography." *International Journal of Comic Art* 10.1: 268–279.

Varnum, Robin, and Christina T. Gibbons, eds. 2001. *The Language of Comics: Word and Image*. Jackson: University Press of Mississippi.

PART IV

Specific Graphic Novels and Comics and Their Application in Educational Settings

Teaching "The Auto-Graphic Novel"
Autobiographical Comics and the Ethics of Readership

Rebecca Scherr

It is a given that our media-saturated world is overflowing with images of war and trauma, from the daily news cycle to films and books and TV. Susan Sontag claims, rightly so, that such a proliferation of representations of atrocity shapes modern perception in the West. Sontag theorizes the politics and ethics lurking in this form of spectatorship, in particular examining the ethical questions that arise when it comes to looking at the pain of others. While Sontag writes about the role of photography in mediating this encounter, I find such a focus equally illuminating when applied to graphic narrative. In fact, the ideas Sontag formulates in *Regarding the Pain of Others* provides an ideal platform for talking about the ways in which graphic narratives shape an ethics of looking at — and therefore of reading — other people's pain.

In putting these ideas into a format for teaching a seminar on graphic narrative at my university, I found myself turning to autobiographical graphic narratives, a sub-genre of the graphic novel that Gillian Whitlock calls "auto-graphics" (Whitlock 2007). Some auto-graphic texts are among the most critically acclaimed of all graphic narratives, enjoying widespread prestige both in the academy and in popular culture. For the course syllabus, I chose four of these critically acclaimed texts — Art Spiegelman's *Maus*, Joe Sacco's *Palestine*, Marjane Satrapi's *Persepolis*, and the up and coming *Fun Home* by Alison Bechdel — for the inventive ways in which these authors use narrative and visual methods of representing pain, suffering, and the trauma of war and/or loss. Autobiographical works such as these powerfully blend the personal and political, and related to this, they question the boundaries of private and public pain. When it comes to the personal dimension of these four texts, all four artists draw on visual and verbal techniques that evoke the reader's empathy; at the same time, the political content contextualizes our reactions and feelings as readers, creating a meta-commentary on what it means to read about, look at, and empathize with the pain of others. The traumatic and sometimes shocking content of these works unambiguously communicates the importance of interrogating our own ethical stances vis a vis the images of atrocity we see on a daily basis. And because of the graphic narrative's association with juvenilia and pleasure, these texts allow us to analyze the often awkward co-existence of desire and discomfort that is part of the act of looking at other people's suffering.

With these ideas as background, I formulated some simple guiding questions for the course: how does the auto-graphic novel represent the self as shaped by history and trauma?

In terms of representing pain and trauma, what does the graphic novel do that other genres cannot? How do these particular auto-graphic texts construct an ethics of readership? Asking such questions is an important part of my teaching philosophy: to get students to see how literature and the world connect and constitute each other. Literary works are not simply aesthetic objects but are transitive; they enlarge our frames of understanding ourselves as constituted by and within larger contexts. To paraphrase Merleau-Ponty, texts and readers are situated, both create the world and are created by it, and in my view ethics are an important dimension of understanding situatedness.

While I designed the course as a seminar for MA students, it could work equally as well as an advanced BA level course. I think what makes my particular version a more advanced course is the secondary literature I assigned: articles and book chapters that focus on the ethics of representation, including work by among others, Linda Anderson, Gillian Whitlock, Susan Sontag, Nancy Miller, and Hillary Chute: some of this secondary literature deals specifically with graphic narrative (Miller, Chute), others with autobiography more generally (Anderson, Whitlock), and some about the ethical questions that arise in the encounter between self and other (Sontag.) I think a shorter secondary list would be suitable for lower-level BA students, with articles by Chute and book excerpts from Sontag among the more accessible of the theoretical writing.

The classes themselves were based on a traditional seminar model: each class consisted of discussion and one or two student presentations on the week's reading, and throughout the course the students developed and wrote a research paper. The presentations mostly focused on the visual aspects of the texts in the form of close readings of individual panels. In order to encourage this close reading focus, the first book we read for the class was Scott McCloud's *Understanding Comics*, which provided an excellent ground from which to build our discussions. The students enthusiastically embraced and challenged McCloud's explanations of the genre, and I found in the final research papers that each and every student came back to this foundational work in order to make sense of their chosen topics. Based on the students' keen interest in the formal constructs of comics, I would consider, when teaching the class in the future, to include some drawing exercises and to have the students themselves draw a panel or short sequence about their own lives, and then weave these drawings into our larger discussions about authorship and readership. Then the formal and theoretical questions we discuss really would become personal for them.

The seminar focus on intertwining form, thematic content, and theory is particularly important because I teach in a literature department. I find that one of the biggest challenges in studying the graphic novel for both me and my students is finding a vocabulary for discussing visual work and culture. We are very good at analyzing language and themes, of finding historical and cultural references in the various texts, but less skilled at really looking at the visual building blocks of the graphic form. In this respect, the seminar focus on the ethics of readership turned out to be a crucial site for forging these links. As McCloud emphasizes, one of the distinguishing features of the comics genre is the way in which it calls such vivid attention to reader participation in two important ways. The first is through the iconic nature of comics; McCloud focuses on the icon of the face (Chapter Two) and argues that the more iconic and less realistic a facial drawing, the more we interpellate ourselves into the text, a strategy important to the efficacy of both *Maus* and *Persepolis* particularly. But what proved more interesting to the students and to the class theme generally was McCloud's discussion of the act of closure in Chapter Three. It is closure — the necessary act of using the imagination to connect individual panels, to use our full range of sensuousness in order to surmise what happens when we move from panel to gutter to panel again — that McCloud argues "fosters an intimacy" and acts as "the silent, secret contract between creator and audience" (McCloud 1993, 69). Thus questions of readership sit right on the visual surface of comics and need not be forcibly sought after as a component of meaning making, as sometimes happens when discussing more traditional literary texts. In other words, while the ethics of readership is always an issue regardless of the genre of a given text, graphic narratives hold the potential to render this ethical engagement as particularly affective, since the processes of interpellation and closure (both of which are unique to the comics format) frame the reader as a co-creator of the narrative (McCloud 1993, 68). Comics demand a particular kind of personal investment.

In the following, I will briefly discuss the four primary texts (*Maus, Palestine, Fun Home,* and *Persepolis*) in the context of the ethics of readership, drawing most of my points from what came up in the classroom. I have also based much of what I say on direct and indirect quotes from the students' final papers with the hope that the inclusion of student research demonstrates what they find interesting about studying the graphic novel. Their insights can therefore be of general use in beginning the process of developing aims and objectives for the inclusion of the graphic novel as an essential part of literary studies. In addition to this, I include a number of questions as suggestions for ways to direct classroom dialogue. In this way, the following discussion is designed as 1) a brief exploration of the myriad questions that arise when we focus on *reading* autobiographical graphic narratives, and 2) as a loose guide for teaching a course with the same or similar focus.

Maus

After first reading McCloud's book, we turned to Art Spiegelman's *Maus*, as it is absolutely foundational to the development of the auto-graphic novel more generally. *Maus* is justifiably famous for many reasons, not least because it is seemingly simple to read yet extraordinarily complex in terms of thematizing how history, memory, trauma, and kinship intersect with each other to construct selfhood. That it does so by examining the Holocaust in particular gives it emotional and traumatic weight, but as one student noted, the presence of trauma is situated in such a way as to invite the reader into Spiegelman's emotional world. This invitation is especially significant given that representations of concentration camps, and of the intense human suffering that occurred during the Holocaust, can often move readers but still keep us at a distance, as the depth of the trauma can be seen as too far removed from most people's ability to comprehend it. However, as this student writes:

> Spiegelman lets the reader approach his father's experience of the Holocaust through the combination of text and image ... without alienating or shocking the reader, and allows for the reader to be active and take part in his graphic narrative. In doing so, he renders the Holocaust ... available to readers who might lack "entitlement" to such narratives [Hole 2010, 4].

Here the student focuses on reader agency, and later links this to the act of witnessing trauma more generally and to the act of closure in comics more specifically, both of which render the reader as complicit in the creation of the narrative. To argue this, the student looks at the artist-narrator Artie's self-reflexive images, those moments when he shows himself recording his father's stories. In such moments Artie acts as a kind of buffer in the text, what the student calls "the filter or mediator needed for the reader to become a co-owner of Vladek's trauma." She continues, "Artie's insistence on hearing more of the stories can be linked to the reader's urge to hear and read more" (Hole 2010, 16). This clearly links to the notion of the reader as witness, and points to the strategies auto-graphic artists use in addressing trauma: in this particular case, Vladek's trauma becomes manageable precisely because of the role of the creator, Artie, as buffer; we are witnessing the witness as he collects the story, tries to put it down in graphic form, all the while grappling with his difficult relationship to his father. The student suggests that graphic closure, however, counters this witnessing at a remove and pulls us close to the text, and it is through this act of closure that Vladek's story also becomes "ours." Is this kind of move—to keep the reader at a distance through the creation of a buffer, *and* to simultaneously erode that distance through closure—unique to the graphic form? It seems that the combination of text and image allows for the graphic narrative to communicate two different messages or to move the reader in two different directions nearly simultaneously. This becomes important in relation to the act of witnessing other people's pain, for this simultaneity mimics and thus addresses the reader's dual role as witness: to at once be an outside observer listening or reading someone else's story; at the very same time, to be enmeshed within the narrative, helping it come into being. Such a stance exposes our personal investment in looking at the pain of others.

Some other questions we formulated as they relate to *Maus* included the following: In what ways does this work about trauma position the reader within a discourse of public feeling and memory? Is it problematic in some ways to make such a trauma, in the words of the student, "available" to readers? Such questions implicitly address the ethical imperatives that are not unique to *Maus* but to all Holocaust narratives, such as, what is the role of memory in Holocaust representation? How do we understand this up against the insistence, found in the critical literature about the Holocaust, that the truth of such a trauma is ultimately un-representable?

In one of our class discussions about *Maus* as a postmodern text that interrogates the notion of the self, an astute student asked, is *Maus* even an autobiography? Isn't it, rather, a biography? This question led to a larger discussion about the ways that *Maus*, in alignment with postmodern theory, allows us to comprehend how the self is a product of disparate discourses. In particular, what *Maus* does is examine how the self can only be understood in relation to other selves. Kinship—especially one's relationship to parents—is shown as a primary place from which to examine the self, so graphically and poignantly explored in Spiegelman's depictions of his relationship with his father and in his discussions with his psychiatrist. This is certainly one of the many aspects of the text that all readers can identify with on an affective level, as many students in the class expressed, and thus what allows such a traumatic experience to become more "approachable" and "available." At the same time, the famous masking effect in *Maus* complicates this notion of comprehending the self as based solely on parental forms of kinship ties. The genius of the masking technique in *Maus* is how Spiegelman graphically shows that larger historical forces also construct selfhood relationally; that is, all the mice "look" similar so that a kind of visual kinship between all mice, all cats, pigs, etc. is established in the text. In this vein, one way to approach *Maus* is to discuss how it constructs the self as relational, and as an effect of disparate discourses of race, religion, ethnicity, nation, war, hatred and ignorance; having the students find particular panels that address this construction and sometimes fragmentation of self proved very fruitful for our discussion. Looking at the self as produced within specific political, historical, and psychological contexts allowed us to probe the ethical underpinnings of this production, in that selfhood is not a thing in itself but is instead situated within a contingent framework; our responses to the limits and possibilities of these frameworks is where the ethical dimension lies. While many kinds of texts, not just auto-graphics, explore the production of the idea of self within a larger context, the iconic dimension of the graphic form allows us, at least in the case of *Maus*, to quite literally *see* this construction.

Palestine

I chose Joe Sacco's *Palestine* as a follow-up to *Maus* because of both its form and content. There is an oblique resonance between the two graphic novels. While Spiegelman does not address Zionism, the fact of the Holocaust structures much of the discourse around Jewish identity in the latter half of the 20th century, and of course it is directly linked to the establishment of the state of Israel. One of the student presentations focused on the *pictorial* resonances between the two texts, especially in Spiegelman's and Sacco's images of barbed wire and spaces of confinement more generally. This is not to say that the students were interested in making facile links between Israel's Palestinian policy and Germany's Jewish policy, but, in dialogue with *Maus*, there is an unmistakable irony in the visual landscapes Sacco draws in *Palestine*.

Again, though, what proved more interesting to the students were questions regarding readership and graphic strategy. While there was only one research paper that addressed *Palestine*, and it did so only briefly, this student's comment sheds light on the link between form and readership:

> the subject matter of *Palestine* simply doesn't lend itself well to poetic composition, and that trying to make it elegant and musical would be directly counterproductive to Sacco's project of relentlessly piling on the ugliness of war. Probably Sacco knows what he is doing, and is entirely capable of using more poetic techniques if he wants to, but instead chose something more overt, something impossible to miss, so that we cannot deny having seen it after we have read the book, just as we cannot deny having seen the situation of the Palestinian people. If so, if the choice of a fairly simple form was intentional, then that too becomes an example of a form deliberately designed to enhance the theme of the text. It is not true, after all, that a thing has to be complex in order to be good [Bjørkan 2010, 8–9].

This student implicitly links Sacco's documentary aims with a simplicity of form, which, interestingly, Hillary Chute contradicts in an article we read for class: "the formalism of [Sacco's] pages presents a thicket that requires a labor-intensive 'decoding'— a term ... connoting difficulty" (Chute 2008, 460). Clearly this student sees Sacco's strategy quite differently, and these variant points-of-view could provide the basis for a good discussion on what constitutes simplicity and difficulty in Sacco's visual style, as well as the strategic effects of simplicity and complexity in graphic composition more generally. Such questions about style came up repeatedly throughout the entire course of the seminar, and became especially compelling when we interpreted *Persepolis*, where, as I discuss later, the child-like, naïve style functions strategically.

In the pages of *Palestine*, Sacco, while compassionately representing the plight of the Palestinian people, consistently returns to representing himself and his methods of collecting material for the book, a clear link to the self-reflexivity and witnessing aspects central to *Maus*. In these scenes, Sacco paints himself as a certain kind of reader and witness, one who is perversely addicted to stories of real human suffering. For example, in the single-page sequence titled "Where is Saburo?" Sacco reunites with his photographer friend Saburo who has been missing for several days. Saburo tells Sacco that while he was gone, he witnessed Israeli soldiers destroying the home of a "suspect" in the Balat Camp, and also tells Sacco he saw a baby whose head was enlarged, a direct result of the pregnant mother sickened from tear gas. Sacco, in the next panel, uses a thought box to tell his readers: "Man, I wish I'd seen the soldiers firing tear gas ... wish I'd seen that baby" (Sacco 2001, 77). This is an attitude Sacco repeats at various junctures in *Palestine*; at one point he calls himself "a vulture" because of this desire to witness, in person, the pain of others (Sacco 2001, 71).

To contextualize Sacco's insistence on his role as eager witness, I had the students read Chapter Three from Susan Sontag's *Regarding the Pain of Others*. In this chapter, she investigates the "iconography of suffering" (Sontag 2003, 40) and especially a reader or viewer's desire for looking at the pain of others: "It seems the appetite for pictures showing bodies in pain is as keen, almost, as the desire for ones that show bodies naked" (Sontag 2003, 41). We applied Sontag's ideas and questions specifically to *Palestine*, asking if we indeed become voyeurs, "whether we like it or not" (Sontag 2003, 42) in reading this text — mimicking Sacco to a certain extent — and if so, what kind of responsibility do we have when it comes to looking at images of trauma? This led to a more general discussion based on the question: what might be the motivating factors in our desire to look at pain and suffering in the first place? What is at root of the *pleasure* we get out of it? Why do we like to do our looking from a distance, through visual media? Connected to this last question, in what ways do we depend upon people like Sacco and Spiegelman to act as mediators? I was also interested in having the students develop Sontag's ideas further by reading the introductory chapter of Gillian Whitlock's *Soft Weapons*, which explores the implications of what it means when the pain and suffering we are looking at is not just the pain of others, but of THE other. Sontag also indicates the politics of this form of spectatorship when she writes, "the other, even when not an enemy, is regarded only as someone to be seen, not someone (like us) who also sees" (Sontag 2003, 72). We discussed what it meant that we were sitting in a classroom in a very white, very rich country (Norway) with its ideas of Western and Eastern cultures, white and brown bodies: how does our cultural upbringing also structure this mode of looking? This last question was one we discussed in-depth, for it would also become integral to our later discussion of *Persepolis*.

Fun Home

The third primary text we covered in class, Alison Bechdel's *Fun Home*, proved to be by far the students' favorite graphic novel, at least as evidenced by the number of research papers devoted to it. Thinking about why this may be so, I have come to the conclusion that it is Bechdel's particular use of closure that draws the reader in, as I will discuss below; perhaps, too, as the least "traumatic" of the graphic novels, it seems closer to the students' own lives and therefore appears easier to relate to. However, its placement following *Palestine* was, I admit, somewhat random. In retrospect, I would place *Persepolis* after *Palestine* because we could then continue our discussions about the politics and ethics of looking at "the other" within the rhetoric of the war on terror and its demonization of Islam and the Middle East more generally.

One student brought up Bechdel's particular use of closure in her class presentation and continued to develop these ideas in her research paper, linking *Fun Home* directly back to McCloud's thoughts on closure. Having watched a video of Bechdel discussing her methods for creating *Fun Home* (mindtv.org), the student pointed out that Bechdel devised the full textual narrative *before* she conceived of the drawings. In the first stages of development Bechdel created pages with written text and blank spaces for the panels. And indeed, a cursory look at *Fun Home* shows this: most panels are accompanied by text above and outside the actual frames. In comparison, there are few speech bubbles within the frames, and added to this, much of the text within the frames consists of archival material: maps, letters, book pages, all re-drawn by hand. The student's argument, then, was that it becomes obvious quite quickly that the textual narrative and the images often have no direct relationship to each other, calling extreme attention to the fact that most of the links we make between narrative text and image are created by the act of closure. That is, the student argues in her paper that the "bigger picture" Bechdel paints is made in the reader's mind by the act of closure, which occurs, paradoxically, "through the connectedness" of text and image, a connectedness which we must actively produce since there is a "lack of natural sequence" between these two levels in the text. And since it is closure that creates intimacy between reader and text, these constant and large leaps of imagination are what interpellate us into Bechdel's world; through "closing the gap" between extremely disparate text and images, we must always be active agents in creating, in a sense, this story; in this act of creation, we feel close to the story. I found this an extremely plausible explanation for the power of this work. In this vein, I think that asking the students to apply McCloud's theories on closure to Bechdel's project would be an excellent way to structure group work and a larger discussion about form and readership. One could ask, while closure is essential in reading any graphic narrative, how does Bechdel's extreme use of it produce a particularly affective response?

Another aspect of *Fun Home* that interested the students was Bechdel's use of archival material, as mentioned above, and this dimension of the text has been discussed at some length in academic articles written about the book. Ann Cvtekovich, for example, claims that the fact that Bechdel draws these fragments of her archive by hand, and does not simply scan the items into the text, imbues the things she draws with an intense emotionality that adds a kind of "witnessing" dimension to them; they do not merely serve as information for the reader, but also as affective and thus connective sites of identification (Cvetkovich 2008, 120). Such a claim can lead into a discussion about the style and line of drawing in graphic narratives: how do line and style call attention to the presence of the memoirist's hand, and thus arguably to the perception of a kind of physical trace of the artist's presence? What are the effects of this kind of presence on our ways of reading graphic narrative, especially in contrast to our perception of an author's presence in purely textual autobiographies? Is there something more personal, more human, in someone's line drawing than, say, in a type-set text? And does this lend itself to an empathic response on the part of the reader? For in all these texts even the language dimension is drawn by hand — how does that fact shape our reactions as readers?

When we covered *Fun Home* in class, I had the students read an article by Nancy Miller in which she explores Lejeune's concept of "the autobiographical pact," referring to the persuasive techniques an autobiographer uses to convince a reader of his or her honesty or authenticity (Miller 2007). One student in the class became intrigued by the questions raised by Miller, and wrote a research paper exploring the concept of "truth" in *Fun Home*. In the course of the paper he asked a series of questions that could be used to stimulate classroom discussion or writing: *how* has Bechdel chosen to present truth in her memoir, and related to this, what tropes and figures does she use to construct a meta-discourse about truth in the text (Kleivane 2010, 3–4)? Chapter Five, "The Canary Colored Caravan of Death," with its depiction of the child Alison's existential dilemmas as expressed in her diary entries, is an exceptionally good place to begin when covering this issue with the students. In addition, the student asked, while Bechdel accuses her father of "making things appear what they are not" (Bechdel 2006, 17) in terms of shaping the public face of the family, is she perhaps doing the exact same thing in her memoir (Kleivane 2010, 15)? If we do however "buy" her perspective on her family's past, why do we do so and what are the consequences of this? It is clear to see from these questions that an exploration of the ethics of making "truth claims" becomes a necessary part of reading auto-graphic works, and is a productive site for interpreting what graphic memoirs do and how they do what they do. Finding ways to link this discussion of truth claims to both the notion of closure and the affective dimension of line and style can tie all of these aspects of *Fun Home* together: for example, do we "buy" Bechdel's perspective because she has brought us so close to text (closure), and simultaneously "touched" us on a deeply emotional level (through her affective visual style)?

Perhaps the ethics of reading come across less obviously in *Fun Home* than in *Maus*, *Palestine*, and *Persepolis* because Bechdel's trauma — if it even is trauma — is one that is primarily familial, while the other texts engage with the ways that familial lives are shaped by "public" traumas linked to war and atrocity. However, I still think that Bechdel's work engages powerfully with ethics, and not just with the ethics of truth claims as discussed above. Bechdel's ethical project is political in that she asks her readers to question the naturalness of the heterosexual family, and her work also asks us to consider what it means to transform very private suffering into a text for public consumption. In doing so, *Fun Home* asks, how are the power dynamics of the larger culture reproduced within the family? Why do so many of us maintain a line between public and private forms of family and feeling? What would happen if we begin to erode these distinctions; would power dynamics then shift? One could approach *Fun Home* as a text that actually empowers readers to rethink and reclaim their own familial histories: the ethics of readership, and its link to the personal and political, then becomes quite clear.

Persepolis

Our last graphic narrative of the semester was Marjane Satrapi's *Persepolis*, which rivals *Maus* in its general popularity and critical reception. The one student who focused on *Persepolis* for his research paper paid particular attention to the stylistic device of direct readerly address and how this trope functions paradoxically. This aspect of the text was also mentioned by those who gave presentations on *Persepolis*, with one chapter, "The Cigarette," pointed out as especially illustrative of this dynamic. In this sequence, our narrator Marji begins with a tale of cutting class one afternoon when she was 12 years old, and follows with depicting her mother yelling at her for this digression. Beautifully tying in the larger discourse of war and politics with the private sphere of the family, and thus breaking down the artificial divide between public and private, young Marji responds to her angry mother: "Dictator! You are the guardian of the revolution in this house!" (Satrapi 2006, 113). Following this, Satrapi does something very interesting, a textual act that fascinated the students in terms of the possibilities of the graphic form: Marji turns and speaks directly to "us," the readers, while descending into her basement hideaway. But this is not all; in this address, the figure "speaking" to us is still the 12-year-old Marji, but the "voice" coming from her is the adult Marjane, the author, who speaks retrospectively of both the outcome of war and her own young rebellion. The student who wrote about this in his paper argued: "To me it seems that by virtue of its medium ('comics'), the artificiality of *Persepolis* is made apparent ... by the narrator whenever she descends from the extra-diegetic level of the narration to the diegetic, and also whenever the character breaks the fourth wall" (Kuo 2010, 6). In other words, this "breaking of the fourth wall" points to the existence of several levels of address happening simultaneously: how can we untangle (or perhaps we cannot untangle) these layers of narration? And how do these intricate layers of readerly address also link the past and present, as well as the public world of war and suffering with the private sphere of family emotion? Importantly, how is this complex form of address unique to the graphic narrative, and what are its possibilities?

This student argues further that this method points to the text as text, to its construction and in a sense to its artificiality, yet he says that Satrapi does this at the exact same time as "she requires us to read it as nonfiction" (Kuo 2010, 7). So she requires us to approach the auto-graphic narrative as constructed and real, fictional and nonfictional, the main protagonist as both present and absent. Reading the auto-graphic narrative, then, we must manage and navigate these seemingly oppositional concepts; paying close attention to these oppositions is one way to approach the book in the classroom.

Alongside *Persepolis*, we returned to the work of Gillian Whitlock, who discusses *Persepolis* in the final chapter of *Soft Weapons*. She addresses two major issues in Satrapi's text: first, the discourse of the veil which, when pursued in class, allows the discussion to touch upon very contemporary social and political debates centered on identity and rights. What we focused on in our seminar, though, was the second major aspect Whitlock addresses, which is the specifically nostalgic element of the comics genre more generally: "Essential to the haunting effects and the uncanny art of comics is its association with juvenilia: its unique implication in childhood memory" (Whitlock 2007, 196). Edward Said, in his forward to Sacco's *Palestine*, echoes this: "Comic books are a universal phenomenon associated with adolescence" (Sacco 2001, i). This haunting and uncanny effect Whitlock mentions comes across in a dissonant form in *Persepolis*, through the voice of the adult author accompanied with the figure of the child Marjane, as mentioned above. Less jarringly, like with *Fun Home*, *Persepolis*'s focus on childhood aligns it with the more classic, Romantic classification of autobiography: that is, it is a self-story that charts "coming of age" as a coming into being of the artist, with the autobiographer exploring the private and public influences that have gone into shaping one's art. But importantly in *Persepolis*, more so than in *Fun Home*, it is the (seemingly) simplistic style of the drawing itself that most powerfully evokes childhood. The scenes within Satrapi's panels lack perspective and are thus exposed as two-dimensional; all of the other books we read utilized the rules of perspective to some extent. In addition, Satrapi's images are black-and-white and blocky, and altogether, these signify naiveté. That is, the drawing style itself is reminiscent and evocative of children's drawing; however, this is of course a strategic use of a naïve style. The small details, especially the use of a single line or the position of a feature on a face, actually reveal the artist's skill and sophisticated application of expressionism. In other words, through the tiniest details, Satrapi infuses her characters and scenes with emotion and intensity.

Some students suggested in the seminar that perhaps Satrapi's childlike representational method, when applied to drawings of horror, death, and trauma — especially her images of dead and decapitated bodies, of firing squads and physical torture — are positioned as they would be imagined in the mind of a child. And as the child is often used to invoke the notion of "universality," this is one strategy that makes this particular story — so far removed from most Westerners personal experiences as well as historical consciousnesses — emotionally "available" to readers. Thus the question can be asked: how does the figure of the child mediate one's reading of the auto-graphic novel? What political work is done through this figure, and what are the ethical implications of this method? Another student expressed a more politically slanted reason for why so many readers find *Persepolis* approachable and enjoyable: that it tells the story of escape from an Islamic regime, and that it is a reaffirmation of Western values of freedom and autonomy, and thus tells a story of the "East" that Western readers most want to hear (Kuo 2010, 5). I think there is something in that idea.

Conclusion

This essay covers, very briefly, one major theme we developed over the course of 10 weeks: the strategies artists/writers use to communicate with an audience, or more to the point, the various ways that the figure of the reader becomes a part of the graphic text. Yet I find this one strand touches, to a certain extent, on all the other aspects of the graphic novel we also explored in the seminar: the strategies artists use to represent trauma; the role of emotion in both graphic narrative and autobiography; the power and uncanniness of images to invoke pain and pleasure, thought and feeling; the complex interactions that both unite and divide text and image; the ways that "the self" is constructed in pictorial and linguistic narrative. What emerged most clearly from the collectivity of papers and classroom discussions around this theme is that the auto-graphic narrative teaches us how to think about the ethics of readership not from a detached perspective, but from one that is fully immersed in the emotional world of the text. It seems the graphic novel — through its nostalgic reminder of childhood, through the continual act of closure we perform on its surface of frames and gutters, and through the labyrinth of emotions it leads us through — encourages us to see our crucial role as readers as resulting directly from our affective engagement with the text.

On the first day of class I asked the students to discuss what the graphic novel does, or can potentially do, that purely literary texts cannot. Again and again, over the course of the semester, we came circling back to the issue of closure as a particularly powerful attribute unique to the graphic narrative. While the ethics of readership most definitely can and should be taught using other literary and visual genres, the auto-graphic narrative's particular framing of the reader as an active part of the text itself calls attention to, in rich and detailed ways, our investments as readers: what it means to read and how it is we engage with the act of reading. Graphic texts can, therefore, simultaneously call attention to other investments we have that relate to the act of reading: our investments in looking, feeling, questioning, and desiring. These investments take on particular political force when we are dealing with reading about other people's suffering and pain; having "co-created" someone else's story through closure and therefore having experienced that story on an affective level of comprehension, we can no longer claim, in the same ways as before, distance from the images of pain that saturate our everyday lives.

Acknowledgments

I wish to thank all of the students who took "The Auto-Graphic Novel" course in the Autumn of 2010 at the University of Oslo, and also an extra thank you to the students who gave me permission to quote from their unpublished seminar papers.

References

Anderson, Linda. 2001. *Autobiography*. London and New York: Routledge.
Bechdel, Alison. 2006. *Fun Home*. London: Jonathan Cape.
_____. 2011. "Creating Fun Home: A Family Tragicomic." *Mindtv.org*. Accessed February 28, 2011. http://mindtv.org/cgibin/display_asset.fcg?member_id=1776;ordinal=924;file=vodind.ttml;style=mind.
Bjørkan, Kristian. December 2010. "Shaped Like Itself: Where Forms and Theme Intersect." Seminar paper. University of Oslo.
Chute, Hillary. 2008. "Comics as Literature? Reading Graphic Narrative." *PMLA* 123.2: 452–465.
Cvetkovich, Anne. 2008. "Drawing the Archive in Alison Bechdel's *Fun Home*." *Women's Studies Quarterly* 23.1–2: 111–128.
Hole, Siren Elise Frøytlog. December 2010. "Mediation of the Holocaust and the Comics Medium." Seminar paper. University of Oslo.
Kleivane, Helge Engeseth. December 2010. "The Truth in *Fun Home*." Seminar paper. University of Oslo.
Kuo, Adam Tyrsett. December 2010. "A Postmodernist Study of Identity, Subjectivity, and Self-Representation in *Persepolis* by Marjane Satrapi." Seminar paper. University of Oslo.
McCloud, Scott. 1993. *Understanding Comics*. New York: Harper Collins.
Miller, Nancy. 2007. "The Entangled Self: Genre Bondage in the Age of Memoir." *PMLA* 122.2: 537–48.
Sacco, Joe. 2001. *Palestine*. Seattle, WA: Fantagraphics Books.
Satrapi, Marjane. 2006. *Persepolis*. London: Jonathan Cape.
Sontag, Susan. 2003. *Regarding the Pain of Others*. New York: Farrar, Straus and Giroux.
Spiegelman, Art. 2003. *The Complete Maus*. London: Penguin.
Whitlock, Gillian. 2007. *Soft Weapons*. Chicago: University of Chicago Press.

Teaching Theory Through *Y: The Last Man*

Timothy D. Arner

While the serious study of comics and graphic novels has been increasingly recognized as a valuable critical enterprise by professional scholars in academia, the idea that these types of works would show up on the syllabus for a college course still surprises many students. Unaware of the canon wars of the 1980s, the emergence of cultural studies as a discipline, and the ways in which various literary theories opened up new ways of thinking about what counts as literature, it seems that students are more likely than many of their professors to insist upon the separation between high and low culture or the difference between Literature with a capital L and books that one reads simply for fun. Perhaps we have reached a point where we no longer need to defend graphic fiction as a legitimate field of scholarly inquiry, as suggested by the recent boom in academic journals, edited collections, and monographs dedicated to the subject. We may, however, still need to justify the introduction of comics or graphic novels into our classrooms, where students arrive expecting to focus solely on "the classics" or, at least, types of Literature that they might not otherwise read on their own (i.e. poetry, Shakespeare, big, thick tomes with no pictures). The initial surprise expressed by many students, which fortunately registers more often as amusement rather than serious resistance, provides an opportunity to discuss the ways in which our society defines Literature versus popular culture, how we experience and evaluate art, and the practical value of using literary and cultural theories to examine all kinds of media.

In an effort to foreground these issues, I recently assigned the first two volumes of Brian K. Vaughn's *Y: The Last Man* in my literary analysis class at Grinnell College. A prerequisite for any student who wants to take higher-level literature classes, literary analysis introduces students to literary terms, the principles of close reading, and the basic tenants of a number of literary theories, including feminism, psychoanalysis, and critical race theory. For a useful overview of theoretical concepts, we read and discussed *How to Interpret Literature: Critical Theory for Literary and Cultural Studies* by Robert Dale Parker, who explains, "This is a book about how, every day, we interpret — and can enjoy interpreting — the dialogue between art and daily life" (2008, 3). Applied to a selection of poems, short stories, drama, and novels, the questions raised by various theoretical approaches allowed us to consider how theory opens up new ways of reading literature and helped us better understand how literary texts address contemporary social issues. At the conclusion of my latest version of the course, the class spent the final two weeks of the semester interpreting *Y: The Last Man* through the three theoretical approaches previously mentioned. By reading graphic fiction, students were asked to apply these literary theories to both text and image and to reflect upon the artificial divide between Literature and popular culture. This essay describes one approach to teaching theory through *Y: The Last Man*, and, in so doing, demonstrates the benefits of using graphic fiction in the literature classroom.

Y: The Last Man is a 60-issue comic book series that ran from 2002 to 2008. Set in the aftermath of a worldwide plague that instantly kills every mammal with a Y chromosome except for a young man named Yorick Brown and his pet monkey, Ampersand, the series depicts the new challenges and opportunities afforded to women living in a world devoid of a male population. After the plague hits, Yorick travels from New York City to Washington, D.C., to find his mother, who is a U.S. congresswoman. His mother assigns a covert government agent known only as Agent 355 to protect Yorick and help him locate a bio-engineer named Dr. Alison Mann, whose research may hold clues as to what caused the plague and why Yorick and Ampersand were able to survive. As Yorick, 355, and Dr. Mann travel across the country to retrieve genetic samples stored in a laboratory in San Francisco, they are pursued by two groups of women who want to capture or kill the last man on Earth.

As with any post-apocalyptic literature, the depiction of a radically different fictional world asks readers to evaluate the operation of a new kind of society against the norms that govern their own. In *Y: The Last Man*, gender is the most obvious and immediate point of thematic concern, as the plague eliminates the male population and cripples the American government and infrastructure, which had been controlled almost entirely by men.[1] By imagining the effects of a worldwide "gendercide," the series foregrounds the ongoing gender inequalities that result from a society that has always been, and remains to this day, largely patriarchal. The stories of how individual women and the small communities that form after the plague cope with and exploit their new circumstances not only speaks to the broadly-defined notion of feminism as a mode of critical inquiry and call to political action but it also highlights competing schools of thought within feminist theory. As a comic book series, *Y: The Last Man* also forces the reader to confront the issue of how gender has been typically represented within that particular medium.

In the fourth issue of the series, Yorick has his first direct encounter with the Amazons, a paramilitary feminist organization dedicated to the eradication of all lingering aspects of male culture. Yorick slips away from 355 to visit the Washington Monument, which has become "an ad hoc memorial for all of the men" (*Unmanned*: 88). While a group of women at the memorial are reflecting upon what has been lost, four women burst onto the scene and spray paint "Good Riddance" on the base of the monument. Yorick says that until this point he had only heard rumors about the Amazons, and he asks, "They're like roving packs of pissed-off lesbians, right?" A woman explains, "Nah, they're not gay. They're insane. Someone told me that they all burn one of their boobs off" because "supposedly, that's what the real Amazons did. Makes it easier to shoot an arrow or something" (94). Yorick's snide comment about "pissed-off lesbians" echoes the types of vitriolic accusations hurled against feminists by those who have sought to trivialize and discredit their political and social agendas. The woman's correction of Yorick's remark dismisses the notion that feminism is linked to one kind of sexual identity, yet she classifies their militant brand of feminism as "insane." The destructive impulse of the small group of Amazons in *Y: The Last Man* stands in contrast with the peaceful mourning of the other women, who disapprove of the Amazons' actions. My students quickly identified the Amazons as the villains of the story, noting that their extremism is always depicted as counter-productive. Still, rather than simply condemning the Amazons' actions, we used their role in *Y: The Last Man* to discuss the ideological spectrum of feminism as a theoretical school and social movement.

The Amazons' act of self-mutilation provides a sign of solidarity that invokes their historical counterparts from ancient Greece, perhaps to remind the reader that the feminist movement did not spontaneously appear in the early 1970s but arose from a long tradition of women seeking alternatives to patriarchal hegemony. Because the medium of graphic fiction allows the reader to study and evaluate both text and image, the visual depiction of the Amazons emphasizes the body as a site of biological and social gendering. This is most clearly and effectively illustrated on the final page of Issue Four, where we learn that Yorick's sister, Hero, has joined their cause. In a full-page panel, Hero wears a loose-fitting and mostly unbuttoned shirt that allows the reader to see part of her right breast and the fresh scars that mark the removal of her left breast (*Unmanned*, 104). My students noted that this image functions not only to display Hero's new identity as an Amazon but it also suggests a violent rejection of maternalism that is both symbolic and literal. Readers can use the brutal physicality of the Amazons to think through how control over one's body, represented here at its most extreme, speaks to fundamental issues of female empowerment, individual self-identification within a gender binary, and the social performance of gender as it relates to notions of biological imperative.

The issue of female empowerment in *Y: The Last Man* is troubled by the fact that the Amazons operate under the brutal control of Victoria, who is only ever seen wearing an army jacket that both signifies her dictatorial leadership and makes it ambiguous whether she has actually undergone the same act of self-mutilation that she demands of her followers. Victoria first appears in Issue Four as she stands onstage addressing a crowd of women at the Baltimore Convention Center. She tells the women, "Bobby Fischer once said that he could defeat any woman at chess hands-down ... playing blind-folded and without his knights. I beat him in a private match when I was thirteen." Victoria's anecdote describes a personal moment of triumph in countering Fischer's misogyny that also functions as one small battle in an ongoing war. She goes on to explain, "Our opponents are gone now ... but that doesn't mean we've won. There are misguided women out there who will attempt to remake this world exactly as it once was" (*Unmanned*, 102). This statement begins to seem ironic as the reader learns more about the extent and effects of Victoria's tyrannical rule over the Amazons; as my students pointed out, she replicates the very power structures she would seem to be fighting against. Victoria recognizes this contradiction, however, and she justifies her role to Hero in Issue Five, claiming, "I despise barking orders like a patriarch. Rest assured, when the game is over, the queen and the pawn go back into the same box" (*Unmanned*, 114). For many of my students, the chess metaphor failed to justify Victoria's decision to order the execution of a woman who had insulted her, but her comment moved the class to consider the relationship between motive and method as they relate to struggles for power and equality.

The hierarchical structure of the Amazons provides one model of community organization in the post-plague world of *Y: The Last Man*, but Yorick and his companions find an alternative model in Marrisville, Ohio. In the second volume, *Cycles*, Yorick and 355 are injured after being forced to jump out of a moving train. They are cared for by a group of women who have managed to restore electricity to their town and have set up a communal society that functions democratically. When Yorick expresses surprise at their standard of living, an elderly woman explains that some of these women have had "plenty of experience making do without any men around" and she cites her experience during World War II when women made up most of the town's workforce (*Cycles*, 44). It is later revealed that the women who live in this town had all been incarcerated in a nearby penitentiary, and their cooperation functions as a necessity born from their time as prisoners (68–9). While the Amazons rely on a governance system that replicates patriarchy by locating power in a central authority figure, the women of Marrisville respond to freedom from their imprisonment by removing hierarchical structures as they create a new community.

When a group of Amazons arrive in Marrisville, Victoria tries to convince them to hand over Yorick so that the Amazons can kill him. She points out the ways in which men were directly or indirectly responsible for their incarceration, citing a series of facts about the relationship between gender, crime, and the penal system: "The vast majority of you convicted of violent crimes were merely defending yourselves or your children from an abusive male… Those of you who killed your husbands served prison terms twice as long as men who killed their wives… Most of you were in for 'economic crimes,' literally stealing to feed you families … but while you rotted in prison, men who embezzled billions went free" (*Cycles*, 79). Victoria's speech provides a stark reminder of the very real injustices of our patriarchal pre-plague world and adds an important context for thinking about the circumstances that shaped her agenda. By considering the contrasting social structures and agendas of the Amazons and the women of Marrisville, students debated the ways in which women should respond to a history of unfair treatment by male-dominated institutions.

Discussions of feminism in *Y: The Last Man* need to address not only the text's narrative but also the representation of gender through the medium of graphic fiction. Any consideration of the series as a feminist text is troubled by its adherence to popular conventions of comic storytelling that attempt to appeal to the medium's primary audience of adolescent males through the visual representation of female characters. In the opening pages of the series, we are introduced to Yorick and his girlfriend, Beth, as they talk on the phone. Beth is hiking in the Australian Outback while wearing a purple bikini top and very short shorts, revealing a curvaceous bust, an impossibly flat and trim stomach, and perfectly toned legs; her long blond hair is flowing in the breeze (*Unmanned*, 6). Like the typical Barbie doll, her proportions reflect a male ideal of beauty, an ideal that has been reproduced on the pages of comic books (particularly superhero comics) since their earliest days. I posed these questions to my class: To what extent does this series replicate or critique the ways in which the female body is figured in comic books or other visual media? Is the text's ostensibly pro-feminist message of female empowerment belied by the ways in which women are pictured? And should the fact that the series is drawn by a female artist, Pia Guerra, affect how one evaluates these images?

Given the similarities between comics and film as types of sequential art (Eisner 1985, 40; McCloud 1994, 8), Laura Mulvey's discussion of voyeuristic pleasure and the male gaze in her seminal article "Visual Pleasure and Narrative Cinema" can provide a way of analyzing gender representation in *Y: The Last Man* through both feminist and psychoanalytic lenses. Mulvey cites Freud's work on scopophilia, which describes the pleasure one experiences "in using another person as an object of sexual stimulation through sight," as she considers the ways in which women appear on the screen "as an erotic object for the characters within the screen story, and as erotic object for the spectator within the auditorium" (1975, 10) In the post-plague world of *Y: The Last Man*, erotic tension is ever-present both for the protagonist, because of his status as the last potential hope for sexual reproduction, and for the reader, who bears witnesses to Yorick's new role and can find pleasure in the way the medium of graphic fiction, to an even greater extent than film, "freeze[s] the flow of action in moments of erotic contemplation" (Mulvey 1975, 10–11). The personal and political implications of gender and sexuality are pushed to the extreme in *Y: The Last Man*, and the narrative's focus on how Yorick responds to his circumstances allows the reader to consider his character from a psychoanalytic perspective.

When we first see Yorick, he is wearing a straightjacket and hanging upside-down in a door frame in his apartment while chatting with Beth on the phone. His confinement is juxtaposed against the image of Beth discussed above; as Beth is freely running through the vast expanse of the Australian Outback, Yorick struggles to escape from his self-imposed restriction (*Unmanned*, 5). After working his way out of the straightjacket, he explains to Beth that he has become increasingly agoraphobic, and he notes the irony that he is now "the escape artist who can't escape his apartment" (17). Yorick's conversation with Beth leads up to him proposing marriage but the phone connection is lost when the plague hits before Beth has a chance to answer. Throughout the remainder of the series, Yorick's intensely monogamous devotion to Beth puts his personal desire to find her at odds with the larger social demands of the post-plague world, which would seem to require him to partner with numerous women. His willingness to put himself at risk as he tries to make his way to Australia creates conflict between him and his traveling companions, who want him to guard his life more carefully and put the world's needs ahead of his own. Like 355 and Dr. Mann, many of the students in my class were frustrated by Yorick's selfish pursuit of Beth, but we could turn to psychoanalysis to help us evaluate Yorick's decisions and consider the psychological drives that might explain his behavior.

From a psychoanalytic perspective, much of Yorick's behavior can be explained as a manifestation of his latent desire for a closer relationship with his mother. The agoraphobia he acknowledges during his conversation with Beth suggests a growing need to seek comfort in a womb-like state. Yorick's chosen profession serves as a convenient plot device as he possesses a set of skills that allow him to find a way out of difficult situations, but it also symbolically represents his neuroses.[2] His work as an escape artist allows him to reenact the birthing process as Yorick encloses himself in various sorts of symbolic wombs (the straightjacket is a particularly powerful symbol) and then uses his own power to emerge into the larger world, where he finds affirmation in this individual achievement. Forced out of his home and into a hostile world after the plague, Yorick fixates on finding his potential wife, who, according to Freudian theory, has become a symbolic mother who stands in for the biological parent. The tension between the conflicting male desires to both return to the mother and establish an individual identity separate from her is, to some extent, relieved by Beth's absence, as Yorick must exercise his own agency as he undertakes the difficult journey to Australia. Of course, the sexual drive remains a powerful influence, particularly as Yorick's only social interactions are with women and he faces temptation on a number of occasions. Yorick's attempts to control his libido as he comes to terms with his unique personal and social circumstances provides an interesting look into the operation of the id, ego, and superego—the forces that pit desire against conscience.

Freud's work on dream theory has proved useful for literary critics because deciphering dreams and explicating texts both involve finding meaning in symbols. Issue Five opens with two-page depiction of a disturbing dream Yorick is having (*Unmanned*, 106–7). Beth and Yorick are together in the Outback; Beth is naked, her arms and hands covering her breasts and genitals in a pose that recreates Botticelli's famous painting, *The Birth of Venus*. Yorick is kneeling on the ground next to her, also nude but wrapped up in a pile of chains. Beth says to Yorick, "Don't come, baby," to which Yorick replies "I can't come. I ... I can't even touch you." The meaning of their exchange is complicated by its double-entendre, as Beth's warning about Yorick's attempt to travel to Australia ("Don't come, baby") is understood by Yorick to be a reference to sexual climax ("I can't come. I can't even touch you"). Beth clarifies her meaning in a panel at the bottom of the page, which provides a close-up of what appears to be a red tear-drop falling from her eye while she says, "Don't come, Yorick. Don't come for me. Stay away. You know why..." The full-size panel on the facing page shows blood flowing out of Beth's eyes, nose, and mouth and cascading down her entire body as the trees and grass in the background are engulfed in flames. This image recalls the effects of the plague, which similarly caused blood to erupt from the faces of all of the men on the planet (*Unmanned*, 31). Students were eager to interpret the details of the images as well as the wordplay to posit theories about how the dream reveals aspects of Yorick's psychological state and comments on the larger themes of gender, trauma, and annihilation in *Y: The Last Man*.

While Yorick struggles to understand his individual identity and need for social attachments in the post-plague world, his sister, Hero, embarks on her own journey in response to the crisis. When Hero first appears in Issue One, she is wearing her paramedic's uniform while making out with a fireman in the back of an ambulance. Their tryst is interrupted by a phone call from her mother, who reminds Hero that today is her father's birthday. Hero retorts, half in jest, "Well, if the professor wanted kids who loved him, he shouldn't have given us such stupid names." As Hero and her boyfriend are seen exiting the ambulance, another female EMT remarks, "What ... a ... whorebag. Has 'Zero' effed every firefighter from last year's calendar now?" (*Unmanned*, 28) These few panels establish Hero as someone who craves male attention and companionship to compensate for a strained relationship with her father. Further indication of Hero's troubled past with the most prominent male figures in her early life, her father and her brother, can be seen in Issue Ten where Hero tells Yorick, "Dad always liked you best because you were 'the smart one'" (*Cycles*, 100). The moment of the plague's appearance creates a particular trauma for Hero, as she watches blood burst from her boyfriend's face and soon realizes that, despite her EMT training, she cannot save him (*Unmanned*, 31). All of these factors provide clues that help explain Hero's decision to join the Amazons and desperately seek the approval of Victoria, who, in her patriarchal role, functions as both mother and father to Hero. Considering these characters through a psychoanalytic lens allowed the class to recognize how art and language in graphic fiction can effectively present complex characters who demand careful interpretation.

The issue of character depth and complexity in graphic fiction has particular resonance when dealing with the representation of race, which has been a fraught subject since the earliest days of comic strips and books in America. A recent study of newspaper comic strips found that "minorities make up only 3 percent of all human cartoon characters, a percentage far below their real-life representation of about 25 percent of the U.S. population" (Glascock and Preston-Schreck 2004, 429). Scott McCloud attributes the lack of racial diversity within comic books to a lack of diversity amongst their writers and artists, and he points out that although Jewish creators have been "hardly underrepresented within the New York-based comic book industry, Jewish tradition was nevertheless completely invisible to comic book readers for many years" (*Reinventing Comics* 2000, 107–9). Countering this trend, two of *Y: The Last Man*'s major protagonists are ethnic minorities; Yorick's companions are an African-American government operative, 355, and an Asian-American geneticist, Dr. Alison Mann. The hero of the series is a straight, white, middle-class man, which replicates a dominant theme of many other comic series (and other popular media), but in the post-plague world of *Y: The Last Man*, Yorick has fallen from a position of social privilege to become a minority of one, the ultimate Other. Because of his status, Yorick is targeted by a group of soldiers from the Israeli military who believe that possessing the last man would help them preserve their ethnic, religious, and national identities. The series thus provides occasion to consider how critical race theory helps readers examine the ways in which ethnic, cultural, and national differences are represented in graphic fiction and function as important issues in the world outside of the text.

Because of the material limitations and artistic conventions of the medium, stereotyping has long been a feature of comics. Will Eisner remarks that stereotyping is "an accursed necessity — a tool of communication that is an inescapable ingredient in most cartoons" (1996, 11). A class might be asked to consider the validity of that statement and to examine the methods and effects of certain representational strategies in comics and other forms of media. I posed the question: By casting Yorick's companions as ethnic minorities, to what extent does *Y: The Last Man* propagate or challenge certain racial stereotypes? Some students felt that 355's role as bodyguard and Dr. Mann's work as a genetic engineer reinforce the stereotypes of the "tough black woman" and the "smart Asian." Other students noted that the long-form nature of the series allows these characters to be fleshed-out as multi-dimensional individuals who have complex personal narratives of their own. The series directly confronts the issue of stereotyping in an exchange between Yorick and Dr. Mann. Yorick tells Dr. Mann that he and 355 have had a number of difficult and violent run-ins with groups that are pursuing them, namely "kidnappers, Amazons, Republicans. Nothing someone like *you* will have any trouble handling." Dr. Mann responds with indignation, "Why? Because I'm Asian? You think that automatically makes me some kind of ... of martial arts master? Because I don't know the first thing about karate or kung fu." Yorick tells her, "I just mean that you looked pretty ripped, that's all," to which Dr. Mann sheepishly replies, "Oh. Thank you. I ... used to be into pilates." (*Cycles*, 11) Dr. Mann's assumption about Yorick's meaning speaks to the ways in which individuals must often work against cultural stereotypes in order to preserve and express their own identities, an issue to which many students can easily relate and connect to personal experience.

As Yorick and Dr. Mann's conversation continues, Dr. Mann comments on the difficulty of defining the terms by which individuals and groups are classified. Yorick asks, "But since you bring it up, what nationality are you?," a question that suggests that one's national identity relates to biological markers of racial difference. Dr. Mann clarifies, "My *nationality* is American. My *ethnicity* is Chinese and Japanese" (*Cycles*, 12). She points out that race, ethnicity, and nationality are distinct and separate aspects of identity that can refer to different markers of one's hereditary and social origins. The relationship between race, ethnicity, and nationality also plays a significant role in the series as a group of women from the Israeli military pursue Yorick, believing that securing the only male on earth will empower their own cause. We are first introduced to their leader, a colonel who goes by the name "Alter," before the plague when she is patrolling a street in the West Bank (*Unmanned*, 14–16), a place where issues of race, ethnicity, and national identity have been particularly fraught. Keenly aware of the political and material implications of identifying individuals and groups according to particular conceptions of classification, Alter continues to fiercely defend Israeli interests in the post-plague world. Representing a diverse group of characters who continue to feel the weight of history in this alternate vision of the future, *Y: The Last Man* invites its readers to examine both the characters' world and their own from different perspectives that have been shaped by complex notions of identity. A number of my students connected the series' foregrounding of these types of conflicts to the events and aftereffects of 9/11. This led to a discussion of racial profiling, which brought us back to the issue of how characterization and stereotyping function in both on the comics page and in the real world.

While political divisions continue to be drawn along ethnic and national lines in *Y: The Last Man*, the personal relationships and family dynamic formed by the diverse characters of Yorick, 355, and Dr. Mann serves as the central focus of the narrative. As we discussed above, the three protagonists' different backgrounds can produce moments of tension, but their racial identities do not inhibit their intimacy or overwhelm their shared goal of discovering the cause of the plague. Still, one might ask whether the fact that the series' primary hero is a white male should affect how we read its handling of race. Some students noted that 355 and Dr. Mann are, in some ways, relegated to supporting roles because their role is, essentially, to ensure the survival of Yorick. Others pointed out that 355 and Dr. Mann really possess most of the power in their trio and Yorick depends on them to keep him alive so they can find a way to reverse the effects of the plague. We might also ask how the text might be read differently if Yorick was not the "typical" American comic book hero but if the last man on Earth was, instead, represented as a member of a minority group.

In this essay, I have focused on three theoretical approaches that provide useful ways of interrogating the language and images of *Y: The Last Man*, but the text invites a host of other approaches that allow readers to create meaning. While this essay treated each theory in isolation, many of our class discussions revealed the intersections between these theories, as students often noted that psychoanalysis can help explain Victoria's particular brand of feminism or that feminism provides a particular perspective for thinking about how characters like 355 and Dr. Mann experience and express their racial identities. Because we had begun the semester reading *Hamlet*, the intertextual resonance of the name Yorick also became a topic of conversation and allowed us to see the comic book as a response to Shakespeare's play. As we put these two texts in conversation, the line between the celebrated Literature of high culture and the popular medium of graphic fiction not only blurred but disappeared completely. Similarly, we were able to see how literary theories both inform and are informed by the works to which they are applied, creating a dynamic relationship that generates important and exciting methods for thinking about the apocalyptic world of *Y: The Last Man* as well as the world outside of the text.

Notes

1. As Vaughn explains in the deluxe edition, "This 'gendercide' instantaneously exterminated 48 percent of the global population ... 495 of the Fortune 500 CEOs are now dead, as are 99 percent of the world's landowners. In the United States alone, more than 95 percent of all commercial pilots, truck drivers, and ship captains died... Internationally, 99 percent of all mechanics, electricians, and construction workers are now deceased ... though 51 percent of the planet's *agricultural* labor force is still alive" (2008, 39).

2. The fourth volume of the series, *Safeword*, involves an extensive exploration of Yorick's psychology, particularly with regards to his sexuality.

References

Eisner, Will. 1985. *Comics and Sequential Art*. Tamarac: Poorhouse Press.
_____. 1996. *Graphic Storytelling and Visual Narrative*. New York: W.W. Norton.
Glascock, Jack, and Catherine Preston-Schreck. October 2004. "Gender and Racial Stereotypes in Daily Newspaper Comics: A Time-Honored Tradition?" *Sex Roles* 51.7–8: 423–31.
McCloud, Scott. 1994. *Understanding Comics: The Invisible Art*. New York: HarperPerennial.
_____. 2000. *Reinventing Comics*. New York: HarperPerennial.

Mulvey, Laura. 1975. "Visual Pleasure and Narrative Cinema." *Screen* 16.3: 6–18.
Parker, Robert Dale. 2008. *How to Interpret Literature: Critical Theory for Literary and Cultural Studies.* Oxford: Oxford University Press.
Vaughn, Brian K., and Pia Guerra. 2003. *Y: The Last Man, Volume 1: Unmanned.* New York: Vertigo.
_____, and Pia Guerra. 2003. *Y: The Last Man, Volume 2: Cycles.* New York: Vertigo.
_____, and Pia Guerra. 2008. *Y: The Last Man, The Deluxe Edition, Volume 1.* New York: Vertigo.

Approaching Literary Features Through the Graphic Novel *Logicomix*

Marianna Missiou *and*
Yiannis Koukoulas

Introduction

In the educational arena, comics have crossed a route from absolute demonization to jubilant acceptance and actual creative uses. Today, comics are attracting the interest of the education community. More than ever, comics have been explored, analyzed, criticized, and consequently they have broaden their perspectives. Comics are not only about graphic art but also about literary art. Although there is some skepticism on whether or not comics are "true" literature, undoubtedly both literary and artistic characteristics of comics are in the core of this medium's essence (Groensteen 2006; Morgan 2003).

In this essay, we will deal with the Doxiadis et al. (2009) graphic novel *Logicomix*. The purpose is to use *Logicomix* in the classroom, as a case study through which to teach some of the important theoretical concepts in literary studies. We will focus on biography as literary genre, and metafiction and intertextuality as literary techniques.

While the definition and term of "graphic novel" are still evolving and controversial, some of its features are generally accepted (Baetens 2001; Gabillet 2007; Tabachnick 2009). *Logicomix* appears as one of the characteristic manifestations of the graphic novel, not only by its length (310 pages) and the quality of the illustration and binding, but also by its complex visual and written narration, the dynamic and fully delineated characters and the sophisticated settings. In this sense, graphic novels appear as one of the newest manifestations of literature and by its quality, *Logicomix* continues the innovative establishment of new routes pioneered by emblematic graphic novels, such as *Maus*, *Persepolis*, *Palestine* and *Blankets*.

Logicomix has witnessed a worldwide sensation and has been already translated to several languages since its release in 2008. In 2009, the book made the *New York Times review, Sunday Book Review*, Editor's Choice list, and it was number-one on the *New York Times Graphic Novel Best Seller List*. The book sold out on the day it was released in Greece, the Netherlands, the United States, and United Kingdom, and it got into the Top 10 on Amazon.com and Amazon.com.uk. The story is about the great philosopher and mathematician Bertrand Russell and his epic quest for the foundations of mathematics, in order to show what logic is and what the science of logic is. In a parallel narration, the authors of the book cooperate for the creation of the story we attend. Although the Logicomix's theme might appear too complex, the book can be read by a wide range of ages, from young adolescents to adults.

As far as literary pedagogy is concerned, various researchers have pointed out the benefits of studying comics and the graphic novel (Groensteen 1998; Versaci 2007;Tabachnick 2009) . With the radical and continuous changes in technology, the easy access to information, and the plethora of images, reading books is an activity less and less favored. However, based on the appeal to and attraction of young audience, comics can constitute what Groensteen calls the "last fortress against analphabetism" (1998, 15), and be used as a tool to enhance not only reading, but also reading literature. Tabachnick considers the graphic novel "a perfect fit with modern reading habits" (2007:4) that challenges students to re-examine how they interpret texts (2007, 3–5). Versaci (2007) discusses ways in which comic books expand the boundaries of literature. He stresses the complexity of comics as a format that can express ideas, create characters, address issues, and tell stories in ways unmatched by other forms. Furthermore, comics introduce a special polysemy that demands audience engagement qualities. McLuhan calls comics a "cold medium," for they offer little data but demand high audience participation to fill the gaps (1994, 164). As Scott McCloud has shown, comics panels "fracture both time and space," resulting to "unconnected moments" (1994, 67). The reader has then to "fill in the intervening moments" between the panels (1994, 94). Thus, the system of the panels in a comic book is open to various interpretations and allows more than one possible reading. The potential of different interpretations is particularly useful in the educational process. Today, it is argued that texts "resistant" to meaning can shape a literary reader (Tauveron 1999; Tauveron 2000). Far from being transparent, such texts demand the collaboration of the reader because by their semantic gaps, the meaning is double and/or ambiguous. Comics promote their narration by complex ways, and the reader has to construct the storyline filling in the gaps. He has to generate predictions, move back and forth between text and images, and draw inferences to build meaning. He has the opportunity to invest in the book in his own way according to his age and experience. Reader goes as deep into the several levels of the narration as his experiences and skills allow him. Thus, comics can be considered as "cross-over" literature (Becket 2009), for they transcend age boundaries.

In this context, we infer that *Logicomix*'s textual and visual nature offers a rich ground of application having to do with reflection and expansion upon important features of literature. We will suggest some ways of exploiting in the classroom the potential of *Logicomix* to illustrate and teach the literary notions of biography, metafiction and intertextuality. Those suggestions should be considered rather as an encouragement to teachers, as it is up to them to adjust and possibly expand the possibilities raised in this paper, according to the particularities, age and abilities of their students, as well as their specific teaching goals. Because comics by their nature are open to interpretation, *Logicomix* can potentially be addressed to a broaden readership. Therefore, within the scope of the present article, we would not limit the potentials of *Logicomix* to a specific educational audience.

Logicomix: *A Fictionalized Biography*

One of the main literary characteristics of *Logicomix* is the biographical and auto-biographical elements that the book contains (229 — Figure 1). As a form of narrative, biography

Figure 1. The author and the fictional characters share a common passion for mathematics.

is not just a presentation of facts, but a ground for critical controversy around the division between fact and fiction (Lee 2009). Relative to its closeness to the truth, biography includes biographical fiction, fictionalized biography, authentic biography, and autobiography (Russell 2004). Because it is based on real facts, *Logicomix* can be classified as biography, a literary genre that, at least in the Western world, is witnessing its period of prosperity (Hamilton 2008). Hamilton stresses today's vivid popularity of the depiction of real lives in every contemporary medium (2008, 1). In addition, some of the most noteworthy graphic novels and comic book of recent years have been entirely autobiographical. Chaney (2011) investigates the distinctive way that comics present and shape autobiographical narratives and discourses and Chute shows how the visual and verbal form of comics favors the representation of memories, by their images fragmentations and the pauses or gaps of the narration (2010, 2–4).

In *Logicomix*, as in fictionalized biographies, the authors dramatize some of the facts and imagine scenes and dialogues. This is because the story covers a long period of time and is animated by an important number of characters. Its adaptation to a unified narration requires subtraction, abstraction, and synthesis, and, thus, a large dose of fantasy. As *Logicomix* is based on reality while at the same time remaining intensively fictional, it is interesting to analyze with our students the nebulous line between truth and falsehood in biographies. According to Lee, the biographer has the responsibility to tell the truth about what actually happened in the life of real people, but this rule is continually broken (2009, 6). Thus, students can examine the many ways of distorting the facts in *Logicomix*. Considering that the creative team members of *Logicomix* are the biographers of Russell's life, then students can explore the way they dramatize their visual and textual narratives with descriptions or emotions, colored scene-setting, or strategies of suspense. Students can also detect fictional methods as imaginary episodes and hypothetical conversations. For example, it is interesting to see how dates and events have been fluctuated to let Russell exchange information and ideas with contemporaneous figures he never met, but whose ideas influenced his theories. For example, Russell has not actually attended David Hilbert's speech on the problems of mathematics at the 1900 International Congress in Paris (150). In the supplemental pages at the end of the book, the authors themselves make clear that the biography should not be read as history but as fiction. They even invite the readers to amuse themselves by trying to detect more of such inaccuracies.

Salmon (2007) wrote that today's storytelling is slightly compromised to exercise power. It is thus stimulating for students to search the meaning of storytelling. They can then be aware of the power of any text as consumers or as producers. Searching for and exchanging information on Russell's life, together with critical analysis of the way such information appears in *Logicomix*, gives the opportunity for a critical debate among the students. For example, students could discuss Russell's attitude to the anti-war movement during the First War. They can then look for information on this movement in other sources and compare the way Russell's ideas are presented in *Logicomix*. For older students, a possible activity could be to investigate and discuss the relationship of the important mathematicians shown in *Logicomix*, such as Wittgenstein, not only within their inter-personal relationship with Russell, but also within their social life and attitudes such as their tension to psychological diseases.

Lee argues that every biography is a form of autobiography (2009, 12). She states that "the driving energy for the book may come from loathing of fear, a need to understand some monstrous career, or a reversionary desire to set the record straight" (2009, 12). The choice of the subject has been made for a reason and there is likely to be some shared experience between the writer and the subject. Apostolos Doxiadis, the creator of *Logicomix*, has a lot of common elements with the story. For example, Doxiadis was drawn to mathematics. At age 15 he entered Columbia University in New York City to study mathematics. He thus has the experience and the understanding of that profession to write about the life of another mathematician. Searching for the similarity of the biographer's and his subject's life, students could be encouraged to explore the lives of their own heroes and discover what they may have in common with them. They could talk about themselves and their own experiences. For example, they could choose a notable person from the fields of sciences, arts, or letters and undertake the role of the biographer. In a discussion group, they could argue about their selection and the person's characteristics that they would like to highlight. On a second level, students would choose characteristics of their own personality and life, to write their auto-biography. Furthermore, they could proceed to a selection of characteristics of the external appearance of the notable person in question, and attempt to make a sketch of him, or even to reproduce their own auto-portrait.

Reading a biography, students can empathize with the real problems of notable people and can learn both problem-solving and how to overcome obstacles (Rovin-Murphy 2001). They can also go through a deeper understanding of life in general (Russell 2004). Logic and madness, pursuit of a dream, failure of realizing dreams, lonely childhood, privileges and borderline abuses, failed marriages, and prioritization of work over family are just some of the daily life instances found in *Logicomix* that can be discussed with and among students. For example, students could discuss Russells' struggle to find what logic is and the consequences in his private life and psyche. Then, they could write a list of advices they would give to Russell, in order for him to have a better life.

The open end of the graphic novel frustrates traditional reading expectations. Not accidentally, Russell's narration begins as an attempt to help participants in a demonstration of isolationism to take the correct and logical decision (31). At the end of the book while recounting the Holocaust (293 — Figure 2), Russell does not act on the participants' behalf, but he says that, having knowledge of the imperfect tools of logic, the responsibility of the decision lies within each of them separately (294–298). This outcome constitutes an opportunity to set an ethical dilemma and to establish a debate among students in order for them to understand life. They can analyze, for example, the consequences of Russell's exhortation and the associated benefits and harms. The book concludes with the creative team watching the last act of Aeschylus' *Oresteia*, where Athena has transferred the responsibility of judging whether Orestes is innocent or guilty to the citizens (307–312). Students can associate the actual conclusion of the story, as given by the creative team, with the end of Russell's narration. Obviously, they would relate the Furies, seeking blood and revenge, with the audience of Russell, seeking for the right answer. Athena asks the Furies to become part of the jury, while Russell exhorts his audience to see the failure of the foundation of logic. Because *Logicomix* resists interpretive closure, it invites the reader in more active interpretive roles. Students can then elaborate their own end, and, in this process, their abilities to imagination, to verbal or written expression, and fictional competence are developed.

Logicomix *and Metafiction*

According to Waugh, metafiction is a term given "to fictional writing which self-consciously and systematically draws attention to its status as an artefact in order to pose ques-

Figure 2. Recounting the Holocaust.

tions about the relationship between fiction and reality" (1980, 2). Or, simply, metafiction is "fiction about fiction" (Hutcheon 1980, 1). Metafiction is used in *Logicomix* and detected in both verbal and visual text. Images and words reveal either independently or synergistically how the fictional reality of the story is constructed.

Metafiction been particularly exploited by children's literature in picture books (Nikolajeva 1998;). The instructive potential of metafiction has been emphasized by many theorists (Hutcheon 1980; Mackey 1990; McCallum 1999; Hunt 1991; Pantaleo 2005). Metafiction can involve the reader in the production of textual meanings, it can implicitly teach literary and cultural codes and conventions, as well as specific interpretive strategies. As McCallum wrote, metafiction "empowers readers to read more competently: more explicit forms often seek to teach readers conventions and strategies with which to interpret metafiction as well as other more closed texts" (1999, 139). Young and old students have the potential to learn all the necessary literary and cultural codes and conventions to recognize metafictive devices (Hunt 1991; Pantaleo 2005). Metafictive devices can draw the attention of student-readers to how texts work and to how meaning is created. They can trace the strategies through which metafictions play with literary and cultural codes and conventions. Then they can use these techniques to make themselves producers of metafictive expression. By studying metafiction, they are "studying that which gives the novel its identity," and are involved in the creation of meaning (Waugh 1980, 5). Through students' textual engagements with metafiction, students can understand complexities in any narration. They can sharpen their metafictive awareness and detect similar devices in other contemporary productions, printed or digital (Pantaleo 2005).

Logicomix uses several metafictive techniques. From the very first pages, the reader is in front of an "overly obtrusive narrator who directly addresses readers and comments on his own narration" (McCallum 1999, 139). An assignment would be for students to detect all those self-referential instances. For example, the writer, Apostolos, in an in-actor role, is presented in front on the reader-viewer (11). Apostolos holds a draft of the graphic novel in the course of creation. He then yawns and immediately feels embarrassed for letting the reader catch him at this personal moment. He stares at the reader, apologizes, welcomes him, presents himself. He introduces the original concept of seeking the foundations of mathematics, and argues over the developing logic and madness theme and how to approach it (11–15). He even anticipates the reaction of the readership by stating that the book is not a typical comic book, and that the creators' friends either considered them as fools for writing it, or took them as serious people trying to write a "book for beginners" on logic (Doxiadis 2009, 12). He then invites the readers to meet computer scientist Christos Papadimitriou, from whom he asked assistance with the book. When Apostolos tells Christos the story he would like to write, the readers get to hear it too. He anticipates the reaction of Christos and, staring at the reader in a whispering posture, he says that he will not tell Chistos that the "transmission" is "live," so that Christos would look more "natural" (14). Also, the presence of Apostolos' dog and an owl on the olive trees in the historic centre of Athens (17 — Figure 3), is another sign addressed to the reader. Those sympathetic creatures, presented to sleep and snore during the creative team's endless discussions on the construction of the story, draw attention to *Logicomix* status by implicitly posing to the reader the question of whether or not the book is boring.

As Waugh wrote, "the lowest common denominator of metafiction is simultaneously to create a fiction and to make a statement about the creation of that fiction. The two processes are held together in a formal tension which breaks down the distinctions between

Figure 3. A metafictive device: the presence of the owl enhances the reader's attention.

creation and *criticism* and merges them into the concepts of *interpretation* and *deconstruction"* (1984, 6). In this sense, the dialogues of *Logicomix*'s creative team about how to develop the story make the creation of the graphic novel as the crafted object rather than an attempt to reproduce Russell's reality. Students could analyze the novel for the presence of such statements. For example, the creative team's debate on how to move forward with the story (97–100) consist an instance of how the authors make the fictionalized biography conscious of its own proceedings and make it its own subject. Furthermore, strategies which draw attention to the physicality of texts are interspersed within the graphic novel, and students are invited to detect them. For example, panels like pins (26–27) that hold white and black cases of the graphic novel under construction and a deliberately mixing of literary and extra-literary genres such as various intra-texts (newspapers of the time of Russell, letters of an exchanging correspondence, protestors' placards, pages from books and scripts). Students could be asked to distinguish what elements belong to the story under construction and what elements concern the story itself. They could then imagine and suggest other graphic ways to be inserted as metafictive elements.

Multiple narrations are another technique of metafiction present in *Logicomix*. Different narrative and pictorial techniques, often visually mixed, are utilized to tell the story of the in-story authors, who tell a story about Russell. In turn, Russel tells the story of his life. In discussion groups, student can attempt to detect and discuss the presence of the interconnected narrative strands and the way they differentiate through the graphic novel's specific codes and conventions. In order for them to realize how a story works and how a text is structured, they can make categories of the techniques used, such as the use of colors and frames, to represent the various narrative strands. For example, grey scale colors are used in Logicomix to refer to the past and contrast the vivid colors of the present (15–20— Figure 4). Often the two levels are juxtaposed lying one over the other, but in any case the narrative strands are perceived by the colors' differentiation. Students could also produce inferences on why the panels are designed without any framing and the reasons that this technique is used by the authors.

As Kress and Van Leeuwen (2002) wrote, ideational function of the color denotes places and things. Color, at its textual function (Kress and Van Leeuwen 2002), creates unity and coherence into the various levels of the graphic novel. Color coordination also promotes textual cohesion. The same degree of brightness and/or saturation is used in the various colors of a page or a larger section of a text. For example, when Russell gives his lecture, dark colors such as olive-green and brown predominate (31–34). Therefore, as colors are used to make the different parts of the story more distinct, by reading the graphic novel, students are not only introduced into semiotic practices important for the age of multimodality, such as visual literacy, but also into literary techniques such as metafictive devices. A suggestion for an educational activity would be for the students to associate colors, brightness, and saturation to the levels of the narration and discuss the reasons for which the authors have opted for the selection of those specific techniques. On a second level, students could propose their own colors, applying their choices on white and black photocopied pages of *Logicomix*. They could then compare their choices among them and discuss the effectiveness of their propositions.

The various narratives are also linked by the use of repeated images, story elements, and different frames, which imply that they might constitute aspects of the same story. An activity could be for students to detect those elements and construct the logical, temporal, and causal relations between the strands. For example, when Apostolos explains the historical

Figure 4. Greyscale contrasts vivid colors to mark past and present time.

context of the story to Christos, his words are limited within speech bubbles (14). Then the words move into caption boxes, marking the switch from the present of the creative team to the historical past of Russell (15). Furthermore, framing as another convention through which narration is unfolded, has been pointed out by theoretical works in comics (Groensteen 1999). Frames in comics can speak and convey information by their form, width, and style. Frames also function as a node for other strands of narration. In *Logicomix*, for example, the differentiation of narrative strands and time period are marked through the use of different shapes in frames.

Although framing itself is not a metafictive device, it can enhance critical thinking, just as metafiction. A reading from "frame to frame" (Legrady 2000, 85) can liberate the page as a closed structure in itself. The page becomes an open space in which "frames can be potentially interconnected from all angles, resulting in greater narrative complexity" (Legrady 2000, 85). In addition, framing in art, is a concept that has preoccupied in a philosophical level intellectuals like Jacques Derrida. He writes of how, when we look at a painting, we take the frame to be part of the wall, yet when we look at the wall the frame is taken to be part of the painting (Cited in Marriner 2002, 351). The "contrast and opposition between what is intrinsic and what is extrinsic to the work" (Marriner 2002, 352) could constitute a field to be exploited in the educational process. Sometimes repeated frames, juxtaposed one over the other, are used to give a dramatic tone to the narration. This is the case of the forbiddances, rules and limitations imposed by Russell's grand-mother upon the arrival of young Russell to her castle. Every rule is shown in a single frame and all the rules together are synthesized to form a bigger frame, that of the page (35 — Figure 5). But even the page is a frame by itself. We can thus analyze with our students what forms the frame, what are the boundaries of the frames, how they divide the work, what is internal and what is external of it. Possible questions to raise could be about the panels placed on the ground plan of Russell's residence, the figures drawn as black one-colored shapes, the unequal sizes of the panels and their apparent disorder. Borrowed from film criticism, the technique of shooting could also be used to talk about framing and meaning. We could use for example a piece of paper that will unmask only a small part of the subject page. Each time, a bigger part of the synthesis will be revealed. The students can then describe the effects caused by the differentiation in focusing.

Intertextuality in Logicomix

Logicomix exhibits one of the prominent features of postmodernism, as we are confronted with the literary notion of intertextuality and its visual, iconic equivalent of intericonicity. Although the term "intertextuality" is complex (Kristeva 1969; Barthes 1970; Bakhtin 1973; Culler 1981) today, it is often used simply to refer to literary allusions and to direct quotations from literary and non-literary texts. In general, the comics' medium is propitious to the emergence of intertextual or intericonic elements that contribute to the economy of the narration, evoking the reader's prior experience. The intertextual dimension of a text can "cause readers to recognise how they are being (have been) textually constructed in and by this intertextual playground" (Wilkie 2002, 131). The benefits of intertextuality in education have already been pointed out (Cairney 1992; Dresang 1999; Pantaleo 2006). Teaching intertextuality is about stressing the reading experience of the student-reader on the images of texts already encountered and on their role in the construction of meaning.

Figure 5. Framing as metafiction: looking for the boundaries of the frame/frames.

Students' referencing, be it visual or textual, to the wider world of cultural expression and the created complex layering of meaning, can consist the base for the analysis and study of all contemporary productions. In *Logicomix*, intertextual and intericonic elements are used to promote narration. By their operational function, not only they invite students to recognize them, but challenge them to weave their presence with their own interpretation and construction of meaning.

The book offers the opportunity to familiarize students with emblematic works of art. Discussions can be held about famous paintings and sculptures of the past as well as literary works, and about how they are used by new forms of art, such as the graphic novel, in a new context and with a new meaning. Furthermore, this new use not only preserves the value of the original work, but, in addition, it brings it forth to the scene and it develops it for new purposes. The students can place themselves in a detective role, trying to recognize sources and influences, in order to approach the complex relations among genres and/or among art, and discover the meaning absorbed and transformed in the network of the intertextual space. It is particularly noteworthy that in the very first frame of the first page of the first chapter of *Logicomix*, immediately after the Introduction, we see the *Thinker* (1902) of Auguste Rodin (31). The students can develop their awareness of the different discourses that converge in a text, written or visual, and their interdependence by searching the history and meaning of this sculpture and trying to associate it with the aspect of the *Logicomix*'s story, which has to do with human thinking and understanding. This globally recognizable image, can lead students and teachers in search of further information on this work of art and the new meaning earned by this new contextualization.

Such associations can be done in several pages of *Logicomix*. When young Bertrand Russell suffers from nightmares after the death of his grandfather in 1879, just before the emergence of expressionism in art, he is shown between frightening creatures drawn in Baroque style (50— Figure 6), while his face and body posture imitates the frenzied, screaming, and ossified expressionist figure of *Scream* (1893) of Edvard Munch (50). A few pages later, Bertrand has come of age and has settled important life decisions. The didacticism and the terror of the baroque, as well as the expressionistic exteriorization of a troubled inner world, are replaced with a romantic mood (54). Lyrics of Shelley (83–85) are cited and in parallel a full-paged panel derives from the romanticism of Caspar David Friedrich showing *Wanderer above the Sea of Fog* (1818) (85 — Figure 7). When Russell visits with Alfred North Whitehead, the retrospective exhibition of the Pre-Raphaelites, the mythological *Danaïdes* (1903) of John William Waterhouse serve as pretext for Russell to make a decision (187–188 — Figure 8). The analogy is clear. The *Danaïdes* were condemned by the gods to endlessly throw water in a leaking jar. Russell has continually postponed the publication of *Principia Mathematica* (the three-volume work on the foundation of mathematics written by Russell and Alfred North Whitehead). Munch's *Scream* is back when Russell is going through a crisis of pessimism, but this time his emotional situation is clearly designed and based on Munch's model; the work is now completed by the Norwegian artist and Russell can dream by the terms and the pictorial representation of Munch (234 — Figure 9). *The Ready Mades* of Marcel Duchamp, such as *The Fountain* (1917) (266 — Figure 10) and *Black Square* (1915) (267) of Kazimir Malevich, together with the nonsense of the Dadaist theatre (267), are used as pretext for Russell to realize that the values of the old world and the positivistic illusion can no longer express the man of the 1920–1940 war. For all these works, we can exhort the students to look for information in history or art books, about creations and their creators, the era that they have been created and their meaning. Furthermore, stu-

Figure 6. Edward Münch's *Scream*, in an incomplete form, is associated to young Russell's troubled inner world.

"EARTH, OCEAN, AIR,
BELOVED BROTHERHOOD!
MOTHER OF THIS UNFATHOMABLE WORLD!
FAVOUR MY SOLEMN SONG, FOR I HAVE
LOVED THEE EVER AND THEE ONLY!!!"

I was strong enough to cry out.

At last, I could turn my back on my dark legacy.

Figure 8. John William Waterhouse's *Danaïdes* reflects Russel's hesitation in publishing his *Principia Mathematica*.

dents can attempt to analyze and discuss the reasons why the authors of Logicomix have opted for such selection of pieces of art and the way these works are used in the graphic novel to promote narration. They could then detect the reasons why the specific work is chosen by the Logicomix authors, its significance originally and the significance it takes in *Logicomix*.

Besides artwork, *Logicomix* offers plenty of references to theatrical and literary works of the past. The *Divine Comedy* of Dante is drawn based on the illustrations of Gustave Dore (1861) and is converted in the eyes and mind of the young Russell to the forbidden knowledge that must be conquered somehow (44–45 — Figure 11). This image is in contrast with another image, showing Russell's grand-mother forcing his intellectually challenged uncle to read the Bible (52). Furthermore, books like Ivan Turgenev's *Fathers and Son* (81— Figure 12), Tolstoy's *Anna Karennina* (81), and Dostoyevsky's *War and Peace* (81), confirm and validate Russell's decision for quest, as these books helped him overcome the fear from his grandmother's moral commands. Lewis Carroll's *Alice in Wonderland* (101), Sterne's *Tristram Shandy* (166), Vonnegut's *Breakfast of Champions* (166), Calvino's *If on A Winter's Night a Traveler* (166), the Stevenson's *Dr. Jekyll and Mr. Hyde* film adaptation (231), become integral parts of the plot that unfolds over them as well. We are aware that those works demand a skilled reader/viewer. However, we would propose their reading or watching selectively, according to the age and skills of the students. If this is not possible, then a simple reference on the above mentioned oeuvres, even if it just to mention the title and give a summary of the story, it might consist into a first contact with the leviathan of the classical literary and artistic production. And maybe this first initiation, through *Logicomix*, would awake in the students the curiosity to read those books or to watch the performance later, in some other moment of their lives.

Opposite: Figure 7. Lyrics of Shelley and Caspar Friedrich's "Wander Above the Sea of Fog" imply Russell's coming-to-age romantic mood.

Figure 9. Edward Münch's *Scream*, in its complete form, illustrates adult Russel's emotional state.

Figure 10. Marcel Duchamp's *Fountain* makes Russell realize the fading of the old world's values and positivistic illusions.

Figure 11. Gustave Doré's *Divine Comedy* incites young Russell's quest for knowledge.

Figure 12. Ivan Turgenev's *Fathers and Son* implies the validation of Russell's decision for the quest for knowledge.

By Way of Conclusion

In this article, we tried to show how a graphic novel can be seen not only as an art form but also as a subject of literary analysis in the classroom. Although it might seem that the graphic novel is used as an instrument to promote a specific educational agenda which is an acceptable and common practice among teachers who deal with comics essentially, it carries its own weight as an autonomous work and can be defended as a worthy subject of study. By reading graphic novels and comics with a literary perspective, students can simultaneously approach a multimodal contemporary production and literature enjoyment. They thus come closer to the duality of the medium: art and literature.

References

Anstey, Michele, and Geoff Bull. 2006. *Teaching and Learning Multiliteracies*. Newark, DE: International Reading Association.
Baetens, Jan. 2001. *The Graphic Novel*. Louvain, Belgium: Leuven University Press.
Bakhtin, Mikhail. 1973. *Problems of Dostoevsky's Poetics*. Ann Arbor, MI: Ardis.
Barthes, Roland. 1975. *S/Z*. London: Cape.
Beckett, Sandra. 2009. *Crossover Fiction: Global and Historical Perspectives*. New York: Routledge.
Cairney, Trevor. 1992. "Intertextuality: Inferious Echoes from the Past." *The Reading Teacher* 43.7: 502–507.

Culler, Jonathan. 1981. *The Pursuit of Signs: Semiotics, Literature, Deconstruction*. London: Routledge.
_____. 2009. *Literary Theory: A Brief Insight*. New York: Sterling.
Chaney, Michael. 2011. *Graphic Subjects: Critical Essays on Autobiography and Graphic Novels*. Wisconsin: University of Wisconsin Press.
Chute, Hillary. 2010. *Graphic Women: Life Narrative and Contemporary Comics*. New York: Columbia University Press.
Doxiadis, Apostolos, Christos H. Papadimitriou, Alecos Papadatos, et al. 2009. *Logicomix*. New York: Bloomsbury.
Dresang, Eliza. 1999. *Radical Change: Books for Youth in a Digital Age*. New York: H.W. Wilson.
Eisner, Will. 2005. *Comics and Sequential Art*. Tamarac, FL: Poorhouse Press.
Gabilliet, Jean-Paul. 2007. "Aux sources du graphic novel." *Le Collectionneur de Bandes Dessinées* 111: 39–37.
Groensteen, Thierry. 1998. *La bande dessinée en France*. Paris-Angoulême: Ministère des Affaires Etrangères, ADPF/CNBDI.
_____. 1999. *Système de la bande dessinée*. Paris: PUF.
_____. 2006. *Un objet culturel non identifié*. Editions de l'An 2: Paris.
Hamilton, Nigel. 2008. *How to Do Biography, a Primer*. Cambridge, MA: Harvard University Press.
Hunt, Peter. 1991. *Criticism, Theory and Children's Literature*. Oxford: Blackwell.
Hutcheon, Linda. 1980. *Narcissistic Narrative: The Metafictional Paradox*. New York: Methuen.
Kress, Gunter, and Theo Van Leeuwen. October 2002. "Colour as a Semiotic Mode: Notes for a Grammar of Colour." *Visual Communication* 1.3: 343–368.
Kristeva, Julia. 1969. *Semiotiké*. Paris: Editions du Seuil.
Lee, Hermione. 2009. *Biography, a Very Short Introduction*. Oxford: Oxford University Press.
Legrady, George. 2000. "Modular Structure and Image/Text Sequences: Comics and Interactive Media." In Anne Magnussen, and Hans-Christian Christiansen, eds., *Comics & Culture: Analytical and Theoretical Approaches to Comics*. Copenhagen: Museum Tusculanum Press.
Marriner, Robin. 2002. "Derrida and the Parergon." In Paul Smith, and Carolyn Wilde, eds., *A Companion to Art Theory*. Oxford: Blackwell.
McCallum, Robyn. 2002. "Very Advanced Texts: Metafictions and Experimental Work." In Peter Hunt, ed., *Understanding Children's Literature*. New York: Routledge.
McCloud, Scott. 1994. *Understanding Comics*. New York: Harper Perennial.
McLuhan, Marshall. 1994. *Understanding Media, the Extensions of Man*. London: Routledge.
Morgan, Harry. 2003. *Principes des Littératures Dessinées*. Paris: Editions de L'An 2.
Nikolajeva, Maria, Scott, Carol. 2001. *How Picturebooks Work*. New York: Garland.
Pantaleo, Sylvia. Feb 2005. "Young Children Engage with the Metafictive in Picture Books." *Australian Journal of Language and Literacy* 28.1: 19–37.
Pantaleo, Sylvia. 2006. "Readers and Writers as Intertexts: Exploring the Intertextualities in Student Writing." *Australian Journal of Language and Literacy* 29.2: 163–181.
Rovin-Murphy, Deborah. 2001. *30 Biography Book Reports: Easy and Engaging Hands-On Literature Response*. New York: Scholastics.
Russell, David. 2004. *Literature for Children: A Short Introduction*. Boston: Pearson/Allyn & Bacon.
Ryan, Marie-Laure. 2004. "Introduction." In Marie-Laure Ryan, ed., *Narrative Across Media. The Languages of Storytelling*. Lincoln: University of Nebraska Press.
Salmon, Christian. 2007. *Storytelling. La machine à fabriquer des histoires et à formater les esprits*. Paris: La Découverte.
Tabachnick, Stephen, ed. 2009. *Teaching the Graphic Novel*. New York: The Modern Language Associations of America.
Tauveron, Catherine. 1999. "Comprendre et interpreter le litteraire à l'ecole primaire: du texte reticent au texte proliferant." *Repères* 19: 9–38.
_____. 2001. "Relations conjugales dans le couple infernal comprehension/interpretation : un autre drame tres Parisien." In Catherine Tauveron, dir., *Comprendre et interpreter le litteraire à l'ecole et au-delà*. Paris: INRP.
Versaci, Rocco. 2007. *This Book Contains Graphic Language: Comics as Literature*. New York: Continuum.
Waugh, Patricia. 1980. *Metafiction: The Theory and Practice of Self-Conscious Fiction*. New York: Routledge.
Wilkie, Chistine. 2002. "Relating Texts: Intertextuality." In Peter Hunt, ed., *Understanding Children's Literature*. New York: Routledge.

Manga, the Atomic Bomb and the Challenges of Teaching Historical Atrocity
Keiji Nakazawa's Barefoot Gen

Jeremy R. Ricketts

Hadashi no Gen, or *Barefoot Gen,* by Keiji Nakazawa, is a work of manga that explores the World War II atomic bombing of Hiroshima and its aftermath. Manga is a traditional Japanese art form that melds the fundamentals of American comics with a traditional Japanese style of narrative. *Barefoot Gen* is a work of *hibakusha* (survivor of the bomb) literature, but its aesthetic expression in the form of manga lends it a rhetorical power not available to more conventional forms of atomic bomb literature such as a written testimonials or documentary accounts. The portrayal of the events of August 6, 1945, through manga adds another layer to the complex aesthetic of bearing witness and makes *Barefoot Gen* useful in multiple classroom situations. Manga allows what Kyo Maclear (1990) calls a "prolonged gaze" (12), a gaze that lingers long after the media's cameras go home, and a gaze well-suited to the classroom experience. *Barefoot Gen* is at once visual testimonial and documentary, a work both political and humanistic. The representation of the bomb through manga also leads to unique challenges. Well-known *hibakusha* writers like Yoko Ota and Tamiki Hara struggled to put their experience into words. In the midst of such unprecedented destruction and horror, these writers faced the difficulty of articulating atrocity and adequately bearing witness within the abruptly narrowed confines of human language. Keiji Nakazawa's challenge as a writer and artist is thus doubly daunting. He must not only put words into the mouths of his characters who are in what he describes in his introductory note as an "atomic hell," but he must also find ways to draw the unprecedented visual events he witnessed in the hours, days, and months after Hiroshima.

    History teachers in particular face the related pedagogical problem of how to illustrate the depth of devastation in the aftermath of the bomb. This essay shows that by using manga as his aesthetic vehicle for representing the bomb and its effects, and by employing various binaries such as documentary and testimony, Nakazawa overcomes many hurdles faced by other *hibakusha* authors and delivers a powerful work that bears witness to the atrocity of Hiroshima. His rhetorical and artistic choices can be very effective for classroom usage. I have used this text in interdisciplinary humanities courses, advanced expository writing courses, as well as a class that dealt with literature and autobiography, and my students have always responded with enthusiasm. *Barefoot Gen* offers a strong range of interdisciplinary opportunities to middle school, high school, and university instructors alike. To fully understand the dynamics playing out in *Barefoot Gen*, some background information on Nakazawa's life and *Barefoot Gen* itself is in order.

On August 6, 1945, at 8:15 A.M., six-year-old Keiji Nakazawa was just outside of his school in Hiroshima, Japan, when his life, like so many others, was forever changed by an atomic blast. As he tells the reader in his introductory note to *Barefoot Gen*, despite being just one kilometer from ground zero, Nakazawa was largely unhurt thanks to his proximity to a concrete wall. After the blast, he quickly made his way through the ruined city in search of his family. He was reunited with his mother only to discover that his only sister had been instantly killed by debris, and his younger brother and father had been trapped under their house and killed in the fire that engulfed much of Hiroshima in the hours after the bomb. Nakazawa's mother had been spared because she was outside hanging laundry, and one older brother was in the countryside while another was out of the country in the navy (fateful choices such as these haunt much of *Barefoot Gen*). Nakazawa's mother had been in the process of essentially committing suicide, refusing to leave her husband and two children to the flames when a Korean neighbor dragged her away. Amazingly, just a few hours later she gave birth on the side of the road. Nakazawa had a new sister in the midst of atrocity, a new life to cling to in the midst of all the death. Tragically, however, the sister died four months later. Nakazawa lost much of his family and much of his hair due to radiation sickness, but he survived the bomb and its aftereffects. He has the ethos of a witness and survivor, and students often respond with interest to his lived story of the bomb.

Like so many other artistically inclined *hibakusha*, Nakazawa channeled his talents into trying to find a way to represent the horror of the atomic bomb. He chose manga as his vehicle of expression. In 1966, when his mother died of radiation-related causes, he turned to the horrors of nuclear war and the challenges of representing history. After her cremation, he went to collect his mother's bones, but there were none to collect due to the corrosive effects of radioactive cesium. He relived the shock and horror of August 6, and he dedicated his life to documentary and testimony as well as to ensuring that no one would ever forget the atomic bombing of Hiroshima.

The saga of *Barefoot Gen* spans some ten volumes and 2,000 pages, and thus poses somewhat of a logistical challenge to instructors. What to include? What to leave out? In my own courses, I have found that the first four volumes form a coherent narrative arc that can be covered in the course of a unit or even an entire semester depending on the precise focus of the class. The first four volumes cover from April 1945 to two years after the bombing of Hiroshima. Volume one details Gen's wartime life from April until August, and the bomb's destruction ends the work. Volume two deals solely with the day of and the day after the bomb. Volume three covers the weeks after the bomb, while volume four takes the reader through several vignettes lasting almost two years, ending the work two years to the day after the atomic bomb exploded over Hiroshima. Using these volumes in a class thus imparts the immediate history of the bomb itself while also developing some of the social and cultural history experienced by the Japanese as a result of the aftereffects of the bomb.

Nakazawa's most successful aesthetic choice that always makes for compelling class discussion is the mixture of a documentary style deeply concerned with historical facts with an alternately virulent and sublime antiwar testimonial from someone who was there to bear witness to the bombing. In the words of Art Spiegelman, who wrote the introduction to the English translation of this book as well as the seminal graphic book rendition of the twentieth century's other great atrocity, the Holocaust, "[*Barefoot Gen*] stands at the intersection of personal and world history." The book's point of view constantly shifts from the wide-eyed wonderment of Gen to an all-knowing narrator's didactic voice warning of unfathomable technological advances. By interspersing this documentary voice into scenes of domestic tranquility, Nakazawa gives the narrative a frantic urgency. The omniscient narrator collapses time and space and moves from the small-town troubles and joys of Hiroshima to the Trinity test in the New Mexican desert in the space of one panel, a visceral movement within history largely unavailable to other texts. Yet the first half of volume one has very little to do with the bomb. The story remains largely within Gen's perspective, which is telling, as in Japanese "Gen" means "source" (as well as "elemental," which Nakazawa admits in his introductory note was an ironic play on words).

The book opens with a metaphor about wheat that echoes Emperor Hirohito's postwar poem about a pine tree bent with snow: "Wheat pushes its shoots up through the winter frost, only to be stepped on again and again. The trampled wheat sends strong roots into the earth, endures frost, wind and snow, grows straight and tall ... and one day bears fruit" (Nakazawa 1, 1). This opening suggests a nationalist work, but Nakazawa's relationship with Japan has been compromised by what he sees as the Japanese military's role in bringing about the war. The Americans are not exonerated either. In Nakazawa's perspective, the Japanese and American military (as well as American scientists) share equal blame for the atomic bombing of Hiroshima. Nakazawa also pays heed to the atrocities Koreans in Hiroshima faced after being brought into Japan as slave labor. These nuances make his work more comprehensive than many historical texts.

Nakazawa's antiwar stance is embodied and personified in Gen's father, Nakaoka Daikichi. Nakaoka is vociferously antiwar and makes his views known throughout the neighborhood, eventually landing in jail for antiwar comments. Members of the military and Nakaoka's jailers are depicted as soulless automatons; drawn without pupils, they are vapid examples of groupthink and ready to die for a war which Nakaoka sees as already lost. These scenes open up a space for classroom dialogue about the morality of war in general and can be connected to modern and ancient struggles alike.

The family's life and by extension the narrative itself is fractured when eldest son Koji enlists in the Navy. As Nakaoka curses Japan for starting the war, the narrative sharply breaks from a moving testimonial of individual sacrifice to documentary as the reader is transported into the sky where a squadron of B-29s drop bombs and set a city on fire. Then the reader's eyes move directly from the flames of Japan to a lab in Los Alamos. The narrator states the simple facts of the Manhattan Project's progress, and then shows a map of Japan with the atomic bomb hovering ominously above the four target cities of Kyoto, Niigata, Kokura, and Hiroshima. The next panel shows Gen and his younger brother Shinji standing outside, with Shinji wondering when the war will be over (Nakazawa 1, 104–105). The aesthetic effect of this sequence of panels is devastating and carries a power unavailable to conventional histories. Maclear notes that expressive culture facilitates "new sites of possibility by providing opportunities to see and hear what has become familiar differently" (86). Nakazawa repeatedly shows himself a master of visual literature and students' exposure to his unique text opens oft-unexplored avenues of critical engagement.

The shift from testimonial to documentary voice is jarring and often sparks classroom discussions on historical methodology and questions about angles of vision. The reader has been drawn into the lives of the Nakaoka family and literally sees their fate but is powerless to intervene. After the panel with Gen and Shinji, the narrator again interrupts and documents the advance of the American army up the islands of the Pacific. The narrative moves into May 1945 as corpses pile up and Japanese villagers commit suicide en masse in the face of the American advance (Nakazawa 1, 106–109). Yet these horrible scenes are rendered ironic in the face of what the reader knows is to come: a weapon that has the ability to completely annihilate human bodies.

Nakazawa marks narrative breaks with a drawing of the sun. As August 6 looms ever nearer, the sun grows increasingly brighter and more ominous. The sun, which once would have stood in for the rising sun depicted on the Japanese flag, now becomes a metonym for the bomb and stands in silent and ominous contrast to the spoken words elsewhere on the pages. In other panels, a ticking clock repeatedly chimes with increasing urgency as the story moves into July 1945. It is almost as if the adult Nakazawa is trying to reach through history and break through the wall of the narrative to save his younger self and his family. But only Nakaoka has any foreboding of what is to come. He notices that Hiroshima has been largely spared by bombing and senses something sinister in the works. Yet even he cannot grasp the full magnitude of the atomic bomb. In another gesture of irony, Gen sees that American POWs have painted a large "P" on the roof of their prison to keep American bombers at bay. Gen decides to paint a "P" on his roof, little knowing that nothing can stop the approaching bomb (Nakazawa 1, 164–165; 178). Small but crucial details such as these tend to electrify classroom discussion by bringing the past into the present and helping students make meaning out of atrocity. These details also underscore how unprecedented the scale of destruction in the atomic age would be.

As the narrative continues, Gen and his family encounter hardship due to Nakaoka's antiwar activity, but everything is finally settled on July 17 and the family is at peace. As they sing songs and laugh, the narrator interrupts to tell the reader that it is July 16 in America, and the world's first atomic test is about to commence. In rapid documentary succession, the test bomb is detonated, the Potsdam Declaration is issued, and Japan rejects the Allies' demands (Nakazawa 1, 202–206). Again, the narrator collapses time and space to create a sense of inevitability as the Americans prepare to drop the bomb. The sun grows ever larger, the clock ticks ever louder, and on page 243 of the first volume, three panels depict a ticking clock, the sleeping Nakaoka family, and a huge Enola Gay flying across the night sky. Nakazawa moves seamlessly from personal to world history, a technique not as easily accessible in other forms of literature. Nakazawa thus fuses the literal truth of world history with the truth of his personal experience to create a moving work of *hibakusha* literature that is accessible to students, especially in an increasingly visual age.

On August 6, the family awakens to an air raid. The all-clear signal is sounded as the Enola Gay flies closer to the city. The omniscient narrator ruefully notes that if the all-clear signal had not been given, many more would have lived. The people of Hiroshima go about their business, and Gen notes the beauty of a lone B-29 flying overhead. The Americans flying the plane are never seen, but dialogue emanating from the B-29 talks of the attack as if the B-29 is speaking itself, as if humans have been taken entirely out of the equation. The narrative moves in rapid succession from testimonial to documentary and back, until Gen sees something fall from the B-29. The bomb has been dropped and in the next panel it explodes. Nakazawa draws the explosion with stark, dark lines (Nakazawa 1, 246–252). The omniscient narrator makes futile attempts at simile, describing the flash of the bomb "like a million flashbulbs going off at once" (Nakazawa 1, 249), and the mushroom cloud "like an eruption from the pit of hell" (Nakazawa 1, 251). Despite these powerful words, the visual representation of the bomb and its effect on people are far more effective than the limits of simile in the face of the atomic age.

For example, on page 253 of volume one, Gen sees people whose flesh is completely burned off, drawn with their skin hanging in ribbons. Formerly ordered panels now stretch across the entire page in an attempt to show the damage done by the bomb. A horse on fire literally breaks through the panel (Nakazawa 1, 256), as if to suggest there is no logic or order left in an atomic world, echoing Robert Jay Lifton's claim that after Hiroshima, "there were no limits to destruction" (qtd. in Maclear 1999, 6).

The randomness of the bomb leaves Gen completely unhurt while a woman standing next to him is killed in the blast. Gen sees that the destruction stretches for miles and runs off to find his family. After encountering the dying and the dead, Gen finally reaches his house where the most moving moments of the series occur. This scene represents the simple but powerful voice of witness. And yet, ironically, this scene is also the voice of imagination. In reality, Nakazawa never reached his house. He found his mother only after his brother, sister, and father had perished. In reality, his sister died instantly and his father begged his mother not to leave them. In *Barefoot Gen*, Nakazawa cannot betray reality by saving his family members, but he can slightly alter the story to more effectively bear witness for the reader. That is why the series would work best in an interdisciplinary classroom: it is simultaneously manga, history, memoir, and fiction.

As Gen reaches the house, he sees that his father, brother, and sister are all trapped under beams but still alive. The scenes are painful as Gen's mother Kimie screams in futility, "I hate it! I hate this beam!" (Nakazawa 1, 263). Younger brother Shinji screams, "It hurts, Gen, it hurts...." (Nakazawa 1, 265). Nakaoka tells Kimie that she must leave them and save herself, Gen, and their unborn child. Gen finds Shinji's toy boat and places it into his brother's hands. The fire closes in yet Kimie remains. In another jarring narrative shift, the scene moves from the pain of Gen's individual family to a full-page panel showing the enflamed streets of Hiroshima. Horribly burned people scream for help, establishing a collective memory to go with Nakazawa's imagined personal memory. The next panel shifts back to Gen and his mother watching their family burn to death. The fire is about to consume them as well when a Korean neighbor intervenes and drags them to safety. They walk through panel after panel of chaos and horror until Kimie collapses and tells Gen she is in labor. In reality, Nakazawa did not arrive in time to see his sister born, so in what surely must be a gesture to Sadako Kurihara's famous poem "Bringing Forth New Life" (see Treat 1995, 162), Gen runs through the streets of Hiroshima calling for a midwife. No midwife is to be found, so Gen heeds Kurihara's advice to "Let us all be midwives!" and delivers the baby himself. Kimie tells the baby, "When you grow up, you must never, ever let this happen again!" (Nakazawa 1, 284). In the final panel of volume one, Kimie holds the baby up against the backdrop of ever-growing flames, and the baby cries, a visual cue for the dangers of letting history repeat itself.

Perhaps only an artist who was a child when the bomb exploded could render such scenes. Unlike author Yoko Ota, who was an adult on August 6, 1945, Nakazawa strives to simultaneously share awareness *and* experience with the reader. By interspersing documentary with testimony, the reader *and* the victims occupy a central place within the narrative. Nakazawa seems to believe that the experience belongs to the world that allowed the bomb to be made almost as much as it belongs to *hibakusha*. Of course, it belongs to those two disparate groups in very different ways. As Maclear notes, when spectators feel themselves thrust into testimonial art, they might feel an array of emotions ranging from empathy to guilt (22). Nakazawa does not overtly seek a *specific* response from modern readers; he only asks that they bear witness with him.

Nakazawa is hardly alone in his search for a relevant narrative structure, and choosing a classroom text to discuss the bomb or any historical atrocity should involve a careful process, as well. As John Whittier Treat (1995) notes, Ota also experimented with both documentary and testimony, though crucially, not within the same book. Treat argues that in her testimonial *City of Corpses* the reader is marginalized, while in her documentary *Human Rags*, the reader is empowered and thus open to critique *hibakusha* (209–219). Nakazawa solves this problem by weaving the two styles of documentary and testimony together, giving readers omniscient knowledge and then jarring them with emotional, individual, and empowered testimony. He makes the audience simultaneously complicit in the creation of the bomb and victim of that very same bomb. This type of historical critique makes *Barefoot Gen* ideal for classroom situations in that it fosters complex discussions and also makes for compelling reaction papers.

Yet Nakazawa does not let the actual bombing end the story, as the effects of the bomb lingered for years. As volume two opens, Nakazawa paints a stark and horrific landscape. He begins with a panel of the sun surrounded by black smoke from the fires raging in the city, recalling both the flash of the bomb and the rising sun of Japan's national flag, now on an inevitable wane. The next panel shows burned people, their skin hanging in shreds, begging for water. After the triumphant birth of Gen's sister, Nakazawa is clearly reminding the reader of the human cost of the bomb. Gen and his mother struggle for meaning, wondering about the nature of the bomb and cursing the Americans for dropping it. The reader is then removed from Gen's story and Hiroshima completely and transported to Nagasaki where another atomic bomb explodes, the mushroom cloud literally pushing its way outside the boundaries of the panel. The narrator solemnly intones, "As it has always been, it is the powerless, nameless, ordinary people who die in wars waged by a handful of men in power" (Nakazawa 2, 5). These words are placed above living bodies with their flesh hanging off in tatters.

Before the reader can adjust to this new horror, the narrative shifts back to Gen, who is having a dream about his dead family members. He awakens and refuses to believe that they are dead, holding on to an impossible hope. If there had been no intervening occurrence at this point, Gen might have descended into nihilism. However, unlike author Tamiki Hara in *Summer Flowers*, Gen (and by extension Nakazawa) is not rendered passive by the bomb. The tension between hope and despair is maintained to advance the horrific collective memory of the first hours after the bomb. My students have often noted that such techniques bring visceral immediacy to history.

Despite his despair, Gen's baby sister needs food, so he sets off to the countryside to seek sustenance. On the outskirts of the city he encounters for the first time what Joseph Masco (2006) calls a "nuclear uncanny;" that is, a Freudian dread of the unseen effects that the bomb can cause. Soldiers are incinerating bodies as fast as they can to try and stop the spread of mysterious deaths. In rapid succession an apparently unhurt soldier loses his hair, vomits blood, and dies in front of Gen, and soon after, Gen loses his own hair. These panels illustrate for students the lingering effects of this new kind of bomb. In another difficult scene, Gen comes across a river filled with dead bodies. The putrefying bodies periodically burst open. In this moment, he battles between utter nihilism and an existential understanding of the indifference and ultimate absurdity of the universe in general, and the bomb in particular. After taking several moments to process this new horror, he is ultimately freed from fear of death and turns to issues of survival (Nakazawa 2, 16–51). Nakazawa continues to simultaneously establish a collective and personal memory of atrocity through techniques such as juxtaposing Gen's resilience with horribly mangled corpses.

From this moment until the end of volume four, Gen becomes a hero in the sense Joseph Campbell has described. Gen continues his search for rice to help feed his mother and new baby sister and later embarks on a series of quests to aid his family and others in Hiroshima. He has passed through anxiety and dread, he has a keen awareness of death, and after the pivotal breakthrough mentioned above he spends the rest of the series in a kind of existential freedom. He is not dominated or defeated by the bomb or by the Japanese people who refuse to help his family. This factor arguably elevates *Barefoot Gen* above historical texts as well as many other examples of *hibakusha* literature and *hibakusha*-inspired literature such as Masuji Ibuse's extended lament *Black Rain* (1966). In other words, it is important for students to know the terrible history of the bomb, but it is also important that they see the stories of perseverance that led the Japanese out of World War II into a prosperous and peaceful nation.

Gen's first encounter on his quest for food, and the first post-bomb survival story within *Barefoot Gen*, is with a young girl named Natsue who wants to grow up to be a dancer. She is disfigured, but Gen tells her she is beautiful. When she catches a glimpse of herself in some water, she despairs and twice tries to commit suicide. Gen chastises her and points out that since she has almost died twice (in reality three times if one includes the bomb), then she should consider herself reborn. Natsue realizes that others are dying who desperately want to live and decides to embrace life on her own terms rather than those dictated by the bomb. These themes of survival resonate throughout the series.

Gen eventually finds food for his family and they leave the ruins of Hiroshima and find shelter in the countryside. Volume three picks up directly where volume two left off as Gen starts a job caring for an erstwhile painter who believes he will never paint again due to his extensive burns. Gen convinces him to paint by using his mouth. The man's family is haunted by the nuclear uncanny and they avoid the painter in fear of contamination. They call him "monster" and seek to construct him as such, but Gen inverts their language. Recognizing the construction inherent in language and the political implications of naming, he calls the painter by his name, "Seiji," thus making it clear to the reader who the real monsters are. The pedagogical possibilities contained in such scenes are vast. These narrative sequences have the ability to teach complicated history to middle and high school students, and in my college classrooms this scene in particular has ignited important discussions about the social construction of identity.

Gen spends most of volumes three and four experiencing themes of heroic survival. Kimie adopts a boy orphaned by the bomb. Gen retrieves the bones of his dead family members and honors them in prayer. Akira, Gen's older brother, returns from the countryside, and his eldest brother Koji returns from the navy. Gen and his family are forced to live in a shed, but they still find the ability to sing traditional Japanese songs.

Despite these examples, Nakazawa never descends into mawkish sentimentality, and he does not let the reader forget that an atrocity has occurred. For example, in volume two, he has Gen, and by extension the reader, stumble across a trolley filled with dead bodies crawling with maggots (53–55). The aesthetics of manga allow Nakazawa to heed Jonathan Schell's advice and show atrocity from the point of view of the corpse (qtd. in Treat 1995, 199). Treat underscores this argument by pointing out that the seminal American narrative of the bomb, John Hersey's *Hiroshima* (1946) "repealed the degrading effects of earlier wartime propaganda," but, in the words of Mary McCarthy, "[did not] interview the dead" (54–55). In *Barefoot Gen*, the corpses are rendered anonymous by the Japanese army as they try to bury them as quickly as possible, sloughing their skin off by the pound as they throw them into graves. But Gen bears witness to these mass burials and humanizes the dead via Buddhist prayer. Nakazawa uses corpse-eye views throughout the series to give agency to these bodies that were human just seconds earlier. Equal care is given to the living. Natsue and Seiji both have maggots crawling in their burns and are objects of disgust to some, but through Gen's compassion, these characters are redeemed. He relieves sufferers of their fear of death and sets them free to choose a life — and in several characters' cases, a death — of dignity.

When working through this text, instructors should remind students that *Barefoot Gen* is a work of memory. As Treat points out, "anything processed by memory is already fiction" (139), but Nakazawa's situation is unique among other well-known *hibakusha* artists. Grieving over the loss of his mother, Nakazawa sat down in 1966 to write about the events he experienced leading up to August 6, 1945, as well as the aftermath of those events. Rhetorical choices had to be made. Marita Sturken (1997) argues that cultural memory stands at the intersection of personal memory and history, and we can see this dichotomy played out on the pages of *Barefoot Gen*. That juxtaposition is what makes Nakazawa's series such a useful classroom text. History can be as selective as memory, and by uniting the two, Nakazawa creates a historically important work of literature. Depending on the course, *Barefoot Gen* can either be a supplement to a historical text or a stand-alone document that serves as testimony from a survivor.

Prior to the bomb, Gen is an average, carefree boy. After the bomb, he learns Buddhist prayers to honor the dead. The casual violence he displayed against his younger brother is rendered ironic by the force of the bomb and is replaced by sincere prayers for those who died. Among the living, Nakazawa creates monsters and saints, and the reader moves from seeing the burn victims as monsters to seeing those who refuse to help them as those in need of redemption. Gen's family meets several saints along the way, and their stories are not always mediated by Gen, thus creating a collective memory that is passed on to the reader. A woman offers her breast milk to Kimie's baby because Kimie's malnutrition prevents her from producing any. An officer speaks of the futility of kamikaze runs and urges Gen's brother Koji to choose life. Kimie's childhood friend stands up to her tyrannical mother-in-law and gives Gen's family a place to stay. All the while the narrator keeps track of time, slowing it down after the bomb, speeding it up to mark the passage of history. Personal memory, collective memory, and history all collide and in fact collude in *Barefoot Gen* to create a powerful work of manga.

This strategy calls to mind other attempts at collectivity, such as Hiroko Takenishi's short story, "The Rite" (see Treat 1995, 77–79), but I would argue that Nakazawa's visual mediation makes his work more powerful and more accessible to students. Treat writes at great length about the multifaceted dangers of mediation: of pushing the reader too far away, of bringing the reader too close and thus taking experience away from victims. Visual mediation adds an entirely new layer of peril for the artist. However, Masco writes of the banality of the bomb, and this banality is what Nakazawa successfully avoids. Many Americans, and some Los Alamos scientists, feared that the world would end during atomic and hydrogen bomb tests. When the world survived, the bomb was rendered banal and incorporated into the fabric of everyday life (Masco 2006, 13). In other words, when reading about the atomic bomb, the scale of destruction is difficult to grasp. Nakazawa closes that gap by drawing corpses and burn victims in new ways that speak to the atrocity of the bomb. Furthermore, by using visual techniques such as one on page 200 of volume four, in which a flashback shows the bomb exploding over two Hiroshima residents, he creates a collective memory that meshes powerfully with his personal one and in essence creates a narrative of history itself.

Throughout the work, Nakazawa creates tension between modernity and tradition that often generates classroom discussion about the promise and peril of technological advancement. Guns, tanks, and of course, the bomb, shred or annihilate bodies indiscriminately. As mentioned, in *Barefoot Gen* B-29s are anthropomorphized into a human instruments of death. The work of the Manhattan Project is contrasted with simple scenes of traditional Japanese home life. As fires burn across Tokyo, Gen and his family sing folk songs, plant wheat, and attend to ancient Japanese ceremonies. Gen initially mocks the traditional Japanese treatment of giving ground-up bone dust to burn victims, but what does the "progression" of modernity offer but more effective ways of killing? He goes to a Buddhist temple to learn prayers for the dead, and in a moment of irony, the Buddhist priest mistakes his radiation sickness for devotion, not realizing the true reason he is bald. And in the final panels of volume four, Gen sings a traditional Japanese folk song as he walks past intact village homes on one side, and a decimated modern building on the other. This type of symbolism is rarely lost on students.

If, as Treat argues, the atomic bomb is the negation of culture (138), then *Barefoot Gen* stands as a reaffirmation of it, while simultaneously never letting the reader forget the atrocity that occurred on August 6, 1945. In many ways, the most powerful panel in the series is the panel in volume one representing the explosion of the bomb over Hiroshima (250). It is a relatively small panel with the word "FLASH" in its center in all capital letters. Circular shock waves spread across the panel like ripples in a pond, extending potentially infinitely off the panel into the distance. The point is that the bomb changed not just Hiroshima, but the world. The circles call to mind the literal sun whose power the scientists captured and used on civilians, the rising sun of the Japanese flag that began the war, and the frantically ticking clock that Michael Geyer reminds us is still ticking today (qtd. in Treat 1995, 75). But Nakazawa does not just leave it at the "FLASH," as many photographs would leave it at aerial destruction, devoid of human cost. Nakazawa's next panel shows the people on the receiving end of that flash, the humans who became ashes as the anthropomorphized B-29 ironically calls the shockwave "like being inside a tin can that's been hit with a baseball bat" (Nakazawa 1, 251). In the next panels, Nakazawa shows what it was "like" for those on the ground.

The first four volumes of the series are book ended by metaphors of growing wheat. At the end of volume four, Gen's sister perishes from effects of radiation, and he nearly gives in to despair. But he remembers his father's words about wheat, and Gen, now clearly transformed into Nakazawa, makes a pledge. He says, "Papa, I won't forget. I'll go on living, whatever it takes!" (Nakazawa 4, 281). He removes his cap and his hair is growing back, standing as metonym for the rebuilding both of Hiroshima and of the self. Neither will ever be completely the same, nor should be, but neither will let the bomb dictate life, either. Nakazawa thus marks the moment of his sister's death as the moment his memory of the bomb begins. In that instance, he creates a framework of remembrance that he would employ years later as he began his series.

Art Spiegelman argues in the introduction to the English translation of *Barefoot Gen* that while a success, the series is perhaps "too pleasurable for American and British readers."

But this comment ignores the purpose of the tale. *Barefoot Gen* is not meant to be a work of suffering. To be sure, it is a work dedicated to documenting the suffering of the Japanese people. But it simultaneously offers testimony about how they transcended their hardships. Nakazawa wants readers to understand that humans invented the bomb *and* humans transcended it. And Geyer's warning is still understood: even though volume four has a defined ending, the end is not so much what Paul Boyer calls a "cathartic end-point" (qtd. in Maclear 1999, 44) as it is a beginning of life in the nuclear world. Even though there is narrative closure of sorts, the reader must remember that *Barefoot Gen* ultimately spans some 2000 pages in recognition that the "true" story of the bomb, whatever that may be, may never be told in full as long as the potential for nuclear holocaust still exists. In the final analysis, the story does not descend into sentimentality; rather, it transcends the destructive force of the bomb while promising the world to never forget — a powerful message for any classroom.

Instructors who choose to use this text have many decisions to make. In my courses, I have used the four-volume arc and I have also used volume one alone as a way to model a transnational interdisciplinary approach to understanding the atomic bombing of Hiroshima — as much as it can ever be understood. Our classroom treated the work as memoir, history, and literature, but it also has powerful philosophical content that could be used in a philosophy classroom. That is what makes the series so ideal for interdisciplinary courses. When paired with other powerful yet accessible anti-war texts such as Kurt Vonnegut's *Slaughterhouse Five* (1969) and Joseph Heller's *Catch-22* (1961), *Barefoot Gen* represents for students a different mode of understanding the history of World War II from a transnational perspective. Indeed, those instructors with the time and the inclination could cover all ten volumes of *Barefoot Gen* in one semester. The series concludes some eight years after the war and continues to blend themes of atrocity, peace, hope, and resilience. The combination of written and visual and the conflation of memory, outright fiction, and lived history conveys the end of the war in a way more conventional texts simply cannot. Japanese imperialism is condemned, American imperialism is condemned, but life is affirmed from one who lived through atrocity, and that carries power for students as well as instructors.

References

Gravett, Paul, 2004. *Manga: Sixty Years of Japanese Comics*. London: Laurence King.
Heller, Joseph. 2004. *Catch-22*. 1961. Reprint. New York: Simon & Schuster.
Hersey, John. 1946. *Hiroshima*. New York: A.A. Knopf.
Maclear, Kyo. 1999. *Beclouded Visions*. Albany: State University of New York Press.
Masco, Joseph. 2006. *The Nuclear Borderlands: The Manhattan Project in Post-Cold War New Mexico*. Princeton: Princeton University Press.
Minear, Richard H. 1990. *Hiroshima: Three Witnesses*. Princeton, NJ: Princeton University Press.
Nakazawa, Keiji. 1975. *Hadashi no Gen*. 10 vols. Tokyo: Sekibunsha.
_____. 2005. *Barefoot Gen*. Project Gen. San Francisco: Last Gasp of San Francisco.
Spiegelman, Art. 1996. *Maus*. New York: Pantheon.
Sturken, Marita. 1997. *Tangled Memories: The Vietnam War, the AIDS Epidemic, and the Politics of Remembering*. Berkeley: University of California Press.
Treat, John Whittier. 1995. *Writing Ground Zero: Japanese Literature and the Atomic Bomb*. Chicago: University of Chicago Press.
Vonnegut, Kurt. 2001. *Slaughterhouse Five*. 1969. Reprint. Philadelphia: Chelsea House Publishers.

Information Comics
Risks and Pitfalls

FELIX KELLER *and*
DOROTHEA OECHSLIN

Can educational comics ameliorate the public understanding of a science that may transform our lives, but whose basics only the experts understand? Synthetic biology (Nature 2004) is a new science in this sense. The concept *synthetic biology* sounded like science fiction just a few years ago. Synthetic biology not only manipulates genetic information, as does the well-known field of biotechnology; it also claims even to create new life forms by combining molecular biology, chemistry, and engineering techniques. Synthetic biology is therefore faced with a challenge to convince the public not only of its global benefits, but also of its harmlessness.

Searching for new ways to present the new science in Switzerland, the Swiss Academy of Sciences, an institution committed to dialogue between science and society, became aware of a U.S. comic about synthetic biology which had received a lot of attention and acclaim from experts in the field: *Adventures in Synthetic Biology* (Endy 2005). In the U.S., scientific comics have been the subject of experimental research for some time (Gerstner 2003), so the decision to try this new mode of communication is obvious.[1] But the adaptation of this comic that had received excellent reviews in the U.S. resulted in a debacle in Switzerland.[2] It was this debacle that prompted us to investigate the risks and pitfalls associated with knowledge communicated through educational comics.

The Problem

What was the intention of creating, publishing and adapting a comic about synthetic biology and how was its public reception in Switzerland? Similarly to the Swiss Academy of Sciences, the MIT Synthetic Biology Working Group, namely the group of synthetic biologist Drew Endy,[3] invested a lot of time and energy to find better methods to communicate information about synthetic biology in an easily understandable way. These efforts mainly targeted students, but anyone who might be interested should be given access to this topic and to the new methods by which the concept and the potential of synthetic biology could be assessed and outlined. It soon turned out to be a difficult undertaking, to introduce college students to the concept of "common signal carriers," for example. To better convey the idea, the MIT scientists visualized their ideas through abstract graphics, such as this:

As they were discussing the problems of this visualization, a new idea was born: that synthetic biology and its contents could only be conveyed in a narrative form that also uses visual representations, e.g., in a comic. Drew Endy, who was convinced of the potential of comics for knowledge transfer, made a first draft of the comic. Drew Endy and Isadora Deese wrote it. Comic artist Chuck Wadey was asked to do the drawings. He suggested adding an introductory chapter to familiarize both students and laypeople with this new science.[4]

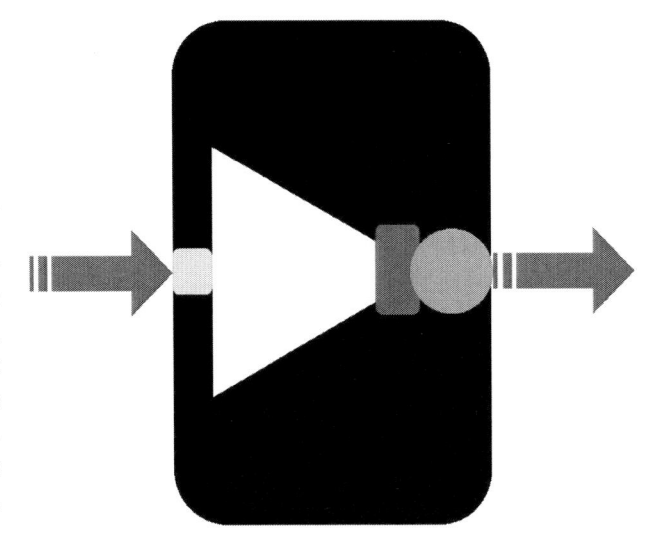

Figure 1. Abstract depiction of genetic inverter, http://openwetware.org/wiki/Adventure_Background

The result of this project, *Adventures in Synthetic Biology*, is a hand-drawn educational comic in the style of a conventional American adventure comic, with use of onomatopoeia, speech bubbles, and many other typical characteristics of comics. Despite the fact that its main task is knowledge transfer, it also contains fictional elements. The comic tells the story of a curious young guy, Dude, a novice in the domain of synthetic biology, whose features resemble those of Drew Endy himself. Under the critical eye of a mother-like mentor he is experimenting with the techniques of synthetic biology, while the mentor explains (to him and to the reader) the scientific background, the principle of genetic inverters, how to correctly connect modules, how to enable DNA programming. After a failed experiment with exploding objects and after being equipped with new systematic methods and the basics of engineering technology, Dude shows his genius by creating some kind of genetic balloons, only the first step for future genetic engineers building new "stuff" like "engineered insulin-producing cells."

The story and its characters are full of vivid exaggerations: bacteria as large as pets, humongous injections, a journey to the core of a cell, a boy in the role of an ingenious and brave scientist who finds the solution that will lay the foundation for a new science. The idea was that students in the field of synthetic biology could now learn about this concept by reading an educational comic, an idea that attracted attention quickly. The comic was even introduced in a 2005 edition of the journal *Nature*, No. 238, and got front page coverage (Endy 2005). Regardless of its original target public (American biology students), the Swiss Academy of Sciences perceived the comic as an ideal medium to introduce synthetic biology in Switzerland.

The decision makers never considered modifying parts or even whole chapters of it — perhaps due to its success in the U.S. In addition, copyrights might have prohibited modifications anyway. The comic was translated from U.S. English into French and German (the two most widely used official languages in Switzerland) and presented at a media event which was part of a synthetic biology conference at the Swiss Federal Institute of Technology, Zurich. However, the comic's U.S. success could not be repeated in Switzerland. The media reacted with skepticism or even harsh criticism to this project launched by the Swiss Academy

Figure 2. "Researchers promote gene technology with monsters,"—an example of a media critique of the comic. "Blick," June 13, 2007.

of Sciences (Hofmann 2008). *WOZ*, a weekly newspaper for a young, progressive audience, criticized the naiveté with which the comic approached artificial life, and how it downplayed the dangers inherent in biotechnology. Even the traditional newspaper *Der Bund* dedicated an entire article to it, dismissing as a failure the academy's endeavor to stimulate discussion of a "sensitive topic" and to visualize complex subject matter in a comic (Imhasly 2007). The article states, "We inevitably feel discomfort when we see a boy inject a humongous syringe into a slimy bacterium that is squeaking in fear and does not stop growing until it finally bursts."

These reviews of the academy's endeavor to promote synthetic biology and to use the comic for this purpose were surpassed by an article about it in the tabloid *Blick*.[5] Above an extract of the comic, we can see the large header in bold letters: "Researchers promote gene technology with monsters." The article calls it a "bizarre gene technology comic" and a "serious researchers' weird attempt to be 'funny.'" The attempt to interest the wider public in gene technology went down the drain. According to the paper, quite the opposite was happening: the comic ridiculed people's fears. "Despite rereading the comic several times, it does not make sense," a Greenpeace spokesman is cited saying: it may only leave the reader perplexed.

Faced with such harsh public criticism, the Swiss Academy of Sciences decided to suspend the project and withdrew its decision to publish the comic for young people, the intended target population. A research group (the authors of this article) was commissioned to investigate the perception of the comic and, in their results, try to identify potential communication pitfalls. Did the target population, young people, perceive the comic equally negatively? Considering the well-known arguments used against biotechnology, why did the comic evoke such harsh criticism of science, scientists' responsibilities, and the economization of science? What role did the medium of educational comics play?

Some Theoretical Reflections on the Information Comic

But first: What is an educational comic and what are the crucial points of this media form? An educational or information comic can be seen as a form of persuasive communication, which uses the cultural form of the comic as its medium. The comic itself, following the famous definition of Will Eisner (Eisner 2008), is a kind of "sequential art": it uses pictures and textual elements, mixing them together into a storyline. Based on this definition, Scott McCloud proposes, in his oeuvre "Understanding comics: the invisible art," an extended definition of comic. For him, a comic consists of "juxtaposed pictorial and other images in deliberate sequence, intended to convey information and/or to produce an aesthetic response in the viewer" (McCloud 1993, 9). In this definition, McCloud integrates the informational aspect of the comic, and his historical investigation of sequential images shows the long tradition of using sequential pictures for knowledge transfer, going back even to the hieroglyphs of Egypt. This extension of the concept of the comic is important for our research, showing that there is a long tradition of connecting pictorial storytelling with information transfer. However, this long history may hide the historical foundation of the reception of the picture sequence itself, or in other words: this definition perhaps leaves out the fact that the way of reading and seeing images and text is not constant over the decades, nor among different social milieus.[6] Eisner points out that consequently, the comic superimposes "the regimens of art (e.g., perspective, symmetry, line) and the regimens of literature (e.g., grammar, plot, syntax)." As a consequence, the reader is "thus required to exercise both visual and verbal interpretative skills." (Eisner 2008, 2).

Following Eisner's insight, we are falling into a paradox: it seems the reception of the comic requires even more skills than the reception of a more homogenous medium like literature and art. Why are comics then usable to communicate knowledge? A closer look at the logic of the semiotic function of visual narratives like comics and graphic novels shows that they hold possibilities for communication that are unique, exactly because they combine the regimens of art and literature. Pictures, generating a holistic "presence" of something where a word-for-word description would be very extensive, represent a form of "thinking" that is different from one that language can communicate. Susanne K. Langer calls them presentational forms, in the sense that they create a meaningful presence or imaging of something. But pictures as presentational forms have their own logic: nobody can translate one picture (a Van Gogh) into another (a Picasso). A picture shows something, but what is showing lacks a clear definition, because the potential meaningful elements of pictures are genuinely polysemous. In contrast, the domain of words, the discursive forms, are explication, argumentation, translation, and the analytical, as Susanne K. Langer explains (Langer 1942). One can translate words into words of another language. One can make precise definition with verbal syntax.

But these regimens of presentational and discursive forms are often not isolated. Moreover, the combination of pictorial elements and words generates new possibilities that aren't just additive; they can explain themselves reciprocally. It is Roland Barthes who has discussed the Comic as a specific form of a combination of words and images in this sense (Barthes 1977). If text is combined with pictures into a new form, the text can have two different functions: *anchorage* and *relay*. Anchorage means, that the text guides the reader through the picture, elucidating its meaning. Texts may have a supportive function to deliver clearly identifiable messages mediated by pictures. The text prevents the floating chain signified that an image contains from getting out of control for the reader, helping him to choose the correct level of perception. This combination of picture and anchor enables a form where text and image complement each other; even if the perceiver lacks skills in pictorial or textual interpreting of the message.[7]

The other function of text is relaying the images. The picture as a presentational form is static, as Langer wrote, while discursive forms are dynamic, and they tell a story in time, leading the eye through chains of signifiers. So text can combine fragments of presentational forms into a greater synthetic form, a new syntagm, a new semiotic unity. Where description by words is enormously costly, the pictures, as presentational forms, may bear a wide range of information efficiently, while the text fits the isolated pictures to the greater story. Especially in comics, Barthes tells us, "the costly message and the discursive message are made to coincide so that the hurried reader may be spared the boredom of verbal 'descriptions,' which are entrusted to the image, that is to say to a less 'laborious' system."

But for whom is this kind of reading valid? A combination of explicitly designed verbal and iconic signs can never cover all the possible meanings of a picture and its elements. There is always a "the rest" of the possible significances that undermines a semiotic system intending the integration of text and images. The connotation is always wider than intended. The example of the comic *Synthetic Biology* shows how the possible connotations that this educational comic evokes are quickly integrated in the political field of "battles" that accompanies the rise of a new biological science (Hall 1996): the question of manipulating and economizing life itself, lack of trust in the power of science, etc.: discourses that are "waiting" to interpret the surplus of meaning in a picture-text system as that presented in the comic "adventures in synthetic biology."[8]

However, according to Barthes, each dimension of symbolic signifying of an image (denotative pictorial elements, connotation of style, literal meaning of integrated words) is an object of interpretation that varies with the number varies depending on each specific act of reading and each different reader. In other words: balancing a productive combination of text and images in a pictorial storyline is difficult insofar as the kind of reading and combining them may vary not only between different groups of persons, but also in the different reading acts of one person, depending on which element of knowledge he is willing to activate, since a plurality and a co-existence of lexicons, or knowledge forms, coexists in one and the same person. (Or in other words, the "language of the image is not merely the totality of utterances emitted (...), it is also the totality of utterances received" (Barthes 1977, 47). But which instance determines what is received? It is not the symbolic form of the pictures and texts (the comic) itself. Receiving and interpreting a message generated by symbolic forms is also a question of the recipient, the individual combination and processing of symbolic forms and their meaning. But this "variation in reading," the activation of a lexicon, is never "anarchic": "it depends on the different kinds of knowledge — practical, national, cultural, aesthetic — invested in the image,"[9] therefore a variation that can even be "brought into a typology," as Barthes believed (Barthes 1977, 46).

With this horizon in mind, the question whether a comic is a "good" media for knowledge transfer can never be answered by discussing the medium of the comic itself. Moreover, the question of which forms of reading and seeing, which skills are affected and which lexicons are activated, when an educational comic is read by different individuals, leads to the pitfalls that gave rise to the public critique of the concrete comic *Synthetic Biology*, as our thesis had in mind.

Researching Reception: Some Reflections on the Method

However, to our knowledge, perception research has not yet provided any instruments to measure perception of educational comics that would allow for a comparison of the comic in question with comparable media. Following our theoretical reflection, we first wanted to understand and explore the processes of reception of the educational comic. Consequently, we focused on the active individual who processes the reading act as a kind of "information" or semiotic processing on the basis of his knowledge and interests.[10] In this sense, we were interested in differences in reading and interpreting, for the purpose of observing how reception or "information processing" varies on the basis of the same media form, to see what communicative forces of the form itself (the comic) can be identified. Empirically, we analyzed the reception of the educational comic using a qualitative inductive approach based mainly on *Grounded Theory* (Strauss and Corbin 1997). To gather data about the reception of the comic, we used focus groups, a traditional method used in communication and social science research (Bloor et al. 2001; Schäffer 2005). Focus groups seemed to be an ideal method because people tend to express criticism or a lack of understanding more openly if they see that others share their perceptions and attitudes. In addition, it can prevent participants from feeling as if they are being made to take an exam, such as in a one-to-one interview. The group dialogue promotes mutual inspiration to contribute to the discussion spontaneously and openly and invites reactions (Lamnek 2005).

The general method of focus groups first had to be adjusted to fit our research questions. The selection process when creating focus groups should generate the largest possible amount of assessments and perception patterns, rather than an imaginary average public. For this reason, we decided to work with four focus groups, each different in terms of relevant aspects/characteristic features of the educational comic, which would allow us to identify specific pitfalls and obstacles. In our design, we distinguished between participants with different competences and affinities: first, young people with an affinity to either the natural sciences or arts/graphics; second, experts in these two areas. This division allowed us a direct observation of the target population, while the expert groups were expected to articulate potential pitfalls and obstacles with precision, based on their prior knowledge. Consequently, our research design consisted of a matrix which distinguished between experts / target population and visual arts/graphics and natural sciences.

Qualitative Research Design: Focus Groups

	Natural Sciences	*Visual Arts/Graphics*
Target population: adolescents between 16 and 18 years	High school students — biology/chemistry	High school students — visual arts
Experts	Biologists, engineers	Graphic artists, advertisers

To avoid the bias of national visual culture and national discourses about science, we decided to expand the design of our comparison groups, all of them from Switzerland (CH), by adding a focus group in the U.S., the origin culture of the comic. A collaboration with the Monterey Institute of International Studies in California enabled us to have eight U.S. students from different academic tracks discuss the original American English version of the educational comic.

Each focus group had between six and nine participants. The number of participants should ideally be between five and twelve, as shown in previous research. A focus group should not be too small (minimum of five), so that a variety of opinions can be gathered; and it should not be too large either (maximum of twelve), so that all group members stay motivated to actively engage in the discussion (see Lamnek 2005). Focus groups are facilitated by a moderator. The moderator raises key questions from a prepared outline so the statements of the different focus groups can be compared. At the same time, the moderator should try to keep the conversation flowing so that key themes can emerge. Towards the end of the discussion, there is an opportunity to ask specific questions that may have remained unanswered. In our research, the discussions were videotaped and transcribed. Each discussion lasted between 55 and 90 minutes. All participant names used in the essay are pseudonyms.

First Results and a Research Strategy to Investigate the Material

The following example will show how difficult it is for the producers of a comic to predict and assess the pitfalls of the medium without communicating with the target public. The images have, as postulated by Barthes, a series of floating elements whose significance is hardly foreseeable. To exemplify this phenomenon and its meaning for educational comics, we will explore a tiny detail of *Adventures of Synthetic Biology*: the glasses of our young researcher's motherly friend and mentor. They are mirrored, which prevents us from seeing her eyes.

In addition, the glasses do not have temples, as if they were implanted in her face. Surprisingly, this minor detail was noticed by all focus groups even though it has no content value, and caused confusion, as illustrated by the following comments from the focus group in the U.S.:

And then her eyes. I didn't even notice it. But first I thought they were glasses but they... (Amy, graduate student, U.S.).

They're glasses (Jennifer, graduate student, U.S.).

No, they're not. There's no connection to her ears (Amy, graduate student, U.S.).

And she has some kind of cotton pads or something else on her eyes. I don't know what it is. And I keep asking myself: What role does it play in the story? (Wanda, graphic artist, CH)

It's totally strange that this woman should only have

Figure 3. A minor detail only? The mirrorshades. From Endy et al. 2005, 12.

two white [glass plates], a kind of glasses. Without these, she'd look much nicer (Elizabeth, high school student visual art/graphics, CH).

These glasses are really awful (Selena, high school student visual art/graphics, CH).

This confusion about the glasses, i.e., the inability to interpret their shape, led to rejection, even aversion towards the character (and her creator), as illustrated by the following snippets from a conversation among biologists/engineers:

Let's take the woman's glasses. Why can't you look her in the eyes, it's so ... (Betty, biologist, CH).

She herself is synthetic, almost like a robot (Christina, biologist, CH).

A graphic artist says:

That really also bothered me very much: You can never see her eyes. It totally confused me. It's so anonymous (Hannah, graphic artist, CH).

The high school students' reactions are similar:

It seems a bit negative, a bit evil. You don't see the woman's eyes. Yes, she seems a little mean (Selena, high school student visual art/graphics, CH).

What makes her seem so unfriendly? (moderator); Reply: The glasses (Lewis, high school student natural sciences, CH).

And most of all, the glasses she's wearing, she's so stupid (Peter, high school student natural sciences, CH).

Based on these statements, it is evident that this alienation also reflects on the reader's willingness to allow the mental processing of the comic's message. But then again, these statements cannot be generalized: the U.S. group, which was more open toward the medium of comics, expressed their confusion about the glasses, but they did not express negative feelings toward the researcher's character. Even the smallest details, which may go unnoticed by most, may have hidden meanings for readers. So, is it impossible to investigate the reception of the comic, because its floating signifiers will be processed completely by heterogeneous audiences, as they form the public of today?

This evidence we see as a result; nevertheless, we tried to search for some regularities, that might help to identify the pitfalls of an educational comic, without saying that we are able to create a guide to a well-performing comic. For a further analysis of the material we followed the methodological principles proposed by *Grounded Theory*. They consist of identifying the recurring arguments, patterns of statements, experiences, and evaluations recorded in the focus group conversations, which we tried to distil by concentrated discussion in our research group. This process of open coding is followed by a phase of "axial coding" for an aggregation of core themes to establish global categories that would facilitate interpretation. Thence the name of the method: the purpose of grounded theory is to extract general insights "grounded" in the collected data. Through this process, new dimensions and relations emerge that cannot be perceived at first glance.

The Cultural Background of Comic Reception and Further Questions

One core dimension shows, not very surprisingly, the significance of cultural background for reception and information processing, the different knowledge and lexicons that are invested to read the comic as a whole form. The focus group in the U.S. had a much more positive attitude towards comics than the Swiss focus groups: As a matter of fact, they even consider comics an integrated part of their (visual) culture.

> It's a format that we'll recognize, at least here in America, we recognize the format, we recognize the genre... I believe they are an integrated part of the American society, they are part of our culture (Sheila, graduate student, U.S.).

An American student who immigrated to the U.S. at the age of eleven explained that she had her own experience of this visual culture: she had not internalized the medium and language of comics to the extent that other Americans had.

> I never grew up with comics until I came to the U.S. and that's when I was introduced to it. But I never got into it because I felt there was a gap between my cultural knowledge and the knowledge here. There would be jokes, and I would think, "Wait, that's funny? I don't get it." That was a demotivating factor for me. So I just kind of never got into comics (Mary, graduate student, U.S.).
>
> Consequently, much more skepticism was felt among the Swiss focus groups. The following were typical statements:
>
> I like comics ... it's a good way to explain complex topics. But I think this comic here is a bad example (Betty, biologist, CH).
>
> I think they have chosen the right medium but maybe not the right kind of language (Rose, advertiser, CH).
>
> I feel that knowledge cannot be transferred through comics. Comics are for fun, leisure, and fiction (Peter, high school student natural sciences, CH).

However, the Swiss participants' attitude was not generally negative towards comics. Consequently, the evidence of a cultural difference leads to further questions: what is exactly the reason for this skepticism towards this *educational* comic? What are its dimensions and what causes it? The above statements merely show that there must be barriers somewhere that prevented knowledge transfer and caused the participants to refuse active engagement with the material.

Visual, Narrative and Knowledge Dimension of the Comic

We searched for further categories and dimensions that determined perception and assessment of this comic. After examining the data, we believe we can distinguish aspects of the perception of this educational comic which are common to all the groups. For us, three main dimensions of messages were identifiable whenever group members discussed acceptance of the comic and its perceived quality. It also became evident that the interaction among the three dimensions constituted a crucial momentum, which led the participants to reject this comic as a medium for knowledge transfer.

The first category of impressions was based on the *visual aspects* of the comic: Here, we refer to the images that were evaluated and questioned, and which either attracted the readers or put them off; this dimension corresponds in some ways to the paradigmatic dimensions of images (style, effect, colors) (Barthes 1977: 41). The comic also tells a story; it is a narration with a cast of characters, and with a specific dramatization. We call this second dimension the *narrative dimension;* it corresponds to what Barthes calls syntagmatic component pictures, of relaying pictures and texts, integrating the reader into a story he can "live with." Finally, educational comics have an independent *dimension of knowledge transfer*: The readers feels themselves challenged to identify what kind of knowledge is provided, what exactly they are supposed to learn.

The readers did not process the three dimensions in an isolated manner. And it is also the perceived relation between them that determined how the readers handled the comic as a whole, influencing the intention to learn from it, as our research showed. Nevertheless, they form independent dimensions with specific properties and specific messages perceived by the readers, as the following examples should illustrate.

As aspects of the *visual dimension* we recognized that the drawing style, the elaboration of details, and the colors that create different atmospheres are core themes which can be seen. These clearly emerged when the appeal of the images was discussed.

> When I started to read, then I got into it because it's pretty with these pictures (Mary, graduate student, U.S.).
>
> Everybody here when you asked what we liked about the comic said, "Oh, pretty colors, pretty images." I don't think that they're distracting because we still all read it (Sheila, Jennifer, graduate students, U.S.).
>
> I totally dislike the style. It doesn't appeal to me at all. For example the fingers, the hands, the way they're drawn (Michael, graphic artist, CH).
>
> Everything looks so menacing. The woman on page 8 against the explosive background. On page 9 the woman who just enters the room, green like a nuclear reactor (José, engineer, CH).

The *narrative dimension*, i.e., the story, is less evident to the extent that it almost disappears behind the images, but still remains important for the assessment of the comic. The narrative dimension is based on the same dramatization used in literature and in movies to establish a narrative structure, with suspense, events, twists in the plot, and characters with whom we can identify. This refers to the relationship that is established between the readers and the characters, and the extent to which the readers recognize themselves in the characters, start to be interested in them, and thereby experience the story together with the characters. Two examples will illustrate what happens when this dimension is not given careful consideration.

> I think it's not only about contents, but also about the characters in comics. If you are interested in a comic, you identify with the characters. But this comic does not even have an introduction. Who are these two characters? That's why I thought it was difficult. I just read it without knowing what it was about (Edward, engineer, CH).
>
> [The characters] would need to be introduced at the beginning of the comic, or there should be an explanatory text. Otherwise, they just exist and the reader has no idea who they are and that's why you just don't care (Inez, high school student visual art/graphics, CH).

Regarding *knowledge transfer*— or matter-of-fact communication — the third dimension, the question of an immediate comprehensibility, emerged as the key criterion for perception. Participants didn't concentrate for minutes on a difficult text segment, asking what it could mean. Confronted with a comic they obviously have a different expectation of comprehensibility, compared to a book with text only. Immediate comprehensibility seems to be a decisive factor in the reader's desire and motivation to further engage in reading a comic.

> They talk about "When the input signal is high, the repressor protein is kicked up and that turns off the output signal." I wasn't sure. What are you talking about, input and output? It didn't seem connected to what was previously happening, actually (Amy, graduate student, U.S.).

Even experts in biology couldn't completely understand the information presented in the comic. Only after they were prompted to engage in further research were they able to distinguish between gene technology and the new science of synthetic biology.

Figure 4. Confusion between scientific content and comic language. From Endy et al. 2005, 11.

Inverter, yes, I can relate to that, height and depth etc., but why we should need this to prevent [the bacterium] from growing, this is something I didn't understand. How is this related to the gene activity that is introduced later on and that we want to stop? (Rita, biologist, CH).

The perception of knowledge and its presentation was the only dimension that was not only identified in all the groups but also assessed with similar negativity.

Processing Visual and Narrative Information

Despite this similar evaluation of the knowledge dimension, each focus group assessed the quality of the other two dimensions differently. For example, their assessment of the visual dimension was by far what most distinguished the Swiss focus groups from the focus group in the U.S. While the discrepancy in their assessments of the narrative dimension was not as strong.

But one of the remarkable results shows that understanding comics is based on a competence that must be learned (by getting familiar with the language of this medium). High school students interpreted the images with reference to the medium itself; they were able to recognize and contextualize comic-specific language. The picture where the bacterium is about to burst, which, incidentally, is the picture that the Swiss Academy of Sciences believed caused the rejection of the entire comic, provided entertainment for connoisseurs of comics:

> I think if it hadn't burst, it would have been even more boring (Elizabeth, high school student visual art/graphics, CH).
>
> You read a comic because everything is totally exaggerated. That's why it didn't bother me that it burst (Lawrence, high school student visual art/graphics, CH).

The broad tendency of the focus group in the U.S. was also to assess the images against the background of the kind of pictures and language typically used in comics. Just like the Swiss high school students, they had internalized the specific competence to decipher the medium and its language. This turned out to be a key requirement to enable successful communication through this medium. The adult experts in Switzerland, however, interpreted the images against the background of the "explosive" topic of gene technology: They perceived them as menacing and deterring.

> That's extremely negative. I would never do this. I'd draw the attention elsewhere rather than blow it up and let it burst (Rose, advertiser, CH).
>
> I find the chromosome injection repulsive (Rita, biologist, CH).

Despite their heterogeneity, these results let emerge a "picture" of what caused the obstacles and pitfalls of this comic despite the generally positive attitude toward the comic.

Ambiguity Between Knowledge Combination and Pictorial Message

Our theory based on this investigation is not only that the successful knowledge transfer of an educational comic hinges on the quality of the three message dimensions. The most important factor is the *interaction* among the three dimensions. In other words: Appropriate coherence of the three levels of an educational comic—visual, narration and knowledge transfer—is crucial for the perception of a comic. Unless the reader perceives the three message dimensions as coherent, the comic will not be accepted as a serious or valuable medium for knowledge transfer; instead, it will evoke confusion or even rejection, even if one dimension is recognized as being high-quality (the attractiveness of one dimension seems not to be able to fade out a perceived weakness of another). This relation became evident in the focus groups' discussions, only. Both in terms of country of origin (Switzerland or U.S.) and in terms of generations, the focus groups have shown different perceptions of the coherence of these dimensions.

Because of the naturalness with which they regarded comics, the focus groups in the U.S., who generally had a positive attitude towards this medium, did not seem to have an issue with the interaction among the dimensions. But all the Swiss focus groups were concerned about the lack of coherence, which prompted them to criticize the comic. According to the Swiss sample, the dimension of knowledge transfer contained statements that contradicted both the narrative and the visual dimensions. The perception of this discrepancy not only prompts ambiguity and confusion. It also affects the interpretation of the comic and a reader's motivation to engage in intensive reading:

> The pictures are suitable for little kids, but the content is more suitable for our age (Inez, high school student visual art/graphics, CH).

> I look at the visuals [and I think] the target population should be kids between ten and 12. But it's too difficult for them anyway (Wanda, graphic artist, CH).
>
> The knowledge that is to be transferred needs to be adjusted to the level of the pictures. The contrast between knowledge and pictures is much too big (Alexandra, high school student visual art/graphics, CH).

Based on this mismatch, the Swiss focus groups kept wondering about the actual target population of the comic. Who had this educational comic been produced for? The readers did not respond to the pictures; rather, they felt degraded, treated as children. As a consequence, the confusion about the highly complex, cognitive messages on the one hand and the child-like pictures on the other hand resulted in the readers' loss of motivation.

The Commingling of Fiction and Reality

The Swiss sample was also confused by the discrepancy between the content level, which is supposed to transfer knowledge, and the narration, which is similar to that of an adventure or fantasy comic.

Figure 5. This hero appeals to whom? From Endy et al. 2005, 11.

Due to the entanglement of the content level with the fictional story, the readers, who are not yet experts, have difficulty in distinguishing between fiction and reality when it comes to the interpretation of the messages. This ambiguity about the validity of the content is unsettling for the readers, particularly — but not only — the high school students, who absorb, process, and store information on a daily basis:

> There is no way of telling what is real and what is fiction. To check whether it's real what they say, you'd have to look it up in a reference book (Peter, high school student natural sciences, CH).
>
> If the comic seems unrealistic, then you don't think that what the comic says is true (Shannon, high school student natural sciences, CH).
>
> As a layperson, you wonder whether the jargon has been made up (Edward, engineer, CH).
>
> The science fiction genre is just not adequate to deal with this topic. It is confusing too; what's real? It doesn't seem serious (Paul, engineer, CH).

As illustrated by the latter statement, the participant felt that the genre was ill-chosen, both in terms of knowledge transfer and gene research.

In the eyes of the Swiss readers, the adventure genre (with its fantasy elements and strong exaggerations) gives the science of synthetic biology the nimbus of incredibility, of a dangerous, even apocalyptic aura. Graphics experts were surprised by the choice of the genre and how it was put into practice:

I find it extremely strange, the topic and how it was implemented. That is totally new and unfamiliar for me. The fact that this topic is conveyed in this way is almost a little uncanny, with this kind of language ... with this nonchalance, the easiness with which one reads comics, but this topic is hard to digest (Michael, graphic artist, CH).

If I imagine a more serious style, such as a factual graphic organizer, then [the comic] would get its seriousness back (Ashley, advertiser, CH).

The readers' prejudice against gene research (a horror science that may create strange life forms) is confirmed by this type of narration with its fantastic elements, and thereby promotes a negative attitude in their processing of this new science. The choice of the genre through which knowledge is transferred (an inadequate relationalization of content dimension and visual narration), can affect the publishers' credibility and the perception of their degree of seriousness. This interplay has been a subject of discussion in social psychology (Güttler 1996; Petty and Wegener 1999, 44–57), which asks for further research concerning the acceptance of knowledge transfer presented in information comics.

Conclusion

Why does the interplay among a variety of signal levels or semiotic dimensions constitute a pitfall for the medium of educational comics? We believe that a possible pitfall may be caused by the initial perception of comics as being mainly a visual media. It can be disastrous to focus on one dimension only of the three we have identified, e.g., by presenting appealing images to optimize knowledge presentation, but neglecting narrative elements. Each picture has its own rhetoric, and the use of comic images may disturb a reader who only knows comics from his childhood, in the case of a comic intended to communicate important information to him. In addition to the investigation of whether educational comics are the appropriate medium for the target population, it is important that images, narration, and knowledge constitute a coherent unity for the readers, so that they feel they are being taken seriously. Otherwise, readers will respond neither to the images nor to the narration. Why then should they want to engage with the knowledge that the comic intended to convey?

Unlike comics designed for the purpose of entertainment and art, educational comics have a clear objective: knowledge transfer. If comics are viewed from the angle of art, their openness to interpretation and their richness of allusions constitute a fascinating integral part of this medium. But in educational comics, ambiguity and richness of allusions, even though they can make a comic more appealing, entail dangers: They may confuse readers, even to the extent that they will not know exactly what they are supposed to be learning. Ultimately, the result can be their unwillingness to actively engage with the presented material.

It is rather unlikely that a dictum like the one formulated by Edward Tufte (1983) for the visual display of quantitative information also makes sense in the realm of educational comics: that each spot of paint has a clear, unique meaning. The incorporation of knowledge into a visual narration, where pictures and narration are a medium of knowledge rather than a representation of knowledge, is probably a generic moment of the comic medium itself. Full control over possible meaning is not thinkable, as even theoretical reflections show.

From our perspective, the particular challenge of this medium is the fact that the three dimensions of communication — visualization, narration, and knowledge communication — are pivotal, and need to be balanced out. This means that they may surprise and amaze the reader, but should not confront him with contradictory messages. It is precisely this balancing act that entails pitfalls. Even if the visualization of the knowledge can be appealing, the reader may not respond well to the narration, may even feel repulsion. Consequently, knowledge acquisition will be impaired.

Whether or not the balancing act was successful is something that may not be predictable by authors and distributors. It only takes small visual details to trigger an unexpected reader response, as we have attempted to exemplify theoretically and empirically. In contrast to a comic intended to be an art form, in the case of educational comics it is necessary to carefully investigate reader perception, for as long as educational comics are not an integral part of learning and even knowledge culture.

Notes

1. "You can use them [educational comics] to teach chemistry; you can even use comics to teach law," Kakalios enthuses. "Students are so busy enjoying their superhero ice-cream sundae that they don't notice that I'm sneakily getting them to lower their guard and eat their spinach at the same time" (Gerstner 2003).
2. We assume that this applies to all German-speaking readers. We hope to include French-speaking cultures, where the art of comics is much more deeply anchored, in our next investigation.
3. Today, he is an assistant professor in the Department of Bioengineering at Stanford University.
4. Cf., concerning the background: http://openwetware.org/wiki/Adventure_Background.
5. The tabloid *Blick* is comparable to the British newspaper *The Sun* or *The Globe* in the U.S.
6. In contrast, there are, as for example Martin Jay showed, historic different "scopic regimes," different ways of seeing and interpreting images (Jay 1988). Even the development of new media techniques (Crary 1992) affects how the recipients perceive sequential picture-stories.
7. Especially biology, showing the complex form of organisms, has profited from this advance of the connotative power of combining text and image since more than hundred and twenty years ago, for example with class wall charts to teach a great mass of children with no educational background for the first time (Bucchi 2006).
8. In a large-scale survey carried out in February 2010 to measure people's knowledge about this new technology in Europe, 83 percent of all respondents reported that they had never heard of "synthetic biology." Eight percent said that they had come across this term before and only eight percent stated that they had concerned themselves with this topic (Gaskell et al. 2010, 29).
9. This is the domain of cultural studies as the study of "cultural representation and signifying practices," which is not the primary subject here. See Hall (1997).
10. See the broad discussion of various ways to define the educational comic in: Jüngst (2010, 11f).

References

Barthes, Roland. 1977. "Rhetoric of the Image." In Roland Barthes, *Image, Music, Text*. New York: Hill and Wang.
Bloor, Michael, Jane Frankland, Michelle Thomas, and Kate Robson. 2001. *Focus Groups in Social Research*. London: Sage.
Bucchi, Massimiano. 2006. "Images of Science in the Classroom. Wall Charts and Science Education." In Luc Pauwels, ed., *Visual Cultures of Science. Rethinking Representational Practices in Knowledge Building and Science Communication*. Hanover, NH: Dartmouth College Press.
Crary, Jonathan. 1992. *Techniques of the Observer: On Vision and Modernity in The nineteenth Century*. Cambridge, MA: MIT Press.
Eisner, Will. 2008. *Comics and Sequential Art: Principles and Practices from the Legendary Cartoonist*. Tamarac, FL: Poorhouse Press.
Endy, Drew. November 2005. "Foundations for Engineering Biology." *Nature* 438.24: 449–453.
_____, Isadora Deese, Chuck Wadey, and The MIT Synthetic Biology Working Group. 2005. *Adventures in Synthetic Biology*. Accessed November 3, 2011. http://mit.edu/endy/www/scraps/comic/AiSB.vol1.pdf, 2005.

Gaskell, George, Sally Stares, Agnes Allansdottir, et al. 2010. *Europeans and Biotechnology in 2010—Winds of change? A Report to the European Commission's Directorate-General for Research*. Luxembourg: Publications Office for the European Union.

Gerstner, Ed. 2003. "Superheroes Make Physics Fun: Comic Books Impart Common Sense and Critical thinking." *Nature Online*. Accessed March 3, 2011. http://www.nature.com/news/2003/030312/full/news030310-3.html.

Güttler, Peter O. 1996. *Sozialpsychologie: Soziale Einstellungen, Vorurteile, Einstellungsänderungen*. München: Oldenburg.

Hall, Stuart. 1996. "Encoding/Decoding." In Stuart Hall, Dorothy Hobson, Andrew Lowe, and Paul Willis, eds., *Culture, Media, Language*. London: Hutchinson: Centre for Contemporary Cultural Studies.

_____, ed. 1997. *Representation: Cultural Representations and Signifying Practices*. London: Sage.

Hofmann, Markus. 2008. *Die veröffentlichte Wahrnehmung der Synthetischen Biologie—Und Was Man Daraus Schliessen Kann*. Accessed March 3, 2011. http://www.gensuisse.ch/focus/synth/#ref3.

Imhasly, Patrick. June 29, 2007. "Das Leben vom Reissbrett. Biologen Wollen Künstliche Organismen Schaffen—Bereits Kommen Proteste Auf." *Der Bund*.

Jay, Martin. 1988. "Scopic Regimes of Modernity." In Hal Foster, ed., *Vision and Visuality*. New York: The New Press.

Jüngst, Heike Elisabeth. 2010. *Information Comics. Knowledge Transfer in a Popular Format*. New York: Peter Lang.

Lamnek, Siegfried. 2005. *Gruppendiskussion—Theorie und Praxis*. Weinheim: Beltz.

Langer, Susanne Katherina Knauth. 1942. *Philosophy in a New Key; A Study in the Symbolism of Reason, Rite and Art*. Cambridge, MA: Harvard University Press.

McCloud, Scott. 1993. *Understanding Comics: The Invisible Art*. Northampton, MA: Tundra.

Nature. October 7, 2004. "Futures of Artificial Life: Researchers Involved in Synthetic Biology Need to Take Steps to Engage More with the Public." *Nature* 431.7009: 613.

Petty, Richard. E., and Duane. T. Wegener. 1999. "The Elaboration-Likelihood Model: Current Status and Controversies." In Shelly Chaiken and Yaacov Trope, eds., *Dual-Process Theories in Social Psychology*. New York: Guilford Press.

Schäffer, Burkhard. 2005. "Gruppendiskussion." In Mikos Lothar, and Claudia Wegener, eds., *Qualitative Medienforschung*. Konstanz, Germany: UVK.

Strauss, Anselm, and Juliet Corbin. 1997. *Grounded Theory in Practice*. Thousand Oaks, CA: Sage.

Tufte, Edward R. 1983. *The Visual Display of Quantitative Information*. Cheshire, CT: Graphics Press.

Graphic N-extbooks
A Journey Beyond Traditional Textbooks

JEREMY SHORT, DAVID KETCHEN
and JEFF SHELSTAD

The first Saturday of each May is embraced by comic enthusiasts as Free Comic Book Day. This promotional invent is the brainchild of Joe Field, a comic book store owner in California. The event is now supported by key industry distributors and often timed to coincide closely with other key media events such as the opening of the second Spider-Man movie in 2002. The event has attracted considerable press, and serves to call both new and old comic readers to remember and appreciate this key form of sequential art.

But what if every day could be Free Comic Book Day? And, what if the comics focused not simply on intriguing characters in dynamic situation, but material that would take important but otherwise droll prose and engage the college aged reader to learn material often relegated to textbooks that often go unused throughout the semester? Textbooks are anything but free—often costing upwards of two hundred dollars.

This goal has been embraced by open-sourced textbook publisher Flat World Knowledge and a number of books in its catalog that rely on the graphic novel format to enhance several classes common in colleges nationwide and internationally. These graphic novel "textbooks" are free online and apply to courses ranging from a primer in freshman success, to general courses in management/ entrepreneurship, and more specific niche business classes such as family business and franchising.

In this essay, we note applications of graphic novels to university education—with particular emphasis on material relevant to business education. We detail a number of specific examples of various graphic novel materials and how they might be integrated into a number of pedagogical applications in higher education. Our goal is present an increasingly popular application of the graphic novel that has great potential to revolutionize how textbooks are perceived and used in higher education.

Graphic Narratives and University Education

> "We must go beyond textbooks, go out into the bypaths and untrodden depths of the wilderness and travel and explore and tell the world the glories of our journey."
>
> —*John Hope Franklin, historian and winner of the Presidential Medal of Freedom*

Although textbooks still have a place within the modern educational system, Professor Franklin's quote challenges educators and students to stretch beyond textbooks. This challenge can be met in a variety of ways. The most obvious is experiential learning — actually getting out in the world, working through successes and failures, and distilling lessons about why good and bad outcomes occur.

Another option, and one that we have pioneered, is trying to create books that share the strengths of college textbooks but avoid textbooks' weaknesses. On the plus side, textbooks offer rigorous treatment of ideas that have been developing by leading scholars within a field. Unfortunately, textbooks also tend to be "dry" and boring, especially when viewed from the perspective of the typical college student. In response to this situation, we went into a literary bypath that promised to provide the academic rigor of textbooks but that can deliver this content within the context of an enjoyable fictional journey.

As we examined our field — business management — we found that books do exist that engage the reader and, not coincidentally, often sell like the proverbial hotcakes. Books that are derisively described as "pop management" books rely on catchy titles, up-tempo writing and simple (and simplistic) messages in order to lure readers. Unfortunately, these books also tend to advocate fads while ignoring decades of research on business (Ketchen and Short, 2011). We wondered if books could be created that transcended boring, expensive textbooks on the one hand and pop management books on the other.

We refer to the specific innovation we created as the "graphic novel textbook" or, more simply, the "graphic n-extbook." A graphic n-extbook (GN) conveys ideas from a field of study within the context of a narrative. In creating our GNs, we have tried to combine the academic rigor of textbooks, the fun factor of pop management books, excellent artwork, and a compelling storyline. Together, we have created three GNs: *Atlas Black: Managing to Succeed* (Short, Bauer, Ketchen, and Simon, 2010), *Atlas Black: Management Guru?* (Short, Bauer, Ketchen, and Simon, 2010), and *Tales of Garcón: The Franchise Players* (Ketchen, Short, Combs and Terrell, 2011). Below we describe the evolution of this innovation. In doing so, we hope to inspire you, the reader, to travel the metaphoric wilderness that Professor Franklin described. Whether our journey or yours will offer the glory that his quote promised remains to be seen.

Atlas Black: Managing to Succeed

Atlas Black: Managing to Succeed is the first graphic novel that encompasses key concepts and theories from the management field. The book was designed for potential use as a supplement or complementary text for principles of management, organizational behavior, strategic management, and entrepreneurship courses. It could also be used as a replacement for a traditional text in an experiential or short course; or a primer on business, management, and entrepreneurship for incoming freshmen within the "overview of business" classes that are offered at many colleges and universities.

The story follows the protagonist — Atlas Black — a fifth year college senior who is finally about to graduate. Unfortunately, Atlas has no job lined up, and his job prospects are less than ideal given his relatively low GPA and his series of part-time jobs. Atlas faces problems with his landlord and ex-girlfriend. Atlas is not unintelligent, but he is somewhat of a slacker. In short, he provides a portrayal of a certain type of student we have witnessed in our careers. One with great potential that often goes unchallenged — especially during

Above, Opposite and following page: Figure A, excerpt from *Atlas Black: Managing to Succeed*

Did you know that the Samurai believed that the warrior keeps death in mind at all times, all hours, all days, all years?
Are you going to kill me?
No, kid - it's a *metaphor*. That's how scared you ***should*** be if you're going to start your own business. Any mistake can kill you at any time.
Who are you?
Do you know what a *White Knight* is?
Someone who gives money to help a company that's about to go bankrupt, right?
That's about right.
page 35

204   Part IV: Specific Graphic Novels and Comics and Their Application

the formative college years where academic learning is viewed as dry prose and boring and irrelevant examples. It is exactly this type of student, among others, that we hope to reach with the graphic novel n-extbook.

The plot of the graphic follows Atlas and his struggle to navigate his college career and plan his new life. With the help of his sidekick, the more brainy David Chan, in conjunction with regular visits with their local barrista, Tess, and the academic insights of his management professor, and the mysterious "Black," Atlas will work to fund his college expenses, start a new business, and act as a nascent entrepreneur, along the way illustrating key concepts from a number of theories and frameworks common to management textbooks. *Atlas Black: Managing to Succeed* brings concepts to life using through in graphic novel format in a manner that undergraduates, MBA's, entrepreneurs, and anyone interested in more deep knowledge of business is certain to find both educational and entertaining. The Atlas Black series has received favorable portrayal at media outlets whose readers include those interested in higher education (Wojciechowska, 2010), graphic novels (Monin, 2010), business communication (Short and Reeves, 2009), as well as more general audiences (Pierleoni, 2010). Figure A shows the initial encounter between Atlas and the mysterious "Black." This scene helps to establish both a mentor/protégé relationship that will evolve and the fundamental challenge of entrepreneurs — avoid the red ink of financial losses and stay in the black ink of profit.

Atlas Black: Management Guru?

The second book in the series, *Atlas Black: Management Guru?* picks up to continue the storyline of *Atlas Black: Managing to Succeed*. College student and soon to be graduate, Atlas Black is ready to take his business idea to the next level. This book examines Atlas and his sidekick David as they transition from entrepreneurial dreamers to new venture managers. This book incorporates elements such as effective organizational communication (which is applied in a scene where Atlas and David venture on a double date and watch others engage in speed-dating), and their knowledge is later applied to successfully attaining a business loan.

Elements of motivation and leadership are also found in *Atlas Black: Management Guru?*, as shown in Figure B. In this scene, David acquires a new puppy and the training of this new pet is described following the type of reinforcement common to management and psychology classes. The introduction of the puppy is also used as a plot device to demonstrate that motivating individuals is often far more complex than the training of a new pet. For example, Atlas later visits a local baseball coach who discusses that how individual players process their rewards (often by making mental comparisons to others that they perceive are performing higher or lower) can often be as important as the actual amount of the reward being provided. These examples are helpful to students, many of whom have no experience in business but who have trained pets and participated in team sports.

Tales of Garcón: The Franchise Players

Tales of Garcón: The Franchise Players covers key concepts from family business management, small business management, and franchising. As noted on the back cover, the

Above, Opposite and following page: Figure B, excerpt from *Atlas Black: Management Guru?*

Oh yeah right! Your smile.
It's the same with workers. Tips and rewards immediately follow behavior and form a strong link between action and consequence.
But you have to monitor a puppy constantly to make **positive reinforcement** work!
Negative reinforcement increases desired behavior by removal of unpleasant outcomes once desired behavior is demonstrated.
Taking off a puppy's leash once he learns to not run away, for example.
How's that going?
Not so good.
I had a waitress job where we had to pay for broken dishes until we went 10 days without an accident.
Uh, apparently Puppy cannot go 10 minutes without an accident...
Oh Puppy!
I'll get a wet rag for you.
page 3

208   Part IV: Specific Graphic Novels and Comics and Their Application

Third, extinction decreases the frequency of negative behaviors by removal of rewards following negative behavior.

Dude! He just peed!

For example, I learned last night to not comfort Puppy every time he barks at night or he'd just keep doing it forever.

Finally, punishment reduces the frequency of undesirable behaviors by presenting negative consequences following unwanted behaviors. Like when I tap Puppy on the nose when he bites down on my fingers too hard.

Maybe you shouldn't put your fingers in his mouth?!

Positive Reinforcement
-add a reward following good behavior-

(give a puppy a treat when he does something good)

Negative Reinforcement
-remove deterrent after good behavior is established-

(take off leash when a puppy learns to not run way)

Extinction
-do not reward or otherwise encourage bad behavior-

(ignore a puppy when he barks needlessly)

Punishment
-add a negative consequence following bad behavior-

(tap a puppy on nose if he tries to bite someone)

page 4

Above and following: Figure C, excerpt from *Tales of Garcón: The Franchise Players*

210   Part IV: Specific Graphic Novels and Comics and Their Application

MANY CORPORATIONS ARE JUST LIKE THAT ARMY I AVOIDED: BIG, CLUMSY, AND SLOW TO REACT.
COMING SOON! YET ANOTHER CHEEP! MOTEL
AND YOU CAN HEAR THEM COMING FROM A PROVERBIAL MILE AWAY.
LIKE MY TINY BAND OF FUGITIVES,SMALL BUSINESSES SUCH AS HOTEL GARCÓN HAVE IMPORTANT ADVANTAGES.
YOU ARE NIMBLE AND YOU CAN MAKE FAST DECISIONS!
EXACTLY, SEÑORITA.
AND AS A FAMILY BUSINESS, WE WILL KEEP OUR SPIRIT OF FUN AND CUSTOMER SERVICE ALIVE ACROSS MANY GENERATIONS. A CHAIN HOTEL IS SUBJECT TO THE WHIMS OF EACH NEW CORPORATE PRESIDENT THAT COMES ALONG.
Your local Hotel
Ritz and Glitz
is now a Hippie Hostel
ALL ROOMS $20 A NIGHT!
ENOUGH OF THIS BUSINESS TALK, AMIGOS.
LET ME BUY ALL OF YOU A DRINK.
SOME OF YOU, PERHAPS MORE THAN ONE.
25

book visually addresses a number of questions relevant to family businesses. "Should our family firm expand, or should we be content with the success we enjoy now?" "Which of my children should succeed me at the helm?" "Is franchising a viable source or growth, and is it really a form of entrepreneurship?" "How can I ensure that my family firm thrives in the future?" The founders of family firms wrestle with complex questions like these every day, and the answers are elusive. *In Tales of Garcón: The Franchise Players*, a charismatic entrepreneur named Garcón tries to direct the destiny of the family-owned hotel that he created. As shown in Figure C, each night Garcón holds court to entertain his guests—while providing pithy anecdotes that are highly relevant to business.

The family's plans take an unexpected turn when a mysterious investor offers to become the hotel's first franchisee. Garcón's carefree son Ramón readily embraces the opportunity, while his cynical daughter Isabel questions the investor's motives. This graphic novel can serve as the main text for a college course in family business and/or franchising, as a supplement to a traditional textbook in these topic areas, as a reading within an executive program, and as a primer for entrepreneurs who simply want to learn more about how to be successful.

The Graphic N-extbook as Bricolage

On the surface, our GNs may seem like the products of profound or pathbreaking insights. Instead, like most innovations, they are an example of bricolage. Bricolage refers to a process of creatively using whatever materials happen to be at hand (Baker and Nelson, 2005). Many of civilization's greatest inventions are acts of bricolage. The elements that made up the Gutenberg press, for example, were far from original: "Each of its key elements—the movable type, the ink, the paper and the press itself—had been developed separately well before Johannes Gutenberg printed his first Bible in the 15th century. Movable type, for instance, had been independently conceived by a Chinese blacksmith named Pi Sheng four centuries earlier. The press itself was adapted from a screw press that was being used in Germany for the mass production of wine" (Johnson, 2010).

Bricolage is increasingly being recognized as an important concept within business courses, but mastering the concept is difficult for college students. In *Tales of Garcón*, we address this opportunity by presenting a colorful and tangible illustration of bricolage. When two of the main characters, Ramón and Audrey, are stranded by the unreliable "Ramón Cruiser" on the way to an important meeting, they are forced to hail a taxi. As shown in Figure X, they are given a ride by the "Tapas Taxi." The fictional entrepreneur behind the Tapas Taxi created a memorable new business by combining a traditional taxi with a lunch truck. This example, along with a description of how actor Johnny Depp created his Captain Jack Sparrow character by combining aspects of guitarist Keith Richards and cartoon skunk Pepe LePew, brings the bricolage concept to life for students. The most insightful students also notice that, ironically, the GNs themselves are examples of bricolage. In creating each GN, we sought to combine the best elements of textbooks and graphic novels into one package. Student feedback to date suggests that this journey has not been in vain (e.g., Randolph-Seng and Short, 2010).

University Life: A College Survival Story

The previous books we have co-authored illustrate the potential to apply the graphic novel format to business education. But the possibilities of this medium extend to numerous

Above and following page: Figure D, *The Tapas Taxi: An Example of Bricolage*

DON'T WORRY, I SPENT FOUR YEARS AS A CHEF AT THE FINEST RESTAURANTS IN SPAIN.
THERE I LEARNED THE SPANISH TRADITION OF TAPAS - SNACK SIZED PLATES OF CULINARY DELIGHTS.
YOUR TRUCK AND THIS FOOD ARE INCREDIBLE.
HOW DID YOU COME UP WITH THIS IDEA?
LIKE MOST ENTREPRENEURIAL IDEAS, MINE WAS NOT TRULY NOVEL.
INSTEAD, IT WAS AN EXAMPLE OF BRICOLAGE.
IS THAT FRENCH FOR TACKY?
BRICOLAGE INVOLVES OFFERING A FRESH TAKE ON EXISTING IDEAS.
THIS IS OFTEN DONE BY COMBINING ELEMENTS OF TWO OR MORE CONCEPTS INTO SOMETHING NEW.
INTERESTING. I READ ABOUT ACTOR JOHNNY DEPP DOING SOMETHING LIKE THAT.
HE CREATED HIS CAPTAIN JACK SPARROW CHARACTER IN THE PIRATES OF THE CARIBBEAN MOVIES BY COMBINING PERSONALITY TRAITS FROM ROCK'N'ROLL BAD BOY KEITH RICHARDS AND CARTOON SKUNK PEPE LE PEW.
EXACTLY. IN MY CASE, I COMBINED A GOURMET LUNCH TRUCK WITH A TAXI.
IN TODAY'S FAST-PACED WORLD, CUSTOMERS SEEM TO WELCOME THE CHANCE TO EAT SMALL PORTIONS OF GREAT FOOD WHILE ON THE ROAD.

Above and following page: Figure E, excerpt from *University Life: A College Survival Story*

SO, YOU MUST BE MY NEW OOMMATE, MASON CARVER? RIGHT?
HOPE YOU DON'T MIND, I TOOK THE BED BY THE WINDOW.
AND, UH, I'VE GOT A LOT OF POSTERS, BUT I LEFT YOU A LITTLE SPACE ON BACK OF THE DOOR. I MOVED IN LAST WEEK... HAD TO GET HERE EARLY FOR FOOTBALL. I'M TRAVIS HELTER.
WHAT'S UP BRO?
UH, NICE TO MEET YOU.
DUDE, YOU CAN UNPACK LATER. YOU KNOW WE HAVE A DORM-WIDE MEETING IN A FEW MINUTES?
IN A FEW MINUTES? I DON'T THINK I CAN GO TO THAT, I'VE GOT TO FIX MY SCHEDULE.
THERE'S BEEN A MISTAKE. I'M NOT REGISTERED FOR A COURSE REQUIRED BY MY MAJOR.
RELAX, MAN, YOU GOT TIME. GOT TO GO TO THE DORM MEETING, IT'S "MANDATORY." WE BETTER GET GOING, COME ON!
2

courses at the university level. For example, *University Life: A College Survival Story* (Payne, Short, and Austin, 2011) is a graphic novel that extensively addresses key issues and challenges faced by incoming college freshmen. Various issues that are deemed particularly relevant to this demographic — romance, alcohol use and abuse, study habits, and depression — are presented in the graphic narrative format so that dialogue can be established between students and parents, instructors, and/or counselors. As such, this graphic n-extbook may be utilized as: a complementary information source for freshman orientation courses; a supplement for potential students visiting universities for recruiting events; a primer for high school seniors anticipating attending college the following year; and/or a resource for parents wanting to create a dialogue with children regarding university life.

In the formative early weeks of college, a number of "common sense" strategies can often tip the balance between success and failure in the first semester of college, and *University Life* provides such tips and advice while facilitating dialogue about key issues through its character development and storyline. Within this graphic novel, the reader is introduced to a varied cast of freshmen characters including an athlete, an activist, a sorority member, an international student, a resident assistant, and others — as they manage their first semester in college, making both admirable and questionable decisions along the way. The opening pages of *University Life*— portraying the initial moving of the protagonist Mason Carver into his first university dorm experience — are presented in Figure E. The brief excerpt illustrates the all-too-common anxieties associated with "helicopter" parents, domineering roommates, and scheduling mishaps. The message to the reader is twofold: you are not alone in facing these challenges and these challenges can be overcome.

Conclusion

The opening quote from Professor John Hope Franklin reminded educators and students that they "must go beyond textbooks." We close with a far less eloquent yet no less useful quote. *Rich Dad, Poor Dad* author Robert Kiyosaki (2010) was blunt in his reaction to an interview of one of us about the Atlas Black books. Via Facebook and Twitter, Kiyosaki wrote, "Here's a professor who gets it. Textbooks suck. Make school fun and the learning increases." In seeking to go beyond textbooks, our goal indeed has been to increase student learning by making our books engaging and fun.

References

Baker, Ted, and Reed E. Nelson. 2005. "Creating Something from Nothing: Resource Construction Through entrepReneurial Bricolage." *Administrative Science Quarterly* 50: 329–366.
Johnson, Stephen. September 25, 2010. "The Genius of the Tinkerer." *Wall Street Journal.* Accessed March 1, 2012. http://online.wsj.com/article/SB10001424052748703989304575503730101860838.html.
Ketchen, David J., and Jeremy C. Short. 2011. "Separating Fads from Facts: Lessons from the Good, the Fad, and the Ugly." *Business Horizons.*
_____, Jeremy C. Short, Will Terrell, et al. 2011. *Tales of Garcón: The Franchise Players.* Nyack, NY: Flat World Knowledge.
Kiyosaki, Robert. October 7, 2010. *Robert Kiyosaki@TheRealKiyosaki Twitter* feed. Accessed March 1, 2012. http://twitter.com/#!/theRealKiyosaki/status/26670275389.
Monin, Kate. 2010. "An Entertaining and Educational Graphic Novel Textbook." *Graphic Novel Reporter.* Accessed October 27, 2010. http://www.graphicnovelreporter.com/content/entertaining-and-educational-graphic-novel-textbook-op-ed.

Payne, Tyge G., Jeremy C. Short, and Rob Austin. 2011. *University Life: A College Survival Story*. Nyack, NY: Flat World Knowledge.

Pierleoni, Allen. September 8, 2010. "Business Textbooks Meet The Graphic Novel." *Victoria Advocate.com*. Accessed March 1, 2012. http://www.victoriaadvocate.com/news/2010/sep/08/bc-book-textbookssa-_-books-350-words/?entertainment.

Randolph-Seng, Brandon, and Jeremy C. Short. August 2010. "A Graphic Novel Approach to Teaching Strategic Management." *Academy of Management Annual Meetings*. Montreal, Canada.

Short, Jeremy C., Talya Bauer, David J. Ketchen, et al. 2010. *Atlas Black: Management Guru?* Nyack, NY: Flat World Knowledge.

———, Talya Bauer, David J. Ketchen, et al. 2010. *Atlas Black: Managing to Succeed*. Nyack, NY: Flat World Knowledge.

Short, Jeremy C., and Terrie C. Reeves. 2009. "The Graphic Novel: A 'Cool' Format for Communicating to Generation Y." *Business Communications Quarterly* 72: 414–430.

Wojciechowska, Iza. August 20, 2010. A Graphic Text. *Inside Higher Ed*. Accessed March 1, 2012. http://www.insidehighered.com/news/2010/08/20/graphic.

Part V

Cultural Implications of Graphic Novels and Comics

Beyond Borders
Teaching Global Awareness Through the Graphic Novel

Lan Dong

Using the undergraduate course, ENG 330 Graphic Novel, at the University of Illinois–Springfield as a case study, this essay examines how the graphic novel can be an effective teaching tool in helping students to acquire verbal and visual literacy and engage with texts analytically and critically, to discuss and interpret primary materials within their social, political, and historical contexts, to identify and analyze global issues and their impact, and to practice awareness of and respect for diverse cultures within and outside the United States. Despite the increasing critical attention given to the graphic novel in recent years, the term itself lacks a commonly agreed definition.[1] Coined by Richard Kyle in 1964 to refer to comic books in general, this generic category was introduced to a broad range of readers thanks to Will Eisner's *A Contract with God and Other Tenement Stories* (1978), one of the first American graphic novels. This essay uses the term "graphic novel" to loosely refer to book-length comics, including graphic narratives, graphic memoirs, comic travelogue, journalistic comics, and hybrid genres.

The University of Illinois–Springfield is a small, public liberal arts institution of about 5,000 students. Its general education curriculum specifically emphasizes interdisciplinary approaches and highlights a broad engagement in public affairs. The campus in general offers small classes, substantial student-faculty interaction, and a technology-enhanced learning environment. The student body includes traditional, transfer, long-distant learning, and international students, although the majority of the students on campus are from Illinois. When I offered ENG 330 Graphic Novel in the fall of 2009, the first and only class on comics and graphic novels at this institution, the course had full enrollment. The majority of the students were English majors and about one-third of them were teacher education minors who took this class to fulfill the world and multicultural requirement in accordance with the state teaching certificate. When I taught ENG 330 again in the fall of 2010, it was offered online using the course management system Blackboard. I had to offer two sections to meet the high demand and ended up with two full classes. Students enrolled in this online class had various majors, ranging from business administration, English, history, liberal studies, sociology, and social work to biology, computer science, and mathematical science. They hailed from Arkansas, California, Colorado, Florida, Idaho, Iowa, Louisiana, Nebraska, Nevada, New York, North Carolina, Texas, Washington, Wisconsin, and Germany. The class included both traditional college students and non-traditional long-distant learning students. For non-traditional learners, the online format with asynchronized class instruction and discussion made it possible for them to attend school while working full time, raising families, or traveling. While I can model close reading and guide students through discussion with enlarged images and excerpts from selected graphic novels that are projected on the screen in the traditional classroom, teaching visual literacy as well as textual analysis in the virtual classroom in an asynchronized manner presents more challenges. As a result, I had to adjust pedagogy and adopt different strategy in my teaching practice.

As the title of this essay suggests, the course ENG 330 explores the concept of border on multiple levels: guiding students to analyze primary materials and topics across geographical and cultural borders, facilitating discussion on the meanings and implications between the borders of the comics panels themselves, as well as providing class activities and learning experiences in the traditional face-to-face class and online through Blackboard (the latter literally extending the classroom beyond borders). This essay argues that teaching the graphic novel at the university level, in a traditional and a virtual classroom setting, helps prompt critical thinking and improve students' analytical skills in interpreting textual and visual representations as well as boost their awareness of global perspectives and issues.

In the past, comic books — "originally an offshoot of the comic strip"— were regarded with "considerable suspicion by parents, educators, psychiatrists, and moral reformers" (Inge 1990, xi). During recent years, however, several studies and references for teachers and librarians have argued that comics can be used to inspire students to acquire reading comprehension and critical thinking skills, become engaged readers, and understand social and cultural issues (Thomas 1983; Crawford 2003; Gorman 2003; Cary 2004; Xu 2005; Frey and Fisher 2008; Thompson 2008; Krajewski and Wadsworth-Miller 2009; Rourke 2010; Stafford 2011). These studies, albeit valuable in gathering resources and arguing for comics' legitimate place in classrooms and libraries, focus mainly on primary and secondary education. Stephen Tabachnick's *Teaching the Graphic Novel* (2009), an edited volume recently published by the Modern Language Association in its Options for Teaching series, examines the pedagogical, theoretical, aesthetical, social, and cultural issues related to teaching the graphic novel at the university level. Robert Weiner's *Graphic Novels and Comics in Libraries and Archives* (2010) collects librarians' and scholars' ideas related specifically to the graphic novel in the libraries and archives, including those housed in colleges and universities. Moreover, the National Association of Comics Art Educators (NACAE), a collaboration of teachers, librarians, artists, and scholars, has a website that aims at providing resources for educators in response to the growing influence of comics on education (*www.teachingcomics.org*). Following these scholarly leads and combining theoretical approaches and classroom practice, this essay discusses how the graphic novel can teach college students about historical events, political affairs, and cultural exchanges, thus raising their awareness of issues that potentially have a global impact.

Gretchen Schwarz has argued that the combination of media literacy, graphic novels, and social issues within and outside the United States can effectively engage students in rhetorical analysis as well as "democratic learning" in the classroom (2007). The course ENG 330 Graphic Novel fulfills an "Engaged Citizenship Common Experience" requirement in the area of Global Awareness and is open to all majors at the University of Illinois Springfield. Housed in different departments, courses in this category generally are designed "to help students understand and function in an increasingly globalizing environment and to develop an appreciation of other cultural perspectives;" they aim to "foster an awareness of other cultures, polities, or natural environments at present or in the past" in order to help students "develop knowledge of global economic, political, technological, social, environmental, cultural, artistic, or health dilemmas" (General Education Council). Some of the common learning outcomes for Global Awareness courses include to help students "describe and analyze the effects of global phenomena on individual nations or cultures;" "practice awareness of and respect for the diversity of cultures and peoples of the world;" "analyze the impact (e.g., economic, political, historical, artistic or cultural) of nations, regions, or cultures upon other nations, regions or cultures and the response;" and "demonstrate an informed and reasoned point of view while perceiving and reacting to differences" (General Education Council).[2]

Heeding to these preferred learning outcomes, I also guided students to engage with scholarship in comics studies. Hillary Chute and Marianne DeKoven have proposed that the graphic novel (or, using their terminology, the "graphic narrative") encompasses "a range of types of narrative work in comics" and is viable for serious academic inquiry (2006, 767–768). Using graphic novels as primary texts for "serious academic inquiry," the objective of the interdisciplinary class ENG 330 was twofold: firstly, through reading, discussing, and writing about the graphic novel, students examine issues, phenomena, and controversies that have a global impact and secondly, through this learning process, students come to understand the profound and multivalent importance of the graphic novel. During the semesters of the fall of 2009 and the fall of 2010, we discussed a list of selected graphic novels — attending to their historical, political, cultural, and critical contexts — as well as examined the format and content of these texts with a focus on global perspectives. In addition, we read history, theory, interviews, critical essays, and internet sources that are related to each week's topic. Through reading primary and secondary materials arranged by themes, we explored in-depth how a graphic novel can cross the boundaries between history and memory, or between fiction and memoir; how a graphic novel can be a tragedy and comedy at the same time; and, how a graphic novel can take the form of reportage or travelogue that reveals complex regional, national, and international issues.

Supplemented by articles and book chapters on reserve, books on the class reading list took students on literary and visual journeys to different geographic locations and various historical periods: from Japanese immigrants' experience in San Francisco at the beginning of the twentieth-century to Jewish American life during the Great Depression; from humanitarian efforts in war-torn Afghanistan in the 1980s to the political conflicts in Eastern Bosnia in the 1990s as well as the role of the United Nations and the United States in these conflicts; from the mythological setting of the valley of the wind to the documentary-like chronicles of life in Burma. The class reading list included *Understanding Comics: The Invisible Art* (1994), *The Four Immigrants Manga: A Japanese Experience in San Francisco, 1904–1924* (1999), *Nausicaä of the Valley of Wind* (2001), *Safe Area Goražde: The War in Eastern Bosnia 1992–1995* (2003), *Fun Home: A Family Tragicomic* (2007), *Life, in Pictures: Autobiographical Stories* (2007), *Bound by Law?: Tales from the Public Domain* (2008), *Burma Chronicles* (2008), *The Photographer: Into War-Torn Afghanistan with Doctors without Borders* (2009), and *Berlin City of Stones: Book One* (2009).[3] Besides engaging with these texts, the class discussion also addressed the limitations and strengths of the authors' perspectives since some of them presented their experiences and reflections after traveling to other regions. Based on assessment of students' essays and projects as well as their reflections, these texts indeed appeared to promote critical thinking among the students and discussion on social issues such as the United States immigration history, copyright law and fair use, and the international impact on regional conflicts. This chapter will discuss two of the required readings below as examples to illustrate how the materials were used in the classroom and what students learned in the process of conducting research and preparing for class, participating in class discussion, and completing assignments and self-designed projects.

Global Awareness in Graphics

For the exploration of the graphic novel's effective and powerful representation of materials and topics across geographical and cultural borders in ENG 330, Henry Yoshitaka Kiyama's *The Four Immigrants Manga: A Japanese Experience in San Francisco, 1904–1924* provided an effective example. The book was first published in a bilingual format (English and Japanese) by the artist himself in San Francisco in 1931. Frederik Schodt's English translation was released in 1999. The narrative is loosely based on the experience of Kiyama and three friends, all immigrants from Japan. The story begins with the arrival of Henry, Charlie, Fred, and Frank in San Francisco in 1904 and ends with two of the main characters preparing for their visit to Japan two decades later. Using comic panels, Kiyama's work represents historical, political, and social issues while incorporating elements that are autobiographical, biographical, and historical in nature.

Mary Louise Penaz examines historical biography in the space between public and private, between truth and imagination: "I posit that historical biography is a narrative that contains historical, fictional, and personal/autobiographical elements, but the historical elements dominate the text in that they implicate, re-inscribe, or contest an authorized/dominant historical discourse of a people or nation in a specific epoch as individuals or groups of individuals" (2009, 93–94). *The Four Immigrants Manga* is of significance not only in reflecting the Japanese American experience and revealing multiple aspects of the Japanese immigrant community, but also in documenting historical events in American and world history, for example: the San Francisco Earthquake in 1906, school segregation in California, the Panama Pacific International Exposition, picture brides, World War I, and Spanish influenza in 1916, to list only a few. In terms of artistic style, the book has a standard layout: twelve panels on two pages make up each one of the fifty-two episodes. As a result, the narrative is episodic rather than linear and covers a broad range of social, political, and cultural topics in the context of Japan, San Francisco, and migration in a period of two decades.

For instance, *The Four Immigrants Manga* includes four episodes on picture brides. In the early twentieth century, a number of Japanese immigrants living in the United States were hesitant to go back to Japan to get married, partly out of financial concerns. Considering the fact that many Japanese immigrants had low-paying jobs, the cost of the trans–Pacific passage was high. Some of them were also concerned about the possibility of losing their deferred military draft status if they stayed in Japan for more than thirty days. Therefore, a number of Japanese men relied on families and relatives to arrange their marriages by an exchange of photographs. Once a marriage agreement had been settled, usually by a go-between, the prospective groom would pay the cost of the voyage and the bride-to-be would travel across the Pacific Ocean to Hawaii or the continental United States to marry a man whom she had never met. These women were known as picture brides.[4] It was not uncommon for young couples in such arranged marriages to have mass wedding ceremonies at the dock or in a nearby place immediately after the brides' arrival. The Gentlemen's Agreement of 1907 allowed wives and children to receive visas to join their husbands and fathers in Hawaii and the continental United States. This practice ceased around 1920.

In class we discussed Episode 40 of *The Four Immigrants Manga* panel by panel in which students analyzed text narratives, visual representations, and the historical context. This episode relates how a friend of one of the four main characters (Fred) sends his photograph to Japan with his face in profile; from this photographic angle, he knowingly avoids showing his pronounced horse-shoe-shaped scar. Episode 41 jumps to the day of his bride's arrival in San Francisco. Upon seeing the scar, the bride is shocked beyond consolation. With this image enlarged and projected on the screen, we discussed the visual details in Kiyama's work. In the panel on the left, the characters' physical gestures enhance the emotional intensity: the bride, whose face is hidden, is on the floor with puddles beneath her face that are formed by curvy lines, indicating that she has been crying for an extensive period of time. Although her dialogue bubble contains only three words: "Sob ... Boo hoo..." (Kiyama 1999, 111), her reaction to the truth could not be clearer. The intended husband is visibly frustrated. The plaster that he has used to cover his scar has partially peeled off, revealing the scar and reminding the reader of his failed attempt, and at the same time calling the reader's attention to his previous effort of hiding the truth by sending a photograph with his face in profile. The exaggerated size of his perspiration in both panels reflects his frustration and helplessness. As we moved on to the next panel, I pointed to the food left untouched and a wedding ring in the "puddle of tears" and reminded students how these objects suggest a further time lapse. The husband's narrative confirms the passage of time by telling the reader that he has "bought her clothes and a diamond ring, but she hasn't eaten for three days and nights" (Kiyama 1999, 111).

Following his friend's suggestion, the husband invites a Buddhist priest to counsel his new bride. The priest's sermon is so inspiring that the bride decides to "follow Buddha's teachings" (Kiyama 1999, 111). In the last two panels of this episode, the reader witnesses a dramatic twist. The bride, now smiling, wraps her arm around her husband's shoulders. Her face seems content and happy, which poses a sharp contrast to that of her man marked by an open mouth and an expression of surprise and disbelief. Using six panels, Kiyama documents moments of intensive emotional swings, which are both personal (for the husband and his new bride) and historical (for many Japanese immigrants in arranged marriages based on a mere exchange of photographs). Infused with exaggeration and humor, this episode nonetheless provides serious insight into the reality that picture brides had to deal with at the time.

In his study of Keiji Nakazawa's *Barefoot Gen* (2004, 2005), W. G. Sebald's *The Emigrants* (2002), *Austerlitz* (2002), and *On the Natural History of Destruction* (2003), and Art Spiegelman's *Maus: A Survivor's Tale* (1986, 1991), Jeff Adams focuses on these works' "visually oriented pedagogy" and examines how the authors document "moments of extreme social crisis" and recount traumatic incidents from the past for a contemporary audience (2008, 35–36). Similarly, panels in *The Four Immigrants Manga*, such as those discussed above, generated an animated discussion among students in my class not only on immigration, legislation, international policies, and United States–Japan relations, but also on religion, social class, and gender. The visual details, sometimes complimenting the textual narrative and other times undermining it through the creation of disparity and ambiguity, prompted questions during the class discussions. Such questions led to students' further inquiry outside the classroom in the process of preparing for their presentations, conducting research for research assignments, writing midterm essays, and completing final projects. For example, some students examined the economic situation in San Francisco and Japan at the turn of the twentieth century and its effect on the relationship between the two countries, or conducted research on Japanese and American women's rights at the time in a comparative framework, or addressed religious beliefs in Japan and in Japanese immigrant communities and their impact in early twentieth century, or investigated policies and legislations regarding immigration and immigrants at the local, state, and federal levels. In their midterm essays, some students argued that the graphic novel is an effective way to represent history, using Kiyama's book as the primary text. As Bradford Wright has pointed out, a cultural history seeks to "deepen our understanding of the interaction between politics, social change, and popular culture" (2003, xv). In this case study Kiyama's work presents such a cultural history in the form of a graphic novel that prompted the students to think about complex social issues within and outside the United States borders. If stories of Henry and his friends, set in San Francisco and told in comics panels, provide cultural references that students may be familiar with, the next text shifts the geographical location to Afghanistan and presents the narrative in a combination of photography and comics, thus challenging students' preconceptions of the "unfamiliar" literally and figuratively.

The Space In-Between

Currently, graphic novels are reviewed regularly in the *New York Times Book Review* while many bookstores have identified comics as a growth area and publishers have begun launching new lines to publish or distribute graphic novels; moreover, an increasing number of scholars and general readers realize that "comics are stories with pictures that are not limited by genre or stylistic constraints" (Sturm 2002). In order to examine the collaboration and at times tensions between textual narratives and visual representations and to scrutinize other elements beyond panel frames (such as the gutter), this chapter now turns to Emmanuel Guibert, Didier Lefévre, and Frédéric Lemercier's *The Photographer: Intro War-Torn Afghanistan with Doctors Without Borders*. Just as the translator Alexis Siegel has stated in his introduction, "through the alchemy of this rare collaboration, *The Photographer* ushers us into a deeper understanding of a fascinating country and a truer appreciation of humanitarian workers who risk their lives in the service of others" (2009, xi). Upon reading this book in the course ENG 330 Graphic Novel, many students were surprised and considered it unique due to its content (i.e., a medical team carrying out humanitarian efforts in Afghanistan despite constant threats imposed by warlords, bandits, Wahhabi fundamentalists, Soviet soldiers, and harsh living conditions) and its format (i.e., a combination of photographs and comic panels).

In class I first introduced images from other graphic novels so that students understood the usage of visual elements other than comic strips in a graphic novel is by no means exclusive to *The Photographer*. Art Spiegelman's *Maus*, an indisputable landmark in the history of the graphic novel, incorporates photographs, maps, and diagrams. Maps, photographs, excerpts from literary works and the dictionary, as well as pieces of handwritten personal correspondence and diary entries play an important role in Alison Bechdel's *Fun Home*. What makes *The Photographer* unique is its seamless fusion of the moments captured by Lefévre's cameras during his trip to Afghanistan with Doctors Without Borders/Médecins Sans Frontières in 1986 and Guibert's artistic reflection in comic panels inspired by Lefévre's narrative years later. Originally published in three volumes in France in 2003, 2004, and 2006, this book in hybrid format further testifies to the versatility and potential of comics as a medium. Its literary and artistic complexity, paired with its emotional intensity, provides a reading experience like none other. When discussing comics as a vessel "that can hold any number of ideas and images," Scott McCloud has noted that "icons demand our participation to make them work" (2004, 6, 59). Combining comic icons with documentary photography, *The Photographer* presented a new challenge for the students to comprehend Afghan people, the local landscape and cultural customs, political affairs, military conflicts, and international negotiation not only through Lefévre's photojournalist view but also through Guibert's creative perspective as well.

Accompanying a Médecins Sans Frontières (MSF) mission in Afghanistan and documenting the trip with his cameras, Lefévre (identified by his first name Didier in the book) is the photographer referred to in the book's title. In his introduction to *The Photographer*, Siegel states: "Didier's innocence, openness, and eagerness to learn make him an ideal guide for us as readers. His reportage has a depth of honesty that comes from a passion for service — service to his art, first and foremost, and, second, to the mission that he has agreed to be part of: a humanitarian expedition of Doctors Without Borders" (2009, v). Even though some students had heard about this humanitarian organization before taking ENG 330, none of them knew much about its founding in 1971 in France and awarding of the Nobel Peace Prize in 1999, let alone the group's undertakings in Afghanistan during the Soviet occupation. As Siegel has pointed out, witnessing an MSF mission in a war zone through reading *The Photographer* is a "humbling experience" (2009, x). As many students commented in class discussion, the reading experience was not only humbling but also inspiring. The exposure to various aspects of Afghan life challenged their preconceptions of the country and broadened their understanding of its culture and people well beyond what the media have been reporting on: Taliban and extremists.

For instance, prior to reading and discussing *The Photographer*, most students had associated Afghan women with social oppression, a restrictive dress code, gender bias, and lack of equal rights without further interrogation of the subject matter. In class we discussed how *The Photographer* uses photographs, comic panels, and textual narratives to demonstrate contrasting aspects of women's lives in Afghanistan, thus drawing the reader's attention to the complexity of gender relations. Shortly after his arrival in Peshawar, Pakistan, Didier documents his adjustment to the unfamiliar environment while recording the MSF team's preparation for the long and dangerous journey across the border into Afghanistan. What surprised Didier as much as the students was the fact that the leader of this mission is a woman, Juliette Fournot. Having spent her teenage years in Afghanistan, Juliette is fluent in Afghan Persian and is knowledgeable about the country and its culture.

For class discussion, we analyzed the hybrid layout on page 42 as an example to examine how the book enables the reader to observe Juliette carrying out her task effectively when negotiating and coordinating with the local Pakistanis and Afghans despite her gender. As McCloud has pointed out, the space between the panels, known as the gutter, is "the host to much of the magic and mystery that are at the heart of the comics" (2004, 66). Figure 1, including photographs and comic panels arranged in deliberate sequence, uses these gutters to capture repeated action within limited space and to emphasize the extraordinary out of the ordinary. On top of this page, two photographs show Juliette talking to small groups of men from two different angles: one from behind and the other from the side. In both frames, Juliette stands out as the only woman. The background details on these photographs lead to ambiguity: they could be two meetings that happen at differing time and settings; they also could be one meeting in one location shot from different angles.

As the students continued to read down the page, they found four comic panels portraying a conversation between Juliette and Didier probably sometime after one of such dealings, in which she explains how she manages to perform her duties both as a chief and as a woman. These panels seem sequential and continuous in terms of the characters' action. Besides asserting her authority through a certain tone, Juliette emphasizes the importance of knowing the cultural norms: "you'll never see me reach out my hand to them, stare at them, or do anything that could humiliate them" (Guibert, et al. 2009, 42). Then this scene concludes with another photograph of Juliette interacting with a group of men. This time she is facing the camera, again the only female in view. "Although movement and meaning *can* be shown and articulated *within* a panel through a variety of techniques, more frequently action is evoked in the space *between* frames" (Berlatsky 2009, 174; italics in the original). The juxtaposition among the seemingly linear narratives, the visual representations in the comic panels, and the implied temporal and spatial gaps in the photographs all suggest a time lapse. Thus, such photographs and comic drawings are "visual interventions" providing layers of interpretations overlain with text narratives (Adams 2008, 40). The particular arrangement of the frames—two photographs on the top, followed by three comic panels, and then followed by a comic panel side by side with a photograph—complicates the notion of time. Juliette's dialogue with Didier could have happened after her interactions with the local men; it also could have occurred during an interval, indicating tasks as such were common day-to-day routines for her, although they may seem unusual to the reader. Such a combination allowed the students in this case study to take a glance at Juliette's experiences in Afghanistan in only a few frames.

In another village, after Didier has witnessed and documented medical procedures performed under impossible circumstances—children severely injured, sick, or passing away, as well as other heart-wrenching events—his conversation with Juliette introduced the students to Afghan women within the context of their family life. Figure 2, for instance, portrays the last section of the two characters' conversation. As the dialogue bubbles indicate, Juliette provides most of the narrative in this scene. "Graphic narrative, through its most basic composition in frames and gutters—in which it is able to gesture at the pacing and rhythm of reading and looking through the various structures of each individual page—calls the students' attention visually and spatially to the act, process, and duration of interpretation" (Chute and DeKoven 2006, 767). Even though all but one panel portrays both Juliette and Didier, the characters' gestures and facial features distinguish their roles clearly: Juliette leads the conversation while Didier is a listener for the most part. Juliette's hand gestures and facial expressions change from panel to panel, corresponding to the specific conversational topics. When she mentions how her best friend from a westernized family in Kabul once resorted to *chadri* to hide her identity when meeting with her boyfriend, her finger is pointing to her head scarf. Her smiling face compliments the narrative tone and helps to emphasize the irony of the common yet biased understanding of *chadri* in Afghan women's life. In comparison, Didier's posture hardly changes across the nine panels on this page. One of his hands is holding his chin in the first two panels; on the rest of the page, he is sitting next to Juliette with his head turning toward her and arms folded on his knees.

Because of her gender and her ability to communicate and gain trust, Juliette has access to Afghan women, thus supplying valuable information about women's family life before and after marriage as well as their social roles. Contrary to the common American and European view of the "poor helpless woman under her *chadri*," an Afghan woman can take advantage of *chadri* to seduce her love interest, to gain freedom of stepping outside her home in urban areas, and to carry weapons and participate in resistance (Guibert, et al. 2009, 144–

Figure 1. Emmanuel Guibert, Didier Lefévre, and Frédéric Lemercier. Trans. Alexis Siegel. 2009. *The Photographer: Into War-Torn Afghanistan with Doctors Without Borders.* New York: First Second, 42.

145). Juliette's personal encounter with Afghan women reveals that they have a strong influence on the local leaders and are generally the custodians of values and moral reference points. Gaining their support and obtaining inside information are of particular importance for her effective interaction with Afghan men. Juliette's comments—"And they're funny. You should hear them gossiping about the men, you'd split your sides laughing"—not only adds a humorous touch to the narrative but also demystifies and portrays Afghan women as human beings who share many characteristics in common with women from other cultures (Guibert, et al. 2009, 145). Didier's response, "I'm going to grow some boobs so I can come with you next time" (Guibert, et al. 2009, 145), concludes this conversation. This commentary, juxtaposed with Figure 1 discussed above, uncovers the ironic complexity of gender

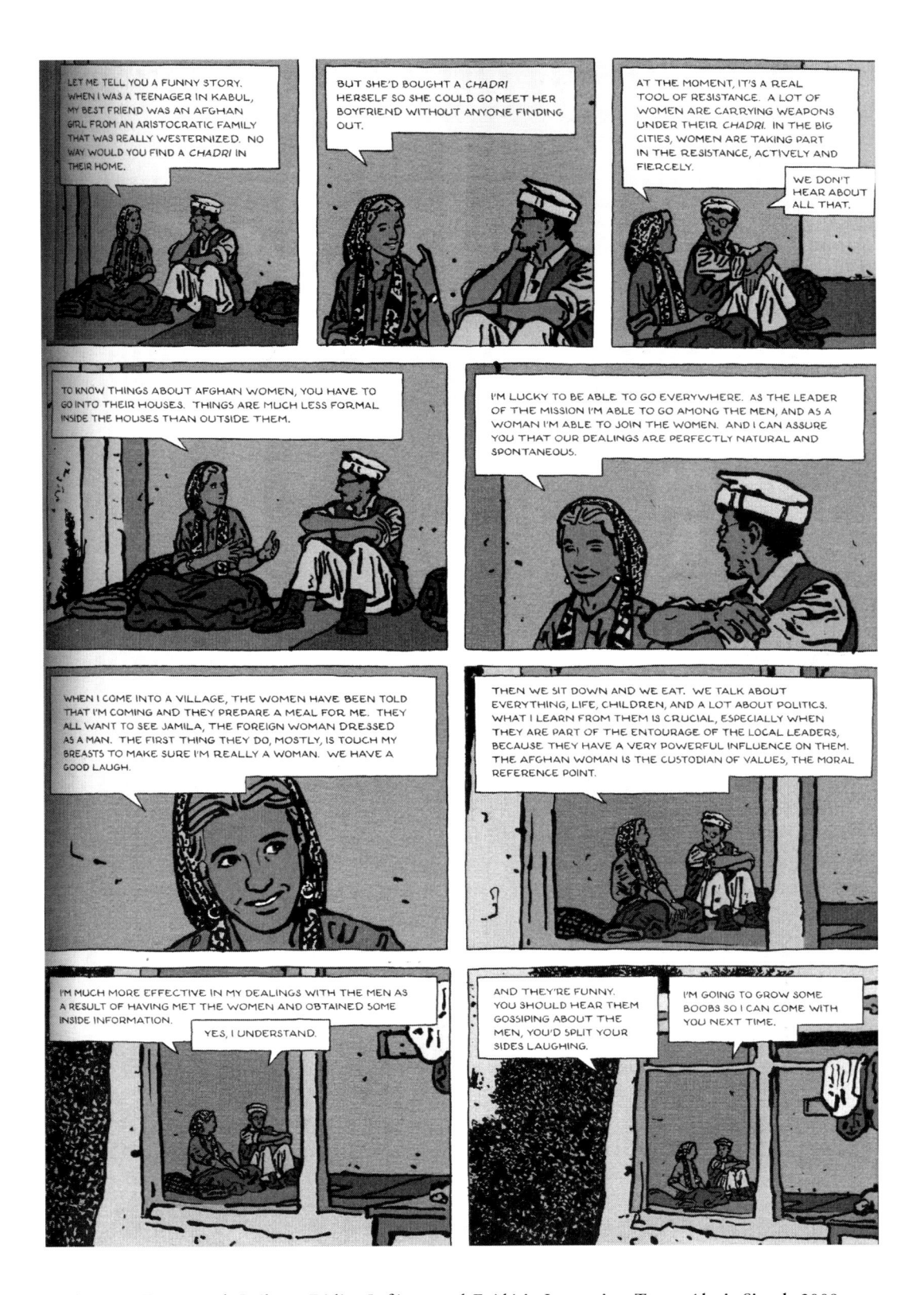

Figure 2. Emmanuel Guibert, Didier Lefévre, and Frédéric Lemercier. Trans. Alexis Siegel. 2009. *The Photographer: Into War-Torn Afghanistan with Doctors Without Borders.* New York: First Second, 143.

in Afghan society. If Juliette's female identity is an implied disadvantage in the previous scene, here it becomes a privilege that has worked to her benefit and sheds light for the students on the multiple layers of Afghan women's life.

Conclusion

Besides helping students practice awareness of and respect for diverse cultures and peoples, global awareness courses at the University of Illinois Springfield also aim at guiding student to recognize their social responsibilities in a larger community at the local, regional, national, and international levels. To that end, ENG 330 Graphic Novel requires not only close reading papers, analytical essays, and oral presentations but also research assignments and a final project with open possibilities. For instance, one student wrote, drew, and designed a pamphlet of comics panels on suicide prevention for LGBT youth. Some students chose to do lesson plans for secondary schools using graphic novels as primary texts and hoped to implement them in their student teaching practicum that is part of their teacher education minor curriculum. Some wrote research papers exploring the educational values of graphic novels or examining the generic interrelation between the graphic novel and life writing. Collectively, these projects not only serve as tools to assess students learning, but they also indicate the impact of this course well beyond the classroom.

Most students, in their reflection essays, wrote positively about their learning experiences. One student commented on the study of the graphic novel: "I became amazed by the fact that a series of graphic novels gave me a better understanding or further curiosity about international issues that a magazine article or a textbook could not." Another student wrote about the graphic novel being literature beyond words: "The graphic novels we read this semester really opened my eyes up to a literary field that is both exciting and powerful.... To interpret a graphic novel, we need use that same literary theory but also add a close reading of the visual pieces of the novel. The interpretation now becomes more complex because it must go beyond words." Yet another student reflected how the appreciation of the graphic novel acquired through the course has affected his view of literature in general:

> From the beginning of our Graphic Novels class, I was given an opportunity to look at literature from a new perspective. By *seeing* as well as reading the assigned narratives, my expanded perspective forced me to consider the wide variety of available material and enabled me to pay more attention to alternatives to the literary canon.... Rather than limiting my perspective with words on a page, the physical layout of graphics suggests an intellectual exercise that promotes a way to read, a new angle that provides a more complete picture both mentally and physically.... While not surprised at the diversity of the publications, I was enlightened by the level of sophistication compared to what I expected from "comics" at the onset of the class.

These students' comments and reflections suggest the particular objectives, reading materials, and coverage of a class on the graphic novel have opened many intellectual doors to explore further: global awareness, comics' literary and creative potential, and genre crossing, thus expanding the horizons of their learning experience and fostering civil engagement and responsibility.

Scholar James Sturm has stated: "despite the growing critical recognition and commercial success of cartoonists' work and the fervent interest in the medium from young artists, academe does not recognize the medium's legacy." In studying the transformation of American youth culture, historian Bradford Wright considers comic books as one of the few "enduring expressions of American popular culture" that are so instantly recognizable yet so poorly understood (2003, xiii). Thus, the findings of this case study suggest that the introduction of the graphic novel in university classrooms may be one way to foster recognition and understanding of this medium's complexity as well as its potential as a valuable teaching tool for the exploration of both local as well as global issues.

Notes

1. Philip Charles Crawford, for example, considers the graphic novel "a sophisticated story, told in comic book format, in one full-length book" growing out of experimentation in the late 1970s and early 1980s (2003, 1). Approaching the term from a different angle, Stephen Tabachnick defines the graphic novel as "an extended comic book that treats nonfictional as well as fictional plots and themes with the depth and subtlety that we have come to expect of traditional novels and extended nonfictional texts" (2009, 2).
2. More information about the engaged citizenship common experience curriculum and the global awareness requirement is available at: *http://www.uis.edu/academicplanning/curriculum/EngagedCitizenship CommonExperience.html.*
3. In the fall of 2009 I used *Fun Home* and in the fall of 2010 I replaced it with *Berlin City of Stones.*
4. It is worth noting that there were a number of Korean women who entered the United States as picture brides in the early twentieth century as well. Moreover, after Japan annexed Korea, all Koreans were considered Japanese subjects until Korea gained its independence in 1945.

References

Adams, Jeff. March 2008. "The Pedagogy of the Image Text: Nakazawa, Sebald and Spiegelman Recount Social Traumas." *Discourse: Studies in the Cultural Politics of Education* 29.1: 35–49.
Berlatsky, Eric. May 2009. "Lost in the Gutter: Within and Between Frames in Narrative and Narrative Theory." *Narrative* 17.2: 162–187.
Cary, Stephen. 2004. *Going Graphic: Comics at Work in the Multilingual Classroom.* Portsmouth, NH: Heinemann.
Chute, Hilary, and Marianne DeKoven. 2006. "Introduction: Graphic Narrative." *Modern Fiction Studies* 52.4: 767–782.
Crawford, Philip Charles. 2003. *Graphic Novels 101: Selecting and Using Graphic Novels to Promote Literacy for Children and Young Adults.* Salt Lake City, UT: Hi Willow Research and Publishing.
Frey, Nancy, and Douglas Fisher. 2008. "Introduction." In Nancy Frey, and Douglas Fisher, eds., *Teaching Visual Literacy: Using Comic Books, Graphic Novels, Anime, Cartoons, and More to Develop Comprehension and Thinking Skills.* Thousand Oaks, CA: Corwin, 1–4.
General Education Council. "ECCE Course Approval Criteria — Area: Global Awareness." Accessed September 26, 2011. http://www.uis.edu/academicplanning/curriculum/EngagedCitizenshipCommonExperience. html.
Gorman, Michele. 2003. *Getting Graphic: Using Graphic Novels to Promote Literacy with Preteens and Teens.* Worthington, OH: Linworth Publishing.
Guibert, Emmanuel, Didier Lefévre, and Frédéric Lemercier. Trans. Alexis Siegel. 2009. *The Photographer: Into War-Torn Afghanistan with Doctors Without Borders.* New York: First Second.
Inge, M. Thomas. 1990. *Comics as Culture.* Jackson: University Press of Mississippi.
Kiyama, Henry Yoshitaka. Trans. Frederik L. Schodt. 1999. *The Four Immigrants Manga: A Japanese Experience in San Francisco, 1904–1924.* Berkeley, CA: Stone Bridge Press.
Krajewski, Sarah, and Melissa Wadsworth-Miller. 2009. "Graphic Novels + Teacher Research = Student Success." *The English Record* 50.1: 9–16.
McCloud, Scott. 2004. *Understanding Comics: The Invisible Art.* New York: HarperCollins Publishers.
NACAE: National Association of Comics Art Educators. Accessed February 22, 2011. http://www. teachingcomics.org.
Penaz, Mary Louise. 2009. "Drawing History: Interpretation in the Illustrated Version of the *9/11 Commission Report* and Art Spiegelman's *In the Shadow of No Towers* as Historical Biography." *a/b: Auto/Biography Studies* 24.1: 93–112.
Rourke, James. 2010. *The Comic Book Curriculum: Using Comics to Enhance Learning and Life.* Santa Barbara, CA: Libraries Unlimited/ABC-CLIO.
Schwarz, Gretchen. November 2007. "Media Literacy, Graphic Novels, and Social Issues." *Simile: Studies*

in Media and Information Literacy Education 7.4: no pagination. Accessed January 25, 2011. *http://utpjournals.metapress.com/content/x1611725454724x3/fulltext.pdf.*

Siegel, Alexis. 2009. "Introduction." In Emmanuel Guibert, Didier Lefévre, and Frédéric Lemercier, eds., *The Photographer: Into War-Torn Afghanistan with Doctors Without Borders*. New York: First Second: v–xi.

Stafford, Tim. 2011. *Teaching Visual Literacy in the Primary Classroom: Comic Books, Film, Television and Picture Narratives*. London: Routledge.

Sturm, James. April 5, 2002. "Comics in the Classroom." *Chronicle of Higher Education* 48.30: B14–B15. Reprinted Teachingcomics.org. Accessed January 25, 2011. *http://www.teachingcomics.org/index.php?option=com_content&view=article&id=107:Comics%20in%20the%20Classroom&catid=45:Comics%20in%20Classrooms&Itemid=65*

Tabachnick, Stephen E. ed. 2009. *Teaching the Graphic Novel*. New York: MLA.

Thompson, Terry. 2008. *Adventures in Graphica: Using Comics and Graphic Novels to Teaching Comprehension, 2–6*. Portland, ME: Stenhouse.

Thomas, James L. ed. 1983. *Cartoons and Comics in the Classroom: A Reference for Teachers and Librarians*. Littleton, CO: Libraries Unlimited.

Weiner, Robert G., ed. 2010. *Graphic Novels and Comics in Libraries and Archives: Essays on Readers, Research, History and Cataloging*. Jefferson, NC: McFarland.

Wright, Bradford W. 2003. *Comic Book Nation: The Transformation of Youth Culture in America*. Baltimore, MD: Johns Hopkins University Press.

Xu, Shelley Hong. 2005. *Trading Cards to Comic Strips: Popular Culture Texts and Literacy Learning in Grades K-8*. Newark, DE: International Reading Association.

The Benefits of Writing Comics

DIANA MALISZEWSKI

The benefits of reading comics have been well-documented thanks to many studies (Anderson and Styles 1999; Baker 2011; Biebrich 2006; Booth and Lundy 2007; Goldstein 1986; Graham 2011; Krashen 2004; Kunai 2007; Thomas 1983; Ujiie and Krashen 1996). According to Steven Krashen, students are more engaged, motivated, and increase their vocabulary partly as a result of reading this type of material (Krashen 2004). Studies examining the benefits of writing or creating comics may not be as numerous as their reading counterparts but have begun to appear in the literature more frequently than in the past. There are several reasons for the preponderance of comic reading advocates. Linda Jenkins states "historically reading has been given precedence over writing in the American education system because reading has been considered the gateway to knowledge and a necessary prerequisite to writing" (Jenkins 1994, 1). Further along, she asserts, "theorists in the educational community such as Haugaard (1973) and Alongi (1974) tend to focus on the capacity for comic books to motivate reluctant readers" (Jenkins 1994, 32). Michael Bitz confirms Jenkins' declaration a decade later when he notes, "surprisingly few researchers have focused on the connections between comics creation and conventional writing instruction. ...perhaps the reason for the relative disconnection between comics and writing is that teachers are so much more focused on reading, and even speaking, than on writing..." (Bitz 2010, 51). James Carter, in his article on the power of comics, says that a "concept that often goes unconsidered is that comics and graphic novels needn't only be integrated into the curriculum as additional reading material. ...writing and drawing graphic novels is an authentic composing activity" (2009). Does the medium of comics encourage reluctant writers? How does writing comics differ from creating other texts? What writing skills can be honed by creating comics?

The Ontario Ministry of Education offered grants to various schools to investigate issues pertaining to boys' literacy as part of a project from 2005 to 2008. A small team of teachers at Agnes Macphail Public School studied the link between engagement and graphic novels. The results of that research indicated that reading and writing comics engaged both male and female students (Bodkin et al. 2009, 2009a). Further independent investigation at the school focused on writing comics. This less formal inquiry discovered that writing and creating comics produced similar benefits to reading them, as well as unique rewards. The use of technology as a creation tool helps overcome limitations such as time and drawing talent so that students of any age or ability can become a comic artist and reap the benefits (Albers and Sanders 2010).

Challenges in Creating Comics

There are several justifiable reasons why the benefits of writing comics have not been studied as frequently as the benefits of reading comics. Tuula Meriso-Storm (2006) reports that kids like writing less than reading. She notes that student attitudes towards writing decline with age because students realize that skillful writing takes effort. (Meriso-Storm 2006, 113). Boy students surveyed felt that writing was not a masculine pastime (Meriso-Storm 2006, 114). In addition to the writing portion of comic creation, the artwork required can also intimidate potential creators. Mark Crilley jokes that "you may think one will need a graduate degree in design and an encyclopedic knowledge of human anatomy to get started" (Crilley 2009, 2).

Creating a comic takes much longer than reading a comic; there are many steps to follow and many decisions to make. Michael Bitz reports in his project that devising the manuscript for the comic was the hardest part of the process and that several of his participants dropped out because they were too overwhelmed (Bitz 2004). Bitz also lists limited time, parental support, willing students, available community partners, and the pressures of standardized testing as other challenges (Bitz 2010, 40). Edwin Vega and Heidi Schnackenberg claim that "actual creation of comics by these same [school-aged] children has not been possible until multimedia software and hardware became available to the public and to schools" (Vega and Schnackenberg 2006, 30). Even with the enabling technology, there are still challenges: Collier (as cited in Lawrence, McNeal and Yildiz 2009) states that "First, not all students have technological knowledge; second, even those who do have it need to know how to manage these skills" (Lawrence, McNeal and Yildiz 2009, 484).

Considering all the challenges that exist creating comics, educators may be tempted to abandon such projects, but that would be shortsighted. The benefits for students in creating comics are many and wide-ranging. The benefits can be grouped into four categories: 1) The process of creating comics mirrors the writing process and involves many other skill sets and subject areas. Simply put, writing comics makes you a better writer. 2) Comic writing is purposeful and authentic and honors the voice and experiences of the creator. 3) Creating comics is fun and engaging. 4) It is a collaborative and creative process that, through the use of technology, magnifies the other benefits as well.

CREATING COMICS PRODUCES BETTER WRITERS WHO INCORPORATE OTHER SKILLS AND SUBJECTS

Reading frequently makes students better readers, and similarly, writing often makes students better writers. As an added bonus, writing comics incorporates many other abilities and information "pockets." Edwin S. Vega and Heidi L. Schnackenberg created a program they called "Summer Safari" for 9- to 14-year-old students to create their own comic. At the end of the program, they surveyed their participants' satisfaction with the program using 16 questions. Based on their observations, they found that "comic creation is multidisciplinary and interdisciplinary, which tends to help kids see the links between various subjects, rather than just compartmentalizing knowledge for specific classes" (Vega and Schnackenberg 2006, 36). They witnessed their students using grammar and writing lessons from their English classes so that the readers would understand the character's words and actions clearly (Vega and Schnackenberg 2006, 32).

Michael Bitz founded "The Comic Book Project" in 2002 as an after school program for students in urban schools. His instructors underwent training workshops prior to working with their 10- to 13-year-old clients, so that the workers understood the connection between basic drawing techniques and how they parallel basic writing techniques (Bitz 2004, 578). When the project was completed, all students and instructors completed an 18-item questionnaire. 86 percent of the participants reported that they were getting better at writing because of the project (Bitz 2004, 582). The instructors confirmed the students' self-assessment in this area, as did the manuscripts, which showed evidence of corrections and revisions (Bitz 2004, 584). In his later book, Bitz states, based on his research, that "creating comics enables students to retain creativity in the writing process while reinforcing all the basic writing skills that teachers aim to instill: planning, rehearsing, composing, revising, and editing" (Bitz 2010, 52).

Mark Crilley is a graphic novelist who visits many schools to speak to students and he explains "graphic novel storytelling ... is also a fantastic way of teaching them some of the fundamentals about writing. They learn the importance of conflict, the use of dialogue to reveal character, and how crucial rewriting is to the writing process" (Crilley 2009, 2). Crilley's assertions are echoed by other writers and researchers (Lawrence, McNeal and Yildiz 2009; Sloan 2009; Zimmerman 2008).

CREATING COMICS IS PURPOSEFUL, AUTHENTIC AND HONORS THE WRITER'S LIFE EXPERIENCES

The students creating comics as part of these projects cared about their writing because it held an authentic purpose with a real-life audience. Salika A. Lawrence, Kelly McNeal, and Melda N. Yildiz (2009) gathered a group of 12 urban high school students for a three-week course in the summer of 2007. Their data was accumulated through the collection of student work, teacher plans and reflections. The four university professors teaching the course conducted mini-lessons in reading, writing, math, and technology, and "the writing mini-lessons focused on writing for authentic purpose and real world audiences" (Lawrence, McNeal and Yildiz 2009, 486) as well as informational writing, research and publishing writing. In addition to writing four comics by the conclusion of the course, students had to write comic reviews for the Barnes and Noble's website. Students were more confident about their own writing; they were hesitant to write and upload any negative views of published graphic novels (Lawrence, McNeal and Yildiz 2009, 491).

When reviewing his online comic creation site, Akira Kamiya (2009) referenced Make Beliefs Comix creator Bill Zimmerman's hope that "through making comics and becoming creators of media, we can all find our voices and feel empowered to communicate our stories" (Kamiya 2009, 59). Merisuo-Storm surveyed 10- to 11-year-old boys and girls about their attitudes towards reading and writing and she concluded, based on her findings, that "there should be, from the beginning of school, a meaningful purpose for writing ... as a means of communication" (Merisuo-Storm 2006, 113). Boys were significantly more interested in comics (Merisuo-Storm 2006, 117) and "writing without a purpose does not interest boys" (Merisuo-Storm 2006, 124). Merisuo-Storm recommends that teachers allow boys to write about what they know and like. Willona M. Sloan (2009) summarized three famous studies that had participants make their own comics. All of the examples she cites (Bitz 2001; Cary 2004; Frey and Fisher 2004) link to authenticity and true reflections of life experiences. Bitz's students produced "comic books based on themes that connect to their everyday lives" (Sloan 2009:2). Frey and Fisher (as quoted in Sloan 2009) "realize the power they [comics] have for engaging students in authentic writing" (Sloan 2009, 3). Cary's sample projects for his second language learners include "creating their own cartoons editorializing about personal experiences, family, school, or the local community" (Sloan 2009, 7). Students enjoyed sharing their opinions, through comics, with a receptive audience.

James Carter used a lesson approved by the National Council of Teachers of English and the International Reading Association called "Comic Book Show and Tell" to teach comic book scripting. Through his work promoting graphic novels, he came across a New Hampshire high school teacher who helped her students create an anthology of comics called "Scars" that "produce an authentic and heartfelt exploration of the hard times in their lives" (Carter 2009, 68).

Michael Bitz elaborated frequently on the power of writing comics: "the comics represent their ideas, identities, fears, and dreams for the future." (Bitz 2010, 23). He extols the process that helps students of all ages "find their own voices ... by developing and defining original stories about themselves, their schools, and the surrounding communities." (Bitz 2010, 42). Similar results have been reported by other educators (Kirson in Baker 2011, 15).

Creating Comics Is Fun and Engaging

Comics are fun and engaging to make. Many studies repeat this mantra (Bitz 2004; Bitz 2010; Crilley 2009; Vega and Schnackenberg 2006). Students are more inclined to participate in activities that are fun, which means they will engage in writing, which links back to the first benefit listed—writing comics makes students better writers.

Creating Comics Is Creative, Collaborative and Uses Technology Well

Writing comics is good for students because they work collaboratively with others in a creative venture. Using technology to do it increases the benefits. Published comics are collaborative ventures involving writers, illustrators, inkers, editors, and many other participants—each person brings their strengths to the project. It is a cliché, but together, everyone achieves more. The teamwork motto applies to student productions as well. By working with other students skilled in different areas, students increase their own proficiency (Lawrence, McNeal, and Yildiz 2009, 492). In "The Comic Book Project" the student production teams "let creativity and teamwork guide them" (Bitz 2004, 579) once it was time to move beyond planning their comics, and the final product was "the result of efforts by many people" (Bitz 2010, 71). At home and with their friends, students create and compose through technology via tools such as websites, fanfiction and blogs, often separate from their school-based writing tasks (Miller in Albers and Sanders 2010, 254). Suzanne Miller writes about digital video projects but could just as well be talking about comic creation when she describes how wonderfully "students work in teams collaborating with each other and with cameras, computers, and props as mediating tools (Vygotsky 1978) for the clear purpose..." (Miller in Albers and Sanders 2010, 262). Bitz' final chapter of "When Commas Meet Kryptonite" reminds the readers of the need for creative collaboration with technology: "[digital] technologies can be a wonderful and resourceful tool, but only that. Without creative thinking, instruction with technology is just as passive as instruction with a textbook"

(Bitz 2010, 159). So much more can be said about collaboration, creativity and comics, but it can be summed up by Papert (as cited in Vega and Schnackenberg 2006, 30) who postulates that when individuals design or create things that are meaningful to them, some of the most powerful learning occurs.

Initial School Inquiry Project: Using Comics to Improve Male Attitudes to Reading and Writing

The Ministry of Education for the province of Ontario, Canada, was concerned about the disparity between girls and boys test scores and attitudes towards reading and writing. A branch of the ministry, the Literacy and Numeracy Secretariat, created a boys literacy project, in which schools could apply for grant money to examine ways to improve boys' literacy. Agnes Macphail Public School applied for, and received, a grant that focused on the use of comics / graphic novels. (Bodkin et al. 2009a) The school's essential question was "How can graphic novels used in FRED (Free Reading Every Day) time, incorporated in curriculum areas, and combined with instructional strategies improve attitudes towards reading and writing, and reading preferences?" The teacher inquiry team, consisting of the teacher-librarian and the junior division classroom teachers, focused most of the project on reading comics. However, a portion of the funds were used to invite Richard Comely, the comic artist behind "Captain Canuck," to come and teach small groups of students how to produce their own comics. The junior division collected all the comics made by the student teams into a book that was reproduced for all Grade 4–6 students.

The inquiry team used two methods of qualitative data collection. They collected anecdotal notes and observations based on attitudes expressed by students as they worked on social studies projects, Earth Day comics, a whole-class novel study project and other reading-related tasks. The teacher investigators also analyzed student written and oral reflections. The one method of quantitative data the team employed consisted of checklists of boys reading preferences for twenty randomly selected days. In their social studies classes, their culminating task had several options and creating a comic was one of the choices. When studying the reading response journals, one teacher noted that at least half of the responses were based on graphic novels. The teachers reported that one of their next steps would be to continue to provide students with the opportunity to make comics, using tools such as Comic Life.

Subsequent Library Inquiry Project: Value of Writing Comics Using Technology

Integrating technology with comic creation became even easier when the Ontario Software Acquisition Program Advisory Committee licensed Bitstrips for Schools in 2009. This online comic creation website is free to all Ontario educators. Bitstrips for Schools, found at www.bitstripsforschools.com only requires an Internet connection, rather than any software downloads, so students and teachers can easily work on comics at home and at school. Users can create and modify their own cartoon characters using the templates and controls provided, so students no longer have to be concerned about their supposed lack of artistic ability. Built-in art libraries offer many backgrounds and props for creators to use and change. Photos and copyright free images are easily imported into comic panels and collaborative tools such as share and comment features are part of the Bitstrips class community.

Agnes Macphail's teacher-librarian wanted to collect more quantitative data to further examine the benefits of writing comics (especially using Bitstrips for Schools) and to help with further planning for ICT (Information and Communication Technologies) classes that she co-taught with the classroom teachers. Students in grades 1–8 were surveyed about various technology tools they had used in their first term of the 2010–2011 school year. The Grade 1–4 students used the SMART Board (interactive white board) and its Senteo student response system to register their votes. The Grade 5–8 students filled in anonymous surveys hosted by www.surveymonkey.com.

The results of the survey mirrored the findings from the literature review. In the intermediate division, 39 percent of respondents felt that Bitstrips was useful for learning and 25 percent felt that Bitstrips was very useful for learning. One student respondent commented: "I also like bitstrips because we can use comics for assignments. Is [sic] really fun!" Another commented on the differentiated learning opportunities available using the computer: "We were introduced to many different things like wallwisher, just read it, and bitstrips, instead of just one or two ways to learn."

For the Grade 5–6 students, the results were even more significant. 32.7 percent indicated that Bitstrips was useful for learning and 51 percent indicated that Bitstrips was very useful for learning — the only item on the list that out-ranked Bitstrips on the Grade 5–6 survey was the SMART Board interactive white board and the corresponding Senteo response system. One student wrote: "My 2 favorite things is the smartboard senteos and the bitstrips. The reason I like because they are 2 fun ways to learn [sic throughout]. " Pride in accomplished work was evident in another comment: "I liked bitstrips because I got my own little person that looks good."

The Grade 3–4 students were questioned about how fun, how easy, and how educational each tool was to them. The results for Bitstrips are in the chart below.

	Enjoyment Value	*Ease of Use*	*Educational Value*
Class A	96% = very fun 3% = somewhat fun 0% = not fun 1% = skipped question	84% = very easy 15% = somewhat easy 0% = not easy 1% = skipped question	78% = very educational 4% = somewhat educational 8% = not educational 10% = skipped question
Class B	75% = very fun 21% = somewhat fun 0% = not fun 4% = skipped question	75% = very easy 21% = somewhat easy 0% = not easy 4% = skipped question	54% = very educational 36% = somewhat educational 3% = not educational 7% = skipped question
Class C	96% = very fun 3% = somewhat fun 0% = not fun 1% = skipped question	96% = very easy 3% = somewhat easy 0% = not easy 1% = skipped question	60% = very educational 36% = somewhat educational 0% = not educational 4% = skipped question

Student comic creations were sophisticated, funny, insightful and engaging. Using the comment tool in Bitstrips, students became each other's cheerleaders and supporters, praising and encouraging their peers. If a picture is worth a thousand words, then let the students speak volumes testifying to the benefits of comics through examples of their work.

Figure 1. Appendix A. *London Night* by Youeel Ataalla

Figure 2. Appendix B. *Crazy Rex* by Philo Ataalla

Figure 3. Appendix C. *Plane Headquarters* by Hassan Butt

Figure 4. Appendix D. *Safety in the Winter* by Joyce Cheung

Figure 5. Appendix E. *How to Build Strong Bones* by Helen Qin

References

Alongi, Constance V. May 1974. "Response to Kay Haugaard: Comic Books Revisited." *The Reading Teacher* 27: 801–803.
Anderson, Holly, and Morag Styles. 1999. *Teaching Through Texts: Promoting Literacy Through Popular and Literary Texts in the Primary Classroom.* New York: Routledge.
Baker, Amy. 2011. "Using Comics to Improve Literacy in English Language Learners." Master's thesis. University of Central Missouri.
Biebrich, Janice Leigh. 2006. "Towards a Broader Understanding of Literacy: Comics and Graphic Novels, Seeing the Meaning." Master's thesis. University of Alberta.
Bitz, Michael. 2004. "The Comic Book Project: FORGING Alternative Pathways to Literacy." *Journal of Adolescent and Adult Literacy* 47.7: 574–586.
_____. 2010. *When Commas Meet Kryptonite: Classroom Lessons from the Comic Book Project.* New York: Teachers College Press.
Bodkin, Barbara, et al. 2009. *The Road Ahead: Boys' Literacy Teacher Inquiry Project, 2005 to 2008: Final Report.* Ontario Institute for Studies in Education: Ontario Ministry of Education. http://conted.oise.utoronto.ca/UserFiles/File/RoadAhead2009.pdf
_____, et al. 2009. *The Road Ahead: Boys' Literacy Teacher Inquiry Project, 2005 to 2008: Supplement.* Ontario Institute for Studies in Education: Ontario Ministry of Education. http://www.edu.gov.on.ca/eng/curriculum/RoadAhead2009_Supplement.pdf
Booth, David, and Kathy Lundy. 2007. *Boosting Literacy with Graphic Novels.* Orlando, FL: Steck-Vaughn.
Carter, James Bucky. 2006. "The Comic Book Show and Tell." Newark, DE: International Reading Association. www.readwritethink.org/lessons/lesson%5fview.asp?id=921. http://web.ebscohost.com/ehost/detail?sid=1771907f-906a-4e96-9618-00a7988a75be%40sessionmgr110&vid=1&hid=119&bdata=JnNpdGU9ZWhvc3QtbGl2ZQ%3d%3d — bib3up
_____. 2007. "Ultimate Spider-Man and Student-Generated Classics: Using Graphic Novels and Comics to Produce Authentic Voice and Detailed, Authentic Texts." In James Bucky Carter, ed., *Building Literacy Connections with Graphic Novels: Page by Page, Panel by Panel.* Urbana, IL: National Council of Teachers of English.
_____. 2009. "Going Graphic." *Educational Leadership* 66.6: 68–72.
Crilley, Mark. 2009. "Getting Students to Write Using Comics." *Teacher Librarian* 37.1: 2–7.
Goldstein, B.S. 1986. "Looking at Cartoons and Comics in a New Way." *Journal of Reading* 29.7: 657–661.
Graham, Steven. 2011. "Comics in the Classroom: Something to Be Taken Seriously." *Language Education in Asia* 2.1: 92–102
Haugaard, Kay. 1973. "Comic Books: Conduits of Culture?" *The Reading Teacher* 27.1: 54–55.
Jenkins, Linda. 1994. "The Reading-Writing Connection in the Comic Book Genre: A Case Study of Three Young Writers." Ph.D. dissertation. University of British Columbia: Dissertation. http://www.eric.ed.gov/ERICWebPortal/search/recordDetails.jsp?ERICExtSearch_SearchValue_0=ED369070&searchtype=keyword&ERICExtSearch_SearchType_0=no&_pageLabel=RecordDetails&accno=ED369070&_nfls=false&source=ae
Kamiya, A. 2009. "A Tool for Creative Writing: The Make Beliefs Comix Web Site." *Adult Basic Education and Literacy Journal* 3.1: 59
Krashen, Stephen. 2004. *The Power of Reading.* 2d ed.. Portsmouth, NM: Heinemann.
Kunai, Ikue, and Clarissa C.S. Ryan. 2007. "Manga as a Teaching Tool: Comics Without Borders." *CATESOL State Conference.*
Lawrence, Salika. A., Kelly McNeal, and Melda N. Yildiz. 2009. "Summer Program Helps Adolescents Merge Technology, Popular Culture, Reading, and Writing for Academic Purposes." *Journal of Adolescent and Adult Literacy* 52.6: 483–494
Lueking, Mary. 2007. *Comics in the Classroom.* Accessed 2011. http://www.springfield.k12.il.us/teachers/mlueking/comics_in_the_classroom/?p=8308&i=75152.
Merisuo-Storm, Tuula. 2006. "Girls and Boys Like to Read and Write Different Texts." *Scandinavian Journal of Educational Research* 50.2: 111–125.
Miller, Suzanne M. 2010. "Toward a Multimodal Literacy Pedagogy: Digital Video Composing as 21st Century Literacy." In Peggy Albers and Jennifer Sanders, eds., *Literacies, the Arts & Multimodality.* Urbana, IL: National Council of Teachers of English.
Sloan, Willona M. 2009. "No Laughing Matter: Comic Books Have Serious Educational Value." *Education Update* 51.10: 1–3, 7.

Thomas, James L. 1983. *Cartoons and Comics in the Classroom: A Reference for Teachers and Librarians.* Littleton, CO: Libraries Unlimited.

Ujiie, Joanne, and Stephen Krashen. 1996. "Comic Book Reading, Reading Enjoyment, and Pleasure Reading Among Middle Class and Chapter 1 Middle School Students." *Reading Improvement* 33.1: 51–54. http://www.eric.ed.gov/ERICWebPortal/search/recordDetails.jsp?ERICExtSearch_SearchValue_0=EJ527305&searchtype=keyword&ERICExtSearch_SearchType_0=no&_pageLabel=RecordDetails&accno=EJ527305&_nfls=false&source=ae

Vega, Edwin S., and Heidi L. Schnackenberg. 2006. "Integrating Technology, Art, and Writing to Create Comic Books." *Middle School Journal* 37.4: 30–36.

Zimmerman, Bill. 2008. "Creating Comics Fosters Reading, Writing, and Creativity." *Education Digest*: 55–57.

Multicultural Education Through Graphic Novels

REBECCA M. MARRALL

Introduction

Graphic novels are a combination of art, content, and delivery that engage readers on emotional, cognitive, and visual levels. Consequently, graphic novels are a strong educational medium, precisely because this alternative means of delivering information can effectively school many different types of learners. And because of the format's inherent versatility, graphic novels present another exploratory tool for many undergraduate and graduate courses at the university level.

As an educational tool in the collegiate environment, graphic novels are an especially unique and effective way to explore personal identity and cultural narratives. Briefly, a working definition of the phrase "cultural narratives" refers to historical narratives that chronicle a cultural or ethnic heritage. Examining narratives in novels such as Gene Luen Yang's *American Born Chinese*, or Alison Bechdel's *Fun Home*, can encourage understanding of diverse worldviews.

Furthermore, studying graphic novels introduce all students to diverse narrators or experiences. This essay investigates how using graphic novels in the higher education settings present a unique opportunity for investigating diverse cultural narratives while promoting multicultural awareness. In addition, the essay provides criteria by which to assess graphic novels and sequential art for course use, and ends with an annotated bibliography of recommended graphic novels.

Higher Education and (The Lack of) Representation

In 2007, the National Center for Educational Statistics — affiliated with the U.S. Department of Education's Institute of Education Sciences — published a report on enrollment trends at postsecondary institutions. This report contrasted enrollment data between 1976 and 2007, and remarked on the change over three decades. For example, European American students consisted of 82.6 percent of all U.S. college students in 1976. In 2007, statistics reported that European American students made up 64.4 percent of the collegiate student population in the United States (NCES 2007).

However, African American students only composed 1.4 percent of the postsecondary student population in 1976 and increased to 13.1 percent by 2007. For Hispanic students, enrollment increased from 3.5 percent in 1976 to 11.4 percent in 2007. For Asian Americans and Pacific Islanders, the trend changed from 1.8 percent in 1976 to 6.7 percent in 2007. And for American Indians and Alaskan Natives, the growth varied from 0.7 percent in 1976 to 1.0 percent in 2007 (NCES 2007). Though enrollment in postsecondary institutions has drastically increased for those of non–Caucasoid descent, there remains a large discrepancy between European American postsecondary student enrollment and enrollment into higher education by members from historically underrepresented groups (No data was given on other identities, such as gay/lesbian/bisexual/transgender).

The National Center for Educational Statistics also reports that in 2007 almost 80 percent of college and university faculty are European American. In contrast, 7 percent of faculties are African American while 6 percent identify as Asian American and Pacific Islander. Only 4 percent of college professors are Hispanic, and a low 1 percent of American Indian and Alaskan Native faculty are employed (NCES 2007). Clearly, the majority of college students in the United States are being taught by predominantly European American faculties.

This discrepancy in faculty representation has implications for collegiate course materials. Most course textbooks and articles used in higher education are written by scholars of European American heritage. The sheer numbers of Caucasian faculty ensures that their scholarly output will overwhelm the materials disseminated by faculty from historically underrepresented groups. While faculty of European American heritage can recognize the discrepancy, they cannot change the results of sociological inequity in the United States overnight. But what to do, though? Because the students may learn from educational materials outside their own cultural narrative, these students may not fully identify with the content—and thus, not fully engage with the course curriculum.

Of course, colleges and universities cannot manufacture new faculty overnight, nor can they resolve the underlying social conditions which created this inequity in a few short years. However, faculty can make a choice to include course materials that better represent the classroom demographics (and indeed, those of the entire United States). But what strong educational medium can provide a platform for all students to examine a wide variety of worldviews? A combination of art, content, and delivery, graphic novels engage readers on emotional, cognitive, and visual levels (Heaney 2007). And because of the format's inherent versatility, graphic novels can be an excellent exploratory tool for many undergraduate and graduate courses at the university level.

History of Graphic Novels

Scrutinizing the history of graphic novels provides much insight into why this medium is so apropos for exploring diverse narratives in higher education. Defined as an on-going series of stories based on cartoon renderings, comics first appeared in the United States first appeared in the late 19th and early 20th century (Cornog 2009). By the 1930s, most newspapers in the United States ran daily comic strips, and the popularity of comics soon sparked a demand for more. Out of that demand, grew comic books. Enjoying a wide readership, comic books soon manifested in new genres: horror, detective fiction, and much more. But despite being read by all age groups, comic books were commonly perceived as a medium for youth (Cornog 2009).

In 1954, the text entitled *Seduction of the Innocent* stalled the popularity, and production, of comic books. Written by psychiatrist Frederic Wertham, the text argued that comic books promoted moral evils among youth in the United States (Hadju 2008). A public outcry swept across the United States, and the resulting social turmoil forced U.S. comic book publishers to create the Comics Code Authority. The Comics Code Authority (CCA) enforced censorship of comics, based upon several criteria. Any "controversial" plot elements were removed, as were any depictions of "alternative culture."

However, a new form of comics emerged in defiance to the CCA throughout the 1960s and 1970s: "comix." These underground comics, usually sold outside of bookstores or comic shops, had detailed stories about sex, drugs, and alternative lifestyles—everything the CCA forbade (Skinn 2004). And in 1978, publisher Baronet Books published the graphic novel *A Contract with God and Other Tenement Stories* by artist-author Will Eisner. Often deemed the first of its kind, the graphic novel was a visually-based story with a beginning and an end (Serchay 2008). By the late 1980s, comics publishers broke with the CCA (Hadju 2008). Abandoning the CCA allowed comics publishers to publish content that introduced radically different voices. These graphic novels explored new cultural paradigms. For example, Alison Bechdel's 2007 graphic novel *Fun Home: A Family Tragicomic* examines a woman's assessment of her own lesbian identity and her familial relationships. Or Gene Luen Yang's 2008 graphic novel *American Born Chinese*, which explores mixed ethnic heritage and stereotypes in contemporary teenage United States.

Though these novels are excellent works of art and story—both *Fun Home* and *American Born Chinese* won the prestigious Eisner award—they also demonstrate an increasing awareness of the diverse cultural, social and ethnic experiences found throughout the United States today (Downey 2010). This growing realization, manifested in many mediums but particularly in graphic novels, presents unique opportunities beyond those of personal enrichment. Indeed, these visually-based stories are a strong educational medium because they provide students a platform to explore multicultural narratives while learning with multiple literacies—both of which contribute to an inclusive classroom environment.

Graphic Novels: Explore Diverse Worldviews and Promote Student Engagement

The recent explosion of graphic novels that explore diverse cultural narratives present a timely and unique tool for instructors seeking to include multicultural elements in their courses. Schwarz writes about the multiple reasons to include graphic novels in a collegiate course, and states: "Graphic novels put forward different opinions and notions of society, history, traditions, and life in a more straightforward manner and give minority viewpoints a voice" (Schwartz 2002).

For students who are members of historically underrepresented groups, inclusion of non–European, non-heterosexual, or disabled narratives sends them a message that their voices are recognized and valued (Bucher 2004). For European American students, heterosexual or fully abled students, incorporating graphic novels into the college curriculum may present a new cultural narrative. Both scenarios provide ample opportunity to ask critical questions about race, ethnicity, disability, identity, and sociocultural conditions in the United States (Downey 2010). And while measuring the effectiveness of engaging students on this type of affective learning is difficult without a formal study, the use of non–Anglo materials can promote a sense of inclusion for students of non–European or mixed heritage.

Graphic novels not only address concerns about multicultural education, but also allow students to learn in multiple ways. Many scholars agree that presenting data in a variety of media — visual, text, and more — is valuable for educational endeavors (Thompson 2007). Thus, graphic novels are a strong educational medium precisely because they provide an alternative means of delivering information which can effectively school many different types of learners. Many educators had expressed concern that comics didn't challenge students sufficiently. However, a study which analyzed the concept comprehension and retention of three mediums (a traditional text-only work; a text with few illustrations; and a graphic novel) found no significant difference in test scores — which demonstrated that comics were just as effective as traditional educational media in conveying information (Mallia 2004).

In direct contrast to the historic disparagement that comics are "too easy" for literacy development, analyzing graphic novels require more complex skills than basic cognition (Lavin 1998). Indeed, authors Lyga and Lyga examined graphic novels under the multiple intelligences theory (generated by psychologist Howard Gardner), and concluded that three of seven types of multiple intelligences are engaged when students read sequential art: linguistic, spatial, and interpersonal (Lyga 2007).

Furthermore, graphic novels provide nontraditional examples of plot, scenery, character development, conflict and more. The innovative delivery of different types of information — visual, lingual, and emotional — provides an abundance of material with which students can connect (Krashen 2004). Finally, Heaney (2007) argues that assessing graphic novels falls under developing deductive reasoning abilities, an advanced cognitive function under psychologist Benjamin Bloom's taxonomy (Leckbee 2005). In short, graphic novels provide a platform which begs those basic critical questions (Who, what, where, why, how?), and gives students opportunities to build upon multiple literacies.

Selecting Relevant Materials

Much of the literature on selecting graphic novel for scholastic or curricular use exists in library science and reader's advisory journals. However, a basic rationale can guide professors to most effective selection process. If college and university faculty wish to use to graphic novels for the specific purpose of examining a diverse array of worldviews while delivering that story in a multiple-domain format, there are a few elements to consider: perspective, story format, language, and visual presentation.

Perspective is the narrator's point of view, and often reflects unique insights about the narrator's upbringing or cultural background. Faculty should not only consider ethnic cultural narratives, but those from other identities: gay/lesbian, disabled, mental health, a specific generation, and much more. Story format addresses the way in which the story is delivered to the reader. Format can vary in complexity, and offer students an opportunity to examine literary common devices in a nontraditional situation. For example, Gene Luen Yang's *American Born Chinese* is an interweaving tale of three stories, each of which examines a different character's perspective about ethnicity in the United States.

Language is quite clearly an important factor in selecting graphic novels. Especially in a collegiate environment, faculty should strive for a balance between accessible and challenging language. Finally, visual presentation in a graphic novel is vital because it provides students an opportunity to improve visual literacy. Use of color, placement of objects, and depiction of characters can say a great deal about the story's purpose — and the author's intention in creating the work (O'English 2009).

Conclusions

Authors Stancato and Hamachek write that "Effective teaching ... should encompass and emphasize the interactive nature of cognitive and affective learning..." (1990). Graphic novels do address these cognitive and affective learning needs. The graphic novel format, and its unique method of information delivery, provides multiple domains through which students can learn. Furthermore, the content of graphic novels — particularly those that explore cultural narratives — offers students both an opportunity to become more aware about diversity while promoting inclusion for students who are members of historically underrepresented groups. Finally, being able to address diversity, and what it means to every individual, through graphic novels in a collegiate setting provides a rich opportunity for authentic dialogue in a safe environment. In essence, use of graphic novels results in both affective and cognitive learning to create higher levels of engagement and inclusion.

A key word of that last statement is "inclusion." Inclusion is defined as all of the policies, techniques, and strategies by which all students are encouraged to participate equally in education, and by extension, the world outside academia (Inclusion n.d.). Curriculum and textbook choice is one technique to promote inclusion in education. How does inclusion benefit students? Much of educational curriculum has, until the last two decades, been dominated by European American scholars and cultural narratives.

This one-sided curricular model resulted in an unequal representation in educational materials, which may discourage students from a non–Anglo background from identifying with the cultural narratives presented in class (Inclusivity 2009). Practicing inclusion means providing materials from a wide variety of worldviews in effort to better reflect the diversity in today's collegiate classroom. Ideally, this endeavor would result in widening participation by all students.

References

Bucher, Richard D. 2004. *Diversity Consciousness: Opening Our Minds to People, Culture, and Opportunities.* Upper Saddle River, NJ: Pearson/Prentice Hall.
Cornog, Martha, and Timothy Perper. 2009. *Graphic Novels: Beyond the Basics.* Santa Barbara, CA: Libraries Unlimited.
Downey, Elizabeth M. 2010. "Graphic Novels in Curriculum and Instruction Collections." *Reference & User Services Quarterly* 49.2: 181.
Hadju, David. 2008. *The Ten-Cent Plague: The Great Comic-Book Scare and How It Changed America.* New York: Farrar, Straus, and Giroux.
Heaney, Mary J. 2007. "Graphic Novels: A Sure Bet for Your Library." Collection Building 26.3: 72–76.
"Inclusion." n.d. In *Oxford Reference Online.* Accessed February 17, 2011. http://www.oxfordreference.com/.
"Inclusivity." 2009. *A Dictionary of Education.* Oxford University Press. Accessed February 17, 2011. http://www.oxfordreference.com/.
Krashen, Stephen D. 2004. *The Power of Reading: Insights from the Research.* Westport, CT: Libraries Unlimited.
Lavin, M.R. 1998. "Comic Books and Graphic Novels for Libraries: What to Buy." *Serials Review* 24.2: 32.

Leckbee, J. 2005. "I Got Graphic! Using Visual Literature Works!" *Young Adult Library Services* 3.4: 30.

Lyga, Allyson, and Barry Lyga. 2004. *Graphic Novels at Your Media Center: A Definitive Guide*. Westport, CT: Libraries Unlimited.

Mallia, Gorg. 2007. "Learning from the Sequence: The Use of Comics in Instruction." *Interdisciplinary Comics Studies* 3.3: n.p. Accessed February 16, 2011. www.english.ufl.edu/imagetext/archives/v3_3/mallia/index/shtml.

National Center of Educational Statistics. 2007. "Fast Facts: Enrollment." Accessed February 15, 2011. http://nces.ed.gov/fastfacts/display.asp?id=98.

National Center of Educational Statistics. 2007. "Fast Facts: Race/Ethnicity of College Faculty." Accessed February 15, 2011. http://nces.ed.gov/fastfacts/display.asp?id=61.

O'English, Lorena. 2009. "Comics and Graphic Novels in the Academic Library Collection." In Martha Cornog and Timothy Perper, eds., *Graphic Novels: Beyond the Basics*. Santa Barbara, CA: Libraries Unlimited.

Schwarz, Gretchen E. 2002. "Graphic Novels for Multiple Literacies." *Journal of Adolescent & Adult Literacy* 46.3: 262–265.

Serchay, David S. 2008. *The Librarian's Guide to Graphic Novels for Children and Tweens*. New York: Neal-Schuman.

Skinn, Dez. 2004. *Comix: The Underground Revolution*. New York: Thunder's Mouth Press.

Stancato, F.A., and A.L. Hamachek. 1990. "The Interactive Nature and Reciprocal Effects of Cognitive and Affective Learning." *Education* 111.1: 77.

Thompson, Terry. 2007. "Embracing Reluctance When Classroom Teachers Shy Away from Graphic Books." *Library Media Connection* 25.4: 29.

"So, Joss, why do you always write these strong women characters?"
Using Joss Whedon's Astonishing X-Men *to Teach Feminism*

ERIN HOLLIS

While planning a recently created course on the comics' medium as literature, I was immediately confronted with the problem of women in relation to the medium. First, because I wanted to teach a variety of genres in the class, and not just what Hillary Chute has called "nonfiction graphic narrative," the dearth of women creators within most of the genres posed a problem (Chute 2008, 452). So, while it was easy to choose from the many fantastic women creators of nonfiction graphic narrative, including Alison Bechdel, Marjane Satrapi, and Lynda Barry, it was more difficult in the other genres we were covering in the class to find a work written or drawn by a woman. The superhero genre proved especially challenging, since many of the most celebrated works in the genre are written and drawn by men and do not address the frequently problematic representations of women in the genre. Alan Moore's *Watchmen*, for example, barely pays attention to the issue of the depiction of female characters (Moore 1995). And while it does a good job of questioning many of the conventions of superhero comics, it remains mostly silent about the place of women within that genre. Of course, the class could talk about the lack of nuance in many superhero comics in their portrayal of women, but I wanted to give students a more subtle example of the genre that would allow them to consider more fully the issue of women within the medium. Joss Whedon's recent work on the series *Astonishing X-Men* (2004–2007) provided a perfect solution to this quandary as it both comments on typical comic book depictions of women and encourages its readers/viewers to question such depictions. Further, that a man wrote the series allows students to form a more complicated perspective about feminism—a subject with which many students are frequently uncomfortable. In this essay, I will discuss how I approach teaching Joss Whedon's *Astonishing X-Men* through the lens of feminism.

Joss Whedon, creator of *Buffy the Vampire Slayer* (1997–2003), *Angel* (1999–2004), *Firefly* (2002–2003), *Dollhouse* (2009–2010), and director of the record breaking *Avengers* (2012) has long had the reputation of being a writer who embraced storylines and characters with a feminist slant. Most famously, his creation of *Buffy the Vampire Slayer* was inspired by his desire to question gender stereotypes so common in the horror genre:

> The first thing I ever thought of when I thought of *Buffy: The Movie* (1992) was the little ... blonde girl who goes into a dark alley and gets killed, in every horror movie. The idea of *Buffy* was to subvert that idea, that image, and create someone who was a hero where she had always been a victim. That element of surprise ... [and] genre-busting is very much at the heart of both the movie and the series ["Welcome to the Hellmouth" commentary 2002].

This comment has helped to generate a great deal of scholarly response to Whedon's work from a feminist point of view, including book-length studies like Lorna Jowett's *Sex and the Slayer: A Gender Studies Primer for the Buffy Fan* (Jowett 2005) and numerous articles that frequently appear in *Slayage*, the Whedon Studies Association journal. Whedon's celebrated feminist approach to *Buffy* is reflected in his other work as well, and he frequently addresses his approach to depicting women in his work. For example, in a speech on May 15, 2006, to Equality Now, an organization whose co-founders include a former student of Whedon's mother and that was "founded in 1992 to work for the projection and promotion of the human rights of women around the world" (Equality Now), Whedon offers seven answers to a question he is commonly asked in interviews: "Why do you always write these strong women characters?" (Whedon 2006). Asking students to look at his answers to this question in detail helps to more specifically present his stance on feminism.

His first answer, "because of my mother," highlights how her influence shaped his attitudes on feminism (Whedon 2006). When Meryl Streep introduced Whedon before his speech, she honored his mother, Lee Stearns, as well, saying that his mother's "radical ideas about women's strength and independence and passion and empathy inspired Joss to create not only *Buffy the Vampire Slayer* but many other strong women characters" (Whedon 2006). Indeed, Equality Now was formed in part from Stearns's inspiration, and Whedon's first answer indicates how his mother's approach to equality encouraged his writing not only of female characters, but of male characters as well. Whedon continues with his second answer, saying he writes such strong women characters "because of his father" (Whedon 2006). He goes on further to explain that both his father and stepfather "had a lot to do with it because they prized wit and resolve in the women they were with above all things, and they were among the rare men who understand that recognizing someone else's power does not diminish your own" (Whedon 2006). Whedon's focus on power in this answer demonstrates how he not only seeks to represent female characters as strong, but also seeks to create male characters that are accepting of that strength. This recognition demonstrates Whedon's nuanced approach to the issue. It is not about taking away the power of male characters so that female characters are empowered; rather, his work seeks to make each character he writes accept themselves for the power that they have and accept different iterations of power in the other characters.

As Whedon continues his short speech, his third and fourth answers indicate both how he understands the significance of what he is doing and also his recognition of the paradox of writing such characters. His third answer, "because these stories give people strength," demonstrates his knowledge that his work can affect the lives of his viewers/readers (Whedon 2006). He clearly understands the responsibility he has to his viewers to create characters who can provide models of how better to live in the world. His fourth answer, "because they're hot," may seem flippant and humorous, but he is also commenting on the problematic response of many viewers. Since the representation of strong women characters can be seen as a way of trying to attract a largely male audience who want to watch a woman with outstanding abilities and since these characters are usually quite attractive, there is the risk of merely reinforcing the stereotypes he is trying to question. His answer, "because they're hot," indicates his knowledge of and complicity in these sorts of representations, but because he is aware of the paradox, he can easily question it in how he creates his characters. Therefore, inherent within his representation of strong women characters is an underlying criticism of the necessity of joining sexuality and strength.

Whedon's fifth answer indicates his frustration with the seeming lack of progress in television's representations of women. In the speech, because Whedon had set out to answer the most common question interviewers usually ask him, he created a fictional moment where he is asked the question repeatedly, as so often happens to him on a press junket. By his fifth answer, he demonstrates his frustration with the question, striking back at the imagined interviewer, but at the same time making a significant point about the constant repetition of the question:

> Why are you even asking me this? How is it possible that this is even a question? Honestly, Seriously, why did you write that down? Why aren't you asking a hundred other guys why they don't write strong women characters? I believe that what I'm doing should not be remarked upon, let alone honored, and there are other people doing it. But seriously, this question is ridiculous and you've just got to stop [Whedon 2006].

Hidden beneath his obvious irritation with the question is a serious point. It should no longer be necessary, he argues, to comment on such characters. He wants to reach a point where his work is not even remarked upon for the inclusion of such characters because such strong women characters have become ubiquitous. Since it is still commented on, it demonstrates how little progress has been made.

Perhaps Whedon's most serious and sustained consideration of the question occurs in his sixth response. Here, he zeroes in on the focus of the event for which he is making the speech — equality:

> Because equality is not a concept. It's not something we should be striving for. It's a necessity. Equality is like gravity. We need it to stand on this earth as men and women, and the misogyny that is in every culture is not a true part of the human condition. It is life out of balance and that imbalance is sucking something out of the soul of every man and woman that is confronted with it. We need equality. Kinda now [Whedon 2006].

His argument that equality is a necessity pushes back against the question again as he indicates that he is writing such strong women characters, because, to choose not to write such characters would only serve to reinforce the "imbalance" and "misogyny" he sees occurring in every culture. His comparison of equality to gravity also indicates that equality should be a force that is at once necessary to us, but not something we think about on a daily basis because it just comes naturally. We go through our daily lives without often thinking of the gravity that keeps us grounded, and Whedon would like the same to happen for equality. He wants it to be unquestionably part of our everyday lives. Whedon's seventh and final answer puts his previous answer in context. Pretending to ask himself the question one final time, he responds simply, "because you're still asking me that question" (Whedon 2006). As long as the question is being asked, until such characters become unremarkable, Whedon will find it necessary to continue writing such characters.

In the class, I use this short speech to introduce both our study of *Astonishing X-Men* and our discussion of women in comics. Such an introduction can help to lay the groundwork for many of the issues that are commonly brought up in feminist criticism of the medium, including the frequent overly sexualized portrayal of women and the relative lack of women creators in the superhero genre. Beginning with a discussion of Whedon's fourth answer, "because they're hot," the class discusses the problematic representations of women characters within the medium, and how such characters often risk merely reinforcing typical gender stereotypes (Whedon 2006). As Jeffrey A. Brown argues in relation to "bad girls" in action film and comic books, "on the one hand, she represents a potentially transgressive figure capable of expanding the popular perception of women's roles and abilities; on the other, she runs the risk of reinscribing strict gender binaries and of being nothing more than sexist window-dressing for the predominantly male audience" (Brown 2004, 47). Such a risk is incredibly problematic, but, as Sherrie A. Inness argues, "just by *being*, [the superheroine] suggests that the male stranglehold on the heroic can be subverted. The woman hero serves as a bold new role model for women and girls" (Inness 1999, 143). Thus, by starting with Whedon's speech, students can easily perceive the underlying issues of representing women in the medium. Further, by consciously using a speech made not by a woman, but by a man, I also try to question students' assumptions about feminism. Students often assume that only a woman can be a feminist, and by using Whedon as an example of a feminist, they can move beyond a kneejerk reaction to the movement to a more complicated understanding of it.

Students respond to the speech in a variety of ways. Some students, usually women, make a gesture of solidarity and immediately applaud Whedon's statements, saying, "finally, someone has said what I want to say." These students are often the most vocal, and their response sometimes runs the risk of silencing other students in the class who aren't entirely sure how to respond to the speech. Often, I find students are reticent to discuss certain topics, especially topics related to race, gender, and religious issues. This timidity frequently stems from students' desires not to say something offensive or from their preconceived notions about certain topics. After discussing various reactions to Whedon's speech, and noting some students' discomfort with the discussion, we move on to a more general discussion of feminism. Seeking to confront the issue directly, I ask students their opinions about feminism. Inevitably, many students will have a negative response, mentioning "man-bashing" and militancy as their major objections to the movement. Such a response demonstrates how many students are reluctant to identify as feminist and how they see the movement as particularly anti-male. In order to give students a better perspective on the feminist movement, I give them a brief history of the movement in which I discuss each wave of feminism and what, in general, proponents during each wave sought to achieve. This history helps to establish a better, less reactionary, understanding of the movement.

Beginning by introducing Whedon's own ideas on equality and then by drawing back and discussing feminism in general provides students with a framework through which to explore women in comics. Before moving on to discussing Whedon's *Astonishing X-Men* in particular, I ask students to name all of the female superheroes that immediately come to mind, listing them on the board as students call them out. Because the class generally attracts a large number of comic book fans who have an extensive knowledge of the subject, the list can get quite lengthy. The class also attracts a large number of English majors who have no history with comic books, so these students are often surprised by the amount of female superheroes their peers can name. The list includes a wide variety of characters, including Wonder Woman, She-Hulk, Supergirl, Batgirl, Elektra, Jean Grey, Emma Frost, Kitty Pryde, Huntress, Rogue, and Invisible Girl/Woman. After students have provided the list, I ask them to create a taxonomy for the list, dividing the characters into three categories: superheroines with their own comic book titles whose origins are not related to any other superheroes, superheroines created in relation to a superhero, and superheroines who are part of a team, like the X-Men or the Avengers. It becomes immediately apparent that few of the characters on this list belong to the first category. Unlike superheroes like Batman, Superman, Spider-Man, or the Hulk, most female superheroes were not created for their own original series. Students quickly realize that perhaps the only well known female superhero that strictly belongs in the first category is Wonder Woman. This realization helps lead into the next section of the class, where we talk about Wonder Woman as an icon.

Since it is difficult to find appropriate and widely available collections of *Wonder Woman* comics to study in the class, we instead look at a number of covers throughout the many years and iterations of Wonder Woman as a character in order to discuss the evolution of superheroines within the genre. As Kelli E. Stanley argues, Wonder Woman's "transformations often mirror those faced by her flesh-and-blood 'sisters': her metamorphoses reflect nothing less than the confusion, fear, and constant reformation of American ideas about American women" (Stanley 2005, 145). In other words, because Wonder Woman is so reflective of the transformations that American women have gone through over the years, looking at her transformation helps to provide students with an understanding of the changing place of women within American society.

We begin with covers from the golden age of comic books when Wonder Woman was created by Dr. William Moulton Marston, psychologist and inventor of the lie detector who wrote the comics under the pseudonym Charles Moulton. As we examine the covers from the golden age, students learn the story behind the creation of Wonder Woman. Marston approached his creation of Wonder Woman from both a scholarly and idiosyncratic feminist perspective. In 1943, two years after Wonder Woman's creation, he wrote an article for *The American Scholar* in which he explained his interest in comic books:

> This phenomenal development of a national comics addiction puzzles professional educators and leaves the literary critics gasping. Comics scorn finesse, thereby incurring the wrath of linguistic adepts. They defy the limits of accepted fact and convention, thus amortizing to apoplexy the ossified arteries of routine thought. But by these very tokens the picture-story fantasy cuts loose the hampering debris of art and artifice and touches the tender spots of universal human desires and aspirations, hidden customarily beneath long accumulated protective coverings of indirection and disguise. Comics speak, without qualm or sophistication, to the innermost ears of the wishful self (qtd. in Daniels 2000, 11).

Providing students this context helps to highlight the scholarly reasons Moulton had for creating Wonder Woman. His idea that the medium has the ability to address "human desires and aspirations" is connected as well to his own eccentric take on feminism. In an interview with *The New York Times* in 1937, Moulton predicted that "the next one hundred years will see the beginning of an American matriarchy—a nation of Amazons in the psychological rather than physical sense" who will "take over the rule of the country, politically and economically" (qtd. in Daniels 2000, 19). Moulton's view of a future matriarchy is often reflected in the early Wonder Women comics and, by looking at the covers of those comics, students can see how Wonder Woman was early shaped as a representative of a future matriarchal utopia.

After examining the golden age covers, we move through the years after Moulton died when Wonder Woman became more focused on marriage and domesticity. For many years, Wonder Woman and her comics languished in a sort of prison of 1950s prevailing ideology as women were being encouraged to return home after the war so that returning soldiers would have better access to jobs. And in the later 60s, Wonder Woman became less of a superhero as she lost her powers and her costume. In one notable cover that we look at in class, a modernly dressed Wonder Woman has painted an "X" over her older incarnations as a costumed Wonder Woman and as Diana Prince. The cover reads, "Forget the Old. The New Wonder Woman is Here!," marking an entirely new turn for the character (qtd. in Daniels 2000, 125). In these years, Wonder Woman is often depicted as weak and helpless. In the 1970s, however, Wonder Woman was to receive a makeover through the efforts of Gloria Steinem and *Ms.* Magazine. After looking at several of the covers during Wonder Woman's domestic and powerless periods, the juxtaposition of the cover of the first issue of *Ms.* Magazine from July 1972 can jar some students, who immediately recognize how that cover is a throwback to the golden age Wonder Woman. The cover reads "Wonder Woman for President" and depicts a traditionally-costumed, giant-sized Wonder Woman defending a city against war (qtd. in Daniels 2000, 130). The cover, which was an original drawing for the inaugural *Ms.* Magazine issue, ushered in a new age of Wonder Woman comics in which she was once again a feminist icon. Yet, even though she was returned to her original form, the covers from this time indicate the discomfort many of the writers and artists had with the idea of representing feminism in their comic books. Whereas in the Moulton era of Wonder Woman she is often supported by communities of women like the Holliday girls and the other Amazonians, the comics in the 1970s often made women into adversaries.

Perhaps the most widely known iteration of Wonder Woman is Lynda Carter's portrayal of her in the television series, *Wonder Woman*. After discussing a few 1970s covers, we examine a short clip from the series, discussing how the transition to television affects interpretations of the character. The clip that students watch shows Wonder Woman spinning in order to change her costume. The campiness of the show, much like the *Batman* series from the 1960s, serves to remove the more serious undertones from her character, and she is often depicted as somewhat weak, contrary to how she was depicted in the early Moulton comics. After a quick discussion of her television iteration, we return to looking at covers, examining Wonder Woman's evolution throughout the 1980s, 1990s, and 2000s. Students are able to see how the so-called feminist icon has changed over time and how even a female superhero with her own unique origin is subject to the prevailing ideologies of the times in which she is written. Examining the history of Wonder Woman provides an excellent context for reading Joss Whedon's *Astonishing X-Men* through the lens of feminism.

Whedon's run on *Astonishing X-Men* is notable not only for how he depicts the two main female characters, Kitty Pryde and Emma Frost, but also for how he depicts the male characters' interactions with the female characters. In the class, students read volumes one through four of *Astonishing X-Men*, which include all the issues for which Whedon was the writer. Since students are approaching the series from the context of having discussed Whedon's own response to his "strong women characters" and from having considered the history of women in comic books, they are poised to read the events of the series through the complicated lens of gender. Hopefully, by the time we begin to discuss Whedon's work, students who were uncomfortable discussing gender, and in particular feminism, will feel more comfortable and approach the topic with a more nuanced understanding. After having students read the series in its entirety, I ask them to comment on how the female characters either reinforce or subvert the tradition of women characters in comic books. Students often immediately bring up Emma Frost as a character who reinforced a lot of the negative stereotypes of female superheroes. In the series, Emma Frost always wears the same white costume that usually accentuates her cleavage and leaves her midriff exposed. Unlike the other members of the X-Men, she does not don a distinctive costume when Cyclops tells the group that they must go back to wearing costumes because she was basically already wearing a costume.

In other words, when the other characters are teaching or off-duty, they wear casual, everyday clothes, but Emma is always wearing a white outfit that is specifically designed to show off her body. Because she is the most sexualized character in the series and also the least trustworthy within the X-Men group, she seems to many students an example of Whedon's failure to subvert typical genre conventions. Alternatively, many students point out that her appearance mimics that of many male superheroes, who are almost always depicted as incredibly muscular. These students point out that no one is objecting to the depiction of these male superheroes or how they are overly sexualized. I point out to students that this is a common response to the criticism of overly sexualized female characters, but that having muscles isn't exactly the same as accentuating the curves of a female character. After gauging students' responses to Emma Frost, I ask them to consider her characterization from a slightly different perspective. Keeping in mind Whedon's desire to depict male characters that accept powerful women, I ask students to consider the relationship in the series between Cyclops and Emma Frost.

Throughout Whedon's run on the series, the relationship between Cyclops and Emma Frost is depicted as one in which Cyclops is comfortable with Emma Frost's power. Even when Emma Frost is untrustworthy and turns on the entire team, including removing Cyclops's powers because she is partially possessed by Cassandra Nova, Cyclops still respects her and even remains mostly loyal to her. Notably, she remains a part of the team after her betrayal of them, and this is mostly due to Cyclops's attitude towards her. Students have a number of responses to the Cyclops/Emma Frost relationship. Some students object to the relationship outright because they are long-time X-Men fans, and they are fans of the Jean Grey/Cyclops relationship. Other students point out that Emma Frost could be manipulating Cyclops the entire time. Indeed, Whedon's well-known humor comes to the fore in one scene in which the subject of Emma Frost's manipulation of Cyclops is directly confronted. In the scene, Emma mentions to Cyclops that "Kitty thinks I'm mentally controlling everything you say," and the next panel shows Cyclops with a strange look on his face, not saying anything, representing a hesitating pause on his part (Whedon 2004, n.p.). In the next panel, he says "But you're not, right?" to which Emma responds, "You will never see me naked again" (Whedon 2004, n.p.). That they can joke about it indicates the comfort in their relationship. Even though students often respond negatively to the relationship between Cyclops and Emma Frost, examining it in more detail does provide students with an example of a nuanced representation of a relationship between a powerful woman and man. Cyclops's comfort with the power that Emma Frost demonstrates, even when he has lost his own power, indicates his ability to recognize that someone else's power does not weaken his own power. Discussing their relationship and its negative and positive qualities usually brings up comparisons to the other notable relationship within the book — that of Kitty Pryde and Colossus — and such a comparison also brings up the relationship between Kitty Pryde and Emma Frost, since they are arguably the two strongest female characters in the series.

Unlike Emma Frost, Kitty Pryde is not represented as overly sexualized. She is often depicted almost as a teenager, and her body is never really emphasized, even when she is wearing her costume. Students immediately make this comparison and talk about how these different representations of the bodies of female characters affect their responses to them. Many students dislike Emma Frost from the beginning, preferring Kitty Pryde. In class, we discuss how this preference might be linked to Emma Frost's sexualized representation. In addition, Whedon depicts Kitty Pryde as a sort of stand-in for the reader, urging the reader to identify most with her. Having just joined the group, she doesn't belong like the other main characters. Kitty also constantly questions Emma Frost and her motives, creating distrust in the reader towards Emma Frost and a stronger relationship between the reader and Kitty. Whedon also cleverly uses Kitty's relationship with Emma in order to question typical comic book depictions of women characters. When Kitty arrives at the opening day assembly late, the contentious relationship between her and Emma is immediately set up. Emma comments to the students, "This, children, is Kitty Pryde, who apparently feels the need to make a grand entrance" (Whedon 2004, n.p.). Kitty responds, "I'm sorry. I was busy remembering to put on all my clothes." (Whedon 2004, n.p.). Kitty's response highlights a common criticism of female superheroes, perhaps reflecting Whedon's own criticism of the overly sexualized nature of women in comic books. The relationship between Emma and Kitty reveals these conventions and encourages the reader to side with Kitty's criticism of such conventions.

The depiction of Kitty also highlights how different kinds of power can be interpreted. When she is introduced in the series, Whedon portrays Kitty's power as defensive rather than offensive. When they make their first appearance in costume, Kitty's job is to save the hostages by phasing them through the floor. She does not directly attack Ord or any of his henchmen. Because of her initial use of her power as protective rather than damaging, the character of Kitty can be productively linked to the character Invisible Girl. In many ways, Kitty's evolution in Whedon's short run on the series mimics the evolution of Invisible Girl into Invisible Woman. In her early incarnations, Invisible Girl used her power of invisibility only as a defensive power. Indeed, she was often subject to attacks by villains because of her weakness. Eventually, however, Invisible Girl grew into Invisible Woman as she acquired the power to use her invisibility to shield others and to create force fields that could attack other characters. Invisible Woman now represents one of the most powerful superheroes in the Marvel universe. Indeed, Laura Mattoon D'Amore argues that Invisible Girl's transformation can be seen as a "historical palimpsest of an America coming into feminist consciousness" (D'Amore 2008, para. 15). Giving this historical context to students helps them to interpret Kitty's evolution in this series as a sort of microcosm of the evolution of female superheroes in the medium. In the beginning of the series, Kitty is unsure of her powers and unsure of her place on the team. But she slowly becomes more confident of her powers, realizing that her phasing can be used as a weapon. When she phases a weapon into someone's head, for example, she gains power over that person and is able to negotiate with them. By the end of the series, Kitty uses her power to save the entire planet, and she not only phases but bonds with the gigantic bullet sent from the Breakworld to destroy Earth. She defeats a weapon no other superhero could defeat, saving Earth in the process, but also most likely dooming herself to death as she cannot sever the bond she created with the bullet. Kitty becomes one of the most powerful characters by recognizing her own power. Discussing the development of this character can help students to see Whedon's nuanced approach to gender in this series.

Since discussing issues of gender in the college classroom can often provoke discomfort in students, using the comics' medium to approach the topic helps students to understand the history of the subject and the multiple possible responses one might have to the topic. Whedon's work provides a particularly productive example of how gender is represented in the medium. While many students in the class merely want to read comics for their stories and to escape, looking more closely at the history of the representation of women in the comics and at how Whedon chose to depict women in his comics can highlight for students the underlying ideas of that which they generally perceive as throwaway literature. Hopefully, after discussing Whedon's *Astonishing X-Men* through the lens of Wonder Woman and Whedon's own thoughts on equality, students will develop new ways to read comic book characters that seek to question assumptions about gender and feminism. As long as people are asking Whedon, "Why do you create such strong women characters?," it is important to continually challenge students' perceptions and biases about feminism by asking them to confront and interpret various representations of gender in a variety of mediums.

References

"About Equality Now." 2011. *Equality Now Webpage*. Accessed February 15, 2011. http://www.equalitynow.org/english/about/about_en.html.

Brown, Jeffrey A. 2004. "Gender, Sexuality, and Toughness: The Bad Girls of Action Film and Comic Books." In Sherrie A. Inness, ed., *Action Chicks: New Images of Tough Women in Popular Culture*. New York: Palgrave.

Chute, Hillary. March 2008. "Comics as Literature? Reading Graphic Narrative." *PMLA* 123.2: 452–465.

D'Amore, Laura Mattoon. 2008. "Invisible Girl's Quest for Visibility: Early Second Wave Feminism and the Comic Book Superheroine." *Americana: The Journal of American Popular Culture* 7.2. Accessed February 4, 2011. http://www.americanpopularculture.com/journal/articles/fall_2008/d'amore.htm.

Daniels, Les. 2000. *Wonder Woman: The Complete History*. San Francisco: Chronicle.

Inness, Sherrie A. 1999. *Tough Girls: Women Warriors and Wonder Women in Popular Culture*. Philadelphia: University of Pennsylvania Press.

Jowett, Lorna. 2005. *Sex and the Slayer: A Gender Studies Primer for the Buffy Fan*. Middletown, CT: Wesleyan.

Moore, Alan, and Dave Gibbons. 1995. *Watchmen*. New York: DC Comics.

Stanley, Kelli E. 2005. "'Suffering Sappho!' Wonder Woman and the (Re)Invention of the Feminine Ideal." *Helios* 32.2: 143–171.

Whedon, Joss. 2006. "Equality Now Acceptance Speech." *Youtube*. Accessed 02/11/2011 http://www.youtube.com/watch?v=QoEZQfTaaEA.

_____. n.d. "Welcome to the Hellmouth." Commentary. *Buffy the Vampire Slayer Season One DVD Collection*. Twentieth Century–Fox.

Whedon, Joss, and John Cassaday. 2004. *Astonishing X-Men Vol. 1: Gifted*. New York: Marvel.

_____. 2004–2005. *Astonishing X-Men Vol. 2: Dangerous*. New York: Marvel.

_____. 2006–2007. *Astonishing X-Men Vol. 3: Torn*. New York: Marvel.

_____. 2007–2008. *Astonishing X-Men Vol. 4: Unstoppable*. New York: Marvel.

Sequential Art for Qualitative Research

Marcus B. Weaver-Hightower

Just before hitting the key to advance to the next slide in my presentation, a shock of nervousness hit me. Would the students think what I was about to show them was silly or juvenile? Would they think my drawings amateurish? I was teaching a graduate class in qualitative educational research — using in-depth interviews or ethnographic observations rather than statistics (e.g., Creswell 2007) — and I was about to show them a comic book page, or what Will Eisner (1990) termed *sequential art*.

The class had been studying the nuances of transcribing interviews or observations (e.g., Poland 2003), a key component of the qualitative research process. I wanted my students — many of them practicing educators or administrators — to be thoughtful about their choices: Will you transcribe every "um," "ah," and hesitation? How will you represent gestures? How will you impart sound quality (intonation, pauses)? I wanted to guide students to the conclusion that there were many ways to represent complex social interaction on paper; the key, as researchers, is to choose transcription methods carefully and explain all decisions.

I gave the class an example — using a video of a classroom scene — meant to guide them several levels of abstraction up from real life to video to transcript. In the two-minute clip, an eleventh grade student I call Phillip was supposed to be working with classmates on field trip plans, but he ran afoul of his English teacher by breaking several rules, including having his shirttail out, eating in class, and using poor grammar. The video showed what some teachers might do to force compliance to their authority, for the teacher cited Phillip for several violations — rapid-fire — until he finally relented (or appeared to). After the clip, I show students a simple, typical transcript made from the recording (Figure 1). They read along while I play the video again, checking to see that the transcript is "accurate."

Figure 1. Transcript of Disciplinary Incident

[Teacher walks up to the group]

Teacher: [slowly, enunciating each word] Put the food away.

Phillip: [to Teacher] But the camera ... I was — I was doin an advertisement.

Teacher: You just did. [slow, enunciating] Put the food away.

Yolanda: [to Teacher; Teacher looks at her] (xxx)

[Phillip leans his head back and pours chips from his hand into his mouth. The teacher looks over at him and gives a seemingly stern look.]

Phillip: I'm puttin em in my pocket.

Teacher: [to Phillip] You ever hear the term [enunciated] *ask*ing for?

Phillip: *Ask*in for?

Teacher: Unbutton your shirt. | All the way down | All the way down.
Louis: | | ooooooo

Phillip: [feigning shock] *O::h*! *It is*! *All* them buttons get in there. [to Louis] *Shut up.*

Teacher: (xxx)

Louis: [to Phillip] (xxx) I notice your top button   (xxx)

Teacher: | *Five cents.* | "How'd *them* buttons get in there."

[Teacher walks away]

[Phillip stands and look at camera, smiling. Pantomimes brushing crumbs off shirt for 12 seconds. Flashes index and middle finger (peace sign) and laughs while sitting back down. Looks at Kevin wiping mouth. Kevin laughs, too. Phillip shifts his facial expression to one that looks more *serious*.]

Note: Brackets indicate transcriber comment or gestural cues. "(xxx)" denotes inaudible or indecipherable speech. *Italics* shows emphasis. Double colons (::) indicates drawn out speech. Vertical lines denote overlapping speech. Asterisks (*) mark whispered or quiet speech.

Then I unveiled the sequential art transcript (Figure 2), which I made by inserting still frames from the video into sequential art creation software, *Comic Life* (plasq software 2010). The sequential art transcript provides a rich array of information that the text-only transcript cannot, and it immediately captures attention and conveys verisimilitude. Speech balloons intimate tone through varying borders (dotted for whispers, jagged for intense). Text boxes still provide narration, but images allow these to be more concise. Gestures, body postures, facial expressions, and relative locations are in evidence. The photos' backgrounds provide a visual "thick description" of setting. Particularly helpful, though, the sequential art captures motion and action: Phillip's defiant performance for the camera can actually be seen, frame-to-frame, as he stands and displays his stylized hand gestures.

Despite my confidence for what the comic page could do, I felt as if I were almost daring the students to agree that one can do a transcript in numerous *acceptable* ways. If they can accept a comic book transcript, I suppose I was thinking, they could accept *anything*. At the same time, I wasn't simply using the comic page for shock value or kitsch. It wasn't just a gimmick. I really wanted them to think about the possibilities of representation and how different mediums and layouts structure cognition and shape interpretation.

At first, I wasn't completely sure if students were reacting well. Some smiled broadly. Some seemed surprised. Some just stared neutrally. I felt a sudden impulse to rush through it, like a standup comic bombing on stage and urgent to get to the next joke. As we talked more, though, students began to liven, showing they were more interested and starting to see my point. I explained to them what I saw as the benefits and challenges of sequential art for transcribing (explained below).

Though I was worried that students would think it silly or too "experimental," they really seemed to see that sequential art could be a vehicle for the kind of information they were collecting in their research sites. More than just what students might have taken from this lesson, though, I have come to see myriad uses of sequential art beyond the transcript, especially for practicing social science scholars to represent research. In this chapter I explore the many resources that sequential art provides to both students of research and practicing

Figure 2. Sequential art transcript of a disciplinary incident.

researchers. Most literature on sequential art's educational applications focuses on K-12 contexts and on either integrating existing comics and graphic novels into the curriculum or having students make their own to learn literacy skills or improve engagement (e.g., Bitz 2005; Carter 2007; Gorman 2003; Thompson 2008). Increasingly, though, sequential artists have shown the form's nonfictional, instructional uses beyond K-12 schools, from teaching weight loss strategies (Lay 2008) to teaching about ethnography (Galman 2007). Within this vein I argue that sequential art can provide a serious, scholarly contribution to education at *all* levels — whether the K-12 students who use it to improve their literacy or, for my purposes, the graduate students and researchers who might use it do qualitative social science research. To make this argument, I outline the resources inherent to sequential art that are congruent with the aims of qualitative research and then give other examples from my own work to demonstrate the form's possibilities.

What Sequential Art Can Do for Researchers

Qualitative researchers, more than anything, want to understand the lifeworlds, experiences, beliefs, and behaviors of those who participate in our research. Any new technique is necessarily measured against how it helps to meet that basic goal. Thus, how might sequential art help us better understand our participants? Using sequential art is compelling and useful, I argue, largely because it draws on a unique set of cognitive and perceptual resources. It provides researchers powerful, unparalleled means to capture and present the movement, setting, sounds, and emotion that qualitative methodologies privilege.

Of course, longstanding traditions of graphical representations already exist in *quantitative* (that is, statistically based) research — charts and figures and tables — all with circumscribed means of assessing both aesthetic quality and validity (e.g., Tufte 2001). Qualitative researchers have long used these traditional forms, too (e.g., Miles and Huberman 1994), though anthropology and sociology, particularly, have also relied heavily on pictorial modalities (e.g., Banks 2007; Harper 2003; Pink 2007; Prosser 1998), starting with sketching and painting, then still photography, and, later, film and video. Such visual media fit well the context-oriented, detail-rich nature of qualitative inquiry. I argue that sequential art has similar utility, and it might in some cases exceed what other forms can do.

Just what is it that sequential art has to offer? According to McCloud (1993, 2000, 2006) and Eisner (1990, 2008), practitioners and leading figures in theorizing how comics work, sequential art demands a distinct "form of reading" because the principles of both art and literature are superimposed, creating a unique "grammar" (Eisner 1990, 8). With the co-presence of words and images, particularly, sequential art becomes a multimodal text with meaning resources far beyond either medium singly (Lemke 2002). Images do not only illustrate the words or the words explain the images (though they sometimes do); their interplay creates a vastly richer medium for the conveyance of deep meaning.

Alongside the inclusion of words and images, at its most basic the ability to read sequential art relies on the human tendency toward *closure* (McCloud 1993). That is, when we perceive objects, images, or words that are juxtaposed, we try to make sense of the juxtaposition, to find a connection. Thus, in McCloud's (1993, 66) famous example, when an axe-wielding man menaces another character in one panel, we assume that the scream above the rooftops in the next panel is related, proof of the menaced character's demise. The construction and interpretation of sequential art is not always so easy or straightforward (e.g., Lewis 2010), of course — the scream in McCloud's panel, for instance, could be someone else's scream far away. Nevertheless, closure is a major way that the sequential art provides meaning and thus holds usefulness for qualitative researchers, for researchers also use juxtaposition of data sources (and types) to make meaning all the time. Sometimes, for example, something seen in an ethnographic observation only makes sense when juxtaposed with an interview with those who were observed. Sequential art can prompt meaning making for researchers in the same way by forcing juxtaposition as a requirement of the form.

Another unique feature of sequential art, beyond the co-presence of text and the juxtaposition of images, is its semiotic system of symbols and lines representing motion, sounds, explosions, cursing, smells, and so on. Think, for example, of the dust clouds around Pigpen in Charles Schultz's *Peanuts*. *Beetle Bailey* creator Mort Walker called these symbols and icons *emanata* (see Abel and Madden 2008, 7–8). This visual grammar is not natural but arbitrary (though emanata do sometimes mirror visual events much as onomatopoeia mirrors sounds). These symbols are socially constructed and learned by readers and artists alike over time and experience with the form. The cultural variation of these conventions proves this (cf., Douglas and Malti-Douglas 1994). Japanese manga comics, for instance, often indicate sleep with a large mucus bubble coming from a character's nose (McCloud 1993, 131), whereas in Western comics sleep often is symbolized with a string of Zs above the character's head. Yet even with its cultural specificity, the resource potential of emanata differentiates sequential art from the traditional visual forms used in qualitative research. The researcher can show facets of experience through emanata in ways that photography and video simply cannot.

The epistemological power of sequential art for qualitative researchers lies not only in the available semiotic resources, but also in the *choices* the medium requires of its creators. McCloud (2006) outlines five basic choices: (a) which moment to show; (b) how to frame the moment, including distance, angle, and inclusion or exclusion; (c) what image to include to show mood, convey appearance, and evoke a style; (d) which words to include to effectively advance the story or explain the idea; and (e) how to make the audience's attention flow around the page. Within these basic decisions, of course, are a plethora of sub-choices — about transitions between panels, fonts, dialect usage, word balloon styles, emanata, and so on. The key point is that more decisions means more analytic and representational opportunities for the researcher, more points at which to interrogate data, more possibilities for providing the audience clarity and verisimilitude.

Consider what sequential art can accomplish that are also vital components of qualitative inquiry, things achievable more readily, more easily, or more efficiently than with text alone. The *location and setting* of a study can be shown in a panel and instantly recognized, where in words it could take pages. *Time and motion* (action) can be shown from panel to panel as participants move through space. *Sound* can be implied effectively and quickly, with speech represented in balloons and noises drawn in boisterous word art or simple text. Sequential art might include *color*, or it may be black and white, for varying emotional and visual effects. Visuals might be used to stimulate other senses, like evoking *smells* by, say, showing frying eggs and bacon or someone's face as they smell something. *Emotion* can be effectively realized, too, through facial expressions, hand gestures, and body postures, or even conveying tense feelings through narrow or skewed panels (Eisner 1990). While it can't show everything — it is, after all, still an abstraction of reality — sequential art can clearly show many things that other print forms cannot.

Not only can comic art be used to show these dynamics, but it can do so in varying styles. Sequential art is perfectly suited to fit many points on the continuum between hyper-realistic and impressionistic presentation of qualitative data, for comic art has a wide array of stylistic and tonal resources available. Joe Sacco's work (2005, 2007), for instance, which he calls "comics journalism," sits close to the realist end of this continuum; his introduction to the special edition of *Palestine* (2007) even details his almost ethnographic practices used in constructing the comics, like taking fieldnotes and documenting scenes with photography. Sacco uses vivid cultural detail and much dialogue to show the effects of war and occupation on people in the Middle East and Eastern Europe. At the stylistic continuum's other end lies Drooker's (2007) *Flood!*, which uses impressionistic, metaphoric pen and ink drawings without any dialogue to explore the disconnection and alienation of city life. In the continuum's middle would be Small's (2009) *Stitches,* which combines scratchy inks and overflowing watercolor grays with elements of magical realism to illustrate a painful childhood memoir.

Altogether, then, with its resources of visual grammar, closure, multimodality, emanata, choice requirements, and stylistic openness, sequential art stands as a potentially valuable means of representation for qualitative researchers. In the next section, I discuss the particular applications to which it can be put within the research process.

Qualitative Comics in All Stages

I opened this essay with the example of sequential art being used for transcription in qualitative research. This is just one possible use for the form's many resources. Indeed, I argue that researchers can use sequential art in *every* facet of the qualitative research process, from research design to data collection to data analysis to reporting.

Regarding research design, researchers could plan studies using sequential art, much as a storyboard artist anticipates shots in a movie. One could also design an entire project with the end product of a sequential art report or graphic novel in mind, anticipating all phases of the project to contribute to that result (Maxwell 2005). Observation, protocols and fieldnotes would be somewhat different, for instance, if one planned from the beginning to visually represent scenes, to focus on dialogue for speech balloons, and to provide narration.

Sequential art is relevant in many ways to the data collection stage, as well. Graphic novels and other sequential art, of course, can themselves be data. This includes traditional practices of collecting comic books or comic strips as cultural artifacts or narratives. Someone researching cancer, for example, might use Harvey Pekar's life experiences in *Our Cancer Year* (Pekar and Brabner 1994) as an instance of one family's coping with the medicalization of cancer patients. Comics are also often the center of gravity for certain subcultures (e.g., Bitz 2009; Brown 2001), so their collection and analysis may be crucial for certain ethnographies. Sequential art might be used to elicit interview responses, much like photo elicitation techniques (Harper 2002), or researchers could have participants make sequential art, asking them to represent their experiences and identities. Galman (2009), for instance, has used the elicitation of sequential art to inquire into the identity construction of teacher trainees, developing collaborative "graphic novels" that delve into the teachers' lived experiences. Her pilot study demonstrates powerful potential in accessing data through sequential art in ways that traditional methods might not.

Sequential art provides tools for data *analysis,* as well. Analysis methods are, in reality, just heuristic devices for making decisions about abstracting and sorting data. By requiring the researcher to select, sequence, illustrate, and textualize parts of their data, sequential art provides increased theoretical sensitivity (like the open coding process of Strauss and Corbin 1990) and a means to map out actions and timelines. Choosing layouts, images, and words can provoke analytic insight into the data, forcing the researcher to stop and consider the factual needs and representational politics of the data set—just as analyzing data using "traditional" social science prose (Richardson 2003) or with "scientific" charts and tables (Miles and Huberman 1994) would. I discuss the analytical power of sequential art choices further in the example below.

Finally, qualitative researchers might productively employ sequential art as a non-traditional mode of presentation for research findings. Qualitative research is primarily concerned with telling the stories of participants, and researchers often employ multiple methods of writing and thick description to present the social world of participants to readers. Sequential art is naturally suited to doing these things, and in a way that is possibly more visceral and — perhaps — "less boring" (Caulley 2008). The medium fits well Richardson's (2003) definition of *Creative Analytic Practice (CAP) ethnographies*—and other arts-based inquiry (e.g., Barone and Eisner 1997; Knowles and Cole 2008; Sullivan 2005)—as means of evocatively presenting research through drama, poetry, and creative nonfiction. A graphic novel could be, for the right research question, a fitting way to present and explain findings. Elliot Eisner (in Saks 1996) has argued that novels could be accepted as dissertations (see also Knowles and Promislow 2008), and Carolyn Ellis (2004) has written a research methods text as a novel, so why not dissertations, methods texts, or any other scholarly genre as a *graphic* novel? (Galman 2007, is a good example of a methods text in the graphic novel form.) To show how presentation of findings might be done in sequential art, in the next section I give an example from my own work on infant bereavement.

An Example: Losing Thomas and Ella

To illustrate the resources and applications of sequential art, I present here another example from my own qualitative work, two pages — Figures 3 and 4 — from a narrative research project (Connelly and Clandinin 1990) about the neonatal death and stillbirth (respectively) of twins, Thomas and Ella. As a way to explore the experiences of fathers facing infant bereavement, I conducted an in-depth interview and many informal conversations with Paul, Thomas and Ella's father, about their deaths. I used this data to construct the (what I call) qualitative comic seen in the sample pages.

Narrative researchers commonly "restory" their data, shaping the interview data to be more chronological or compelling (Creswell 2007). In my first passes through the interview with the twins' father, I similarly reordered and omitted parts to construct a narrative with a logical flow, while ensuring the wording and meanings were his. My decisions about what to keep were framed by themes that I identified in the interview — the most common analysis process in qualitative research — and from similar themes found in the literature on infant bereavement (e.g., Weaver-Hightower, in press). The text in panel four (Figure 4), for instance, was chosen because it is representative of what many fathers say about the hospital experience being marginalizing for them.

Indeed, in turning the interview into a sequential art story, I was forced to make all the choices outlined above by McCloud (2006) about moment selection, framing, images to include, words to include, and flow around the page. Which moments from the father's story were important? Which should be described in words, and which could be images? What angles, framing, and color choices would convey the mood Paul felt? How could I show emotional states? These choices — including the restorying done before the construction of the pages — amount to data analysis, for I was using the heuristic choices of the sequential art production to decide what was important and how it should be framed. This is just like identifying themes and selecting quotations is done in traditional qualitative analysis and reporting, except here the heuristics are visual as well as verbal. For the researcher, this analysis could

Figure 3. Page 1, draft version of *Losing Thomas and Ella*.

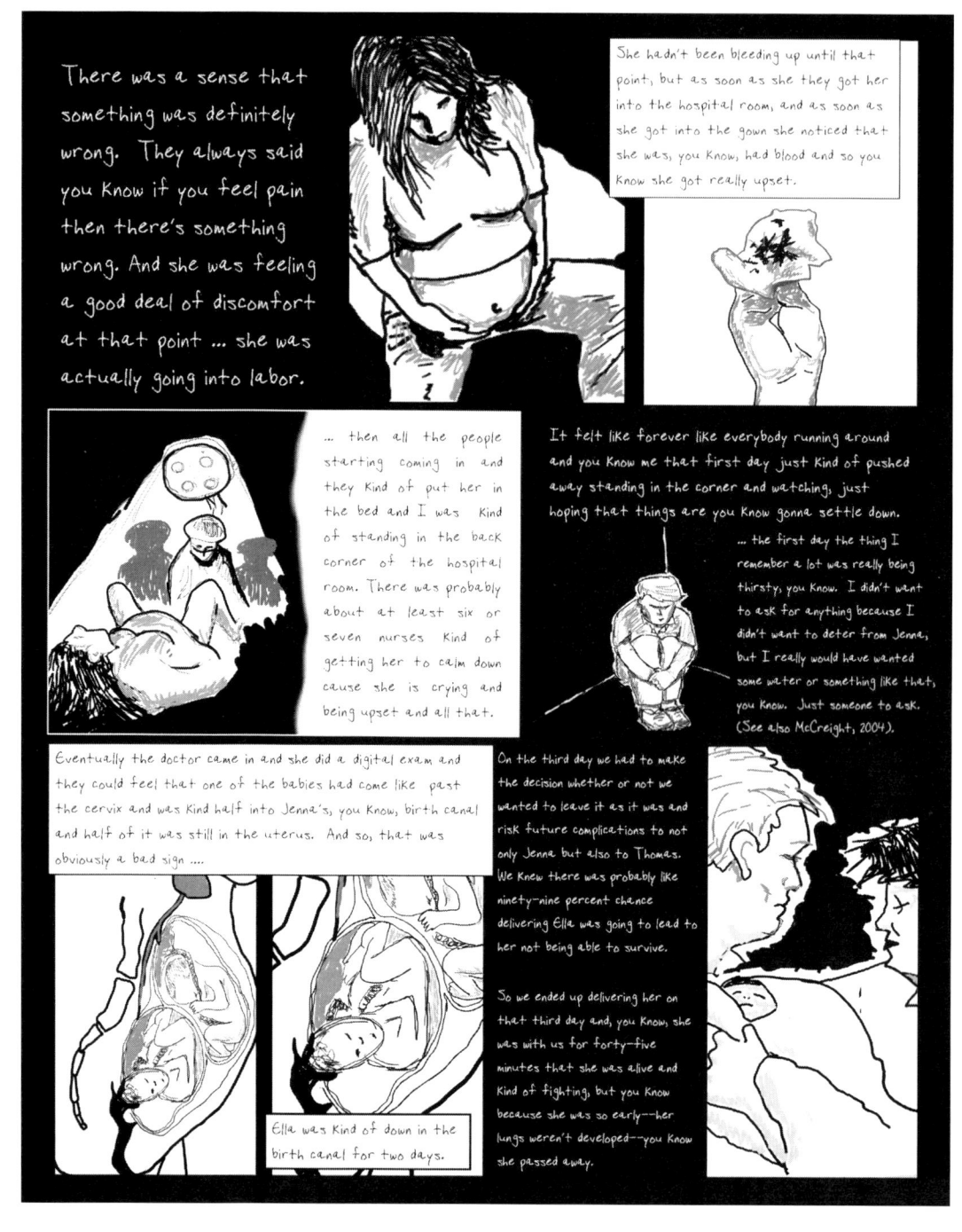

Figure 4. Page 2, draft version of *Losing Thomas and Ella*.

be just a means toward writing up the results — an end product never to be seen — or he or she might publish the sequential art pages themselves as a way to report findings.

Numerous features of the pages demonstrate the potential sequential art has to fit the goals and philosophies underpinning qualitative social science. First, the information presented fulfills many of the characteristics of the chosen approach, in this case narrative research (e.g., Creswell 2007, Chapter Four): it is a narrative based on participants' perspectives and stories, it is factual, and it utilizes the recounted experiences to illuminate a larger social phenomenon. Like other "alternative" modes of research, some creativity is used to evoke emotions that traditional scientific registers cannot or do not. Also, like other scientific registers, I have included footnotes and citations to relevant literature (see panel 4 of Figure 4), acknowledging the interconnection of this work to the field's accumulated knowledge; these are key parts of how social science sequential art might look different from the typical graphic novel.

Sequential art provided me symbolic facilities that traditional qualitative displays could not have. Crucially, the example pages give the reader and me, as researcher, access to events that no one could have seen, inside the womb, particularly in the cross sections on page two. These are imagined scenes, but they are based on the reconstruction of actual events and medical probabilities based on a (layperson's) reading of the medical literature, perusal of medical illustrations, and speculation.

Thought balloons and text boxes echo or explain the images but also illustrate what the images alone cannot. (My pages are perhaps also more text-heavy than traditional graphic novels, reflecting both the source of the data — interview transcripts — the lack of first-hand visuals to work from, and, admittedly, perhaps still working under the yoke of the logocentric traditions of the social sciences [Lemke 2002]). Creating pages with the visual resources of sequential art, importantly, provided me with the emotional language that the words had difficulty conveying. The background gradients from white to black as the story descends into bleakness. The dark, black shapes and lines reference the Expressionist style in Western art, while the simplification of backgrounds on page two eliminates distraction and was intended to give an abstract, almost claustrophobic feeling. On page one, the "Ring!" express sound in words and expressive lines, the car's speeding is conveyed through streaks, and bolts representing sharp pain radiate from Jenna's stomach and are reinforced by her wincing. Perspectives and text boxes are meant to skew in visually tense ways. These are all parts of sequential art's "grammar" that contribute to the qualitative understandings I wanted to convey.

Of course, the preceding description is only my *intention* for what the pages would convey; readers may interpret them in vastly different ways. Still, key to the form's analytical usefulness for me were the choices that had to be made and the visual resources available, requiring me, as researcher, to use different epistemological and cognitive mechanisms than creating text alone would have.

Thorny Issues of Ethics, Quality and Validity

Sequential art can be a powerful tool, as I have argued, but it is not unproblematic. The extra resources provided by sequential art do not guarantee a simple, transparent retelling of information absent of reader (mis)interpretation, ethical challenges, issues of scholarly and artistic quality, and conceptual and factual validity.

First, the use of sequential art suffers a legacy of controversy. Some consider comics and graphic novels dangerous (Wertham 1954), while others view them as solely for children, silly, not to be taken seriously. Though recent changes in demographics and content have bolstered its legitimacy, qualitative researchers who practice sequential art — or any other form of arts-based research (Woo 2008)—may find themselves defending the medium often.

Beyond the annoyance of constant defense, though, such barriers to the use of sequential art suggest a politics of multimodality. As Lemke (2002, 321) says, "'logocentrism' in modern European intellectual and academic culture represents a political ideology. Privileging linguistic meaning to the point of excluding or denigrating pictorial modes of representation has a definite politics; it favors particular interests or modes of social control." These modes of control are not trivial. Tenure and promotion, the availability of publishing venues, and acceptance by peers are serious concerns in using a medium that is often not taken seriously or considered "low culture." Similarly, we must ask whether it is ethical to initiate graduate students into such practices given the professional dangers (Ellis 2004; Knowles and Promislow 2008; Richardson 2003; Saks 1996).

One might also ask serious questions about the ethics for the participants in research (e.g., Papademas 2004). Images necessarily work within and contribute to existing power relations (Harper 2003), and images are used to constitute and reproduce social inequality (e.g., Berger 1972; Goffman 1976; Kress and van Leeuwen 1996), and sequential art could easily be used for these ends, too. More immediately, though, sequential art provokes questions about the ethics of using images of participants to tell stories: How do we protect anonymity in so visual a medium? What methods of disguise might researchers use? (For figures 3 and 4, I made Paul and Jenna look different than they actually do, but is that enough?) How might institutional review boards and ethics panels be convinced of the protections provided participants?

Another challenge of sequential art is that it might draw researchers' attentions too much toward particularly visual data. Sequential art-based research could lead researchers to focus too much on the visually appealing (or, depending on the researcher's position, the repellent) to the detriment of other important elements. Things that might be hard to make images of, particularly concepts and feelings, might be overlooked in favor of things simple to represent.

Sequential art also provokes thorny issues of quality and validity. Because statistical tests can't be run to "prove" its validity and no centralized "eye of the beholder" can arbitrate its artistic quality, sequential art might have a different set of standards by which peers might judge it. This is not to say, of course, that traditional qualitative validity methods—triangulation, member checking, peer debriefing and the like (e.g., Lincoln and Guba 1985, Chapter 11)—are incompatible; indeed, these may be invaluable in shaping the sequential art in a study.

Given its fit with other CAP ethnographies (Richardson 2003), as noted above, sequential art might best be evaluated similarly to other alternative presentations (see especially Finley 2003). Richardson (2000, 254; 2003), for one, suggests that an ethnography, whether traditional or arts-based, should fulfill five criteria: (1) substantive contribution to social and cultural understanding; (2) aesthetic merit; (3) researcher reflexivity; (4) impact on the reader; and (5) expression of a reality. Sequential art can help accomplish all of these when done well. Judging the scientific validity of sequential art, then, may not be much different from the standards for traditional qualitative research.

What of the "aesthetic merit" just mentioned, though? Even those who may be persuaded of sequential art's usefulness may balk at having to draw. While certainly standards of artistic quality exist by which we might judge published art, drawing talent is not a requirement for using sequential art in qualitative inquiry (see Abel and Madden 2008, 9–10). First, not all applications of sequential art have to be published. As I posited above, one might use it at nearly any stage of a project, for any of the many tasks in qualitative inquiry that readers never see, like transcripts. Second, sequential art can convey a great deal without needing highly rendered images. Matt Feazell draws his popular underground comic hero *Cynicalman*, for instance, as deceptively simple "stick figure" compositions, but its nuanced stories belie the illustrations' simplicity (see http://home.comcast.net/~mattfeazell/NAComics.htm).

Furthermore, the technology for producing sequential art has made the process simple for even novices. Computer programs for making sequential art are now readily available, including *Comic Life* (http://www.plasq.com), the application I used for the examples above, which allows for "dragging and dropping" of photos and other digital images; provides page templates; and automatically creates balloons, text boxes, and even word art. There is even a comics creation application for the iPhone, Comic Touch (also from plasq), and Internet-based comics creation tools, like Comiqs (http://comiqs.com), Pixton (http://pixton.com), and ToonDoo (http://www.toondoo.com). These incorporate Web 2.0 tools like blogging and commenting to facilitate collaboration and communication — potentially useful for research processes like member checking, peer debriefing, research dissemination, and more. With these applications and Websites — alongside the profusion of scanners, digital cameras, and stock art on the Internet — one hardly needs to be able to draw to create sequential art. I am not suggesting that technology can substitute for craft (particularly in published work), only that technology allows far greater access to the medium and its methodological and epistemological benefits.

Conclusion

> "What [artistically oriented research] yields at its best are ineffable forms of understanding which can only be conveyed through the figurative or nondiscursive character of the artistic image which such research yields... The working assumption is that with such understanding, both cognitive differentiation and the ability of individuals to grasp and deal with situations like those portrayed in the research will be increased"
>
> — Elliot Eisner (1981, 8).

Sequential art has the potential to increase the "grasp" of qualitative researchers and their readers. By using the linguistic, pictorial, and symbolic resources of sequential art, researchers have added possibilities for conveying facets of human experience, emotion, and even worlds unseen but imaginable. Naturally, not every research project needs sequential art, but for the right studies it can be transformative. In planning research projects, visualizing and analyzing data, and presenting theories, processes, and findings with sequential art, the researcher is able to employ unique ways of knowing, seeing, and saying.

References

Abel, Jessica, and Matt Madden. 2008. *Drawing Words & Writing Pictures: Making Comics from Manga to Graphic Novels*. New York: First Second.
Banks, Marcus. 2007. *Using Visual Data in Qualitative Research*. Los Angeles: Sage.
Barone, Tom, and Elliot W. Eisner. 1997. "Arts-Based Educational Research." In Richard M. Jaeger, ed., *Complementary Methods for Research in Education* 2d ed. Washington, DC: American Educational Research Association.

Berger, J. 1972. *Ways of Seeing*. London: BBC and Penguin.
Bitz, Michael. 2009. *Manga High: Literacy, Identity, and Coming of Age in an Urban High School*. Cambridge, MA: Harvard Education.
Brown, Jeffrey A. 2001. *Black Superheroes, Milestone Comics, and Their Fans*. Jackson: University Press of Mississippi.
Caulley, Darrel N. 2008. "Making Qualitative Research Reports Less Boring: The Techniques of Writing Creative Nonfiction." *Qualitative Inquiry* 14.3: 424–449.
Connelly, F. Michael, and D. Jean Clandinin. 1990. "Stories of Experience and Narrative Inquiry." *Educational Researcher* 19.5: 2–14.
Creswell, John W. 2007. *Qualitative Inquiry and Research Design: Choosing Among Five Approaches*. 2d ed. Thousand Oaks, CA: Sage Publications.
Douglas, Allen, and Fedwa Malti-Douglas. 1994. *Arab Comic Strips: Politics of an Emerging Mass Culture*. Bloomington: Indiana University Press.
Drooker, Eric. 2007. *Flood!* Milwaukie, OR: Dark Horse.
Eisner, Elliot W. 1981. "On the Differences Between Scientific and Artistic Approaches to Qualitative Research." *Educational Researcher* 10.4: 5–9.
Eisner, Will. 1990. *Comics and Sequential Art, Expanded Edition*. Parasmus, NJ: Poorhouse.
———. 2008. *Graphic Storytelling and Visual Narrative*. New York: W.W. Norton.
Ellis, Carolyn. 2004. *The Ethnographic I*. Walnut Creek, CA: Alta Mira.
Finley, Susan. 2003. "Arts-Based Inquiry in *QI*: Seven Years from Crisis to Guerrilla Warfare." *Qualitative Inquiry* 9.2: 281–296.
Galman, Sally A.C. 2007. *Shane, the Lone Ethnographer: A Beginner's Guide to Ethnography*. Lanham, MD: Alta Mira.
———. 2009. "The Truthful Messenger: Visual Methods and Representation in Qualitative Research in Education." *Qualitative Research* 9.2: 197–217.
Goffman, Erving. 1976. *Gender Advertisements*. New York: Harper Colophon.
Gorman, Michele. 2003. *Getting Graphic! Using Graphic Novels to Promote Literacy with Preteens and Teens*. Columbus, OH: Linworth.
Harper, Douglas. 2002. "Talking About Pictures: A Case for Photo Elicitation." *Visual Studies* 17.1: 13–26.
———. 2003. "Reimagining Visual Methods: Galileo to *Neuromancer*." In Norman K. Denzin and Yvonna S. Lincoln, eds., *Collecting and Interpreting Qualitative Materials*. Thousand Oaks, CA: Sage Publications.
Knowles, J. Gary, and Sara Promislow. 2008. "Using an Arts Methodology to Create a Thesis or Dissertation." In J. Gary Knowles and Ardra L. Cole, eds., *Handbook of the Arts in Qualitative Research: Perspectives, Methodologies, Examples, and Issues*. Los Angeles: Sage.
Kress, Gunther R., and Theo van Leeuwen. 1996. *Reading Images: The Grammar of Visual Design*. London: Routledge.
Lay, Carol. 2008. *The Big Skinny: How I Changed My Fatitude*. New York: Villard.
Lemke, Jay L. 2002. "Travels in Hypermodality." *Visual Communication* 1.3: 299–325.
Lewis, A. David. 2010. "The Shape of Comic Book Reading." *Studies in Comics* 1.1: 71–81.
Lincoln, Yvonna S., and Egon G. Guba. 1985. *Naturalistic Inquiry*. Beverly Hills, CA: Sage.
Maxwell, Joseph A. 2005. *Qualitative Research Design: An Interactive Approach*. 2d ed. Thousand Oaks, CA: Sage Publications.
McCloud, Scott. 1993. *Understanding Comics: The Invisible Art*. Northampton, MA: Kitchen Sink.
———. 2000. *Reinventing Comics: How Imagination and Technology Are Revolutionizing an Art Form*. New York: Harper Perennial.
———. 2006. *Making Comics: Storytelling Secrets of Comics, Manga, and Graphic Novels*. New York: Harper.
Miles, Matthew B., and A. Michael Huberman. 1994. *Qualitative Data Analysis: An Expanded Sourcebook*. 2d ed. Thousand Oaks, CA: Sage Publications.
Pekar, Harvey, and Joyce Brabner. 1994. *Our Cancer Year*. New York: Thunder's Mouth.
Pink, Sarah. 2007. *Doing Visual Ethnography*. 2d ed. Los Angeles: Sage.
Poland, Blake D. 2000. "Transcription Quality." In James A. Holstein and Jaber F. Gubrium, eds., *Inside Interviewing: New Lenses, New Concerns*. Thousand Oaks, CA: Sage Publications.
Richardson, Laurel. June 2000. "Evaluating Ethnography." *Qualitative Inquiry* 6.2: 253–255.
———. 2003. "Writing: A Method of Inquiry." In Norman K. Denzin and Yvonna S. Lincoln, eds., *Collecting and Interpreting Qualitative Materials*. 2d ed. Thousand Oaks, CA: Sage Publications.
Sacco, Joe. 2005. *War's End: Profiles from Bosnia, 1995–96*. Montreal, Quebec: Drawn and Quarterly.

_____. 2007. *Palestine (Special ed.*. Seattle: Fantagraphic.
Saks, A.L. 1996. "Should Novels Count as Dissertations in Education?" *Research in the Teaching of English* 30.4: 403–427.
Small, David. 2009. *Stitches: A Memoir.* New York: W.W. Norton.
Strauss, Anselm, and Juliet Corbin. 1990. *Basics of Qualitative Research: Grounded Theory Procedures and Techniques.* Newbury Park, CA: Sage.
Sullivan, Graeme. 2005. *Art Practice as Research: Inquiry in the Visual Arts.* Thousand Oaks, CA: Sage Publications.
Thompson, Terry. 2008. *Adventures in Graphica: Using Comics and Graphic Novels to Teach Comprehension, 2–6.* Portland, ME: Stenhouse.
Tufte, Edward R. 2001. *The Visual Display of Quantitative Information.* 2d ed. Cheshire, CT: Graphics Press.
Weaver-Hightower, M. B. In press. "Waltzing Matilda: An Autoethnography of a Father's Stillbirth." *Journal of Contemporary Ethnography.*
Wertham, Frederic. 1954. *Seduction of the Innocent.* New York: Rinehart.
Woo, Yen Yen Jocelyn. 2008. "Engaging New Audiences: Translating Research into Popular Media." *Educational Researcher* 37.6: 321–329.

Afterword

Mel Gibson

This collection of essays offers a rich resource for anyone interested in the potential of comics in education. The case studies focusing on individual texts or genres, such as that by Jeremy R. Ricketts on *Barefoot Gen*, indicate the potential for exploring theory, ideology and specific subject areas through the medium.

In addition, the first essay, by Carol L. Tilley, in focusing on the history of the relationship between education and comics reveals that presenting comics as a social problem has not been the only way of thinking about them. This serves to counter the perception of the relationship of the two as simply one of antagonism. The dominant discourse in the UK was that of the Comics Campaign Council in the 1950s and 1960s which characterized the medium as dangerous. George Pumphrey, part of that campaign, suggested that all comics fell into one of two categories which he described as "harmful and harmless" (in Barker 1984, 81), adding that the best they could do was no harm to the child. In the USA, Fredric Wertham, whose fears regarding delinquency and comics are well documented was the most dominant voice. It is a great strength of this collection to allow other, less negative voices, to be heard.

My recent research has moved along similar lines to that of Tilley, in that I've been looking at writing from the 1940s about comics. Most interesting for me was the *Journal of Educational Sociology*, which devoted an issue to "The Comics as an Educational Medium" in 1944. Articles included Josette Frank's "What's in the Comics?," a content analysis designed to show the wide range of material in comics and one on the social impact of the medium by Sidonie Matsner Gruenberg. A later edition from 1949 contained articles unpacking the moral panic about comics and directly addressing questions from parents and teachers, most notably, Frederic M. Thrasher's "The Comics and Delinquency: Cause or Scapegoat." This current collection, then, joins a tradition of balanced explorations about the potential of, responses to and uses of comics.

It remains important to explore the perceptions of comics amongst educators and librarians, lest concerns about content, or a lack of confidence in using the medium means it is excluded from the classroom or library. This means that another key element of this collection is very significant; the inclusion of essays such as that by James Bucky Carter, exploring the varied understandings that students, teachers and professors have of graphic novels and comics. These essays show the current range of debates about their value.

To conclude, working with comics in education is rewarding and challenging. It asks that educators get to grips with what may be unfamiliar texts and be creative in using them to get across key ideas, theories and cultural understandings. In showing the diverse possibilities of the medium in a range of educational contexts this collection should both help those wishing to engage with the medium, but are unsure where to start, as well as those hoping to enrich and extend their current practice.

References

Barker, Martin. 1984. *A Haunt of Fears: The Strange History of the British Horror Comics Campaign*. London: Pluto Press.
Frank, Josette. December 1944. "What's in the Comics?" *Journal of Educational Sociology* 18.4: 214–222
Gruenberg, Sidonie Matsner. December 1944. "The Comics as a Social Force." *Journal of Educational Sociology* 18.4: 204–213.
Thrasher, Fredric, M. December 1949. "The Comics and Delinquency: Cause or Scapegoat." *Journal of Educational Sociology* 23.4:195–205.

As a librarian Mel Gibson encouraged the development of collections in the UK, initially through her writing an article for Keith Barker's (1993) edited collection *Graphic Account: The Selection and Promotion of Graphic Novels in Libraries for Young People,* published by the Youth Libraries Group in the UK. As an academic she has written extensively about the medium and runs http://www.dr-mel-comics.co.uk/. She is on the editorial board for the *Journal of Graphic Novels and Comics* and recently co-edited a special issue with Robert G. Weiner on audiences and readership.

About the Contributors

Christina C. **Angel** is currently a visiting assistant professor of English at Metropolitan State University of Denver, where she teaches British and world literature, mythology, children's literature, comics and graphic novels, and writing and rhetoric courses. She sits on the board of directors for Comic Book Classroom.

Timothy D. **Arner** is an assistant professor of English at Grinnell College, where he specializes in medieval literature. In addition to courses on Chaucer and the history of the English language, he has taught the "Craft of Argument," introductory courses on literary analysis, and a first-year seminar on David Foster Wallace's *Infinite Jest*.

Christina L. **Blanch** is a doctoral student and an anthropology instructor at Ball State University. Her research focuses on pedagogical methods using comics as teaching tools in higher education. Some areas of interest include: life histories of comics professionals, qualitative research methods, gender studies, and innovative pedagogies using popular culture.

James Bucky **Carter** is an assistant professor of English education at the University of Texas–El Paso. He edited the best-selling and award-winning collection *Building Literacy Connections with Graphic Novels* (NCTE, 2007) and *Rationales for Teaching Graphic Novels* (Maupin House, 2010), and co-authored *Super-Powered Word Study* (Maupin House, 2010) with Erik E. Evensen.

Roy T. **Cook** is an associate professor in the Department of Philosophy at the University of Minnesota and an associate fellow of the Northern Institute of Philosophy at the University of Aberdeen. He is the co-editor (with Aaron Meskin) of *The Art of Comics: A Philosophical Approach* (Wiley-Blackwell, 2012).

Lan **Dong** holds a Ph.D. in comparative literature and is an assistant professor of English at the University of Illinois–Springfield. She is the author of *Mulan's Legend and Legacy in China and the United States* (Temple University Press, 2011) and *Reading Amy Tan* (Greenwood/ABC-CLIO, 2009), and the editor of *Transnationalism and the Asian American Heroine: Essays on Literature, Film, Myth and Media* (McFarland, 2010) and *Teaching Comics and Graphic Narratives* (McFarland 2012).

Kevin M. **Flanagan** is a Ph.D. student in the Critical and Cultural Studies Program at the University of Pittsburgh, where he teaches film and composition courses. He is the editor of *Ken Russell: Re-Viewing England's Last Mannerist* (Scarecrow, 2009). He is investigating the intersections of comedy and war (on screen) in the post–1945 British context.

Abram **Fox** is a doctoral student studying 18th-century art at the University of Maryland–College Park, where he teaches a summer course on comics and high art in the 21st century. His dissertation is on American-born painter Benjamin West and he is co-authoring an article on classical symbolism in David Mazzucchelli's *Asterios Polyp*.

Erin **Hollis** is an assistant professor in the Department of English, Comparative Literature, and Linguistics at California State University, Fullerton. She is currently working on a book project that examines modernist literature and popular culture and how both teach us to be human. She studies and teaches popular culture, covering topics such as the Harry Potter series, vampire literature, and comic books.

Felix **Keller** is an assistant professor of sociology at the University of St. Gallen, Switzerland. He has taught social science research at several universities in Switzerland. His main fields of interest include sociology of knowledge and science, visual knowledge, utopian thinking, and popular culture.

David **Ketchen** currently serves as Lowder Eminent Scholar, professor of management and as executive director of the Lowder Center for Family Business and Entrepreneurship at Auburn University. He has taught courses at the undergraduate, M.B.A., executive M.B.A., and doctoral levels and has published six books, including three graphic novels.

Yiannis **Koukoulas** is a Ph.D. student at the Athens School of Fine Arts, Department of Theory and History of Art. He has been working as a journalist in newspapers and magazines since 1992, specializing in art and comics. He has curated many comics' exhibitions, has presented many papers in conferences and comics conventions, has edited and written introductions for many graphic novels.

Alice **Leber-Cook** has an M.Ed. in adult education from the University of Minnesota, and is currently pursuing an M.A. in curriculum and instruction, also from the University of Minnesota. She has worked and volunteered with adult learners in Columbus, Ohio; Philadelphia, and Minneapolis.

Diana **Maliszewski** works at Agnes Macphail Public School in Toronto. She is the editor of *The Teaching Librarian*, the official magazine of the Ontario School Library Association. She first discovered comics when she began her master of education degree studies with the University of Alberta. She was Canada's 2008 Teacher-Librarian of the Year and attends the Toronto Comics Arts Festival regularly.

Rebecca M. **Marrall** is the Diversity Resident Librarian at Western Washington University. Through her dual focus on public services and diversity-related topics, she strives to reach out to all campus populations, and the Bellingham community. She earned her master's degree in library and information science at the University of Hawai'i.

Marianna **Missiou** gives lectures on childrens' literature at the University of the Aegean (Rhodes, Greece). She has a B.A. in French literature from the University of Athens in Greece, a master's degree in children's literature and a Ph.D. dissertation titled "René Goscinny: The Reception of His Work in Greece and Its Integration in Greek Education." She is the author of *Comics, from the Newsstands to Classroom* (Kapsimi, 2010.)

Thalia M. **Mulvihill** is a professor of higher education and social foundations of education and director of the Adult, Higher and Community Education Doctoral Program at Ball State University. Her research areas of special interest include: life histories of women educators, graduate student education with a focus on curriculum development for future professors and student affairs administrators.

Dorothea **Oechslin** graduated with an M.S. degree in psychology and German linguistics from the University of Zurich, Switzerland. She has been a research assistant and project manager at the Lucerne University of Applied Sciences and Arts since 2009 where she is investigating educational comics and visual communication.

Maryanne A. **Rhett** is an assistant professor of Middle Eastern and world history at Monmouth University in West Long Branch, New Jersey. She received a Ph.D. in 2008 from Washington State University in world history, with a regional focus in the Middle East and thematic focus on imperialism and nationalism. Her research looks at the global questions related to the *Balfour Declaration*.

Jeremy R. **Ricketts** completed his doctorate in American studies at the University of New Mexico where he is a visiting lecturer in the department of English. His research interests include religion and culture, memoir (including graphic memoirs), and visual culture. He has presented his research at several national conferences and has published articles on subjects such as sacred space and Japanese manga.

Daniel Ian **Rubin** is a National Board Certified Teacher in English/language arts and has been teaching for 14 years (12 of those in high school English). He is a doctoral student at New Mexico State University in curriculum and instruction with an emphasis in critical pedagogies. He is interested in the intersection of English/language arts and critical pedagogy in the secondary classroom.

Rebecca **Scherr** is an associate professor of American literature in the Department of Literature, Area Studies, and European Languages at the University of Oslo. She has published a number of articles on American literature and film, most recently on Alison Bechdel's *Fun Home*.

Jeff **Shelstad** is the CEO and co-founder of Flat World Knowledge, Inc., a publisher of free and open college textbooks. A frequent speaker at industry conferences and educational forums, Jeff is on the board of directors of the Education Division of the Software & Information Industry Association (SIIA). He graduated from the University of Minnesota Carlson School of Management in 1987 and received an M.B.A. degree from Duke University in 2004.

Jeremy **Short** is the Rath Chair in strategic management at the University of Oklahoma. He has published a graphic novel focusing on management and entrepreneurship (*Atlas Black: The Complete Adventure*), as well as a graphic novel focusing on franchising and family business (*Tales of Garcón: The Franchise Players*).

Carrye Kay **Syma** is an associate librarian at Texas Tech University. She has co-authored a forthcoming article with Robert G. Weiner looking at the use of comics and animation in the Library 1100 Information Literacy course at Texas Tech University.

Carol L. **Tilley** is an assistant professor in the Graduate School of Library and Information Science at the University of Illinois Urbana-Champaign, where she teaches courses in comics reader's advisory and youth services librarianship. A former high school librarian, she spends part of her time investigating the intersection of young people, comics, and libraries.

Phillip **Troutman** is an assistant professor of writing at George Washington University in Washington, D.C., where he uses the field of comics studies to teach academic writing and research. His research includes the study of disciplinary/academic discourse and the visual rhetoric of American abolitionists in the nineteenth century

Marcus B. **Weaver-Hightower** is an associate professor at the University of North Dakota. He is the author of *The Politics of Policy in Boys' Education: Getting Boys "Right"* (Palgrave Macmillan, 2008), co-editor of *The Problem with Boys' Education: Beyond the Backlash* (Routledge, 2009) and co-editor of *School Food Politics: The Complex Ecology of Hunger and Feeding in Schools Around the World* (Peter Lang, 2011).

Robert G. **Weiner** is an associate humanities librarian at Texas Tech University where he serves as liaison to the College of Visual and Performing Arts. and is the author or editor of numerous books related to films, comics, music and popular culture. He is on the editorial board of *Journal of Graphic Novel and Comics.*

David **Whitt** is an associate professor of communication at Nebraska Wesleyan University in Lincoln, Nebraska. He has edited and contributed chapters to two books on comparative mythology: *Sith, Slayers, Stargates and Cyborgs: Modern Mythology in the New Millennium* (Peter Lang, 2008) and *Millennial Mythmaking: Essays on the Power of Science Fiction and Fantasy Literature, Films and Games* (McFarland, 2010).

Index

Abina and the Important Men 117–118
Abstract Expressionist Ultra Super Modernistic Comics 98
Academy Award 56
Accelerated Reader (AR) 64
Action Comics 52
Adams, Fay 19
Adams, Jeff 224
ADD 39
Addams, Charles 17
ADHD 39
Adult Basic Literacy (ABE) 29
Adventures in Cartooning 69
Adventures in Synthetic Biology 184–185, 188–190
Aeschylus 158
Afghanistan 225
Akira 55
Alice in Wonderland 169
All Quiet on the Western Front 16
Allusion Approach 107, 108
Alongi, Constance 233
Alvermann, Donna 13
Amazing Fantasy 53
Amazon.com 154
Amazon.com.uk 154
American Born Chinese 63, 245, 247–248
American Imago 126
American Library Association 53
American Popular Culture Movement 122
American POWs 177
American Splendor 36, 56–57
American youth culture 230
Anderson, Linda 135
Angel 251
Angel, Christina 4
Anglo-Saxon culture 18
Anna Karenina 169
An Anthology of Graphic Fiction, Cartoons, and True Stories 93
Apple Macintosh 30
Arakawa, Hiromu 116
Archie 25
Archie 61
Arkham Asylum: A Serious House on Serious Earth (AA) 54–55
Arno, Peter 17
Art of War 3
"Articulation of Elementary-School English with Secondary-School English" 13
Asia 112
Association for College and Research Libraries 5
Asterios Polyp 93, 95–97
Astonishing X-Men 251, 253–254, 256, 259
Ataalla, Philo 240
Ataalla, Youeel 239
Athena 158
Atlas Black 5, 10
Atlas Black (character) 201, 205, 217
Atlas Black: Management Guru? 201, 205–208, 218
Atlas Black: Managing to Succeed 201, 202–205
Atomic age 178
Atomic bomb 182
Attucks, Crispus 3
Auster, Paul 96
Austerlitz 224
Australian Outback 148, 149
Auto-graphics 131
Avengers (film) 5, 251
Avengers (characters) 255

B-29 177, 182
Bachalo, Chris 116
Bakis, Maureen 4
Balat Camp 139
Ball State University 40
Baltimore Convention Center 147
Barbie 61, 62
Barefoot Gen 26, 174–176, 178, 180–183, 224, 274
Barnes and Noble 235
Baronet Books 247
Barry, James 94
Barry, Lynda 251
Barthes, Roland 187–188, 190, 192
Bartholomae, David 129
Bartleby the Scrivner 102
Batgirl 254
Batman (character) 36, 53, 54, 55, 113, 118, 119, 225
Batman (media) 4, 50, 52, 96, 99, 113, 115, 119, 256
Batman and Robin (comic) 113
Batman Inc. (comic) 113
Baum, L. Frank xi
Beatles 50
Beau Geste 16

Bechdel, Alison 63, 92, 139–141, 225, 245, 247, 251
Beetle Bailey 31, 264
Bender, Lauretta 19
Beowulf 17, 18, 101–103, 107–109
Berlin 115
Berlin City of Stones 231
Berlin City of Stones: Book One 222
Bible 109, 169, 212
Big Brother 88
Bilal Asselah 113
Bitstrips for Schools 237–238
Bitz, Michael 64, 233, 236
Bizup, Joe 127
Black Beauty 74
Black Rain 180
Black Square 166
Blackboard 220, 221
Blankets 154
Blast 76, 78
Blick 186, 198
Bloom, Benjamin 248
Bloom, Harold 78
Boccaccio 109
Bohr, Neils 117
Bomer, Randy 28
Botticelli 149
Bound by Law?: Tales from the Public Domain 3, 222
Boyer, Paul 183
Breakfast of Champions 169
Breakworld 258
Brown, Jeffrey A. 254
Brunetti, Ivan 93
Bucher, Katherine T. 85, 87
Buddha 224
Buffy: The Movie 252
Buffy the Vampire Slayer 50, 251–252
Der Bund 186
Burke, Kenneth 129
Burma Chronicles 222
Busiek, Kurt 55

Calvino, Italo 169
Cambourne, Brian 62
Campbell, Joseph 180
Canada 112
Captain America (character) 35
Captain America (media) 1, 35
"Captain Canuck" 237
Captain Jack Sparrow 212
Carr, Constance 16

282 Index

Carracci, Annibale 95
Carrier, David 92
Carroll, Lewis 169
Carry On 73
Carter, James Bucky 4, 8, 60, 87, 233, 236, 274
Carter, Lynda 256
Cassady, John 50
Catch-22 183
Cawelti, John G. 75–76
Chaney, Michael 157
Characters and Caricatures 94–95
Chardi 227
Chasing Amy 56
Chaucer 108–109
Che: A Graphic Biography 26
Cheney, Lynne 113
Cheung, Joyce 241
Child Study Associates of America 36
Childs, Peter 76
Chite, Hillary 222
Christopher Marlowe 74
Chronicle of Higher Education 5, 9, 119, 232
Chute, Hillary 135, 138, 157, 251
City of Corpses 179
City of Glass 96
Civil Rights Movement 3
Civil War 116
Clan Apis 3, 9
Claremont, Chris 65
Classic Comics 15
Classics Illustrated 1, 3, 18, 74
Clowe, Daniel 95
A Collection of Failed Experiments in Comic Book Aesthetics 98
Columbia University 158
Columbus 50
Comely, Richard 237
Comic Book Classroom 4
Comic Book Confidential 53
Comic Book Superheroes Unmasked 53
Comic Books: Conduits to Culture 38
Comic Life 261, 271
Comic Studies 37
Comic Touch 271
Comicbookclassroom.org 114
"The Comics and Delinquency: Cause or Scapegoat" 274
Comics and Ideology 54
Comics and Sequential Art 69, 128
Comics Campaign Council 274
Comics Code Authority (CCA) 24, 50, 247
Comics Magazine Association of America 12
A Comics Studies Reader 122
Comicsintheclassroom.net 114
Comiqs http://comiqs.com 271
Conan Doyle, Sir Arthur 75
Confederacy 116
"Confessions of a Comic Book Professor" 4, 10
Conrad, Joseph 115
"Contemporary Trends and Issues in the Graphic Novel" 59–61

A Contract with God and Other Tenement Stories 36, 220, 247
Cope, Bill 27
Crawford, Philip Charles 231
Crawford, Robert 75
Crazy Rex 240
Creative Analytic Practice (CAP) 266
Crilley, Mark 234–235
Crime Does Not Pay 1
Crumb, R. 98
Cruse, Howard 26
Cvtekovich, Ann 140
CXStudies 124
Cyclops 256–257
Cynicalman 271

Dachau 56
Dalí, Salvador 95, 98
D'Amore, Laura Mattoon 258
Danaïdes 166
Dante 1, 169
Daredevil 96
Dark Knight 54
Dark Knight 128
Darwin, Charles 3
Davco 3
DC Comics 50, 52–53, 55
DC Universe 54
Death 55
Decameron 109
Deese, Isadora 185
DeKoven, Marianne 222
Dénouement 80
Denslow, W.W. xi
Denver Comic Con 4
Deogratias: A Tale of Rwanda 115
DePauw (Indiana) 52
Depp, Johnny 212
Derrida, Jacques 164
Detective Comics 52
Detective Comics Annual 113
Dewey, John 13
Diana Prince 256
Dias, Earl J. 16
Didier 226–228
Divine Comedy 169, 171
DNA programming 185
Dr. Jekyll and Mr. Hyde 169
Doctors Without Borders/Médecins Sans Frontières 225, 226
Dollhouse 251
A Doll's House 98
Don Quixote 50
Doré, Gustave 169, 171
Dorrell, Larry 12
Dostoyevsky, Fyodor 169
Doxiadis, Apostolos 3, 154, 158, 160, 162
Dracula 117
Drawing Words and Writing Pictures 69
Drooker, Eric 265
Duccio 94
Duchamp, Marcel 76, 166, 171
Duchess of Malfi 106
Duke University 114
Du Maurier, Daphne 16
Dunn, Ross 112

Earth 258
Earth Day 237
EC Comics 3
Egypt 187
Egyptian mythology 108–109
Eisner, Will 36, 117, 128, 151, 187, 220, 247, 260, 263
Eisner award 247
Electric Company 3
Elektra 254
Eliot, T.S. 73, 75–80
Elizabeth I 106
Ellis, Warren 50
Emma Frost 254, 256–258
Endy, Drew 185
English as a Second Language (ESL) 23–32
English Journal 15, 16, 17, 90
English Language Learners (ELLs) 85
"Enjoying Humor of Various Kinds" 14
Ennis, Garth 26
Enola Gay 177
Equality Now 252
Eurocentric modernism 77
Europe 112
European modernism 73
An Experience Curriculum in English 12–15, 20
Expressionist style 269
Extrapolation: A Journal of Science Fiction and Fantasy 126

Facebook 102, 109, 217
Fair Use 3, 222
Falbe-Hansen, Rasmus 114
Fallout 3, 9
Family Guy 106
Famous Funnies 14
Fanon, Franz 116
Fathers and Son 169, 172
Fawkes, Guy 87
Feazell, Matt 271
Federal Reserve Bank 3
Field, Joe 200
Fin de siècle 117
Firefly 251
Fischer, Craig 122
Fisher, Douglas 236
Flat World Knowledge 200
Flood! 265
Foster, Spencer R. 114
Fountain 171
Fournot, Juliette 226
Fourth wall 142
Frank, Josette 274
Frankenstein 3
Franklin, John Hope 200–201, 217
Frazer, James George 75
Free Comic Book Day 200
Freire, Paolo 94
Frey, Nancy 236
Full Metal Alchemist 116
Fun Home 63, 135, 139–142, 225, 231, 245
Fun Home: A Family Tragicomic 92, 247
Furies 158

Index

Gaiman, Neil 36, 55, 106, 109
Gaines, M.C. 19
Galman, Sally 265
Gardner, Howard 248
Gaudier-Brzeska, Henri 78
Gendercide 146
Gerde, Virginia W. 114
Getz, Trevor 117–118
Geyer, Michael 182–183
Gibbons, Dave 54–55, 63
Gillray, James 74
Ginsburg, Allen 3
GLAAD 53
Golden Age 123
Golden Legacy 3, 9
Gonick, Larry 3, 9
Gordon, Ian 53–54
Gospels of Luke and Matthew 94
Government Issue: Comics for the People, 1940s–1960 2, 9
Graham, David 30
Graham, Richard L. 2, 9
Grandville 116
Grapes of Wrath 1
Graphic Account: The Selection and Promotion of Graphic Novels in Libraries for Young People 275
Graphic Novels and Comics in Libraries and Archives 221
"Graphic Novels as Young Adult Literature" 59
Graphic Storytelling and Visual Narrative 69
Graphicmedicine.org 3
Graves, Robert 78
Gray, Lillian 19
Great Depression 222
Greco-Roman 109
Greece 154
Green Lantern 36
Greenpeace 186
Grendel 18, 108
Groensteen, Thierry 155
Grounded Theory 189, 191
Gruenberg, Sidonie Matsner 274
Guerra, Pia 148
Guibert, Emmanuel 225, 226
Gulliver's Travels 117
Gutenberg, Johannes 212
Gutenberg press 212
Guy Fawkes 85, 105, 108
GW Libraries 125

Hadashi no Gen 174
Hagood, Margaret 28
Hall, Stuart 198
Halloween 89
Hamachek, A.L. 249
Hamilton, Alexander 3
Hamilton, Nigel 157
Hamlet 106
Hamlet 152
Hara, Tamiki 174, 179
Harris, Albert 18
Harvey, RC 4, 123
Hatfield, Charles 4, 92, 93, 119, 121, 122, 123
Hatfield, Wilbur W. 13, 14, 20
Haugaard, Kay 38, 233

Health Care Reform 3
Heaney, Seamus 108
Heart of Darkness 115
Heisenberg, Werner 117–118
Hergé 128
Hermeneutics 106
Herodotus 111
Herriman, George 17
Hersey, John 180
Hetalia 116
Hezney, Mary J. 248
Hi and Lois 31
Hibakusha 175, 177, 179–181
Hibakusha 174
Hieroglyphs 187
Higgins, Dusty xi
Hillard, Van 119–120, 128
Himaruya, Hidekazu 116
Hinds, Gareth 108
Hine, David 113
Hiroshima 174, 176–179, 182–183
Hiroshima 180
Hirst, Damien 92
Hitchcockian 80
Hochschild, Adam 115
Hogarth, William 74, 94–95
Holocaust 56, 87, 135, 137–138, 158, 176
Holocaust Museum 56
Holy Church 107
Holy Grail 74, 77
Hosler, Jay 3, 9
How to Build Strong Bones 242
How to Create Comics from Script to Print 69
How to Increase Ability 18
How to Interpret Literature: Critical Theory for Literary and Cultural Studies 145
Howl 3
Huey, Edmund Burke 18
Hulk 255
Human Rags 179
Huntress 254
Huston, Warner Todd 113
Hutchinson, Katharine 15
H-World listserv (www.h-net.org) 112

I-BEAM 127–128
IBM 30
Ibsen, Henrik 98
Ibuse, Masuji 180
If on a Winter's Night a Traveller 169
Iliad 111
Image Text 126
Indiana University 4, 10, 272
Inferno 1
Information and Communication Technologies (ICT) 238
Information Literacy 5
Inge, Thomas 4, 221, 231
Inness, Sherrie A. 254
International Journal of Comic Art 122, 123, 126
International Reading Association 18, 236
Introducing Comics and Ideology 53
Invisible Girl/Woman 254, 258

iPhone 271
Iron Man 1, 36

J-STOR 126
Jack Kirby's Renaissance and Baroque periods 92
James Bond 73
James I 106–107
Jameson, Fredric 79
Japanese Manga 50, 52, 55–56, 98, 116, 174, 264
Jay, Martin 198
Jean Grey 254, 257
Jenkins, Linda 233
Jim Wilder 50
Jimmy Corrigan: The Smartest Kid on Earth 95
Johnson, Andrew 3
Joker 54–55
Jones, Kevin 6
Jong-Jen, Chang 128
Journal of Educational Sociology 4, 36, 274
Journal of Gender Studies 126
Journal of Graphic Novels and Comics 275
Journal of Popular Culture 122, 126
Jowett, Lorna 252
Joyce, James 79
Jüngst, Heike Elisabeth 198

Kalantzis, May 27
Kamiya, Akira 235
Kan, Kat 4
Kaywell, Joan 65
Keats, Jonathan 30
Keller, James 106
Kelly, Joe 116
Khaldun, Ibn 111
Kill Bill: Volume 2 56
King James 105
King Leopold's Ghost 115
King Solomon's Mines 116
Kinneman, Fleda Cooper 15, 16
Kitty Pryde 254, 256–258
Kiyama, Henry Yoshitaka 223, 225
Kiyosaki, Robert 217
Kleiner, Fred 91
Koukoulas, Yiannis 3, 154, 278
Kowalik, Jessica 128–129
Krashen, Stephen 65, 233
Krazy Kat 17
Kress, Gunter 162
Kruger, Barbara 92
Kunzle, David 92
Kuskin, William 4
Kyd, Thomas 75
Kyle, Richard 220

Langer, Susanne K. 187
LAS 50, 52, 54, 56
Laser-Robinson, Alex 128
"The Last Comic Standing" 36
Lattuca, Lisa R. 121
Lawrence, Salika A. 235
League of Extraordinary Gentlemen 116–117
Lee, Hermione 157
Lee, Jim 95

Index

Lee, Stan 4
Lefèvre, Didier 225–226
Lent, John 4, 24, 122, 131
Leonardo Da Vinci 95
Lewis, Wyndham 76, 78, 79
LGBT 230
L.H.O.O.Q. 76
Liberal Arts Seminar (LAS) 50
librarians 4
Library 1100 6
Lichtenstein, Roy 91
Lifton, Robert Jay 178
Light, Richard 44
Literacy and Numeracy Secretariat 237
Literatures in English Section (LES) 114
Little Toot 19
Lloyd, David 85
Logicomix 3, 154–155, 157–160, 162, 164, 166, 169
London Night 239
Losing Thomas and Ella 267–268
Lutes, Jason 115
Lyga, Allyson 248
Lyga, Barry 248

Macbeth 104–105, 107
Maclear, Kyo 174, 176, 178
Macphail, Agnes 238
Macphail Public School 233
Maddrey, Joseph 80
Maestà Altar 94
Major, Anya 30
Make Beliefs Comix 235
Make Way for Ducklings 19
Making Comics 69
Mallrats 56
Mallrats 56
Manhattan Project 182
Manning, M. Lee 85, 87
Manning, Patrick 112
Mao, Douglas 80
Market Day 95
Martson, William Moulton 255
Martin, Laura 95
Martin, Steve 36
Martin Luther King and the Montgomery Story 3
Marvel 1602 106, 107
Marvel comics 95
Marvel Comics (Marvel) 3, 4, 9, 50–53, 55, 95, 99, 258, 259
Marvel Universe 55, 258
Marvels 50, 55
Marvel's 2009 Wolverine Art Appreciation Month 95
Masaccio 94
Masco, Joseph 181
Maugham, W. Somerset 16
Mauldin, Bill 17
Maus 24, 36, 38, 50, 55, 62, 64, 103, 127, 134–138, 141, 154, 224–225
Mazzucchelli, David 93, 95–97
McAllister, Matthew 53
McCallum, Robyn 160
McCarthy, Mary 181
McCloud, Scott 25, 36, 39, 53, 55, 69, 92–93, 97–98, 124–125, 129–130, 135–136, 139–140, 148, 150, 155, 187, 226, 263–264, 266
McCullough, Constance 19, 20
McFarlane, Todd 95
McGuinness, Ed 95
McGuire, Richard 93
McKean, Dave 54
McLuhan, Marshall 155
McNeal, Kelly 235
Médecins Sans Frontières (MSG) 226
Medieval 102–104, 109
Medieval Renaissance 107
Melville, Herman 16, 78
Merisuo-Storm, Tuula 234–235
Merleau-Ponty, Maurice 135
Metafiction 160
Metamorphoses 109
Michigan State 114
Microsoft Word 30
Miller, Frank 54, 95–96, 116, 128
Miller, Nancy 135, 140
Miller, Suzanne 236
Milton, John 71
Ministry of Education 237
Minneapolis Public School 29
Minneapolis Public Schools Adult Education ESL programs 28
Missiou, Marianna 3, 154, 278
MIT 114, 184
MIT Synthetic Biology Working Group 184
Moby-Dick 113, 117
Modern Language Association 221
Modern Library 100 Best Novels 88
Mona Lisa 95
Monnin, Katie 69
Monterey Institute of International Studies in California 190
Moorcock, Michael 74
Moore, Alan 24, 37, 54, 63, 85, 104, 109, 116, 251
More Fun Comics 14
Morpheus 55
Morrison, Grant 54
Mrs. Dalloway 79
Ms. Magazine 256
MTV 37, 53
Multimodal 79
Multimodal literacy 23, 27–32, 59
Mulvey, Laura 148
Munch, Edvard 166–167, 170
Mutt and Jeff 16

Nakazawa, Keiji 26, 174–183, 224
National Association of Comics Art Educators (NACAE) 221
National Book Award 62
National Cartoonist Society 31
National Center for Educational Statistics 245, 246
National Center for Research Resources 3
National Consortium of Latin American Studies 53
National Council of Teachers of English (NCTE) 12, 13, 15, 16, 18, 72, 236, 277
National Security Agency (NSA) 86
Nature 185
Nausicaä of the Valley of Wind 222
Navigating World History: Historians Create a Global Past 112
Nebraska Wesleyan University 50, 52
Netherlands 154
New Hampshire 236
New literacy 59
New Media 27
New York Times Book Review 225
New York Times Graphic Novel Best Sellers List 154
New York Times Review 154
9/11 54
Nineteen Eighty-Four 84, 87–88
Nobel Peace Prize 226
North, Sterling 19
Northwestern University 18
Norton, Bonny 24, 29
Nyberg, Amy Kiste 12

Obama, Barack 35, 39
O'Barr, James 106
Of Human Bondage 16
Old English 101–103, 108
Old Possum's Book of Practical Cats 76
Olympics 50
On the Natural History of Destruction 224
Ontario, Canada 237
Ontario Ministry of Education 233
Ontario Software Acquisition Program Advisory Committee 237
Ord 258
Oresteia 158
Origin of Species 3
Orwell, George 84
Orwellian 30, 104
Ota, Yoko 174, 178–179
Otomo, Katsuhiro 55
Ottaviani, Jim 3, 9, 117, 118, 119
Our Cancer Year 265
Overton, Gertrude 17, 18, 20
Ovid 109
Oxford University Press 118

Palestine 26, 131, 135, 138–139, 141–142, 154, 265
Palomar College 52
Panama Pacific International Exposition 223
Papadimitriou, Christos 160
Papert, Seymour 237
Parents' Magazine 16
Parker, Robert Dale 145
Parliament 87
Peanuts 24, 36, 264
Pedro & Me 53–54
Pekar, Harvey 36, 56–57, 265
Penaz, Mary Louise 223
Penrod 16
Pepe LePew 212
Perepolis 26, 64, 131, 135, 138–139, 141–143, 154
Peter Parker 63
PhDcomics.com 1

Index

Phil Sheldon 55
Philion, Thomas 59
Picasso 187
Picture Stories from the Bible 1
Pixton http://pixton.com 271
Planetary 50
The Plot: The Secret History of the Protocols of the Elders of Zion 117
PMLA 80
Pop Art movement 91
Postmodernism, or the Cultural Logic of Late Capitalism 79
Potsdam Declaration 177
The Power of Comics 37
The Power of Reading 65
Pre-Raphaelites 78, 166
Presidential Medal of Freedom 200
Principia Mathematica 166
Problems in the Improvement of Reading 19
Progress of Human Culture 94
PS Magazine, the Preventative Maintenance Monthly 2, 9
The Psychology and Pedagogy of Reading 18
Publisher's Weekly 53
Puck Magazine 15
Pulitzer Prize 17, 36, 55, 62
Pumphrey, George 274

Qin, Helen 242
Quatermain, Alan 116
Queen Elizabeth I 105

The Rabbit's Cat 115
Raymond, John 16, 17
Reading Comics: How Graphic Novels Work and What They Mean 74
Reading in Modern Education 19
ReadWriteThink.org 63
The Ready Mades 166
Real Heroes 1
The Real World: San Francisco 53
Rebecca 16
Reese, Dora 19
Regarding the Pain of Others 131, 139
Reinventing Comics 150
Remarque, Erich Maria 16
Renaissance 102–104, 106, 109
Rethinking History 126
Revenge Tragedies 104
Reynolds, Richard 54
Rhetoric Review 126
Rich Dad, Poor Dad 217
Richards, Keith 212
Richardson, Laurel 266
Ricketts, Jeremy R. 274
Rider, H.R. 116
Rivera, Paolo 95
Robot Chicken 106
Robot Dreams 63
Rocky Mountain Conference on Comics and Graphic Novels 4
Rodin, Auguste 166
Rodriguez, Spain 26
Rogue 254
Rollin, Lucy 54
ROM 50
Ross, Alex 55

Rowlandson, Thomas 74
Rowson, Martin 73–74, 76–80
Royal Society of Arts 94
Russell, Bertrand 3, 154, 158, 162, 164, 166
Russell, David 157
Rutgers 114

Sacco, Joe 26, 131, 138–139, 142, 264
Safe Area Gorazde 64, 222
Safety in the Winter 241
Said, Edward 142
Salmon, Christian 157
Salvation Army 65
Sandman 36, 50, 55–56, 103, 109
SANE Journal 4
San Francisco earthquake 223
Satrapi, Marjane 26, 131, 141–142, 251
"Scars" 236
Schell, Jonathan 180
Schindler's List 56
Schnackenberg, Heidi L. 234
School of Visual Arts in Manhattan 96
Schraffenberger, J.D. 108
Schultz, Charles 264
Schultz, Mark 3, 10
Schwarz, Gretchen 86–87, 89, 221, 247
Scott, Randy 4
Scott Pilgrim 108
Scream 166, 170
Sebald, W.G. 224
Seduction of the Innocent 24, 247
Sequential art 260
A Series of Improvised Comics 98
Sewell, Edward 53
Sex and the Slayer: A Gender Studies Primer for the Buffy Fan 252
Seyfried, Jonathan 85
Sfar, Joann 115
Shakespeare 3, 101–107, 109, 145, 152
She 116
She-Hulk 254
Shelley, Mary 3
Sheng, Pi 212
Sherlock Holmes 117
Sherlock Holmes 75
Shirabu, Murasaki 94
Shoah 56
Shultz, Charles 24
Siegel, Alexis 225–226
Silver Age 123
The Simpsons 106
Singer, Marc 93
Slaughterhouse Five 183
Slayage 252
Sloan, Willona M. 235
Small, David 265
Smalls, Robert 3
SMART Board 238
Smith, Dora 12–14
Smith, Matt 37
Smith, Michael W. 62, 65
Smith, Robert V. v, xi–xii
Snatches 73, 74

Social and Cultural Geography 126
Social Science Japan Journal 126
Sociological Forum 126
Soft Weapons 139, 142
Sones, W.W.D. 36
Sontag, Susan 131, 135, 139
South Park 104, 106
Spanish influenza 223
The Spanish Tragedy 75
SparkNotes 103
Speigelman, Art 24, 36, 55–56, 62, 127, 134, 136–139, 175, 182, 224–225
Spider-Man (character) 3, 36, 53, 200, 255
Spider-Man (media) 52, 53, 56
Spider-Man India 52
Spidey Super Stories 3
Spielberg, Steven 56
Stam, Robert 77, 80
Stancato, F.A. 249
Stanley, Kelli E. 255
Star Trek: Communicating Across Generations 50
Stars and Stripes 17
Stassen, Jean-Philippe 115
Steampunk 116
Stearns, Lee 252
Stearns, Peter N. 112
Steig, William 17
Stein, Gertrude 78
Steinbeck, John 1
Steinem, Gloria 256
Sterne, Laurence 169
Stevenson, Robert Louis 169
Stine, R.L. 63
Stitches 265
The Story of Foreign Trade and Exchange 3
The Story of Inflation 3
The Story of the Federal Reserve System 3
Strang, Ruth 19, 20
The Strange Case of Dr. Jekyll and Mr. Hyde 117
Streep, Meryl 252
Stuck Rubber Baby 26
Studies in Psychoanalysis and Culture 126
The Stuff of Life: A Graphic Guide to Genetics and DNA 3, 10
Sturken, Marita 181
Sturm, James 95, 113, 230
Summer Flowers 179
The Sun 198
Sunday Book Review 154
Super Bowl 30
Super Heroes of Modern Mythology 54
Super-Powered Word Study 5
Supergirl 254
Superman (character) 52, 255
Superman (media) 1, 16, 19, 54, 56, 115
SurveyMonkey (www.surveymonkey.com) 238
Suspended in Language: Neils Bohr's Life, Discoveries, and the Century He Shaped 117, 118

Swiss Academy of Science 184–186
Swiss Federal Institute of Technology 185
Switzerland 185
Sykes-Wolsey 73
Syma, Carrye Kay 1, 3, 5, 6, 7, 9, 10, 279
Synthetic biology 184
Synthetic interdisciplinary 121

Tabachnick, Stephen 74, 104, 155, 221, 231
Takenishi, Hiroko 181
Talbot, Bryan 116
The Tale of Genji 94
Tales from the Crypt 3
Tales of Garcón: The Franchise Players 201, 205, 209–212
"Tapas Taxi" 212–214
Tarantino, Quentin 104
Tarkington, Booth 16
Teaching Children to Read 19
Teaching for the Two Sided Mind: A Guide to Right Brain/Left Brain Education 39
Teaching Graphic Novels 69
Teaching the Graphic Novel 104, 221
Teaching the Graphic Novel (course) 69
Teachingcomics.org 114
Teen Titans 50
Texas History Movies 1
Texas Tech University v, xii
Thinker 166
Thomas, Charles Swain 13
Thompson, Terry 50
Thrasher, Frederic M. 274
300 116
The 300 Spartans 116
Three Studies from the Temeraire 92
Thurber, James 17
Tilley, Carol L. 12, 274, 279
Time magazine's Top 100 Novels 54, 63
Tintin 128
Titus Andronicus 104
Tolstoy, Leo 169
TOON Books 70
ToonDoo http://www.toondoo.com 271
Totalitarianism 88
transmedia culture 5
transmedia phenomenon 76
Traxler, Arthur 19
Treat, John Whittier 179, 182
The Tribute Money 94
Trinity test 176
Tristram Shandy 169
True Comics 1, 16, 20
Tubman, Harriet 3
Tufte, Edward 197
Turgenev, Ivan 169, 172
Tutu, Desmond 39
21st century 5, 277
20,000 Leagues Under the Sea 117
Twitter 217
Twombly, Cy 92
Typee 16

Ultimate Spider-Man 53
Ulysses 79
Unbreakable 56
Uncanny X-Men 65
Underground Comix 50
Understanding Comics 25, 53, 93, 95, 97, 124–125, 129, 135
Understanding Comics: The Invisible Art 222
UNICEF 52
United Kingdom (UK) 154, 274–275
United Nations 222
United States (USA, U.S.) 3, 9, 12–14, 20, 35, 50, 53, 59, 112, 113, 152, 154, 184–185, 189–195, 220–225, 231, 245–248, 274, 277
The United States Constitution: A Graphic Adaptation 3
U.S. Department of Education's Institute of Education Sciences 245
United States Senate 112
U.S. Senate Subcommittee on Juvenile Delinquency 24
University Life 5, 9, 212, 215, 216, 217, 218
University of California–Berkeley 114
University of Chicago 114
University of Illinois–Springfield 220–221, 230
University of Minnesota 52
University of Nebraska–Lincoln 3
Untitled (You Invest in the Divinity of the Masterpiece) 92
Up Front 17
Uslan, Michael 4, 5

V for Vendetta 84–90, 104–106, 108
Vanderheyden, Karen 24, 29
Van Gogh, Vincent 95, 187
Van Leeuwen, Theo 162
Varon, Sarah 63
Vaughn, Brian K. 145, 152
Vega, Edwin 234
Versaci, Rocco 55
Version Approach 107–108
Victorian 78, 117
Visual Literacy 5, 59
"Visual Pleasure and Narrative Cinema" 148
Vonnegut, Kurt 169, 183
Vorticism 78

Wadey, Chuck 185
Waid, Mark 38
Walker, Mort 264
Walkowitz, Rebecca L. 80
Wall Street Journal 113, 128
Wanderer Above the Sea of Fog 166
War and Peace 113, 169
Ware, Chris 93, 95
Warhol, Andy 91
Washington Monument 146
Washington State 52
The Waste Land 73–80
Watchmen 24, 37–38, 50, 54–55, 63, 109, 124, 251, 259

Waterhouse, John William 166
Waugh, Patricia 158, 160
The Way of Oz—A Guide to Wisdom, Heart, and Courage xi
Web 2.0 271
Webster, John 107
Weekly Reader 15
Weeks, Ruth Mary 13
Weiner, Robert G. 1, 3, 5, 6, 7, 9, 10, 221, 232, 275, 279
Wertham, Fredric 20, 24, 26–27, 36, 247, 274
West Bank 151
"What's in the Comics?" 274
Whedon Studies Association 252
"When Commas Meet Kryptonite" 236
The White Devil 107
Whitehead, Alfred North 166
Whitlock, Gillian 131, 135, 139, 142
Whitworth, Michael H. 76, 78
Wikipedia 128
Wilhelm, Jeffrey D. 62, 65
Williams, Linda Verlee 39
Wilson 95
Wilson, Woodrow 3
Winfrey, Oprah 63
Winick, Judd 53–55
Witek, Joseph 98, 104, 115, 123
Wittgenstein, Ludwig 157
Witty, Paul 14, 18, 19
Wolk, Douglas 74, 95
Wolverine 53
Wonder Woman 36, 254–256, 259
Wonder Woman (media) 1, 255–256
Wonderful Wizard of Oz xi
Woo, Benjamin 122–123
Wood, Brian 116
Woolf, Virginia 79
The World of Viruses 3
World War I 223
World War II 56, 113, 147, 183
World's End 109
WOZ 186
Wren, Percival Christopher 16
The Wretched of the Earth 116
Wright, Bradford 225, 230
Wysocki, Anne Frances 25

Xbox 37
X-Men 111, 114–115
X-Men 95, 255, 257

Y: The Last Man 40, 44–45, 145–152
Yang, Gene 63, 114, 245, 247–248
Yildiz, Melda N. 235
Yorick Brown 40
Youth Libraries Group 275
YouTube 102

Zamora, Pedro 53
Zimmerman, Bill 235
Zionism 138
Zzu, Sun 3